The Study of Behavioral Development

THE CHILD PSYCHOLOGY SERIES
EXPERIMENTAL AND THEORETICAL ANALYSES OF CHILD BEHAVIOR

EDITOR
DAVID S. PALERMO
DEPARTMENT OF PSYCHOLOGY
THE PENNSYLVANIA STATE UNIVERSITY
UNIVERSITY PARK, PENNSYLVANIA

THE STUDY OF BEHAVIORAL DEVELOPMENT

Joachim F. Wohlwill

College of Human Development
The Pennsylvania State University
University Park, Pennsylvania

ACADEMIC PRESS New York and London   1973

A Subsidiary of Harcourt Brace Jovanovich, Publishers

To the Memory of My Father

ACADEMIC PRESS, INC.
111 Fifth Avenue, New York, New York 10003

United Kingdom Edition published by
ACADEMIC PRESS, INC. (LONDON) LTD.
24/28 Oval Road, London NW1

Library of Congress Cataloging in Publication Data

Wohlwill, Joachim F
     The study of behavioral development.

     (The Child psychology series)
     Bibliography: p.
     1.   Developmental psychology.   2.   Psychology—
Methodology.   I.   Title.   [DNLM: 1.   Child
development.   2.   Child psychology.   WS 105 W846s
1973]
BF713.W63   155.2'5   72–9341
ISBN 0–12–761550–4

PRINTED IN THE UNITED STATES OF AMERICA

Contents

Preface

Developmental psychology is surely one of the most vigorous, flourishing branches of the field of psychology today. But what, exactly, does this term refer to? For some, it is synonymous with child psychology—the study of the behavior of children. For others, it refers to the study of certain general behavioral processes across different age levels. For still others, it concerns the formulation of general laws of development, transcending the realm of the development of the individual from infancy to maturity.

Despite such differences in viewpoint, most people would probably agree that if the term "development" means anything, it denotes a concern for *change* in the individual's behavior as he grows older. Yet it is surprising how rarely developmental psychologists actually look at change directly, or even obtain the kind of information that would permit inferences concerning the nature of behavioral change and the processes governing it.

This volume has developed out of a growing conviction on the author's part that there is a need for a systematic treatment of the questions of methodology and research strategy that face the developmental psychologist as a student of behavioral change. This conviction is fueled by a decade of teaching, research, and discussion of developmental questions with colleagues and students, which filled my daily life as a member of the Psychology Department at Clark University. Although those steeped in the Wernerian tradition will undoubtedly find much of the content of this volume and the stance toward the study of development taken in it fundamentally alien to them, it nevertheless owes an immeasurable debt to the atmosphere of intellectual stimulation, encouragement, independent thought, and devotion to developmental theory and research, that characterized that department when Heinz Werner asked me to join it in 1958, and has continued to flourish there under the guiding hands of Bernard Kaplan and Seymour Wapner.

The book does not represent a comprehensive survey of methodology in the study of children. Such a survey would, of course, be beyond the capacity of a single individual, and the need for it has been adequately met by the *Handbook of Research Methods in Child Psychology* edited by P. Mussen (1960). It is rather to be seen as complementing this handbook, by a systematic focus on problems of research design and strategy and of data analysis that relate specifically to the study of developmental changes in behavior.

Even within this rather more narrowly defined scope, the book does not claim to completeness in its coverage. Not only are certain designs and techniques that might well have been given extensive treatment (e.g., path analysis; time-series analysis) either omitted altogether, or considered only briefly, but at least one major domain of research, that of the nonexperimental investigation of the role of experience, has been excluded. This omission was dictated by considerations of length and time; indeed, this complex topic could well in itself justify a separate volume.

In regard to the treatment of analytic procedures, it should be noted that the intent is to indicate in fairly general and frequently intuitive terms the place of and rationale for particular techniques in application to particular developmental problems, rather than to provide a detailed exposition of them or an introduction to their use. References are, of course, given to more thoroughgoing expositions of those techniques, to which the reader may turn where they prove relevant to his needs and interests. The value of some of these analytic tools would in many cases have emerged more clearly if it had been possible to provide appropriate, concrete illustrative data. But in many cases such material is simply lacking at this time.

The volume, then, has perhaps something of the flavor of an eighteenth-century Baedeker to North America. Hopefully others to come will not only fill in the details and correct the mistakes, but above all open up this broad and still largely uncharted territory to exploration through research aimed at answering some of the questions which this volume considers as central to the study of development.

Acknowledgments

The idea for this book dates back to 1963–1964, when I was a fellow at the Center for the Behavioral Sciences. That year saw no more than an abortive beginning to the project, as I soon came to the realization that I had much more to learn about both developmental processes and matters of methodology before I could hope to tackle a volume on the subject. A second chance to work on it materialized through the opportunity to spend a year as a Research Fellow at Educational Testing Service at Princeton, in its Human Development Research Group. The first 6 months of this fellowship were supported through a Faculty Research Grant from the Social Science Research Council whose assistance to me in this venture is gratefully acknowledged. Upon its termination, Educational Testing Service extended my fellowship through its own funds, and compounded its generosity by permitting me to work on the completion of this project during the succeeding two summers. The support given me by that institution transcends by far the merely financial side: All its resources, from assistance in data analysis to technical advice, from preparation of illustrations to typing of the manuscript and proofreading proved invaluable to me in this work. But above all, of course, it was the atmosphere of encouragement and stimulation at this institution, and especially in its Institute of Psychological Studies, that provided the impetus for this volume.

It remains to acknowledge the many individuals who in one way or another have made contributions to this book. First and foremost, I am deeply indebted to Walter Emmerich, who not only extended the invitation to me to spend a year at Educational Testing Service, but was a constant source of valuable ideas, criticism, and true friendship that were indispensible forms of support during my work on the book. A number of other persons at Educational Testing Service also gave generously of their time and expertise, notably Michael Lewis, Leonard Cahen, Norman Frederiksen, and Samuel Messick. Charles Hall and Richard Harrison provided valuable assistance in a reanalysis of data from the Harvard Growth Study designed to reveal the possibilities and limitations of trend-analytic techniques with longitudinal and cross-sectional data (cf. Chapter VIII). Among individuals from other institutions who have provided helpful comments and criticisms, John Nesselroade deserves special mention, for his careful reading of an earlier draft of Chapter X and his thoughtful suggestions for its revision. The standard disclaimer absolving all such helpers and critics from responsibility for whatever mistakes or misconceptions are contained in the final product is particularly pertinent in the case of this volume.

Thanks are due, finally, to a large array of individuals who played a role in the production of this volume, including the exceptionally able and conscientious administrative, secretarial and clerical staff at Educational Testing Service, especially Ann King and Mrs. S. H. Runyon, and Chester Tanaka who was most helpful in the preparation of the illustrations for this volume. Subsequently, at my present institution at Pennsylvania State University, Florence Dougherty and Celesta Gates labored skillfully and patiently over the at times impossible-looking task of seeing the manuscript through several revisions and working it into its final shape. I take pleasure also in acknowledging the help I have received from the very friendly staff at Academic Press. I am also most grateful to my colleague at Pennsylvania State University, David Palermo, the Editor of the Child Psychology Series, for his responsive attitude and much-needed words of encouragement.

Last but not least, I should like to express my thanks to my patient and understanding wife Fay, for her assistance with bibliographic work and the index, and especially for grinning and bearing it through the drawn-out period of my work on this book.

Look abroad thro' Nature's range
Nature's mighty law is change.
                    —Robert Burns

As for age, what that's worth
depends on the quality of the liquor.
                    —George Eliot, *Adam Bede*

Die Zeit gehet nicht, sie stehet still,
Wir ziehen durch sie hin;
Sie ist ein Karavanserai,
Wir sind die Pilger drin.

Ein Etwas, form- und farbenlos,
Das nur Gestalt gewinnt,
Wo ihr drin auf und nieder taucht,
Bis wieder ihr zerrinnt.

Es ist ein weisses Pergament
Die Zeit, und jeder schreibt
Mit seinem roten Blut darauf,
Bis ihn der Strom vertreibt
                    —Gottfried Keller

PART I

INTRODUCTION

CHAPTER I
Developmental Psychology, Past and Present

In the recent history of the behavioral sciences, few disciplines have witnessed as phenomenal growth as has developmental psychology during the past 12 to 15 years. As late as the mid-1950s it would have been easy to point to a number of outstanding psychology departments which lacked a single staff member representing the child or developmental area; today, these same departments vie with each other to attract the big "names" in the field, and to set up broad programs of research and graduate training. Perhaps the surest sign of the revolution which developmental psychology has undergone is that it has become equally attractive to psychologists of both sexes. Since the field has never been lacking in outstanding female talent (and there is no indication that the influx of men is changing that picture) developmental psychology today provides perhaps the clearest proof that scientific creativity and productivity are not sex-linked characteristics.

Fascinating though a sociologist of knowledge might find an analysis of the changing balance between the sexes in this discipline, of the reasons for it and the effects it has had, it is of primary significance here rather as a tell-tale symptom of the impressive changes which, in a comparatively brief period of time, have transformed and radically altered the character of the field. Whereas up to the early 1950s *child* psychologists were by and large either clinically oriented, with dominant interests in problems of personality development, or concerned with purely practical aspects of child behavior, today *developmental* psychologists, as they are likely to be called (as we shall see further on, the change in name is itself revealing) may specialize in any of a vast array of problems spanning the entire field of psychology. The subject matter of the field thus ranges from the psychophysical study of

visual illusions to social perception, from discrimination learning to complex problem solving, from studies of differential nonreward to studies of
father absence. This tremendous expansion in the topics dealt with has
inevitably been paralleled by a corresponding increase in the variety of
methodological and theoretical approaches represented in the field.

Indeed, to the initiate, the field of developmental psychology must appear
as a veritable Tower of Babel—a beehive of activity, seemingly lacking in
direction, integration, or evident purpose. While it is certainly true that
the field lacks the cohesion, homogeneity, and relative simplicity of organization which seemed to have marked it in earlier days, the picture of chaos
just referred to is surely misleading. There are, indeed, some fairly clearly
discernible, though by no means easily compatible, forces operating in the
field today. These forces lend to the field a definite aura of progress and
even direction, though in a multiple rather than a unitary sense. But to
unravel the strands requires a brief excursion into the more recent history
of the field.

A Brief Historical Sketch

A fully adequate historical account of the evolution of developmental
psychology remains to be written. We are limited, for the most part, to
individual chapters in general treatises such as Ausubel's (1958) and
Watson's (1965), conference papers such as Anderson's (1956) or occasional
papers such as Dennis's (1949) and White's (1968). To these should be added
the volume of selected extracts from classical sources, representing some
of the major historical precursors of contemporary child psychology which
Kessen (1965) has assembled, and a similar anthology edited by Grinder
(1967), focusing on genetic and evolutionary conceptions of development.
These are necessarily sketchy and incomplete, however, and in Kessen's case
limited almost exclusively to European writers.

These various sources are in general agreement in stressing the roots of
child psychology in the biology and medicine of the nineteenth century.
Darwin is seen as a point of origin from which the major lines of thought
shaping the field depart—one moving via James Mark Baldwin and Clapa-
rède to Piaget; another via Preyer and Hall to Gesell; a third via Freud to
Eriksen and the other branches of the neo-Freudian school. This picture
helps account for several phenomena apparent in the history of child psychology. It is consonant with the strong influence of biological models and
modes of thought in this field, as reflected in the theorizing of Werner and
Piaget, as well as of the Freudians. It explains the strong tradition of the
naturalistic, observational method which has dominated the field, from

Preyer's (1882, German ed.) *The Mind of the Child* to Barker and Wright's (1951) *One Boy's Day;* from Darwin's (1877) biographical sketch of an infant to Piaget's (1952b, 1954b) epoch-making observations of his own children during their first year of life. Finally, it probably determined; in part, the largely practical, applied, clinical orientation which permeated a considerable segment of the field in this country during its early days, and as recently as the immediate postwar years.

Yet if this picture is the truth, it is very far from being the whole truth. Indeed, it provides virtually no clues that might aid us in understanding the state of the field today, particularly in the United States. It fails to do justice to the unique phenomenon that is represented in the work of Piaget, much less explain the reasons for the tremendous upsurge of interest in this work which we have been witnessing during the past decade. It does not encompass the thought and work of another influential developmental psychologist of the recent history of the field, Heinz Werner, or even that of his mentor, William Stern. Moreover, it does not handle some of the major recent trends of thought in the field in the United States, as reflected in the work of psychologists such as Sears, Bijou, or Baldwin.

What this picture of the historical evolution of the discipline lacks, basically, is a sense of the strong, pervasive ties that link developmental psychology to the general field of psychology. These ties are clearly in evidence in child psychology in the United States today—as a quick perusal of the *Journal of Experimental Child Psychology*, or even of the more traditional organ of the discipline, *Child Development*, makes plain. What is less commonly realized, or at least improperly emphasized, is the fact that such ties have been strongly in evidence in European developmental psychology, at least since the turn of the century. Thus we find both Werner and Piaget, though known chiefly for their contributions to developmental theory, working extensively on problems of the experimental psychology of perception. The former's article (Werner, 1946) for the *Encyclopedia of Psychology*, significantly entitled "Genetic Psychology, Experimental," provides an excellent overview of European research on child behavior. This overview bears witness to the extent to which child psychology between the two World Wars was integrally related to the parent field of psychology, rather than to biology, medicine, pediatrics, or education. If, historically, there may still be a basis for looking at these latter disciplines as the putative ancestors of child psychology, it seems that the adopted parent has become the truly "natural" parent, and that, inevitably, is the general field of psychology.

Perhaps nowhere is this point better brought out than in the work of Kurt Lewin. Some may regard his credentials as a child or developmental psychologist as suspect, and one looks in vain for a reference to him in any of the above-mentioned historical sketches. Yet Leonard Carmichael, himself representing the biological legacy and tradition in the field, was apparently able to discern the impact which an ambitious general theory of behavior of the scope of Lewin's could have on the field of child psychology. Thus he invited him to contribute a chapter on his own work and theory (Lewin, 1954) to the *Manual of Child Psychology*, which stands out from the rest in being the only one to represent a particular theoretical orientation, while at the same time drawing heavily on data on diverse aspects of child behavior. More recently, Baldwin (1967) has similarly honored Lewin's contribution to child psychology by devoting a chapter to his work in his survey of developmental theories.

It is not easy to account for the propensity of Lewin and his followers to use children in testing hypotheses derived from his theory. In some instances (e.g., the work on aspiration level), it seems to have been mainly a matter of convenience. Because of their presumed simplicity or naiveté, the use of children allowed basic phenomena to be revealed which might be more difficult to study in adults, or which might be obscured by other factors relating to the latter's greater sophistication, recourse to verbalization, or complexity of value systems and personality organization. In other cases, however, Lewin evinces an explicit interest in the developmental changes to which the phenomena uncovered by his theory were subject. Indeed, the aforementioned chapter contains a set of developmental postulates marking Lewin as the first, and possibly still the most successful of those who have attempted to wed a general psychological theory to a developmental framework. In this respect, he foreshadowed the similar attempts by Wapner and Werner (1957) and Piaget (1969), which were, however, directed at a much more narrowly delimited range of problems, i.e., in the field of perception.

It has always struck this author as paradoxical that a general theorist, priding himself on treating behavior exclusively in terms of the contemporaneous field, should have been apparently so successful in incorporating developmental considerations into his theory (though there are undoubtedly those who would argue that the developmental side of his system is essentially grafted on to it from the outside). Underlying this paradox, however, is another, even more curious one: if we search for the dominant influence on those European psychologists who, like Lewin, occupied themselves with the study of child behavior, we come up with but one possible answer—the Gestalt movement. The Gestaltists themselves, despite their well-known nativist bias, and the agenetic character of their theoretical views (at least those of the Berlin, if not of the Leipzig school), were by no means disinterested in the phenomena of child behavior, as witnessed in Koffka's *The Growth of the Mind* (1924), which bears the subtitle: *An Introduction to Child Psychology*. Both Werner and Piaget, furthermore, however critical they were of the Gestaltists' lack of a genetic focus (cf. Piaget, 1954a), owe a clear debt to them, both in their theorizing and in their research. This is even more obviously true in the case of Lewin, on whom the Gestaltists' agenetic mantle fitted rather more comfortably. A further line of influence of the Gestaltists on European child-psychological research emanates from the empiricism–nativism controversy which was fueled by the views of the Gestalt school, and which led for instance to a whole series of studies on the development of the perceptual constancies in childhood, under the aegis of Brunswik and his associates (cf. Brunswik, 1956).

For reasons which are apparent to any student of the development of psychology in the United States, the Gestaltists failed to exert a similar influence on child psychology in this country, even after they arrived here. But behaviorism provided an alternative theoretical framework which, even though more slowly and until recently on a much lesser scale, did eventually come to play a potent role in the evolution of the field, and to bind it more closely to general psychology. There was first the work of Watson which, while it appears to have had only a limited effect in inspiring child-psychological research, remained for many years a significant force in American theorizing about child behavior (e.g., in Floyd Allport's account of the origin of speech). It undoubtedly contributed to the interest in the maturation–learning controversy, which in the 1930s provided the impetus for a large body of studies on child learning and motor development (cf. Munn, 1954, 1965), much as the empiricism–nativism question advanced research on perceptual development in Europe. But the most significant influence came undoubtedly from the elaboration of Hullian and neo-Hullian S-R behavior theory in the 1930s and 1940s, which, through its extension to social and personality functions by Miller, Dollard, and Mowrer laid the foundation for an extensive program of research and theory of child socialization and personality formation, embodied in the work of Sears and his associates (e.g., Sears, Whiting, Nowlis, & Sears 1953), and in the cross-cultural work of Whiting and Child (1953) (cf. also Child, 1954). Granted that this work bore the marks of the strong influence of the psychoanalytic school, it is undeniable that it was the behaviorist school which in effect captured the child psychology of the 1940s and early 1950s, and brought it into the fold of psychology. The behaviorist school outfitted child psychology with an experimental methodology and a theoretical position, to supplant the observational approach and atheoretical character of much of the child development work current at the main centers of the discipline, most typically carried out under the auspices of institutes of child welfare, or of departments of home economics.

In sum, the image of developmental psychology as leading a sheltered existence as an offshoot of the biological and medical sciences, operating in large measure in divorcement from the rest of psychology, was never valid at all abroad, and only to a limited degree in the United States, and decreasingly as we approach the contemporary scene. It remains to pick up and sort out the main threads which we find in the discipline today, and to map out the structure of the field as it has evolved up to the present.

Developmental Psychology in the 1970s

A glance at the contents of the major journals of the field, or at the programs of professional meetings of the American Psychological Association's (APA) Division of Developmental Psychology, or of the Society for Research in Child Development (SRCD), will disclose a much greater variety and heterogeneity of problems and approaches than the brief historical sketch just presented would lead one to anticipate. The fact is that the discipline has undergone not only very marked growth but substantial structural changes during the past decade, the reasons for which are by no means obvious, though some educated guesses as to how they came about, and their portents for the future may be hazarded.

If we attempt to determine the main trends to be found in the field today, at least five separate strands appear to unravel: (1) the invasion of the experimentalists; (2) the Skinnerian influence; (3) the cognitive and language-development boom; (4) the "retreat" to infancy; and (5) the impact of modern social learning theory.

1. THE INVASION OF THE EXPERIMENTALISTS

It would be misleading to suggest that it is only recently that psychologists with experimental backgrounds and interests have become active in the field of child-psychological studies. In fact, a tabulation of the percentage of the membership of Division 7 of the APA (developmental psychology) holding joint membership in Division 3 (experimental psychology) discloses, rather surprisingly, very little change over the past two decades: In 1951, 8.9% held such dual membership, while in 1968 the figure was 8.5%. In the light of these figures, to speak of an "invasion" in this context will surely seem exaggerated. Yet, if one looks at the content of developmental journals, notably the *Journal of Experimental Child Psychology*, or the series, *Advances in Child Development and Behavior*, or, for that matter, the make-up of the slate of officers of APA Division 7 and SRCD, the growing influence of experimentally oriented psychologists on the major directions of research in the discipline, and on its professional affairs, becomes unmistakable.

The reasons for this development are diverse and complex. To some extent, it reflects the growing dissatisfaction, in the mid-1950s, with the bulk of then current child-psychological research: Most of it was carried out without benefit of experimental controls and techniques; it was frequently atheoretical, and usually dealt with complex variables which were difficult to define or control (cf. McCandless & Spiker, 1956; Terrell, 1958). At the same time, it probably mirrors the decline of Hullian and Tolmanian rat research within the experimental field, and the increasing interest on the part of experimentalists in problems of perception, attention, and mediational processes, for which children seemed to be ideally suited as subjects.

Whatever the reasons, there is little question that it is this influx of the experimentalists which, more than any other factor, has anchored the field of child psychology firmly within the general domain of psychology. There are those who will question whether in the process the baby is being thrown out with the bath: Is research on problems which are specifically related to the development of the child (e.g., sex-role identification) being abandoned, and being replaced by problems borrowed from the experimentalist's laboratory (e.g., discrimination or paired-associate learning), without concern for their relevance to the field of child psychology as such? To the extent that this is true, the field is in danger of losing its identity as defined by behaviors or problems specifically concerning the child and his psychological development, and becomes merely a branch of general psychology, which happens to make use of a particular class of individuals as subjects.

There are, indeed, instances in which experimentally minded psychologists have used children in much the same way that they have used rats: that is, as convenient subjects for their research. An example is provided by Spiker's (1963) ambitious analysis of the problem of stimulus interaction and compounding. It manifests sophistication of a high order in the formulation of programmatic research with children, which is of undeniable theoretical interest for the psychology of learning, but is guaranteed to have no relevance whatsoever for any conceivable aspect of *child* psychology. Yet increasingly we find the experimentalists who have chosen to work with children, including those whose initial motive for doing so was based on the suitability of children as subjects for their research, becoming interested in the developmental aspects of the problems they are investigating, at least to the extent of replicating their work across several different age levels. Thus, while the subject matter of much of their research may smack of the laboratory of the experimentalist, the incorporation of a developmental dimension at least introduces a possible link to the field of developmental psychology proper, and presumably contributes to a total picture of the mechanisms and dimensions of developmental change. In the process, furthermore, the investigator is apt to find himself confronted with problems—even puzzles—relating to the interpretation of the age changes he has uncovered, which may cause him to deviate further and further from the interest of the experimentalist with which he started his research, and to become increasingly immersed in questions of developmental process.

We shall have occasion to concern ourselves with certain unwonted consequences of this experimentalization of our field, and to raise questions as to the compatibility of the study of age differences with the approach to research of the experimentalist. For effective handling of joint investigation of the role of experimentally manipulated variables and of age differences turns out to be a far more difficult, as well as a challenging undertaking than those engaged in such research at the present time appear to realize.

2. The Skinnerian Influence

The spread of Skinnerian research based on the operant conditioning paradigm, which emanates from the field of psychology as a whole, is a further force operating in the developmental area today. This is obviously experimental in nature, and might seem properly to belong in the preceding section. Yet its influence on the field and, indeed, the purpose and aims underlying it appear to deviate sufficiently from those characterizing the work of the experimentalists to warrant its separate consideration. For, while some work with children following the operant-conditioning model may be designed mainly to extend previously derived principles to a child population, or to test out the effects of particular variables on some specified operant response, more frequently the work reflects one of two closely related emphases. Some of the work is conducted to demonstrate the applicability of the operant-conditioning paradigm to developmental problems by showing how typically observed developmental changes may be simulated in the laboratory by subjecting a child to a properly programmed sequence of stimuli. (A closer look at this particular approach to the study of developmental questions will be provided in Chapter XI.) Alternatively, the aim may be to show that some particular problem of a practical or pedagogical nature—teaching a child to read or discriminate forms; "shaping" particular desired social behaviors or traits, or eliminating undesirable ones—is amenable to solution by the application of operant conditioning techniques. This emphasis, which is eloquently set forth in the work of Bijou and Baer (1961, 1965) and of Staats and Staats (1963), is thus of an essentially applied nature, starting from the premise that the principles necessary for behavior change and control in children have been firmly established in the laboratory. Its place on the child-psychology scene today does not appear related to any of the other main trends visible in the field, but appears rather to parallel the spread and popularization of Skinnerian psychology over the whole field of behavioral science.

3. THE COGNITIVE AND LANGUAGE DEVELOPMENT BOOM

The study of cognitive functions in children, along with the closely related but still separate area of child language, has undoubtedly been the subject area that has seen the most vigorous growth in recent years.[1] Unlike the preceding two trends, this one has been intrinsically tied to concerns of a developmental nature. In the cognitive realm this has been largely, though not entirely, the result of the tremendous upsurge of interest in the work of Piaget (the latter's name accounts for more entries in the *Subject Index* of the Psychological Abstracts for the years 1967 to 1970 than such typically "American" headings as "learning set" and "retroactive inhibition" combined!). On the side of language, developments in the area of structural linguistics have afforded the kind of promising analytic tool for the investigation of the acquisition of language in childhood that can hope to advance the field beyond the predominantly normative and descriptive stage in which it had languished since the 1930s (cf. McNeill, 1970). One may speculate at length, though not too profitably, about the whys and wherefores of this phenomenon (surely a contributory factor must be *Homo sapiens'* intrinsic fascination with such problems as the changeover from nonconservation to conservation in early childhood, or the induction of linguistic rules on the part of the young child). More to the point, however, is the observation that this body of research, which as already noted, is of most direct relevance to developmental theory, and to issues arising in the study of development such as those of stages, developmental transitions, and mechanisms of developmental change, should be least closely tied to general psychological theory and research. While one finds occasional attempts to relate Piaget's system to more general psychological principles (e.g., Berlyne, 1965), and work on structural developmental linguistics is conducted in some relation to more general notions of verbal mediation (Jenkins & Palermo, 1964), these efforts have remained sporadic, and not notably successful.[2] We shall find similar

---

[1]The recently published revision of the Carmichael *Manual of Child Psychology* (Mussen, 1970) provides convincing documentation on this point. Cognitive Development represents one of five major sections of this two-volume handbook, and by far the largest, even if the inclusion of two chapters on learning theory and learning research strains the boundaries of this heading.

[2]A significant feature of the most such attempts is that the concepts and mechanisms introduced to account for the phenomena require major extensions, if not revisions of the theory ostensibly being applied to them. An interesting case in point are the attempts of behavioristically oriented psychologists (Engelmann, 1967; Gagné, 1968; Kingsley & Hall, 1967) to apply learning principles to the child's acquisition of concepts of conservation (cf. Chapter XI); the particular techniques applied or suggested for this purpose are typically not at all grounded in learning theory as such, but are justified only on a very general plane by reference to such concepts as learning sets, or operations derived from programmed learning.

idiosyncratic features of work in this area at the level of methodology and research strategy paralleling those at the theoretical level. It is these idiosyncratic features that serve to set this realm apart from general psychology.

4. The "Retreat" to Infancy

Paralleling the sharp upward trend in work devoted to the cognitive area has been the marked increase in studies of the human infant. This increase appears to represent in a very real sense a strategic retreat, in that the aim is ostensibly to go back to the bare origins of behavior to determine the response repertoire available at birth, and more important, the potential for learning or behavior modification in the neonate, and to study the course of development from this point of origin, and the variables affecting it. Defined as it is in terms of a particular population rather than content or approach to research, it is not surprising to find this body of research considerably more heterogeneous than any of the preceding. Though predominantly experimental, it includes an important volume of essentially observational, normative work; where some investigations of infant behavior are directly derived from the laboratory of the general psychologist (studies of operant conditioning, of effects of complexity on fixation), others are more specifically tied to the peculiarities of the infant; though much of the research is limited to a particular age segment (usually the neonate), age comparisons and even longitudinal follow-up are becoming more frequent. Similarly, the theoretical viewpoints represented in this work range from simple empiricism, unfettered by any theoretical position, to orthodox S-R connectionism, to developmental theory of a Piagetian or Freudian stamp. Thus, the net effect of this important trend in contemporary developmental research does not appear to operate in any particular methodological or theoretical direction, though it may operate to create a growing in-group within the discipline, brought together perhaps largely by the unique problems of instrumentation, practical care, etc. demanded of the infancy researcher.

5. The Impact of Social Learning Theory

While overall there has been a noticeable decline in work devoted to the study of child socialization, personality formation, and individual differences in children, a notable exception appears to be the work being carried out within the framework of social learning theory, as represented in the research of Gewirtz, and of Bandura and Walters and their associates. It reflects the increasing place being given to systematic, controlled experimentation on the part of child psychologists, and provides convincing evidence of the power of this approach when applied to problems, such as the study of children's aggressive behavior, which previously were investigated almost exclusively through nonexperimental methods. Lastly, this body of research again indicates the close affiliation between general psychology and this branch of child psychology, while at the same time it appears to afford an illustration of the modification or enlargement of general principles as a result of being put to the test in work with children (cf. Bandura, 1969).

To sum up this obviously superficial and highly selective overview of the main trends in contemporary developmental psychology, it is apparent that the field is highly diverse and relatively lacking in integration. In a very real sense it represents the whole field of psychology in microcosm, which is to be expected of a field defined not in terms of subject matter but in terms of a focus on the child and his development, encompassing every facet of behavior.

One source of ambiguity in any attempt to map out the structure of the field or sketch out its boundaries relates to the use of the term "developmental." The term "developmental psychology" has come into widespread use only fairly recently, replacing, or in some cases supplementing the previous labels of "child psychology" or "child development." (A weather vane in this respect is the change in chapter heading from "Child Psychology" to "Developmental Psychology" effected with the 1957 volume of the *Annual Review of Psychology*.) This change presumably is evidence of a greater interest in questions of change in behavior with age, and in the processes governing such changes. Yet the focus on development, in this sense, emerges in only rather blurred fashion from the disparate trends outlined previously. The interest in developmental change as such ranges from perfectly explicit, as in the Piagetian work on cognitive development, to implicit, as in the personality work based on social learning theory (which rarely includes age as a variable), to entirely absent, as in some of the experimentalists' research. This ambiguity, not to say ambivalence, is unwittingly expressed in the title selected for the impressive series of papers launched in 1963, *Advances in Child Development and Behavior*. Undoubtedly the editors did not intend to imply that work of a developmental nature was not, or could not be concerned with behavior (though the use of this title does allow for the inclusion of work on physical growth), but rather that some behavioral work with children is not concerned with the developmental side. The fact remains, nevertheless, that a major share of the papers published in this serial, as indeed in the field at large, does deal with developmental questions, either explicitly, i.e., by including age as a main variable, or implicitly, by looking for presumed antecedents of behavior observed at a particular age, or attempting to simulate age changes outright.

In view of this dominant developmental concern in the field today, however, which is the main concern of the present volume as well, there emerges a second source of conflict, even of unresolved dissonance, which can be detected in the current approaches to research and modes of thought. As the preceding brief survey should have made plain, a common bond shared by much of the current work is its debt to general experimental psychology. Most of the designs, approaches to data analysis and scientific inference which developmental psychologists are utilizing have been taken over fairly blithely from that domain. In fact, it was to bring out how closely child psychology today is beholden to the model provided by the experimentalist, rather than to the realm of biology or medicine, and to naturalistic or field-type study, that the sketch of the state of the field today was undertaken. The question arises as to the appropriateness of this model to the task of the developmentalist, and, more fundamentally, whether developmental psychology can properly be subsumed under the experimental sciences.

Developmental Psychology: Experimental or Differential?

In his 1957 Presidential Address to the APA, Cronbach (1957) saw psychology as divided into two separate and sharply differentiated disciplines: one experimental, the other differential. In his presentation, Cronbach pointed to a whole set of characteristics distinguishing these two approaches. These relate, most obviously, to the design of research: While the experimentalists subject a single variable of interest to them, or several variables in interaction, to deliberate manipulation under controlled conditions, the differentialists are more prone to study the effects of variables *in natura*, as they find them. This difference, which is so obvious as to appear trivial, has several correlates which serve to accentuate the separation between these two disciplines: The experimentalist is generally disinterested in individual differences, which are conveniently relegated to the status of "error variance," no matter how large in proportion to that contributed by the experimental variable or variables; whereas individual differences are the common coin of the differentialists' research. This creates a further divergence between the two approaches, in the preferred mode of statistical analysis employed: Inferential, hypothesis-testing techniques are the stock-in-trade of the experimentalist, as opposed to the predominantly correlational methods to which the differentialist leans. Yet another integrally related differentiating feature between the two approaches concerns the place accorded to systematic theory: Whereas the experimentalist is apt to base his research on a hypothetico–deductive model of scientific inference, using a generalized theory, a set of principles, or a model to generate experimental hypotheses to be put to the test, the differentialist is typically content to remain at an essentially descriptive level, eschewing formal theory, and indeed encountering difficulties when attempting to adopt the hypothesis-testing mode.

In his address, Cronbach stressed the gap separating not only these two approaches themselves, but along with it the psychologists identified with them, by virtue of the dominant channels of scientific communication, structure of academic and professional organizations and institutions, etc. At the same time, he suggested possibilities for a real integration of the two approaches, by bringing the study of individual differences to bear on the problems of the experimentalist, and vice versa. To a limited extent, we have witnessed efforts in this direction, notably in the field of cognitive styles. In addition, there has, it seems, been some increase in sheer contact between the two sides, for instance, through conferences devoted to the examination of a problem area cutting across the boundary between them (such as the problem of the learning of the culturally disadvantaged child). Yet separatism continues to be the rule, and the organization of courses and texts on research design, and indeed programs of graduate training, as well as the institutional structure of the discipline itself, seems calculated to perpetuate it.

It is in the domain of developmental psychology, however, that the clash between the two approaches is particularly acute. There has been little attempt to deal with, much less resolve the question, to which of the two camps this field should properly be assigned. The result has been that ad-herents of each appear to compete with one another for the attention of their fellow developmentalists, for positions of influence, for control over journals, academic curricula, and the like. Thus, while the confluence of the two approaches within this single discipline has undoubtedly brought about a degree of contact and interaction not found elsewhere in psychology, there are forces at work which are likely to create within the field a schism between them mirroring that which Cronbach delineated for the discipline at large.

This schism in developmental psychology is in part a result of the great diversity to be found in the field today. As noted earlier it ranges from the "pure" experimentalists who happen to select children as subjects for their research, to those who come to the field with a particular interest or concern for the behavior of children (say, for thumb-sucking in the nursery-school child). A question of much more substantive interest, however, is the status of *developmental* research: Is the study of change in behavior with development an experimental or a differential enterprise?

Cronbach includes developmental psychology with the differential branch, presumably on the grounds that the study of differences in behavior which are a function of the age of the individual represents an inherently comparative type of undertaking, in which the investigator clearly can have no control over the main independent variable of interest to him. Ausubel

(1958) has similarly described the field as necessarily nonexperimental. Writing as a representative of the more traditional field of child psychology, he argues that for both practical and ethical reasons, and more fundamentally because of the complexity of forces operating on the behavior of the child in his actual world, the experimental method is inapplicable to the problems of the developmentalist. Russell (1957), on the other hand, writing from the vantage point of the experimentalist, is rather more sanguine about the possibilities of bridging this gap, and applying experimental approaches to solve developmental problems; but it is apparent that he defines developmental problems largely in terms of their relevance for general behavior theory, denying the necessity for postulating any problems that are unique to the developmentalist. Accordingly, he sees one of the main functions of the developmental psychologist to be that of defining and studying the boundary conditions for the operation of the laws formulated by the general-behavior theorist.

To investigators of the effects of early experience on development in animals, this debate may appear academic, if not pointless; from their point of view, surely, an experimental psychology of development is, to paraphrase Russell, neither pipe dream nor possibility, but an accomplished fact. Admittedly the possibilities for such direct, experimental manipulation of development are much more limited in work at the human level which Ausubel and probably Russell had in mind in their discussions. Yet even to the child psychologist the opportunity for such an experimental approach is by no means absent, as we will see in our consideration of this topic in Chapter XI.

One possible, if facile answer to the question of whether developmental research belongs in the differential or experimental camp would be to say that it may fall into either: Comparative analysis of age differences clearly belongs on the differential side, whereas research involving direct manipulation of conditions whose effects on development are under study just as clearly belongs on the experimental side.

To leave the matter thus would, however, be an entirely superficial handling of this question. (It would, incidentally, rob this book of its *raison d'être*!) For, upon closer examination, it turns out that the study of developmental change does not readily fit either of the two models, at least in their simplest form. On the one hand, the study of age changes in behavior differs, in certain important respects, from comparative, differential investigation involving other interpersonal characteristics, e.g., the study of sex differences. On the other hand, even when development is subjected to direct experimental attack by manipulating the conditions of experience in a controlled manner, the situation still deviates in some critical ways from that which confronts the experimentalist dealing with nondevelopmental problems.

Thus, assertions to the contrary notwithstanding (cf. Russell, 1957), the thesis of this book is that the concern with development gives rise to very particular requirements and considerations as regards experimental methodology, research design, and scientific inference. To put it succinctly: The canons of the scientific method, as they have been worked out for the field of psychology at large, require modification when applied to developmental problems.

CHAPTER II
The Age Variable in Psychological Research[1]

The Focus on Change and Its Implications

The blatant assertion with which we concluded the preceding chapter is bound to appear highly debatable to many psychologists. The argument to be advanced in defense of it rests on one core assumption, which may be taken as axiomatic: Change in behavior over time, which forms the subject matter of any developmental investigation, constitutes an inherent characteristic of behavior. Before elaborating further on this assumption and the implications to which it leads, let us see how the focus on change embodied in this assumption causes developmental research to transcend the traditional boundary between differential and experimental modes of investigation.

To clarify this point, let us compare the case of the developmental psychologist with that of the comparative animal psychologist interested in interspecies differences in behavior. The essential difference between them is that, unlike age changes, the evolutionary changes which may be assumed to underlie phylogenetic differences cannot be observed as they are occurring. What would be needed to make the study of the latter more nearly comparable to the study of ontogenetic change is a paleontology of behavior, which we are not apt to see become a reality as long as retrogressive time machines remain in the realm of science fiction. Thus the study of phylogenetic differences is destined to remain a purely comparative enterprise, along with the study of sex differences, socioeconomic differences, etc.

[1]The main argument espoused in this chapter has been previously presented in a briefer version elsewhere (Wohlwill, 1970a).

In what sense is this a difference that makes a difference? It is in several ways. First, the investigator of age changes can make statements concerning the characteristics of the changes themselves, e.g., their rate, dependence on particular events; the phylogenetic investigator, limited to cross-sectional comparisons, cannot. Second, while in both realms, cross-sectional differences confound developmental changes with secular changes modifying the character of the populations over historical time, the incorporation of a longitudinal dimension superimposed on the cross-sectional comparison allows the ontogenetic psychologist to separate out these two factors (cf. Chapter VII). The investigation of phylogenetic differences necessarily retains this confounding: If we ignore isolated instances of "living fossils" such as the horseshoe crab, it becomes evident that we cannot reconstruct an evolutionary sequence from a comparison of species presently in existence. This consideration has led Simpson (1958), in fact, to question whether evolutionary change can be meaningfully studied by such comparative study. Third, paralleling the problem of branching in phylogenetic evolution, which severely limits the possibilities for ordering diverse animal species along a single dimension, the investigator of ontogenetic changes is likewise faced with behavior differentiation superimposed on changes on a developmental continuum, which remain confounded and virtually impossible to separate in any cross-sectional analysis. Again, however, by tracing the changes longitudinally, as they occur, a possibility emerges of separating these two components.

The fundamental respect, then, in which the age variable differs from that of phylogenetic differences, or from any of the usual differential variables, is that the variation in some specified aspect of behavior which is attributable to age can be traced as it is taking place in the individual. What this means, in effect, is that it becomes possible to cut the Gordian knot involved in attempting to apply the experimental–differential dichotomy to the developmental domain by abandoning the conception of age as an independent variable altogether and shifting to one in which it becomes instead part and parcel of the definition of the dependent variable. That is, the phenomena to be studied are the changes in behavior occurring along the dimension of age.

According to this notion, the most fruitful way of looking at the age variable is in a manner equivalent to the time variable in the study of forgetting, adaptation or habituation, etc. These represent a class of behavior changes which occur as a function of time; indeed they are defined in terms of their functional relationships to the time variable. Although these phenomena are the province of the experimental psychologist par excellence, the basic behavioral changes which are to be accounted for are generally observed, rather than produced by experimental manipulation; thus much of the work in this area is in principle as nonexperimental as the study of age changes. To be sure, the investigator of these phenomena is not content with merely observing them, but studies the role of particular experimentally manipulable variables on the *course* of such changes (e.g., the role of stimuli or activities which intervene during the adaptation or forgetting period). As we shall see, the developmental psychologist can and does engage in work of a very similar nature.

Three sets of factors have conspired heretofore against the adoption of this kind of view in developmental psychology, i.e., against a shift from a focus on differences to a focus on change. The first of these is methodological: The nearly universal adoption of the cross-sectional as opposed to longitudinal approach means that the developmental investigator rarely has an opportunity to study change directly, but is generally content to infer it from the differences he observes among his age groups. This encourages a paradoxically static stance in the study of development which appears to render the latter equivalent to the study of inherent, or a least ready-made differences among particular populations.

The second factor concerns the static character of the statistical models which are in vogue in psychology today. It is most clearly illustrated in that most popular statistical tool, analysis of variance. Whatever its power and utility, this model is predicated on the existence of a perfectly constant set of populations providing an unchanging universe of scores from which the investigator obtains samples. This notion may be valid in the case of the experimental psychologist undertaking to compare scores obtained under an experimental and a control condition, both sets being obtained contemporaneously and within a brief span of time. It is apt to become suspect, however, as soon as attempts are made to replicate a study at some later time, since the state of the population may well have changed along relevant parameters. Once we move to the differentialist's domain, the problem becomes increasingly acute, since it is patently erroneous to conceive of any population defined in subject-variable terms as unchanging, there is, in other words, no meaningfully definable universe of scores representing, e.g., adults of the female sex, fixed in time and space.

If the real world thus provides, in general, a most imperfect fit for the conceptions of a fixed population on which models such as the analysis of variance are built, these become altogether inappropriate when applied to data which concern change as such. It is only by sticking to the study of age-group differences that developmental psychologists have been able to developmental psychologist is not typically interested in detecting any significant differences whatever among his age groups, but rather in determining of qualitatively differentiated conditions or populations. In other words, the developmental psychologist is not typically interested in detecting any significant differences whatever among his age groups, but rather in determining whether the group means trace out some meaningful pattern when ordered along the age variable. In recognition of this fact, that the age variable represents, not a nominal, but an ordered and indeed equal-interval scale, we find increasingly frequent resort to techniques which take this feature into account, notably trend analysis. What is not commonly realized, however, is that the resort to trend analysis involves a basic shift in the kind of statistical model involved, from one of testing null hypotheses to one best described as curve fitting. This latter model, though essentially descriptive, is in fact much more effectively suited to the needs of the developmental psychologist, as we shall see.

Finally, we come to the role of developmental theory itself in reinforcing the anomalously static approach to the study of development to which we have been referring. Our major developmental theories, notably those of Piaget and Werner, have been mainly concerned with questions of structure: *What* are the differences in the behaviors observable at particular levels of development, or conversely, what is the formal relationship among these different sets of behaviors? They have thus been relatively uninterested in the study of developmental *change*, i.e., the transition from one level to another. Thus the cross-sectional approach has suited their purposes quite well.

In the hands of Werner and his associates (cf. Werner & Kaplan, 1956; Langer, 1970) furthermore, what is in the present view a vice has been turned into a virtue. Developmental differences are not identified with, much less defined in terms of age differences, but rather defined a priori (Werner and Kaplan are explicit and insistent on this point) as those differences conforming to particular structural relationships, e.g., a difference in degree of hierarchic integration. This has permitted them to apply their version of developmental theory to parameters or populations defined in terms of variables bearing no visible relationship to age; for example, they have utilized it to analyze the effects of exposure time, or instructions in studies of perception, as well as differences between normals and schizophrenics, and diverse other group differences, defined in terms of education, culture, or occupational specialization. It should be apparent that the undeniable gain in generality and scope of the Wernerian developmental framework is made possible only by defining the developmental dimension in response terms; in particular, the age variable is now relegated to the status of one among several which happen to be isomorphically related to the stipulated structural differences in behavior. This has necessarily led to an approach to the study of age differences which is comparative and purely descriptive in nature (cf. the title of Werner's major treatise, *Comparative Psychology of Mental Development*), and consequently has detracted from a concern for change occurring along the age dimension, and for the processes governing this change.

In sum, what we are suggesting is that the developmental psychologist consider changes in behavior with age as the basic datum of his discipline. By shifting age from the status of an independent variable to one which forms part of the definition of the dependent variable, the question whether this discipline is experimental or differential evaporates, and turns instead into one of the modes of approach chosen to investigate particular age changes in behavior, which may be either experimental or differential. More important, this view leads to a reexamination of the task confronting the developmental psychologist, to which we will devote Chapter III.

Change as an Inherent Aspect of Behavior

Let us return to the axiom enunciated at the start of this chapter. It is open to challenge on two fronts: first, in its blithe identification of the subject matter of developmental research with the study of age changes, and second, in the notion espoused of the inherent nature of behavior change, and its intended corollary, that such change is not itself necessarily to be explained by reference to external agents, forces or events. Many psychologists, particularly those of a behaviorist persuasion, will take vigorous exception to such a statement; they will presumably argue that changes in behavior with age not only demand explanation, but will prove readily amenable to explanation by applying principles of learning which have been validated and successfully applied in the analysis of behavior change generally.

To anticipate the argument to be proposed in Chapter XI where this question will be examined at much greater length, the gist of it is that the difference between the two points of view can probably be identified with the level of analysis of behavior change which is being adopted. Learning principles are intended to apply at a microscopic level, i.e., to changes observed in particular individual responses under a defined set of conditions. While these may *in principle* be equally relevant to the kinds of changes which the developmental psychologist is interested in, generally involving a whole class of responses changing under ill-defined and probably undefinable conditions, it will turn out to be more fruitful at this macroscopic level to treat these changes as given, and thus not reducible to particular determining forces.

In support of such a position, furthermore, we may invoke a variety of analogous cases involving changes in behavior over time which are similarly treated. There is, first of all, the neurological fact that the central nervous system is never in a state of rest, even during sleep (Magoun, 1958); in other words, change rather than stability is the norm, even if only in a random or cyclical sense. As behavioristically inclined a psychologist as Hull was forced to give explicit recognition to this fact in his construct of behavior oscillation. To be sure, developmental changes are far from random, and thus surely not reducible to such an oscillation principle. But they are by no means the only directional changes occurring in behavior as a function of time. We need only consider such phenomena as adaptation, habituation, and sensitization: In all of these cases the psychologist studies changes in behavior as a function of sheer passage of time. This does not mean that time is given the status of an independent variable causally related to the observed changes. To the extent that a given study, for example, of dark adaptation, consists in nothing more than a plot of the changes in threshold over time, it would probably be regarded as merely descriptive in nature. Independent variables might be introduced to show the role of particular factors, such as wavelength, on the rate of, for instance, adaptation. These factors could then be said to be causally related to the differences in the respective *rates* of adaptation observed, in other words, time would enter as part of the definition of the dependent variable, just as we have suggested earlier for the age variable. These independent variables would not in any sense account for the changes observed with time. The latter, if they are not to be simply referred to as an "inherent characteristic of the visual system," would have to be explained in terms of physiological processes, i.e., by turning to a lower-order level of analysis.

This point leads to a natural objection to using phenomena like adaptation and sensitization, which are directly traceable to neurophysiological mechanisms, as a model for the study of changes in behavior with age. In partial answer to this criticism, we may note that adaptation occurs in situations in which no known physiological mechanism can be invoked [cf. the perceptual "normalization" phenomena studied by Gibson (1937)]. For a closer analogy, however, let us turn to a different order of changes in response over time, where the role of the time variable is under a cloud of suspicion similar to the case of age changes, namely, the changes in response involved in the study of memory.

Here we find represented in miniature the essential dimensions of the conceptualization of the time variable as it applies in developmental research. Just as in the case of the latter, we can contrast the microscopic level of analysis embodied in the study of retroactive inhibition, in which specific changes in response are traced to specific intervening stimuli, or stimulus–response associations, to the macroscopic level entailed in Jenkins and Dallenbach's (1924) classical study comparing the course of forgetting during sleep with that during wakefulness. The fact that retention dropped off much more sharply over the course of time for the awake subjects as compared to the asleep subjects can be taken as evidence for the role of intervening activity in forgetting; indeed, the authors invoke what amounts to a retroactive inhibition notion to explain their results. However, in view of the fact that no specific relationship between these activities and the material (nonsense syllables) that had been learned can be assumed to exist, it appears at least as profitable to look at forgetting as it occurred in this study as a "fact of life," i.e., as an inherent characteristic of the memory process, given a normal, alive, and consequently, active organism. This characteristic may ultimately be explained in neurophysiological terms (an expectation clearly justified by current advances in the neurophysiology and neurochemistry of learning) but not by invoking assumed psychological forces or antecedent events as causal agents.

One major consequence of the adoption of this point of view in regard to the status of the age variable and the inherent nature of developmental change is that the study of age changes in behavior now appears to take on, to a very large extent, a purely descriptive character. At the same time the shift to a focus on change in behavior, and the deemphasis on mere age-group comparison leads to a host of empirical questions requiring study which, however descriptive, are substantially broader in scope and interest than ordinary descriptive research is usually thought of as being. The resolution of these questions will, in turn, bring us closer to an inductively built model of the developmental process, thus leading progressively to research at the level of model-testing and hypothesis testing. Finally, an experimental attack on developmental problems is by no means inconsistent with the view presented here; it will, however, entail research of a kind very different from the manner in which the experimental study of behavioral development is generally conceived of at present. In particular, the object of explanation in such studies will typically turn out not to be the developmental changes themselves, but rather the variables which modulate or modify the course or character of these changes.

Some Further Objections to the Use of Age as a Variable in Psychology

In view of the stance with respect to the age variable which we are proposing for the purposes of this volume, the equating of developmental research with change in behavior over age should appear logical, or at least justifiable. We should, nevertheless, consider some of the main objections to such an identification which have been advanced. Such objections come from diametrically opposed theoretical positions, ranging from Werner's developmental theory, which aims to apply developmental principles to compare the behavior of individuals varying along diverse dimensions, of which age happens to be one, to that of radical behaviorism, such as espoused by those following the Skinnerian position (e.g., Bijou & Baer, 1963). The latter would minimize the role of the age variable in developmental research:

> We expect that little of the changing behavior of a child is produced by the passage of time alone. *Therefore, a developmental analysis is not a relationship of behavior to age, but is a relationship of behavior to events which, requiring time in order to occur, will necessarily have some correlation with age.* The correlation, of course, will be important to anyone planning, let us say, a program of study for the average ten-year-old; but it will not be important to an understanding of the processes of development as such [p. 198, italics in the original].

Accordingly, these psychologists argue for an approach based on the systematic programming of the developing individual's experience in such a way as to simulate the developmental changes normally occurring as an apparent function of the passage of time.

Both of these objections have already been touched on previously. The Wernerian position was seen to be predicated on a purely structural approach to the study of development; it attains an impressive scope and generality, but only at the expense of throwing overboard an external criterion for development such as provided by the age variable, which could provide a base line for the study of behavioral *change*, and notably its functional aspects. As for the radical behaviorist position, we suggested that the meaningfulness of studying changes in behavior taking place along the dimension of age as such, as opposed to relating them to the conditions or events supposedly determining them, depends on the level of analysis at which the study of development is undertaken.

There remain, nevertheless, certain more general objections to the use of the age variable which warrant discussion. For, as popular as the age variable is in psychological research, dissatisfaction and uneasiness as to the appropriateness of its use is widespread. This malaise is given effective expression in Kessen's (1960) excellent discussion of problems of design of developmental research, which remains the only attempt to date to take a systematic look at the various paradigms of research based on the use of the age variable, and their limitations. Kessen cites three main objections to the use of age as a variable in behavioral research: (*a*) aspects of behavior may be lawfully related to age, but yet "demand" an analysis in terms of other variables (e.g., the child's prior history); (*b*) statements of a relationship of behavior to age involve a lack of control over the variables "determining" the age differences, and are consequently devoid of causal meaning or explanatory power; (*c*) the well-known individual variations in the behavior of children at a given age in effect preclude the possibility of obtaining consistent functional relationships to the age variable. These several objections do not lead Kessen to deny age a place in developmental research (as the radical behaviorists do), but he admits it essentially on a provisional, *faute de mieux* basis, recognizing the insufficiency of the present state of our knowledge concerning the *true* variables determining behavioral development.

The first two of Kessen's objections seem to be virtually indistinguishable since the "other variables," which, according to the first objection, should replace age in statements of functional relationships, are presumably those which have a more direct, causal relationship to the behavioral changes found with age. These two criticisms thus are restatements, in a less dogmatic but correspondingly less positive (and thus ultimately less useful) form, of the radical behaviorist's position already referred to: Changes with behavior observed to occur over age are to be traced to particular determining events. As for the third, it is difficult to take seriously the argument that individual differences within an age group diminish the value of functional relationships of behavior to age; if this objection were to be upheld, the whole edifice of experimental psychology, with the possible exception of operant-conditioning research, would come crashing down with a loud thud! The fact is that in many situations, age accounts for a larger proportion of the variance in a set of measures than is true for most psychological variables considered to have a true independent status, i.e., as causal determinants of the behavior. Why should we insist that it account for 100% of the variance, or even come close to this limit?

Kessen's third objection could be rephrased in a different, but more interesting fashion. Chronological age, it can be argued, is not a useful variable in statements of functional relationships to behavior, since there are considerable individual differences in rates of developmental change, i.e., one child at 4 years may attain a level on some given behavioral dimension which another may not reach till the age of 6. This is, as we shall see, by no means a negligible objection, since it relates to the usefulness of the *metric* provided by the age variable (wherein lies the difference between it and Kessen's original form, concerned with within age-group differences). It may be answered in several ways. First, and least compelling, we may refer to the analogous cases of studies of adaptation and forgetting, where rates of change in the behavior in question are similarly subject to individual differences; yet no one has appeared to challenge the validity of the use of chronological time as a base line in such research. (The same point can be made with respect to the use of an independent dimension such as number of trials to criterion to measure speed or rate of learning.) Second, individual differences in rate of development themselves constitute a fact of great potential interest, so that the adoption of a developmental scale that reveals it (i.e., time since birth) should on that score be recommended. Third, the finding of differences in the rate of development does not preclude the possibility of lawful relationships between age and behavior, either in the purely ordinal sense, or in the sense that such individual differences will hopefully prove to be incorporable as parameters in the expression of these functional relationships.

Age as a Neutral Variable: Vice or Virtue?

On occasion dissatisfaction with the use of chronological age (CA) as a base line along which to measure developmental changes (based on the irrelevance of time since birth as a functionally meaningful variable in the study of behavior), leads to the promulgation of some alternative index as a substitute for CA. The one most frequently proposed in psychological studies is mental age (MA), i.e., level of intellectual development, at least in studies in which cognitive development is thought to determine a child's performance on a given task. This seemingly reasonable procedure is roughly comparable to replacing the clock with a rating of degree of experienced darkness as a base line for plotting changes in absolute threshold to light over the course of dark adaptation. In other words, it is in danger of being a fundamentally circular procedure, in which the development of a specific measure of behavior postulated to have a cognitive component is "explained" in terms of a general, highly heterogeneous measure of cognitive development, whose metric is, furthermore, quite dubious. There is, of course, nothing wrong with studying the *interrelationship* between two measures of behavior taken over some segment of the age continuum, but it should be obvious that such a study conforms to an $R_1 = f(R_2)$ relationship, with neither variable meriting a status of "independent variable" (in the sense that the use of MA in this context generally implies), unless the causal link between the two variables has been established through prior experimental research, or can be assumed on purely logical grounds.

This objection of circularity would not apply, to be sure, if we use as a substitute for CA some index of physical or physiological development, or perhaps some composite of several such indices, such as Olson and Hughes's (1942) "Organismic Age" Index (though presumably stripped of its MA component, for the reasons which were just indicated). This procedure might be of value with respect to behavioral measures suspected to be largely biogenic in nature, although the likelihood of any such index showing a more consistent and closer relationship to any behavioral measure than CA seems remote. Conceivably, this might be true for direct measures of neural functioning, e.g., an EEG-derived measure, but here the problem of potential circularity reappears.

There is a further limitation to any of these substitutes for CA. It applies most clearly to "age" measures (MA, skeletal age, etc.) that have a purely relative meaning, being defined in terms of a set of standardization samples representing successive normative age groups. None of these measures reveals much of value concerning the parameters of growth (rate of growth, shape of the growth curve, etc.), since on all of these measures increments over successive yearly periods are all artifactually equal, on the scale of age units employed.

For these reasons as well as others (for instance, the status of CA as a ratio scale) CA is, generally, to be preferred as a dimension along which to measure changes in behavior with age. The purely descriptive, and consequently causally neutral nature of statements of the $R = f(CA)$ variety is beyond question, but at least there is no ambiguity in this respect. Furthermore, it allows us to proceed beyond the descriptive level, in the manner which we have argued previously, i.e., treating CA as entering into the definition of the dependent variable, so as to permit study of the relationships between other independent variables and behavior *change*.

The Age Variable and the Problem of Control in Differential Studies

Attempts to enhance the meaningfulness of measures of developmental status when placed into relationship with some particular response, frequently take the form of *controlling* for the effects of CA, so as to yield a purer measure of the influence of the variable of interest (e.g., MA) independent of all of the diverse aspects of experience and behavior which covary with age. This procedure entails serious difficulties, of a statistical as well as a logical nature, which can be traced to the common confusion surrounding the conception of the age variable, when it is equated to other variables utilized in differential investigation. It further reveals the fallacy of taking over procedures of design and data analysis employed to advantage by the experimentalist for use in differential research.

To bring out the fallacy, let us examine a case in which the usual procedure of controlling for CA in assessing the effects of MA has been turned around, in order to provide allegedly a measure of the role of chronological age independent of change in intelligence, with patently bizarre results. It is a study by Kounin (1941), well-known to psychologists interested in the problem of rigidity.

Kounin's aim was to test a hypothesis derived from Lewin's theory, which postulates an increase in rigidity with age, in the sense of increasing impermeability of the boundaries separating the parts of a field. Accordingly, Kounin hypothesized that the rate of satiation of an activity, and more particularly of cosatiation of some activity as a function of an ongoing related activity, would be positively related to age. However, since mental development would tend to work in an opposite direction (e.g., of generalization occurring across broader spans of conceptual similarity), Kounin was intent on controlling for the role of mental age in testing this hypothesis. To this end, he selected three groups of subjects which were equated for MA, but whose CA varied from 8 to 41 years; the three groups thus consisted of normal children, feeble-minded adolescents, and feeble-minded adults, respectively. The results of this study ostensibly showed that rigidity increases with age (i.e., rate of satiation and cosatiation decreases), a finding which has led to considerable controversy over the meaning of rigidity, etc. (see Luchins & Luchins, 1959, pp. 43ff). Yet, upon closer analysis it appears that this attempt to hold MA constant while varying CA amounts to a *reductio ad absurdum* of the technique of experimental control, at the least if the variable of interest is that of age.

What is it, more specifically, that has been accomplished in this study? The author has, in effect, selected his subjects in a particular way, i.e., so as to yield groups of particular CA and MA combinations. In view of the fact, however, that these two variables are intrinsically correlated in a population of developing individuals, this selection procedure introduces some obvious difficulties, of a logical, as well as a statistical character.

The logical problem resides in the lack of representativeness, and, indeed, artificiality of the samples obtained through such a selection procedure. By equating for MA groups supposedly representing different levels of CA, samples that are certainly highly peculiar result, if considered as representative of their respective levels of chronological age. The results of this study thus throw very little light on the operation of the variable of age as such; they are relevant rather to the comparison of normal with feeble-minded individuals.

The statistical side of the problem similarly relates to the biased nature of the samples, if taken to represent different age levels. The selection procedure clearly operates to select scores at each age level which represent markedly nonrandom samples from their respective age groups. Indeed, it would be very difficult to define any set of populations from which the samples of scores collected by the investigator may be said to have been randomly drawn, since they were obtained not by defining a population beforehand but rather by selecting from populations of specified ages subsamples such as to equate for the correlated variable of MA. It is thus only in the very restricted sense of these samples as representative of particular *combinations* of MA and CA values that they are interpretable in terms of sampling principles at all.[2]

[2]Kounin (1941) himself is ambivalent on this point, at times seeming to be interested mainly in studying the role of age as such, in order to establish the relationship between age and rigidity stipulated by Lewin, while at other times he appears to be concerned rather with the problem of mental retardation.

The same argument would apply to all cases in which selection designed to equate groups on a variable that is correlated with the independent variable is carried out, although the selection effects may not be as dramatic as in the preceding example. To illustrate, we need only invert Kounin's design, by following the fairly common procedure of equating groups for CA in order to investigate the separate role of MA, as in Hoffmann's (1955) study of generalization as a function of intellectual level. Such a procedure seems defensible only so long as the interest is in the variable of IQ, that is, intellectual level relative to the average for a particular age group, rather than level of mental development. The reason why this procedure gives less of an appearance of a *reductio ad absurdum* than did the formally equivalent one in the preceding case is that here the variable of interest (MA) is positively correlated with the actual variable (IQ), whereas in Kounin's study the relationship between the ostensible and the actual variable (CA and IQ) was inverse. Nevertheless, the procedure in both cases is suspect, and for the same reasons.

The argument presented here against the procedure of controlling for the effects of a variable typically correlated with the one of interest to the investigator, by holding it constant through sample selection, is not confined to the case of MA versus CA. It would apply to any differential variable where sample selection is used to "fix" the control variable at a particular level, as in the selection of samples to represent differences in socioeconomic levels, while holding the amount of education constant. When this control procedure is used in developmental psychology, however, to tease out the role of mental development from that of chronological age, we are presented with a good illustration of the misunderstanding of the age variable, as a consequence of its being assimilated to the general category of differential variables.

In this connection a study by Harter (1965) is of direct relevance. Harter was interested in demonstrating the relationship between speed of learning-set formation and intelligence. Accordingly, she chose nine samples of children representing three levels of IQ at each of three levels of MA. Table 2-1 shows the combinations of MA and IQ, the CA levels corresponding to each combination, and the mean criterion score (number of problems taken to reach the criterion for learning-set formation) for each subgroup. Note that here the two variables, MA and IQ, are uncorrelated.

The results indicate that speed of learning-set formation is highly related to MA (scores decrease from top to bottom within each column) and to IQ (scores increase from left to right within each row); but apparently not highly related to CA, as shown, for instance, in the three diagonal cells, all corresponding to a CA of 7 years, which among them contain the highest and lowest of the cell means in the table. This is borne

TABLE 2-1

Characteristics and Criterion Scores of the Nine Groups of Harter's (1965) Study of Learning-Set Formation

Group[a]	Mean IQ	Mean MA (yr)	Mean CA (yr)	Mean criterion score
L–5	71.4	4.9	7.0	51.8
L–7	68.9	7.0	10.1	38.2
L–9	70.0	9.1	13.2	18.1
N–5	103.9	5.2	5.0	30.9
N–7	104.2	7.2	6.9	23.8
N–9	102.3	9.3	9.1	18.2
H–5	137.1	4.8	3.4	18.8
H–7	135.7	6.7	4.9	16.0
H–9	132.8	9.4	7.1	10.8

[a]L, N, and H refer to low, normal, and high IQ levels, respectively; 5, 7, and 9 refer to the MA levels.

out by the correlation of .03 between CA and the criterion score, compared to a correlation of −.47 between the latter and MA.

These findings can be taken to show that speed of learning-set performance is not a function of CA, but rather of intelligence, i.e., that MA is a better predictor than CA in this situation. Indeed, this was Harter's interpretation of her results, in conformance with her argument that the usual practice of selecting groups varying in CA fails to take the concomitant changes in MA into account, so that behavioral changes appear spuriously related to age, when the true variable responsible for the changes is the child's level of intellectual development.

From the perspective of our analysis of the status of the age variable, however, such a conclusion is based on a misconception of the place to be accorded to this variable. The fact is, first of all, that the cross-sectional comparisons between rather arbitrarily selected groups only obscure what we may consider to be a patent fact: Learning-set performance does improve with age. Presumably, if any of the children included in the top row had been followed up longitudinally, their scores would have improved (decreased) in a fashion similar to that shown within each column, corresponding to increases in MA levels. Thus, rather than asserting that MA and IQ separately influence speed of learning-set formation, independent of CA, a more sensible statement would be (a) that this speed is a monotonically decreasing function of age (a purely descriptive statement, encompassing all variables covarying with CA), and (b) that the rate of this decrease varies in populations differing in IQ, i.e., as a function of the particular constellation of genetic and experiential forces which have been at work in molding the child's ability to form learning sets.

As was noted earlier, little is gained, and much is lost, in shifting from CA to MA as an index of development, since this entails a shift from a descriptive, causally neutral statement to one which relates one aspect of behavior to another, but with an increase in explanatory power which is more apparent than real. For the same reason, attempts to vary MA while keeping CA constant (or vice versa) miss the essential point that CA is an intrinsic component of MA, and that the phenomenon of interest is the change in behavior occurring as the individual grows older, as modulated by such individual characteristics as intelligence.

The Concept of the Developmental Function

By throwing age onto the dependent side of the ledger, we arrive at a definition of the developmental psychologist's dependent variable in terms of the concept of the *developmental function*. This term may be defined simply as the form or mode of the relationship between the chronological age of the individual and the changes observed to occur in his responses on some specified dimension of behavior over the course of his development to maturity.[3]

The definition just stated, however simple-minded and preformal, needs elaboration in at least three respects. First, what is meant by "form or mode" of the relationship? These represent the basic, generalizable characteristics of the function, varying from statements of order or sequence, for purely qualitative variables, through statements concerning direction of change, or general shape of the function, to specifications of the form of the function in terms of a mathematical equation. Thus, with respect to the motor sequence of development, the developmental function would consist of the determination of the discrete steps which make up this sequence, in their appropriate order, coupled with at least approximate indications of the points or intervals on the age continuum corresponding to the appearance of each step. For most quantitative dimensions, the function would refer to the overall pattern of change (e.g., monotonically increasing, inverted U-

---

[3]In principle there is no reason not to extend the developmental-function concept to the whole life cycle. However, the indeterminacy of the onset of aging, the lack of measurable change over an extended period of maturity observed for many aspects of behavior, and the difficulty of applying longitudinal methodology to the entire life-span mitigate against the usefulness of such extension. In any event, the treatment of this book will be confined to the course of ontogenetic development up to maturity.

shaped, etc.), together with an indication of the approximate age periods within which each differentiable phase of the function would be contained. Finally, for certain limited kinds of dimensions, notably those of physical growth, and conceivably certain psychological ones such as intelligence or vocabulary, it may be possible to specify more precisely, in mathematical or graphic form, the exact shape of the function, or at least the particular family of curves (Gompertz, logistic, polynomial of the nth degree, etc.) to which it belongs.

The second point was already anticipated in our discussion earlier in this chapter of the objections levelled against the use of age, based on the variation in behavior found in children of a given age. The point is that developmental functions refer to the pattern of change displayed by the individual, and can only be determined through successive observations on the same individual. It is assumed that corresponding functions for different individuals will have some overall communality, so that modal or prototype functions characteristic of groups of individuals may be determined, but even these generalizable characteristics may not become apparent without reference to the individual function. It may be observed that this focus on the individual is not at all unique to the study of developmental change. It is commonly found in any realm of psychological investigation which, however nomothetic in conception and intent, demands detailed analysis of the form of the function relating response to quantitative continua such as time (adaptation), number of trials (learning) or stimulus magnitude (psychophysics).

A third question raised by the definition of "developmental function" relates to the expression "on some specified dimension." In effect, the definition presupposes that the task of dimensionalizing behavioral development has been carried out, and that a dimension has been isolated which lends itself to the study of developmental change in the manner we are proposing. The implications of this requirement for the definition or discovery of such dimensions, and the approaches to this dimensionalization task will be taken up in Chapters V and VI, respectively; at this point suffice it to note in very general terms the nature of the limitations on developmental research which it imposes, and the kind of behavioral variables which will satisfy it.

In order for the developmental-function approach to work, two conditions must be met: First, the behavior variable must be one with respect to which age changes can be expected of sufficient magnitude to be revealed consistently in the face of the "noise" from variance associated with situational factors, stimulus conditions, and errors of sampling and measurement. Second, these age changes must remain roughly invariant over differences in specific experiential and environmental conditions so as to make possible the determination of a modal prototype function representing their expected form under "normal" conditions of development.

These conditions are most readily illustrated by reference to a nonbehavioral variable: growth in weight. Measures of weight are subject to "noise" from such factors as temporary illness, seasonal fluctuation, short-term dietary conditions, exercise, etc., as well as sheer errors of measurement where measures are taken of the individual clothed. There are, furthermore, important variations in weight associated with general evironmental condition, nutritional factors, genetic constitution, and race. Yet none of these can possibly obscure the basic fact of growth for all individuals growing normally (i.e., excepting cases of gross hypothyroidism, dwarfs, etc.). So it becomes possible to talk of a modal type of function for growth in weight, possessing certain characteristics with respect to form, periods of acceleration and deceleration, etc., which can serve as a prototype against which to compare the growth of any particular individual.

Clearly, many behavioral variables do not fulfill these conditions, and would thus be inappropriate for the application of developmental-function analysis in this sense. Some, like reading skill or speed, factual knowledge, proficiency in a particular sport, etc., require highly specific training or experience for the occurrence of any developmental change. Others, like magnitude of the horizontal–vertical illusion, or amount of cross-modal transfer, are so highly dependent on the specific stimuli and conditions used to obtain the measures that consistent age changes are apt to become obscured. Still others, like emotionality, aggressiveness, strength of affiliative needs, etc., represent chiefly dimensions of individual difference that are orthogonal to development, and with respect to which consistent age changes cannot be meaningfully measured, except perhaps in terms of certain qualitative aspects (e.g., form of expression of aggression or affiliation).

The real question is whether there are any variables which do meet our requirements. The answer is an unequivocal yes, provided we know where to look, or more important, how to define them. Some examples are obvious: vocabulary size (as well as other, more interesting measures of language development), spatial ability, visual–motor coordination, verbal recall, attention span. Others emerge upon proper redefinition of the behavioral variable: Susceptibility to visual illusions, or accuracy of visual discrimination, would be poor candidates, whereas strength of assimilation tendencies, or ability to integrate stimulus information across spatial or temporal gaps may be much more promising.

The fact is that we are just beginning to obtain a reasonably comprehensive view of the ways and directions in which children's behavior changes during the course of their development to maturity, and the dimensions defining these changes. Good developmental data with respect to these changes (particularly those based on longitudinal information), are still relatively meager, so that in many places our treatment in the chapters to follow will have to fall back on the tried and true, but not necessarily most relevant or informative cases of physical growth and changes in intelligence-test performance. But on a more abstract plane, it will not be difficult to indicate the ways in which the approaches which we will consider may be applied to many other variables, taken from the realm of perceptual and cognitive development, language, curiosity, etc.

CHAPTER III
Beyond Age-Group Comparison:
A Programmatic View of the
Task of Developmental Psychology

It seems safe to state that better than 90% of developmental research has consisted of cross-sectional age-group comparison studies.The limitations of this approach to the study of developmental phenomena and of the conception of age underlying it were discussed in the preceding chapter, where we likewise pointed to the widespread dissatisfaction with this type of research. Yet, apart from the research of a small, though growing group of devoted Skinnerians, few viable alternatives have been proposed, let alone employed in research. A focal premise of this volume is that such alternatives do exist, that the task of the developmental psychologist is indeed considerably more complex than has been commonly recognized, and that it can be formulated in terms of a hierarchical series of steps, to be presented shortly.

Before proceeding with the construction of this scaffold for developmental research, let us examine more concretely the limitations of age-group comparison research and the questions it poses for the developmentalist by reference to two studies conforming to this paradigm. They start, as it happens, from diametrically opposite theoretical views; one being in the tradition of S-R behaviorist conceptions of child behavior, and the other originating in cognitive-developmental theory. This contrast serves to indicate that the aforementioned limitations, and indeed the proposed enlargement of the view of the developmentalist's task, cut across major theoretical divisions in the field.

Let us look first at a study by Stevenson and Weir (1959) on probability-learning in children. Here we have an excellent illustration of the importation into the developmental field of a problem taken from the general experimental laboratory—in this case, from the area of mathematical learning theory (Estes, 1950; Bush & Mosteller, 1955). Stevenson and Weir were interested in applying this framework to the developmental realm, utilizing a probability-learning task in which one of three choice stimuli is reinforced according to a random partial-reinforcement schedule. They hypothesized that the rate of responding to the reinforced stimulus would be a function of the strength of the child's expectation of reinforcement. In a prior study, Stevenson and Zigler (1958) had indeed found that expectancy of success, manipulated experimentally by giving pretraining for one group of children with a 100:0:0 reinforcement schedule to the three stimuli, and to another with a 33:0:0 schedule, did significantly affect the children's response to a subsequent 66:0:0 condition: The children in the former group, who presumably had built up a strong expectancy of being reinforced, showed only a 72% asymptotal response rate to the 66% reinforced stimulus, while that for the latter group, apparently content with a lower rate of reinforcement, was 85%. We are interested here, however, in Stevenson and Weir's attempt to investigate this problem developmentally, starting from the premise that between the ages of 3 and 9 years, children's expectancy of success increases as a function of their increasing general competence, that is, they become progressively less satisfied with behavior which yields less than consistent reinforcement. The results did, in fact indicate that, at least under one of their two conditions involving a 33:0:0 schedule, asymptotal response rates to the reinforced stimulus steadily decreased with age.

Quite apart from the fact that under the second partial-reinforcement condition (66 : 0 : 0) the developmental trend was much less consistent, this study discloses the basic limitation of the age-group comparison paradigm: the lack of control over the factors determining the age differences observed. There are, in principle, an indeterminate number of ways of interpreting any difference between subject groups in a nonexperimental study (the area of sex-difference research is a prime example of this point). Thus, though Stevenson and his associates may have had a sound basis for their interpretation of probability-learning behavior, in terms of success-expectancy, the age differences they report hardly represent very incisive evidence for their argument. To mention just one competing interpretation for them, Jones and Liverant (1960) invoked the notion of differential experience with environmental uncertainties to explain the very similar age differences they found in their own study.

The subsequent history of the study of probability learning in children, which has been effectively reviewed by Goulet and Goodwin (1970), disclosed a much more basic shortcoming of the Stevenson *et al.* line of attack on the problem, namely that of the response measure chosen for analysis.

In line with the antecedents of this research in the work of the mathematical-learning theorists, attention was focused almost exclusively on asymptotal response rates. Yet, if Stevenson and Weir's expectancy-of-success hypothesis is examined more closely, it leads to the expectation of a qualitative change in the child's mode of response to the situation: In the face of the intermittent reinforcement for responding to the apparently correct stimulus, the older child engages in systematic hypothesis-testing behavior, in an attempt to arrive at a response strategy that will increase his pay-off rate. Stevenson and Weir (1961) soon came to this realization themselves, and by concentrating on the analysis of systematic *patterns* of responses they laid the foundation for a completely altered conception of the problem in cognitive terms, focusing on the development of problem-solving strategies, which was exploited with considerable success in the subsequent research on this problem by Weir (1964) and Offenbach (1964; 1965).

We see then a double lesson in the type of developmental study represented in Stevenson and Weir's original investigation: the lack of power of age-group difference as a source of evidence on the operation of developmental processes, and the limitations of response measures not specifically chosen to reveal such processes in bringing out the true basis for the observed age differences in the behavior. The second study to be cited (Gollin, 1958), couched as it is in developmental theory, is less vulnerable on the second score, but illustrates the first point with equal force, while suggesting a more generally applicable approach to dealing with it. Gollin was interested in applying a cognitive-developmental framework to the study of children's formation of impressions of others. To this end he obtained data, first, on the extent to which children at ages 10–11, 13–14, and 16–17 years make use of processes of inference in interpreting or accounting for the behavior of others (observed via cinematographic episodes); and second, on the extent to which they attempt to cope with conflicting information. In both respects he found marked age changes, in the hypothesized direction.

Although Gollin selected response measures specifically designed to bear on cognitive aspects of impression formation, his study is no less susceptible to competing interpretations of the age differences reported than was Stevenson and Weir's. Thus, with "inference" being credited for any "attempt to go beyond just the action shown in the movie," in other words, involving reference to a motive or underlying condition for the observed behavior, it is apparent that factors of verbal ability or fluency (to name just one alternative interpretation), could readily account for the data. Similarly, the "concept" measure, which referred to the child's attempted resolution of the apparent conflict between "good" and "bad" behavior observed in the same child, might be expected to be influenced by the child's socialization experiences and developing social values, which would in fact be a prerequisite for the recognition of the conflict itself, given the nature of the behavioral episodes presented.

The value of Gollin's study as a pioneering effort in the investigation of this particular aspect of developmental psychology is certainly not diminished by this purely illustrative critique. But it demonstrates again the inherent ambiguity and insufficiency of age-difference data of this sort. More precisely, what it lacks is direct information on the child's cognitive processes relevant to the situation at hand that could be correlated with his performance. Gollin did obtain information on his subjects' IQ, which pointed to a modest relationship of his two measures to IQ within his age-groups, but this finding is hardly sufficient to establish the cognitive basis for his observed age changes, especially given the highly global measure of cognitive functioning represented by the IQ. Subsequent research on the development of social perception and role-taking in children by Feffer and Gourevitch (1960) and Wolfe (1963), similarly inspired by cognitive theory, proceeded to provide just such information, by recourse to measures of cognitive level based on theories considered to have direct relevance to the development of social perception. These studies are thus potentially much more incisive in their bearing on developmental processes in this area. The qualifier "potentially" must, unfortunately, be inserted in this statement, in recognition of the fact that the correlational approach in this area runs into a major methodological difficulty: How does one deal with the role of age per se, when correlating two age-related measures of behavior in an attempt to show that one set of age changes is reducible to, or interpretable in terms of the other? This point will be brought out more fully in Chapter X, dealing with the correlational paradigm in developmental research.

A Hierarchical Model for the Study of Developmental Problems

With the above mentioned shortcomings of traditional research on developmental problems in mind, we are ready now to present in outline a hierarchical model of the major paradigms of developmental research, which, taken together, might be said to define a programmatic approach to the study of developmental problems. This model is sketched out in Fig. 3-1. A brief overview will be given here, which should serve at the same time as a guide to the organization of the core chapters of this volume, V through XII, in which the successive phases of the program are given detailed treatment.

I. The Discovery and Synthesis of Developmental Dimensions	
I-A. Abstracting invariant age changes from variation in situational variables.	I-B. Specification of dimensions, or factors of age changes and construction of developmental scales.

II. The Descriptive Study of Age Changes	
II-A. Quantitative changes: determination of developmental functions and their parameters.	II-B. Qualitative changes (developmental sequences).

III. The Correlational Study of Age Changes	
III-A. The interpatterning of changes along two or more developmental dimensions.	III-B. The interpatterning of changes with respect to qualitatively defined behaviors (the study of stages).

IV. The Study of the Determinants of Developmental Change	
IV-A. The experimental manipulation of development.	IV-B. The nonexperimental study of determinants of development.

V. The Study of Individual Differences in Development	
V-A. Individual differences in the form or pattern of age changes.	V-B. Stability: invariance of individual differences over the course of development.

Fig. 3–1. Schema for conceptualizing a programmatic approach to research on developmental change.

1. THE DISCOVERY AND SYNTHESIS OF DEVELOPMENTAL DIMENSIONS

The first task facing the developmental psychologist as he sets out to investigate the course of development for any particular aspect of behavior is that of constructing scales with which to chart this course. This, then, represents the road-building phase in the study of development. Developmentalists have, by and large, been content to bushwack their way across the field they wanted to study, and the general neglect of this phase may be responsible for the frequently erratic character of their quest, and above all, for the lack of a clear developmental focus to their work.

The scaling or dimensionalization task can be broken down into two components. The first entails abstracting uniform and consistent developmental changes from the many rival sources of variance in behavior attributable to situational or task- and stimulus-specific factors. The second complements the first by determining the dimensional structure of behavioral development, i.e., the factors that remain invariant over age, as well as the qualitative transformations which a given developmental variable undergoes.

The first of these components involves an extensive survey of variation in behavior as a joint function of experimentally manipulated variables and age. The aim of such a survey is not so much to focus on the resulting interactions themselves, or to extend our understanding of the situational variables manipulated (which has been the main purpose of research of this type to date), but to determine the range of situational variation over which the age changes remain invariant, at least in overall direction or form. This determination will lead us, in effect, to a definition of the behavioral dimensions suitable for the investigation of developmental functions. This problem will be taken up in Chapter V, where we will further point out how potent interactions between situational variables and age can be turned to the developmentalist's advantage, by redefining the dimension under investigation to refer directly to changes in the magnitude of the effect represented by the situational variable.

The second component touches on certain fundamental questions of scaling, as they apply to the study of developmental change, and more particularly to the detection of communalities among age changes with respect to different but related measures of behavior, pointing to an underlying factor or dimension suitable for studying the operation of developmental processes. It thus relies heavily, not only on methods of scaling developed for detecting dimensional homogeneity among sets of responses, but further on the tools which the multivariate psychologist has worked out to reveal structural relationships among a set of responses, the age variable entering as an added dimension. The several steps involved in this synthesis of developmental dimensions will form the subject matter of Chapter VI.

This phase of the program will, of course, reveal much information of intrinsic interest to developmental psychologists, and to experimental or differential psychologists more generally. These findings will recompense the investigator for what might otherwise appear to be an inordinately laborious preliminary step. In the overall scheme of our program of research, however, such information constitutes only fallout incidental to the main aim—that of arriving at a set of scales or dimensions along which consistent age changes may be mapped so that the developmental psychologist may proceed with the further steps of the program.

Chapter VII represents, in a sense, a temporary shift in direction from the elaboration of the steps in a program for developmental research to the consideration of a particular methodological issue which is pertinent to all phases of this program. It deals with the longitudinal method, considered to be an intrinsic requirement for developmental research of the type advocated in this volume. In view of this emphasis, it is necessary to explore fully the benefits as well as limitations of this method in comparison with the more popular cross-sectional approach, the difficulties to be overcome in its use, and possible short-cuts designed to alleviate some of these difficulties while preserving the desired information. Along the way we will likewise consider the problem of assessing change in behavior related to chronological age, independently of secular effects related to calendar time, which is looming increasingly important as a major limitation of cross-sectional designs.

2. THE DESCRIPTIVE STUDY OF AGE CHANGES

With the roadbeds laid out for charting the course of development, the task of surveying the lay of the land begins. This is the descriptive phase of the research program, which, as in any science, represents the lowest level of the research pyramid. Yet a case can be made for the proposition that it is the neglect, not to say disdain, of this phase on the part of psychologists that has held up scientific progress in our discipline by encouraging the construction of elaborate theoretical edifices built without concern for a domain of empirical facts to which they might be applied. These edifices are in danger of turning into monumental blind alleys, as the current state of affairs with respect to the Hullian system illustrates.

If description is important for science generally, it is doubly so in the case of a field whose basic phenomena involve change, as is true of any developmental discipline, or any field involving the analysis of change over time (cf. Wohlwill, 1970a). The case of the study of dark-adaptation may again serve as a useful analog. It took painstaking observational study, devoid of any theoretical pretense, to uncover the phenomenon of the two-phased adaptation curve, which gave impetus to the search for a dual process mechanism in the retina, that is, the rods and cones. The case of psychophysics and psychophysiology provides, in fact, an excellent example of the importance of systematic empirical observational work for the establishment of an integrated body of fact and theory.

As we shall find in our examination of descriptive studies of development in Chapter VIII, it is useful to differentiate between quantitative and qualitative types of changes. The former is concerned with the specification of the overall direction and form of developmental functions, and other quantitative attributes of age changes taking place along a given dimension, by application of curve-fitting methods and related techniques at a lesser level of mathematical refinement. The latter concerns chiefly the determination of sequential patterns in the appearance of discrete responses over the course of development, along with the specification of the forms which these successive responses take. Certain aspects of the schedule according to which these responses emerge are also to be included under this rubric.

Note that the object of such descriptive study is not just any arbitrary aspect of quantitatively or qualitatively defined behavior that may be observed at some point during the course of development, which was the source of endless studies of child behavior in the earlier days of the field, but rather changes in response along the developmental dimensions previously established in Phase I. With the spadework of the isolation of such dimensions already accomplished, it is possible to focus the developmental study on the characteristics of the developmental function, and, at the same time, to reserve this type of descriptive analysis for those aspects of behavior for which age changes of sufficient consistency and magnitude occur to make such analysis profitable.

3. THE CORRELATIONAL STUDY OF AGE CHANGES

If, as most psychologists would agree, it is impossible to understand the behavior of an individual by looking at it as a bundle of discrete, isolated, and unrelated responses, it is even more important to look at the development of the individual along a given dimension of response as occurring in interrelationship to other response dimensions similarly undergoing development. Here again, the fact that we are dealing with developmental change complicates and enlarges the conceptual and methodological problems in comparison with those involved in ordinary correlational research. For superimposed on the questions of the degree of association among particular sets of measures, and the factor space which may best describe them, are the questions relating to the temporal patterning among the changes occurring with respect to a given set of measures. Indeed, a whole complex of separate models turns out to be required to conceptualize and study sets of developmental variables in interrelationship with one another.

Chapter IX and X will be devoted to the methods and models which have been devised to deal with this analysis of developmental patterns. The differentiation between these two chapters preserves the quantitative–qualitative distinction offered previously in connection with the descriptive phase of research; for a number of reasons, however, the qualitative side will be taken up first, in Chapter IX. This chapter examines the methodological implications of the concept of stages, considered as a problem in the analysis of the changing patterns in the interrelationship among qualitatively defined responses. While particular emphasis will be given to the study of stages as conceived in Piaget's system, the presentation has a more general focus on structural models of qualitative change, laying stress on a fine-grained analysis of the changing interrelationships among a complex of structurally related responses or response sequences which is considered the earmark of a stage in process of formation.

Chapter X, in turn, will examine the general problems entailed in adapting correlational models to the study of developmental change, with particular attention to factor-analytic models in which time, or occasions of testing, figures as one of the dimensions of the correlation matrix, as well as others tailored more specifically to data on developmental change. Among these are Tucker's extension of factor analysis to three dimensions, analytic techniques dealing with parameters of the developmental function directly, and certain developments in time-series analysis, autoregression techniques, and related procedures for studying interrelationships among developmental variables across a time gap.

Taken jointly, the study of the patterning of development in these two chapters represents a phase intermediate between the descriptive level and that of the study of the functional relationships aimed at the mechanisms of developmental change. It partakes in fact some of the aspects of both of these levels: Determination of factorial structures, and of the changing interrelationships among component responses associated with a developmental stage may be said to represent a high-level descriptive enterprise, but at the same time the examination of these problems in the context of developmental changes will bring out the internal processes governing such structural relationships as they evolve.

4. The Study of the Determinants of Developmental Change

If the correlational approach considered in the preceding section may be said to lay bare the internal structural dynamics of the developmental system, it remains to round out the picture by specifying the mechanisms of developmental change through a study of the variables on which this change depends, or which exert a determining influence on it. While this would normally call for an experimental approach, to allow for systematic manipulation of such determining variables, this is possible at the human level only for behaviors which develop over a sufficiently narrow time interval to allow for systematic intervention, and even for these only for a limited range of experimental conditions, presumed to enhance rather than interfere with development. For this reason we may subdivide this phase into two complementary approaches, the one dealing with the experimental study of developmental change, based largely on animal research; the other dealing with the study of experiential factors in the development of the child, as studied through correlational and other nonexperimental methods.

The experimental investigation of development forms the subject matter of Chapter XI. Consonant with the proposed view of the age variable as forming part of the dependent variable which is the object of the developmentalist's study, we consider experimentation in this realm to involve the investigation of functional relationships between specified experimental conditions and particular characteristics of the developmental function for the dimension of behavior of interest. This is to be contrasted to the typical experimental paradigm, as employed both in the study of effects of experience and more generally in experimental research on the role of particular experimental treatments in modifying behavior, which generally relies on some absolute response measure at a single point in time following the termination of the treatment. A particular consequence of this redefinition of the experimental method is that the effects of the experimental treatment are regarded as superimposed on a prototype developmental function derived for "normal" conditions. The implications of this statement for the causal interpretation of such experimental effects, and the associated problems of methodology and design are discussed in Chapter XI; of particular importance is the need for follow-up longitudinal designs to allow for an assessment of the effects of the treatment on the course of development.

A comprehensive treatment of methodology in the study of the determinants of and influences on development would extend to a consideration of nonexperimental approaches to the study of the role of experience in the development of the child, i.e., work on effects of institutionalization, child-rearing practices, etc. Original plans for this volume did indeed call for a chapter to be devoted to this topic, but they were abandoned when it became apparent that to do it justice would require virtually a book in itself. Fortunately, the need for such a treatment is lessened by the considerable number of books, monographs, and papers available dealing with methodological issues arising in research on these problems.

5. THE STUDY OF INDIVIDUAL DIFFERENCES IN DEVELOPMENT

By and large, the study of developmental change has remained divorced from the study of individual differences in behavior, just as has the study of the phenomena of experimental psychology. Attempts to integrate the two may take two forms: On the one hand, individual-difference analyses may be applied directly to the study of developmental-function characteristics; on the other hand, the developmental-function view may itself be extended to apply, not to changes in an individual's location on a developmental scale, but to the course of changes in his location on dimensions of individual difference, defined in terms that are orthogonal to developmental change. This difference is most readily illustrated with respect to the case of intelligence, the former involving the study of individual differences in the course of developmental changes in MA, the latter, the study of individual differences in age changes in IQ. The distinction suggests, however, a useful differentiation between developmental and differential variables, the former being represented by dimensions such as intelligence, along which consistent directional changes with age take place; while the latter, best exemplified by bipolar personality traits like aggressiveness, exhibit no such systematic shifts with age.

Chapter XII, which is devoted to this topic, will bring out the relevance of the work on the stability of behavior over the course of development to these questions. It will also argue for the need to enlarge this concept to refer to an attribute of the developmental patterns of *individuals*, rather than to a characteristic of a given trait or variable, as determined via the inter-correlation of responses for a group of children at two age levels.

Two points remain to be discussed in regard to the outline of the program of developmental research which has just been presented, with its blueprint for the core chapters of this book. First, the hierarchy of levels is to be looked at less in terms of the model of the construction of a pyramid than in terms of setting up a series of base camps during the course of the assault on a Himalayan summit. That is, work at each level should be thought of as feeding back on prior work at a lower level, permitting the consolidation or possibly revision of that work. In other words, there is a continual interplay between these various phases of research. Thus irregularities or discontinuities found in the descriptive study of developmental functions may have implications for the success achieved at the preceding developmental-scale construction phase. Experimental research on the determinants of developmental-function properties may lead to a revision of our conception of descriptively derived modal developmental functions, e.g., by revealing the presence of parameters ignored at the descriptive level. This interaction between research carried out at different levels is, furthermore (as befits a feedback loop), a two-way street; thus, correlational study of age changes may establish the presence of functional interdependence between developmental variables which can be obscured or distorted through experimental intervention. If we hope therefore to arrive at a valid total picture of development with respect to a particular aspect of behavior, activity will have to be carried out at each of these levels simultaneously, once a minimal foundation has been laid down for initiating work at any one of them.

The second point is that, while this presentation is intended to convey the sense of a total programmatic attack on developmental problems, following the lines of a perhaps too grandiose design, the discussion of the modes of research conforming to each level in the chapters to follow can be taken on its own merits. The discussion should have relevance to actual research falling into a given paradigm at any level, independently of its place in the schema outlined here. It will not be necessary, in other words, for the developmental investigator to "buy" the total program, for him to find relevance in the treatment of the problems of method and design arising at any particular level with which he may be dealing.

PART II

Quantification, Dimensionalization, and Design

CHAPTER IV

Problems of Measurement and Quantification in Developmental Psychology

In discussions of research relating behavioral measures to the age variable, we frequently find the expression "Behavior as a function of age" used, or in its shorthand version, $R = f(\text{Age})$ (e.g., Kessen, 1960). But since age typically accounts for only a small fraction of the variance on the behavioral measure, and since it is not considered to be a determining variable to begin with, but only a shorthand for the multitude of factors covarying with it, the particular form of this functional relationship is rarely taken seriously, let alone given explicit expression. Occasionally one does find attempts to specify the mathematical form of some behavioral "growth function" (the term itself is probably anathema to many developmental psychologists), but for the most part developmentalists have been content to treat the relationship between age and behavior in much broader terms, such as increasing or decreasing trends, changes in incidence of responses in different categories, etc.

The reformulation of the status of the age variable proposed earlier, incorporating age into the definition of the dependent variable and the concern with characteristics of the developmental function, requires that we give more explicit consideration to the problems of measurement in developmental research and to the possibilities for more effective quantitative analysis of developmental data. Clearly the possibilities for formulating functional relationships which incorporate developmental function characteristics as dependent variables, and the types of statements which such an approach will enable us to make are directly dependent on the nature of our measuring instrument, and the level of measurement represented by our data.

Four Prototype Cases in the Measurement of Developmental Change

A general formulation of the problem of measurement in developmental studies is needed at this point. Basically, the problem can be conceptualized as involving a double isomorphism in which an individual's magnitude or level of development on some behavioral dimension is placed into correspondence with the points on some scale or measuring instrument on the one hand, and with the points on the age scale on the other.

Case I. Let us assume the existence of a quantitative developmental dimension X, that is, a behavioral dimension along which age changes occur which are satisfactorily invariant, at least as to direction, across different populations as well as specific situational or experiential conditions. Let us suppose further that we have a previously constructed quantitative measuring scale Y, which can be assumed to be in isomorphic relationship with X; the exact form of the relationship may or may not be known (in general it would be unknown). For example, X may be visual-form discrimination ability, and Y scores on a particular test of form discrimination. Rejecting the facile definition of X as operationally equivalent to Y (since the choice of the particular measuring scale Y employed is presumably arbitrary, i.e., any number of alternative tests or measures might have been employed), we may assume that scores on Y are not only isomorphic with values on X, but a monotonic function of the latter, though the precise form of the relationship cannot be specified. By contrast, the form of the relationship between Y and the age variable T can be specified in a perfectly determinate fashion by examining the covariation of Y with T. The situation can be schematized as in Fig. 4-1, illustrating, respectively, situations of Y increasing monotonically with T, increasing and subsequently decreasing, and varying in irregular fashion.

The representation of the measurement situation for this case is intended to indicate that for a quantifiable dimension such as X it becomes possible to study its variation with the age variable T and to determine at least the general form of this relationship, but only to the extent that our measures Y utilized as indices of X represent a close approximation to X, or linear transform of it (since the units of X are presumably unknown). This is a major reason for insisting on the distinction between X and Y, the tenets of operationalism notwithstanding.

The distinction is hardly novel, of course—we find it stated in equivalent terms by Guilford (1954), who postulates a continuum of behavioral reaction to a stimulus R underlying a continuum J represented by a set of judgments obtained under a given method. Our distinction is, however, more general than Guilford's, not being tied to psychophysical continua; at the

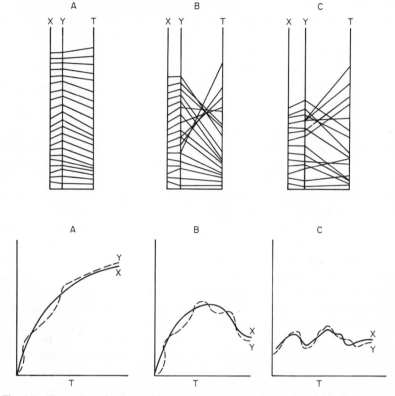

Fig. 4-1. Examples of relationships among a latent behavioral variable X, a measuring scale Y, and the age variable T, for cases of behavior (A) increasing monotonically with age, (B) increasing and subsequently decreasing, and (C) changing irregularly with age.

same time, it is intended for a particular purpose, namely for the study of developmental changes. In other words, X is assumed to refer to a dimension along which individuals are localizable at successive points of their development from infancy to maturity. We may thus look for variance in Y which is unrelated to X, being a function of particular situational factors or other variables which are independent of the individual's developmental status. This does not necessarily affect the isomorphic relationship between X and Y, under constant conditions; nor the possibility that each of a variety of measures Y may all be isomorphically related to X, providing that the differences among these measures either fail to interact with age, or at least do not affect the direction of the age changes. (Ideally they should be reducible to a constant of scale, i.e., m units of change for Y_1 being equivalent to n units of change for Y_2.)

Case II.   Here we come to situations in which our behavioral dimension
X is to be tapped by means of a previously constructed ordinal scale such
as a rating scale, the order of the points having been established beforehand
either by definition or by some suitable stimulus scaling procedure. This
case is equivalent, in general terms, to the preceding in the sense that it
would still be possible to differentiate among the different types of patterns
represented in Fig. 4-1. Necessarily, the particular shape of the age curve,
or the mathematical function relating the scale of behavior Y to T would
become indeterminate. Furthermore, in most instances the number of points
differentiable on the scale available is quite limited, so that the opportunity
for even low-level descriptive statements concerning the relationship of Y
to T, and a fortiori of X to T, is limited.

Two major problems face the investigator wishing to employ ordinal, and
in particular, rating scales in a developmental study. First, responses on a
rating scale may be assumed to represent not discrete points, but rather
intervals of indeterminate width within which X, the variable being assessed,
is varying. This precludes the establishing of point-for-point correspondence
between Y and X, or Y and T, and therefore between X and T. The result, in
fact, is apt to be an erroneous picture of stepwise progression, with the
underlying continuity of the dimension X being lost sight of. More important
for the developmentalist, however, is the lack of any absolute reference
points in the use of the scale, which creates serious difficulties in applying
such scales to different age groups. That is, if one wished to measure age
changes in amount of dependency behavior by recourse to rating scales,
the frame of reference for the use of the points on the scale (assuming these
to be defined in general verbal terms such as "extremely dependent," "highly
independent") cannot be assumed to remain constant across age levels, so
that it becomes difficult to use it to chart developmental changes: The relationship of the measure Y to the psychological variable X would itself be
subject to change. If, on the other hand, the rating scale is defined in terms
of more specific behaviors, e.g., "constantly runs to his teacher for attention
or approval," the context becomes too particularized to permit the application of the scale across an extended segment of the age continuum.

There are, of course, other approaches to constructing ordinal scales,
notably through one or another of the common techniques of scaling (cf.
Torgerson, 1958), although some of these actually yield metric values for the
stimuli scaled. For reasons to be noted more fully in the discussion of Case
III to follow, it is essential that under Case II the scaling be done independently of the responses of the individual whose developmental level is to be
assessed. In other words, we are dealing with Quadrants III and IV, in
Coombs's (1960) schema, rather than I and II, or, following Torgerson's
(1958) terminology, with judgment methods rather than response methods
of scaling.

Most such independently defined ordinal scales, whether constructed through some scaling technique or obtained through direct ranking or rating methods, are severely limited in the degree of discrimination they allow in assessing the level attained by a subject as he changes along that dimension, but they do at least allow us to determine the overall form of the developmental function. Take, for instance, Lewis's (1963a,b) work comparing children's ability to represent three-dimensional space in their drawings with their judgments of the adequacy of such representation in the drawings of others. Lewis initially constructed a set of five prototype drawings for each of three different three-dimensional configurations, these sets being intended to represent successively more accurate and complete degrees of the representation of space. Children between kindergarten and eighth grade were then asked first to make drawings themselves of the same three configurations, and second, to choose from among the five prototypes of each the one they considered "best." The author proceeded to match the children's own drawings to the prototypes so as to assign a level of spatial representation to each child. This level could then be compared to the level he chose as best. In this manner, Lewis was able not only to trace the developmental changes in both drawings and judgments, but to establish a systematic discrepancy between the preferred level and the level indicated by the child's own drawing (cf. Fig. 4-2). The resort to group medians is wasteful of information and the resulting developmental function depicted may bear little relationship to the course of an individual child's progress along the postulated dimension. But at least we have an external criterion against which to evaluate the extent and direction of the changes in these preference judgments, for the group as well as for an individual child, and to compare these against the level attained by the child in his own drawings.

Case III. This case represents situations in which no underlying continuous variable can be hypothesized. The response categories utilized yield scalable response patterns when applied to individuals varying in developmental level, or an invariant sequence when examined longitudinally; however, they are defined in qualitative terms and thus represent a purely nominal scale, in the sense that they do not constitute an ordered set by any applicable *stimulus*-scaling technique. Most observationally derived, and thus response-inferred scales fall into this category, as exemplified in the motor sequences of Gesell, McGraw, etc., as well as such variables as scales of animism or similar cognitively loaded variables, developmental scales of fear-provoking stimuli, etc., wherever these may be found to result in a scalable set of responses.

The distinction being drawn between this case and the previous one, that is, between scales whose ordinality has been established through stimulus-scaling procedures (Case II) as opposed to those which can only be

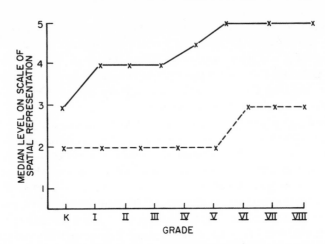

Fig. 4-2. Developmental changes in level of spatial representation in reproduction of a sphere, compared to level of representation of drawings judged as "best" at each age. (———): Choices of "best" drawings; (– – –): Children's own drawings. [Data from Lewis (1963a).]

shown to yield a scalable set of response patterns (Case III), is important. Since in the latter case the response scale Y is not independently defined as a scalable dimension, the order being solely established through the ordering of the subjects (presumed to vary in age) along the latent dimension, statements concerning its relationship to age become circular. Thus, there is no possibility of obtaining anything except a monotonic relationship between the Y categories and T, the age variable. (This statement will be taken up again in Chapter V, where the distinction between Case II and Case III will be considered in relation to the application of scaling methods to developmental data.) Indeed, under these circumstances, in the absence of any independent criterion for ordering responses along the latent dimension, reflected in the finding of scalability, this dimension would become equivalent to the age variable itself.

The example of the motor sequence is a good case in point: The ordinal character of this scale is solely a function of the fact that the appearance of the responses which constitute it is determined by the individual's position on the age scale (considered here in purely ordinal terms). Indeed, it would be difficult to specify any basis on which these responses could be ordered, and if they were to be administered to a psychologically naive set of judges, unfamiliar with their place in the developmental sequence, with instructions to rank-order them, or to apply any standard stimulus-scaling technique to them, it is highly doubtful that anything except a very gross approximation to the sequence would be recovered.

In a purely pragmatic sense, the value deriving from the discovery of such sets of responses for which sequential invariance applies is not to be minimized since it does permit us to differentiate individuals or groups in terms of their rate of progress along this sequence. But, in contrast to the previous case, we would be unable to describe development in terms of a developmental function relating changes in magnitude or relative amount of response along some dimension to age. Any such function would necessarily be altogether indeterminate in shape—any straight line or topological equivalent of it would do (cf. Fig. 4-3 representing the motor sequence).

Case IV. Finally, we come to situations in which an underlying continuous variable may or may not be hypothesized; but the response categories utilized, again representing only a nominal scale, do not approach an ordered sequence, whether considered in terms of longitudinally determined sequential invariance, or in terms of scalability of response patterns. Examples of this case could be taken from a variety of situations in which a set of qualitatively differentiated responses may be age related, but not in any determinate sense; variables such as play interests and occupational preferences would probably fall into this category. In this case, the data

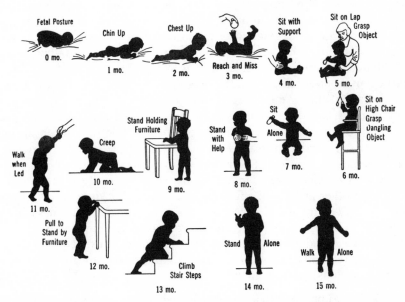

Fig. 4-3. Examples of developmental sequence without independent scaling: Shirley's motor sequence [Reprinted from M. M. Shirley, *The first two years*. Vol. II. Minneapolis: University of Minnesota Press, 1933, Frontispiece. (Reproduced by permission of University of Minnesota Press.)]

obtained would be of the most limited interest for developmental analysis, since they would be confined to the determination of the incidence of each category at successive age levels, for some given group of individuals. The primary value of nominally scaled data of this type is probably in suggesting domains in which more intensive search and study may uncover scales falling at least into Case III, or, alternatively, as supplementary data for the analysis of Case I or II data, to aid in the understanding of the developmental functions uncovered with respect to them. This point will be taken up further in the chapter on the descriptive analysis of developmental change.

1. AN EXAMPLE: STIMULUS COMPLEXITY

To provide an illustration of the four cases just specified for the measurement of developmental change, let us take the variable of stimulus complexity.

Case I. Complexity of stimuli, if artificially constructed, may be specifiable in information terms, i.e., in bits. Accordingly, we ask children at successive age levels to construct patterns from black and red checkers on an expanded checkerboard, and measure the amount of information contained in each. We are now in a position, in principle, to formulate the relationship between the information content H of the child's constructed pattern and the child's age in terms of a growth-curve model or similar quantitative functional relationship. Different children may then be differentiated in terms of rates of growth along this dimension; effects of particular experiences can be described in terms of changes in the parameters of this curve, etc. Clearly, the fruitfulness of such quantitative formulations, and the likelihood that the observed functions do, in fact, conform to any consistent mathematical form, would depend on the adequacy of our particular scale Y as a measure of the assumed underlying psychological dimension of complexity of cognitive functioning X. To the extent that our measure of informational content failed to take into consideration other aspects of cognitive complexity (e.g., integration of parts into wholes, as involved in constructing a meaningful pattern such as a machine, vehicle, or human figure), the observed age-function would have little intrinsic significance, and the results would not be expected to bear any consistent relationship to known patterns of growth, to growth in other domains such as intelligence, etc.

Case II. Suppose instead a Mosaic-laying task was used, resulting in designs which did not lend themselves to specification in terms of an objective measure of complexity such as H. An ordered series of prototype patterns, analogous to the set employed by Lewis (1963a) in the aforementioned study of children's sensitivity to depth in drawings, might be used to define points on the scale of complexity, in terms of mean ratings or rank-order values obtained from a group of judges; the metric of this scale would, of course, be unknown. Assuming that each child's construction can be unequivocally matched to one of these prototypes, we can assign to each child at a given age a complexity value corresponding to the points on this ordinal scale. We may now make statements concerning the general form of change in complexity with age (e.g., monotonically increasing, inverted U-shaped, etc.) Furthermore, we may specify the modal age of attainment of each point, for use in comparing the development of different groups of children along this scale, etc.

In this case the issue of a determinate *quantitative* relationship between X and Y does not arise; we may still postulate an isomorphic relationship between them, however, such that the ordinal relationships between Y and T which emerge from the data can be assumed to hold for the relationship between X and T, providing of course that the underlying variable X (cognitive complexity) is in fact being tapped by our scale Y. Should the judges on the basis of whose judgments the complexity scale was constructed have failed to take into account essential aspects of this variable that are manifested in developmental changes, the obtained results can be expected to reflect this failure: The observed age trends will emerge as inconsistent and devoid of regularity of progression.

Case III.   Suppose that, instead of defining our scale beforehand, we simply administered the Mosaic task to children varying in age, and recorded their responses. From these responses we might arrive at a set of categories which turned out, upon longitudinal investigation, to form a consistent developmental sequence. For instance, the sequence might be defined as follows:

(*a*) Uses pieces in random arrangement.
(*b*) Uses pieces to form a regular geometric shape, with color used at random.
(*c*) Uses pieces to form regular geometric shape, with colors used in solid blocks.
(*d*) Constructs a single meaningful object (e.g., a car).
(*e*) Constructs a group of related objects.
(*f*) Constructs an elaborate abstract design.

The above set of responses would probably not turn out to be scalable along a continuum of complexity; nor would it be obvious what single scale might underlie this sequence. Accordingly, we could not make statements about the character of the developmental function linking complexity, or any other variable, to age. Nevertheless we could utilize the preceding sequence, if it proved consistently replicable, to describe the course of development of children's imaginative constructions, in much the same way as the motor sequence is used in the study of motor development.

This example might seem out of place here, since we started out avowedly illustrating these cases with respect to the measurement of complexity. Obviously, since Case III is defined as involving a set of categories not scalable on any identifiable stimulus dimension, no set of responses conforming to this case could be used to measure complexity directly. It is included here, however, since it applies to many developmental problems, where no a priori response continuum is defined independently, as well as to bring out the limitations of response patterns found to be scalable (in the reproducibility sense) or sequentially invariant, when the continuum presumed to underlie it has not been independently defined.

Case IV. This would be the case if we had rested content with using a set of categories for our scale of complexity which were not in fact scalable, either as stimuli (e.g., in terms of the ratings of independent judges) or in terms of the sequential ordering of the responses obtained longitudinally, or from scalogram patterns. For instance, we might have used various combinations of several independent criteria, such as restriction to rows and columns versus diagonal or angle designs; restriction to one-color checkers versus both colors; restriction to black squares versus black and white. These categories in combination would thus only provide a crude, nominally scaled measure of level of complexity, and little could be hoped for from its use in specifying the nature of the relationship between complexity and age. (Resort to multidimensional scaling would of course reveal any changing relevance of each of the above-mentioned criteria with age, but in this case we would no longer be dealing with a single variable of complexity.)

The Qualitative versus Quantitative Character of Developmental Change

The question whether development should be viewed as entailing qualitative as opposed to quantitative change has been debated at length in the literature. For example, Flavell and Wohlwill (1969) dealt with this question by suggesting that there are many changes which partake of both qualitative and quantitative aspect, the former relating to the structural form or characteristics of the behavior, while the latter concerns the efficiency, consistency, etc. of the operation of a given structural mechanism.

We may take up this question here in somewhat different form, relating it to the framework just presented for conceptualizing problems of measurement. The first and primary issue is simply whether X, the variable of interest to the psychologist, is defined as a continuum, or in discrete terms. As we shall see, much of the controversy over this question emanates from cases in which a continuous, quantitative measure is applied to a variable Y which was either originally defined in qualitative terms, or for which the variations in behavior which were of primary interest could be specified only in qualitative terms. Let us start out with an analog taken from the field of physics: The changes in a quantity of water subjected to heating. If we are concerned with the formal characteristics of the material (e.g., its ability to take on the shape of the container, or to fill a given volume) the qualitative, discrete character of the changes which H_2O undergoes in being changed from ice to water to steam are undeniable. This intrinsic discontinuity is not altered in the least by the fact that these changes are the result of continuously varying forces acting on the H_2O (i.e., heat), or that they are accompanied by changes in the temperature of the H_2O, which are obviously quantitative in nature. Indeed, we could readily envisage an approach to the study of H_2O in its various forms which would focus exclusively on the structural changes in passing from ice to water to steam, and would thus lead to a stage theory of the transformations of H_2O under the action of heat.

The question whether developmental change is qualitative or quantitative is therefore not an empirical matter, but must rather be decided on the basis of the kinds of questions which the investigator is interested in answering, or the aspects of the developmental process that are of most interest to him. Biologists (e.g., Bonner, 1952) have recognized this for some time, in distinguishing between growth, that is, accretionary change, and development, in other words, structural change by differentiation. The mischief that this controversy has wrought in developmental psychology has stemmed from the failure to recognize this point, and the frequently wanton attempts to force a quantitative scale of measurement onto a variable defined in discrete, qualitative terms, thereby obscuring or doing violence to the essential character of the phenomena under investigation. Let us illustrate these points by reference to the following example.

1. The Measurement of Conservation: A Case-Study in the Quantification of Qualitative Developmental Processes

One of the concepts whose developmental history has attracted much attention in recent research in the area of cognitive development is that of conservation. As investigated and discussed by Piaget (1960) in his theory of the development of intelligence, this concept refers to the child's understanding of the fact that certain dimensional attributes of an object or stimulus situation (e.g., the length of a string) remain invariant under changes involving other attributes which are irrelevant to the dimension in question (e.g., the pattern in which the string is laid out). The possession of this concept is, for Piaget, at least, an inherently qualitative phenomenon: At any given time, a child either manifests conservation, or he does not. This follows from the definition of conservation as a logical rule, forming part of the more general system of "concrete operations" which Piaget has postulated, and which necessarily operate in an all-or-none fashion (just as an electrical circuit is either open or closed).

Accordingly, most investigators who have studied the formation of this concept have relied on measurement at a qualitative level, that is, in discrete terms, classifying children into conservers versus nonconservers, or possibly into one of three stages, in which the middle one represents an intermediary, transitional phase characterized by inconsistent responding, failure to give proper explanations, etc. It is apparent that the information yielded in this approach with respect to a given individual is quite limited. At any given time, he may only be classified into one of the two or three response categories. At best, with the aid of longitudinal data, one might specify the age of onset of the conservation concept for any given child, or possibly the interval he takes to move from stage I to stage III, though this would presume a degree of continual monitoring of his progress that would be difficult to achieve in practice.

In situations of this type, several approaches have commonly been employed in attempts to arrive at a quantitative measure of such qualitative change. They are basically of three different kinds. The first preserves the discrete character of the responses, introducing a semblance of quantification by considering the group rather than the individual as the unit of reference, and expressing variations in degree of manifestation of the behavior under study in terms of incidence data, usually in percentage form. The second involves tabulating frequency of occurrence of the behavior, not across individuals, but within a given individual, by administering a series of items or trials representing variants of the same response. The third involves the choice of a quantitative continuum which is thought to reflect differential degrees of strength, efficiency, etc., of the response in question; accordingly, it circumvents the qualitative nature of the X variable presumably under study altogether. Each of these approaches has its own advantages and limitations; they will now be considered individually.

Within-Group Incidence Data. By shifting one's unit of reference from the individual to the group, incidence or relative frequency measures are obtained which allow one to make quantitative comparisons across groups, within a group over time, or before and after some program of experience, etc. For purely descriptive purposes, there can be no possible objection to this approach, provided it is recognized that the quantitative character of such data measures an attribute of the referent group, but not of any individual child. For example, the finding of a difference in the incidence of conservation responses in children of a given age in two different cultures tells us something about the relative probabilities of locating a conserving child in each culture, but tells us nothing that could be applied to a single individual. (This is in contrast to quantitative measures such as IQ, which we can use to make statements, for instance, about the amount of difference between any two children selected from the two groups.)

This point may seem so self-evident as to be altogether trivial. It is stressed nevertheless because group-incidence data of this type are so frequently misused by deriving from them conclusions concerning the development of individual children. A good example was the practice, fortunately less common at present than it used to be, of using information of this kind as a basis for statements concerning the continuity or discontinuity of development. Deutsche's (1937) normative data on stages of thinking about causal relationships, reproduced in Table 4-1, are an example of such group-incidence data, which both the author and others following her (e.g., Watson, 1965) have cited as evidence for the continuity position. (Just what kind of information this question calls for is a problem to which we shall turn later in this chapter.)v

Similarly, it is doubtful that such group-incidence data can shed any light on questions relating to the *speed* or *rate* of development of a response such as conservation. Consider, for instance, the findings of Vinh-Bang (1959), who has plotted functions to describe the rise with age from 0 to 100% in the proportion of subjects exhibiting an understanding of various concepts of conservation and other related concepts. He obtains "bundles" of

TABLE 4-1

Percentage of Answers to Causality Questions Falling in Several of Piaget's Classifications[a]

Type of causality	Age (yr)								All ages
	8	9	10	11	12	13	14	15–16	
Phenomenistic	37.3	32.5	29.5	22.4	16.1	11.9	12.4	10.3	20.8
Animistic	.6	.2	.6	.3	.3	.2	.0	.0	.3
Dynamic	8.3	5.8	6.3	6.2	7.1	6.7	2.9	5.7	6.3
Mechanical	32.5	33.2	37.4	40.5	41.1	41.0	39.5	42.9	38.9
Logical	10.7	11.8	14.1	19.8	28.1	32.0	35.6	31.6	23.4

[a] From Deutsche (1937).

functions such as those shown in Fig. 4-4, including some which appear to converge (conservation of number and area; placing two spatially separated sets in one-to-one correspondence), and some which appear to diverge (conservation of substance and weight, concepts of volume). Still others (not shown in Fig. 4-4) cut across these converging and diverging sets, the rise from 0 to 100% occurring either within a relatively short period of time (e.g., conservation of length), or over a much more extended period (e.g., probability concepts). Vinh-Bang assumes that these curves convey information about the rate of formation of the concepts in question, i.e., within an individual child. But is such an inference warranted? And if not, how shall such findings be interpreted?

The problem is shown graphically in Fig. 4-5, showing how such a group-incidence function can result from a family of individual trace lines of very different shape (i.e., much steeper in slope), the members of the family varying in the age at which the response started developing, according to some presumed normal frequency distribution. Accordingly, differences among group-incidence functions could be attributable either to differences in rate of development of the response within the individual (steep versus gradual curves, Fig. 4-5a), or to differences in the age range over which the trace

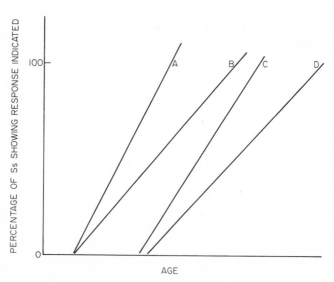

Fig. 4-4. Group trace lines for items developing at different times and over different intervals, showing patterns of divergence (A versus B, C versus D), convergence (B versus C), and parallel progress (A versus C, B versus D). Ordinate values are graphed as on normal-probability paper.

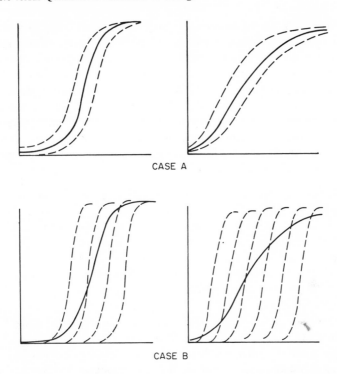

CASE A

CASE B

Fig. 4-5. Development of qualitative responses as a function of age, charted in terms of percentage of subjects in a group exhibiting the response (solid lines) and probability of the response within particular individuals (dashed lines). Upper curves (A) represent two responses developing at different rates in individuals; lower curves (B) represent two responses differing in the width of the age span over which their acquisition is distributed in different individuals.

lines showing the development of the response within the individual are spread (cf. Fig. 4-5b). These two cases would have very different implications for the interpretation of the respective group-incidence curves: In the first, one might suppose that the periods of time required for the transition from absence to full functional presence of the response to occur differs for the two responses. The second suggests, on the other hand, that the timing of the acquisition of the response is determined within narrower limits for one response as opposed to the other, reflecting perhaps a difference in the degree of their functional dependence on some other response, or possibly on particular forces or events in the individual's life history.

We see, then, that the usefulness of group-incidence data as carriers of information about the development of a response within the individual is quite limited. Such data may still be of value for certain purposes, as in

test construction; thus Laurendeau and Pinard's (1957) analysis of the differential rates at which the incidence of passes on items of the Stanford–
Binet changes from 0 to 100% is surely of interest for the determination of
the age-placement of these items (e.g., the meaning of a 6-year-old child
passing an item pegged at the 8-year-old level is different if the item has a
very gradual incidence function, such that perhaps 25% of 6-year-olds pass
it, or a relatively steep function, such that only 5% of children at that age
pass it). But the appearance of quantification which these data convey is
spurious at best, when used for statements concerning the development of
the individual.

The Test-Score Approach.   The most commonly used device for obtaining
quantitative measures for qualitative behavior, such as conservation
responses, while retaining the individual as the object of reference, is to
measure the individual's performance over a set of items or trials, and
count up the number of conservation responses which he makes. This procedure results in a score being assigned to each subject as a measure of his
conservation ability (very much as is the practice in ability testing procedures generally).

Test theory (e.g., Gulliksen, 1950; Lord & Novick, 1968) typically starts
by postulating a universe of items from which a sample is drawn in constructing a given test; this sample of items will typically be of varying degrees
of difficulty, but the assumption is that the responses to the various items
are either independent, or at most only partially dependent. More particularly, the assumption is made of a latent continuous dimension of ability,
with differential amounts of the ability expressing itself in differential
numbers of items passed, most usually according to a normal frequency
distribution, or some variant of it (e.g., positively or negatively skewed).
If, on the other hand, the sample of items all emanate from a restricted
universe, such that there is a high degree of interdependence among responses to the different items, the assumed ability continuum becomes a fiction.
Instead, responses to such a set of items will tend to segregate themselves
into two discrete clusters, representing the two possible modes of response
corresponding to the original discrete categories, or stages, into which the
behavior under study could be divided. The result will be a sharply bimodal
distribution of responses, this bimodality simply reflecting the dichotomous,
all-or-none character of the responses to this universe of items.

It is important to note that it is not the discontinuity of the response
scale that creates this bimodality (responses to individual items of any
test are typically dichotomized on a pass–fail basis), but rather the interdependence among the items. This interdependence will generally hold,
as long as the items are taken to represent a particular concept or nar-

rowly defined skill, such that the correct response will be exhibited whenever an instance of that concept or a situation calling for that skill occurs, providing of course that the concept or skill has been acquired. To the extent, on the other hand, that the behavior measured by the item set is made up of a set of unrelated or only loosely related responses (e.g., items designed to measure orality), the distribution of scores obtained from such items will exhibit continuity.

While the extreme of a determinate, perfectly dichotomized distribution just suggested is rarely if ever observed in practice, the case of conservation does provide us with a good illustration of marked bimodality of responses, where an attempt is made to summate the number of passes on successive conservation items into an overall score (cf. Table 4-2) (Bentler, 1970; Fusaro, 1969; Wohlwill, 1960b; Wohlwill, Fusaro, & Devoe, 1969). The same is found where preferential modes of response generalizable over a series of

TABLE 4-2

Evidence of Bimodality of Distribution of Responses to Sets of Items of Conservation on Different Dimensions

Wohlwill, Fusaro, & Devoe (1969)[a]		Fusaro (1969)[b]		Bentler (1970)[c]	
Score	f	Score	f	Score	f
6	13	13–14	11		
5	15	11–12	4	11–12	33
4	7	9–10	2	9–10	8
3	2	7–8	4	7–8	12
2	3	5–6	9	5–6	7
1	12	3–4	12	3–4	15
0	33	1–2	11	1–2	18
		0	8	0	58
N	85		61		151

[a] Based on responses of subjects, mean age 6 : 4, to 2 items of each of conservation of number, length, and liquid quantity.

[b] Based on responses of subjects, mean age 5 : 11, to items of conservation of number, length, liquid quantity and substance (including 2 equality and 1 inequality trial per dimension, plus 2 prediction trials on liquid quantity).

[c] Based on responses of subjects, mean age about 6 : 0, to 6 items of conservation of length, number substance, continuous and discontinuous quantity and weight; 2 points given per response for correct explanation, 1 for correct unexplained responses. (f values estimated from graphed percentages.)

items are being assessed, as in Klein's (1963) study of texture versus form
dominance in tactual perception. It is apparent that, quite apart from the
problems of statistical treatment created by distributions of this sort, the
impression of quantification which these data convey is not only quite
spurious, but effectively obscures and even obliterates the information in
the data with respect to qualitative differences in performance.

The Shift to Continuous Response Variables.   Just as a physicist might
chart the changes in H_2O from ice to water to steam on the temperature
continuum, so in many cases some continuous variable might be found
along which behavior changes of a basically qualitative type might be measured. For instance, the purportedly qualitative changes in locomotor
behavior in infancy might be indexed in terms of *speed* of locomotion, by
the simple use of a stopwatch. Such a use of the time scale as the dependent
variable would of course obscure altogether the important changes occurring in the *form* of the behavior. Indeed, they would exhibit apparent regression, that is, reduced efficiency of the behavior, as the infant changes from
a quadruped to a biped. Thus, unless it is the continuous variable itself
which is of interest, its use to replace the qualitative response categories
is hardly to be recommended, nor can data derived from it be used in evidence
of the continuity of the behavior changes involved. Such measures may
nevertheless be of some value to *supplement* the qualitative information, as
in the use of reaction time in situations involving the violation of a rule or
principle, as a way of assessing a child's mode of reasoning or cognitive level.
Charlesworth and Zahn (1966) have argued for the usefulness of such
measures, but it seems doubtful that any investigator would feel comfortable
relying on it exclusively—as these authors appear to suggest. In any event,
it is apparent that the course of changes along such a variable can yield
little insight into the characteristics of the underlying developmental
changes in cognitive functioning. At the same time, data of this type may
help us more effectively to measure processes of transition from one type
of behavior to another, and more particularly consolidation of a given type
of behavior. This brings up the point made by Flavell and Wohlwill (1969)
that quantitative changes may and frequently do occur *within* a period
characterized by an unchanging type of behavior, either presaging qualitative changes to come or following such changes. The case of locomotor
development affords a good illustration: Over the period corresponding to
any given type of behavior, there are undoubtedly measurable changes in
speed, strength, smoothness, etc., as the given behavior is perfected.

General Comments.   All of the above approaches to transforming qualitative differences into quantitative change ultimately amount to creating a
silk purse out of a sow's ear, if not vice versa. Of the three, the last one is

probably the least acceptable by itself, since its use tends to draw the investigator's attention away from the qualitative, structural character of the developmental changes under study. The other two approaches by contrast fit potentially into a qualitative conception of these changes, but involving changing probabilities of response. That is, once we look at the change involved in moving from one stage to the next as a probabilistic affair, with one response gradually displacing the previous one, rather than supplanting it once and for all on its first appearance, the transition process can be charted in terms of the changing values of the probability of occurrence of each response, without in the least detracting from the qualitative differences between them. This is essentially equivalent to moving from Guttman's determinate model of scalogram analysis, described in terms of the individual trace-lines shown in Fig. 4-6a, to one of the probabilistic models, notably the normal-ogive model developed in mental test theory (cf. Torgerson, 1958, Ch. 13). The individual trace-lines corresponding to this latter model are shown in Fig. 4-6b. It is important to note, however, that these tracelines are intended to represent the changing response probabilities for particular *items* as a function of the position of individuals along the latent continuum. Here we are using them to represent the changing response probabilities for particular individuals, for some prototype item, as a function of temporal changes in the individual's own position on the continuum. While the graphic representations are transferable to this latter case, the particulars of the analytic models developed to handle actual data clearly are not, since they were developed to deal with purely static situations.

Major Obstacles in the Way of Quantitative Analysis of Developmental Change

As we have seen, the degree of quantitative refinement that one should aim for in principle depends on the type of function to which the variable under study is assumed to conform. It is important, however, to recognize the practical limitations in the collection of data permitting such refinement, which will determine the extent of quantification possible with a given set of data, independently of that ideally permissible or desirable for a given type of function. Indeed, the major challenge confronting the developmental psychologist who is interested in a quantitative approach to the study of age changes is that of overcoming the obstacles which stand in the way of obtaining the kind of data requisite for such analysis. Let us consider the major ones briefly.

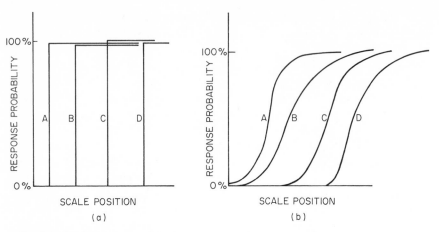

Fig. 4-6. Development of qualitative response in four individuals, according to (a) deterministic and (b) probabilistic models.

The Problem of Precision and Reliability.   It is apparent that any hopes for a refined quantitative approach to the study of developmental functions presupposes that the measures obtained are precise and reliable. In other words, that errors of measurement are small, relative to the age changes which are found with respect to them. The need for reducing errors of measurement represents an important consideration even for physical growth data, as shown in Meredith's (1955) comparison between yearly increment curves from the earliest longitudinal study by Scammon (1927) with those obtained in his own laboratories by methods specifically designed to reduce measurement error to a minimum (cf. Fig. 4-7).

Applied to behavioral data, this requirement in itself severely restricts the range of situations permitting the application of curve-fitting techniques. Elsewhere in psychology, mathematical elaboration in the form of curve-fitting and similar techniques has flourished above all in two areas: that of the study of learning, where discrete responses are cumulated over large numbers of trials, and psychophysical and perceptual measures obtained under highly standardized and controlled conditions. Data of the latter type are very difficult to obtain in work with very young children, so that what might be the most significant portion of the developmental function remains inaccessible. As for the latter type of data, they are, for all their apparent quantitative refinement of limited interest to the developmental psychologist, though the field of probability learning, and that of concept learning (Suppes & Ginsberg, 1963) may provide exceptions to this rule. Nevertheless, it is likely that greater attention paid to questions of reliability

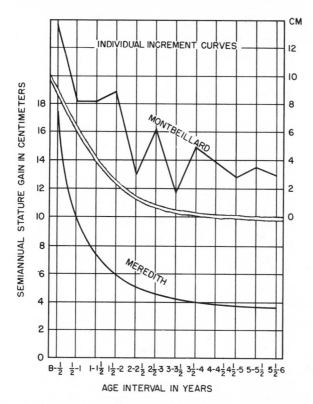

Fig. 4-7. Curves drawn to increases in successive semiannual stature measurements on two boys. [Data for upper curve from Scammon (1927); data for lower curve obtained in Meredith's laboratory (from Meredith, 1955).]

and precision with scales of an appropriate degree of refinement and discriminatory power will reveal possibilities for a quantitative study of developmental functions which have been rarely realized heretofore.

The Problem of Longitudinal Data. Except at the level of determining in gross, general terms the overall form and direction of age changes, little information of value is to be expected from quantitative study of cross-sectional records [a point readily demonstrable by reference to physical growth data (cf. Dearborn & Rothney, 1941, pp. 149ff)]. The loss of information about individual patterns of development which the cross-sectional method necessarily entails can be divided into two components: The averaging process, and the substitution of a set of independent samples stratified by age for a single cohort retaining its identity over the course of growth. The price paid by averaging can be readily shown by comparing longitudinal data treated cross-sectionally, that is, in terms of mean values at different ages, with the results obtained from individualized analysis retaining the longitudinal information. This question will be dealth with more specifically in the chapter on longitudinal methodology (Chapter VII) and in the treatment of growth-curve analysis in Chapter VIII.

The Problem of Comparability of Stimuli or Tasks across Age Levels.   Probably the most difficult problem facing the investigator who hopes to study changes along a single psychological variable over an extended portion of the age continuum is that of constructing a scale that will provide directly comparable scores over this age span. In our discussion of this question we will assume that a constant measuring scale is to be used, based on responses to a constant stimulus on a fixed response continuum. (The case of variant scales, involving changing sets of items as one moves along the age scale, or the use of different tests or tasks at different age levels, raises problems of a very different order, which will be taken up in the chapter to follow.)

Suppose then, that we are dealing with psychophysical and perceptual judgments, time scores, etc., obtained on the basis of a stimulus or task remaining invariant across all subjects. Here, obviously, the main problem is to devise stimuli or tasks which will be indifferently applicable across the entire age span over which the change is to be measured. There are a number of separable aspects to this question, having to do with the perceivability of relevant properties of the stimuli, the understanding of the instructions, the task-set of the subject, and the availability of the required responses in his repertoire. In general, all of these considerations can be reduced to the statement that all influences affecting scores on the behavioral scale in question which are not intrinsically tied to the psychological variable which it is intended to measure must play a constant role across different age levels. Typically careful control studies are required to ensure that this condition is met. Where it is violated, the consequence will frequently be to set lower bounds to the portion of the age continuum which it is feasible to include in a study (e.g., the age at which the child begins to use the required verbal responses consistently, or to be able to understand the instructions). There are often similar upper bounds determined by the nature of the task, e.g., in cases where materials designed for use with younger children become inappropriate for use with an older subject, generating boredom, or task-inappropriate behavior.

The Question of Linearity.   The question whether to transform or not to transform a set of quantitative developmental data, which is typically approached in purely pragmatic terms, usually on the basis of the parametric assumptions (notably normality) underlying the statistical technique to be employed, becomes on occasion of more intrinsic interest. Generally speaking, where a rational basis for the measures employed exists, subjecting the data to some arbitrary transformation can lead to serious distortion for descriptive purposes. For instance, a log–log transformation carried out on growth data to provide a linear plot, however convenient it may be for certain purposes (e.g., for tests of goodness-of-fit, or possibly to meet assumptions of homogeneity of variance), obscures the salient and presumably most significant aspect of the data, namely their negatively accelerated character.

Nevertheless, the problem of linearity, that is, whether equivalent amounts of the variable being measured correspond to unit distances over all portions of the scale, remains a very real issue, and one which may call for particular ways of analyzing data. Above all, this is true of scores such as time scores, error measures, or the like; particularly in any situation in which means and variances are correlated. This is generally the case wherever the scale is effectively bounded at one extreme at zero, but open-ended at the other. For instance, when dealing with time-scores the linearity assumption is generally mistrusted, and a logarithmic transformation is recommended.

By way of example, let us examine developmental trends on the Stroop Color-Word interference test. Data on this test are in the form of time-scores indicating the speed with which a subject is able to name the colors of ink in which a set of color-names are printed (the names being incongruous with the colors, e.g., "blue" may be printed in red). The developmental function obtained for data of this kind [as found from cross-sectional studies, e.g., Comalli, Wapner, & Werner (1962)] are of the form shown in the upper graph (Card C) of Fig. 4-8. However, the increase in speed shown in this graph is obviously not a direct measure of the strength of interference from the incongruous color, since it fails to take into account differences in speed of verbalization, that is, in speed of naming colors in the absence of interference from the meaning of the stimuli. Thus, the strength of the effect has to be measured relative to the base line provided by data on the latter task, shown in the graph for Card B of Fig. 4-8. If we now express the interference effect as the *difference* between these two sets of time scores, we still find a consistent decrease in the magnitude of this effect with age. Yet, if we decide instead to express the effect as a *ratio* of the two times, the resulting values are very nearly constant with age. (For instance, comparing the means at ages 7 and 17–19, the difference values are 117.8 and 46.9, respectively, while the corresponding ratios are 2:1 and 1.8:1.)

There is no simple answer to the question as to which of these two measures constitutes the more valid approach. (Note that the ratio measures are in fact equivalent to carrying out a logarithmic transformation on the data.) One way of deciding it is to rely on a criterion of internal consistency:

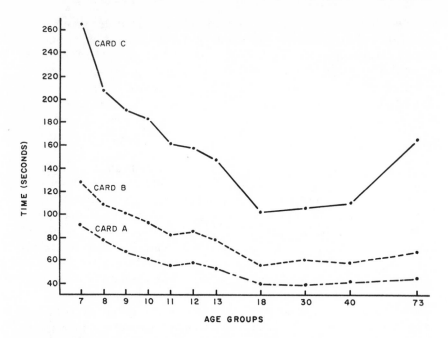

Fig. 4-8. Changes in performance on Stroop Color-Word Test from 7 to 80 years of age. (Card A: Word–reading control card; Card B: Color–naming control card; Card C: Interference card.)

If there are other reasons to suspect that a true improvement in performance is taking place with age—as suggested in the evidence from a study by Rand, Wapner, Werner, and McFarland (1963) for instance, who obtained qualitative indices of performance pointing to an increased ability to maintain the task-set (i.e., to respond to the colors) in the face of competition from the dominant word-reading response—this may be taken to validate the use of difference scores. On the other hand, there is no denying the problematical character of the assumption of linearity of effects, where results converge to or diverge from an origin of zero. The problem is particularly critical where techniques such as trend analysis are applied to the data, since these explicitly treat the data as linear, and indeed ignore the existence of an absolute zero anchoring the scale at one end.

This matter is further complicated by the problem of reliability. In treating a ratio of 40 : 20 as equivalent to one of 10 : 5, we are in effect assuming that the errors of measurement are themselves proportional to the magnitudes of the measurements. This is generally a doubtful assumption, i.e., a score of 5 sec cannot be assumed to be subject to an error of measurement $\frac{1}{8}$th the size of a score of 40. More generally, errors are apt to remain constant, or may even be inversely related to score-magnitudes (e.g., in cases where variable errors may show a trend opposite to constant errors, as in the case of illusions increasing with age).

Units in the Measurement of Developmental Change

For a variety of reasons, investigators studying the course of growth on physical, as well as psychological dimensions, have felt impelled to invent units to measure such growth, whose use raises a number of problems. Generally speaking, the intent has been to arrive at scales that would either yield equal units where the scoring system employed for measuring the responses did not provide for them, or to transform the original raw-score scale onto another one designed to enhance its comparability to other, similar scales. In particular, we may distinguish between *relativized* scales, obtained by translating raw scores onto a new scale, so as to indicate the developmental standing of a given score, relative to some referent group; and *derived* scales, obtained through suitable *transformations* of some raw-score scale.

Age Scales.   The best examples of relativized scales are, of course, the *Age* scores, and the quotient scores derived from them. Although all age scores are comparable in the sense of expressing an individual's standing on a developmental dimension as an equivalent of the CA at which 50% of some standardization or reference group have attained to the same standing, they are arrived at in several different ways, and their status as scales of measurement differs accordingly. In the case of certain age scales, such as height–age and weight–age, it is simply a matter of translating equal-unit scores into such age-equivalents.

In the case of other scales, notably the Skeletal age scale, in its original form (cf. Tanner, 1961), an ordinal scale is constructed whose points correspond to levels of development on the dimension in question attained by 50% of a referent group at each successive age level. Thus, an individual's age score can be read off directly by matching the X ray showing his osseous development to the standard series. (More recent methods of assessing skeletal age involve the allocating of points to represent the stage of development of each bone, and arriving at a total point score by summing these. This procedure results in a more finely differentiated scale, which is more nearly equivalent to the equal-unit scales on which height– and weight–ages are based, although the status of the point system employed here, in terms of the equal-unit assumption, is at least as suspect as it is when dealing with test scores.)

Finally, there are what can only be termed hybrid scales, such as those utilized in the construction of the mental age scale from responses to Stanford–Binet items. They are hybrid in the sense that they start out with a minimum estimate of the child's intelligence, by determining the age-equivalent of a set of items which are uniformly passed. This is clearly a case of placing the child on an ordinal scale of items, much as in the original form of the skeletal-age scale. To this minimum-estimate months of age are then added, according to number of items passed over and above that level (a procedure more akin to the adding up of points in the newer approach to the scaling of skeletal age).

The age-scaling procedure has little to recommend it, except for the comparability it affords to other age scales. With respect to the measurement of growth on the dimension in question, it suffers from some major draw-backs: They force the developmental function onto a purely spurious, and ultimately meaningless linear graph (since on the age-scale the increment between any two adjacent years must be equal to that for any other 1-year interval), and relativize all scores to some arbitrary reference norm. There are undoubtedly important practical uses for such scores, in assessing the progress of an individual's growth relative to a suitable reference norm, but they can convey no information about the course of growth itself, i.e., its form, regularity, or any other characteristics pertaining to the growth func-tion.

In order to arrive at a better picture of the nature of such age-scales, let us refer back to our original schematization of developmental functions, as given in Fig. 4-1 and in the four cases of measurement presented at the beginning of the chapter. In terms of the schema of Fig. 4-1, age-scales represent a derivative Y' of Y, such that $\overline{Y}' = \overline{T}$ for any group of subjects equivalent to the referent group. In other words, the real information with respect to the developmental function proper resides in the relationship between Y and Y'. Where Y is an equal-interval scale (Case I), we can work out such functions in the usual way, and there will be correspondingly little danger of the misuse of age scores to represent absolute developmental status. Where Y is an ordinal scale (Case II) the picture of an individual's function $Y' = f(T)$ will have no more information in it than that of the ordinal function $Y = f(T)$ from which it is derived, so long as the relation-ship between Y and Y' remains necessarily a purely ordinal isomorphism. There is thus some danger of misinterpreting the data obtained from the $Y' = f(T)$ function in this case, since Y' provides a misleading impression of equal-interval measurement.

The most problematical of all, however, are the hybrid cases as already discussed for the Binet, since here the Y function itself is very difficult to define as a scale in and of itself (there are no raw scores obtainable from Stanford–Binet performance). Accordingly, statements of an individual's mental growth curve, or that of a subgroup of individuals, based on such mental age data, are devoid of meaning. A good case in point is provided by Zeaman and House's (1962) analysis of the function describing the growth of intelligence for mongoloid children, as expressed in their triumphant declarative sentence, which is the title of their paper: "Monogoloid MA Is Proportional to Log CA." It is difficult to see this statement as conveying any usable information, except as a convenient expression of the obvious *fact* of the retarded status of mongoloids as a group.

Bayley's 16-D Scale. In contrast to the age scales, which translate standing achieved on some dimension into an age scale, based on some modal CA value corresponding to the age of the average subject of the referent group who has attained that standing, approaches such as Bayley's (1956) and others using *derived* scales represent merely transforms of the original scores onto a new scale. These were designed to permit comparison among different instruments, or scales based on different units.

Bayley's approach is based on a variant of a standard-score approach (which is unsuitable for developmental purposes: If scores are standardized separately for each age group, the growth information is eliminated; while the use of a *SD* unit based on the σ for all groups combined around the grand mean is unsatisfactory, since it confounds variability between and within age groups). Accordingly, Bayley proposes to adopt the $\overline{X}$ and σ for some arbitrarily chosen age group as a reference to determine the origin and unit width of the derived scale. Her procedure is to adopt the values for the 16-year-old groups for this purpose, presumably in order to capitalize on the relative stability of these values, coming near the end of the growth period.

The procedure is straightforward enough, involving as it does merely a linear transform of the original scale values, by means of the equation $X' = 140 + (20/s_x)(X - \overline{X})$, where $\overline{X}$ and s_x are the mean and *SD* of the of the original scores, respectively. At the same time, it presupposes that the original scales subjected to the transformation do in fact constitute equal-interval scales, so as to make such linear transformations meaningful. In short, whatever quantitative treatment of the original scale values could be justified would be permissible on this derived scale. Its main practical value appears to be the fairly limited one of permitting comparison of developmental data based on different scales presumed to measure the same variable (e.g., different kinds of intelligence-test scores). Yet the pooling of data as conceptually diverse as Wechsler–Bellevue raw scores and Stanford–Binet MA scores is surely suspect: For the reasons previously indicated growth-functions based on the latter are altogether artifactual, so that pooling intelligence test scores obtained from this scale together with other intelligence scales can hardly be expected to yield useful information concerning the growth function.

Thurstone's Absolute-Scaling Method. Different from any of the afore-mentioned approaches is that of Thurstone (1925), who has attempted to arrive at an essentially synthetic scale for measuring intelligence based on an absolute zero and equal intervals, starting from pass–fail data, i.e., the percentage of subjects at any given age level passing each of a set of intelligence-test items taken from the original Binet scale. The method is ingenious in its elegance and simplicity. Assuming that ability to pass items of this type is normally distributed, the percentages are transformed into standard scores. Thus, for each age level, a standard-score equivalent for each item is obtained, resulting in an overall mean for that age group. Hypothesizing an underlying continuum on which both items and individuals may be scaled, the differences between mean standard scores of successive age groups for a given set of items can be utilized to locate these age groups on the underlying scale. Thurstone does this by defining a provisional $\bar{X}$ and σ for the youngest age group as zero and one, respectively, and obtaining values for successive age groups by weighting the standard-score means by their respective variances (the latter being inversely proportional to the variance of the standardized item values, as shown by the author in detail). The result is a function for the growth of intelligence as shown in Fig. 4-9, suggesting, among other things, that intellectual growth continues well beyond adolescence, since there is no sign of a decelerating phase up to age 14.

In a subsequent paper Thurstone (1928) proceeds to derive an absolute zero of intelligence for his scale, obtained by extrapolating the age curve backward to the point where variability vanishes. This extrapolation was facilitated by the linear relationship between means and variances for different age groups which was found in Binet test data used in this latter publication. The resulting zero point, interestingly enough, turns out to fall very near the age of conception! Thurstone further discusses the question of the asymptote for intellectual growth, which he does not believe to be determinable on the basis of available scales (Thurstone, 1925; Thurstone & Ackerson, 1929).

Although this and other possible scaling methods that might be proposed for the same purpose (e.g., Thorndike, Bregman, Cobb, & Woodyard, 1927) have considerable intuitive appeal, they present a number of problems. First, the "absolute" character which Thurstone claims for his scale is more apparent than real; any functions derived from it are clearly determined by the particular set of items selected and the particular standardization samples at each age level employed. This is not a very weighty objection,

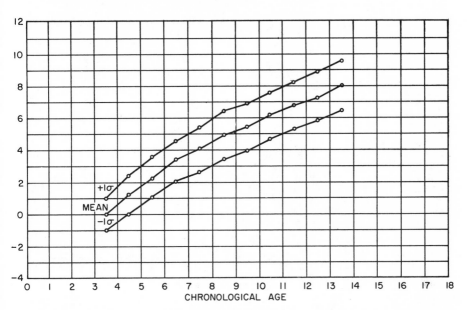

Fig. 4-9. Mean changes in intelligence-test performance, as determined through Thurstone's method of absolute sealing. (Upper and lower graphs represent points $+ 1\sigma$ and $- 1\sigma$ from the mean, respectively.) [From Thurstone (1925). Copyright by the American Psychological Association, and reproduced by permission.]

but it does suggest the need for validating results obtained (particularly with respect to such questions as the location of the absolute zero and asymptote) through replications on new sets of subjects and/or items.

The method is open to criticism, furthermore, simply on the grounds that it yields a rather implausible picture of linear growth over most of the age period from $3\frac{1}{2}$ to 14 years covered by the data. It is interesting to note that from the evidence of a new set of data spanning a similar period, and extrapolating the curves upward and downward, Thurstone and Ackerson (1929) arrive at a rather more idealized S-shaped curve, as shown in Fig. 4-10; they are especially insistent on the positively accelerated form of the curve through infancy and early childhood. The paucity of data to cover this interval (the argument is based entirely on backward extrapolation from the age of $3\frac{1}{2}$ years, using the trends for both $\overline{X}$ and s) detracts from the potency of this argument, but given the difficulty of defining intelligence in such a way as to permit its assessment over infancy and childhood along one and the same scale it will be difficult to either verify or disprove it.

The most severe limitation of the method, however, relates to its failure to provide a ready means of assigning a scale-value to a particular individual. For any individual, we still only have a record of the particular items he

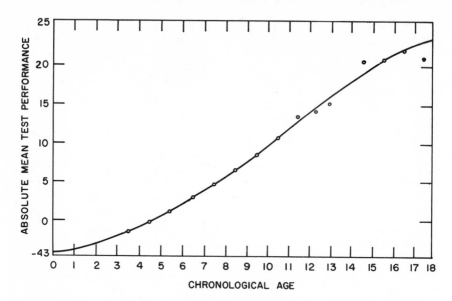

Fig. 4-10. Growth curve for Binet intelligence-test performance, as obtained by Thurstone's method of absolute scaling. [From Thurstone & Ackerson (1929). Copyright by the American Psychological Association, and reproduced by permission.]

passed or failed. The items themselves can be assigned scale-values (e.g., by determining the point on the scale where the curve representing proportion of subjects passing attains the value of .5); but there does not appear to be any determinate way of placing a given subject on the scale, and thus of charting the course of *his* mental growth. In a fashion analogous to a psychophysical threshold, one might define the subject's position as the midpoint of the zone on the scale between the points below which all items are passed and above which all items are failed. But it should be noted that such a procedure would undoubtedly result in age-group *means* deviating to some degree from those originally obtained by the application of the scaling method.

Under the circumstances, it is hardly surprising that Thurstone's method should have found little application in the voluminous literature on the growth of intelligence.

Conclusion.   The emphasis on the study of change which is being urged on the developmental investigator carries with it a responsibility for an approach to the handling of questions of measurement which transcends the pragmatic, rough-and-ready and frequently arbitrary manner in which they tend to be treated in behavioral research. The task of charting the progress of a child along some behavioral dimension presupposes the ability to locate the child's position on that dimension at a given point in time in an accurate fashion. This in turn requires, first of all, that we define the dimension unequivocally, so that the operations required for locating an individual on it, or for ordering a set of individuals, are univocally determined. It further points to the necessity of inventing instruments to achieve such measurement which will yield reliable and determinate results, reasonably free of temporary fluctuation, of influence from extraneous situational factors, etc.

CHAPTER V

The Dimensionalization of Development: The Discovery and Definition of Developmental Dimensions

The writer has been struck by an interesting anomaly in the influential work on the effects of early experience undertaken by Hebb and his associates at McGill in the 1950s. Despite Hebb's extensive training and research experience with a variety of standard animal-learning tasks, such as discrimination-learning in the jumping stand and maze learning, he did not make use of these tasks in assessing the effects of sensory enrichment or restriction. Instead he turned to a measure of animal intelligence obtained from the animal's behavior in a maze especially constructed for this purpose (Hebb & Williams, 1946). This measure is a composite of several different responses elicited in this maze, representing various facets of problem solving behavior. It is explicitly modeled after the standardized intelligence test; to quote Hebb and Williams:

> It differs from a maze-training procedure as a Binet test differs from the learning of nonsense syllables . . . it approximates . . . to the human intelligence test, which uses problems of a familiar kind . . . the subject . . . being asked to answer questions or carry out minor tasks. Our method . . . is comparable to the homogenous performance test, such as the Porteous maze, which uses a number of tasks of the same kind, varying only in difficulty [pp. 59ff].

What Hebb intuitively recognized was that response variables such as number of trials taken to reach criterion of learning in a standard maze-learning or discrimination learning task do not necessarily meet the needs of the psychologist assessing the role of experience on development, especially since the effects of the sensory experience manipulated in this work were, by Hebb's own theory, hypothesized to be fairly broad and pervasive.

The student of development finds himself in the same position, whether he is interested in the effects of experience as such, or in the study of other developmental problems. In order to get a bearing on these problems, an obvious though frequently neglected consideration is that the behavior chosen for study be such as to reveal the operation of significant developmental processes. Measures of intelligence, whether from the Hebb–Williams maze or the Binet or Wechsler tests, qualify in this respect, being sufficiently broad in scope and definition as to be likely to "catch" the major facets of the development of adaptive behavior. In this respect they may actually be too broad, so that it becomes difficult to be sure of the particular processes which enter into the responses obtained on such tests, and of the identity of these processes at different age levels. But the recourse to measures of behavior taken over from the laboratory of the experimentalist invites the opposite problem, that we wind up with responses whose meaning is perfectly determinate and of no relevance for the study of developmental processes. The case of the probability learning literature, referred to in Chapter III, provides an excellent illustration of this point: The asymptotal level of the response rate to the most frequently reinforced stimulus, which was of relevance for the mathematical learning theorists, ceased to be very revealing when applied to the study of developmental changes. If this case represents only a partial illustration of our main theme, it is because the task itself turned out (by pure accident, it would seem) to be still valuable to the developmental psychologist, once the measure of the behavior was shifted to reveal the operation of the subject's problem-solving strategies.

The developmental psychologist is in need, then, of a set of dimensions of response which are homogeneous enough to represent unidimensional continua while still being attuned to significant facets of behavioral development (precisely as Hebb and Williams sought to provide with their measure of animal intelligence). The major portion of this and the following chapter will take up some of the approaches available to him in meeting this need. To begin with let us examine three very different behavioral dimensions, in order to bring into relief some of the main facets of this dimensionalization problem as it faces the developmentalist.

The Dimensionalization of Development Illustrated for Three Response Variables

1. PERCEPTUAL CONSTANCY AS A DEVELOPMENTAL DIMENSION

"Developmental" studies of the various perceptual constancies abound (Pick & Pick, 1970; Wohlwill, 1960a, 1963a); but, as is the case with most research on similar developmental problems, once we go beyond mere statements of the significance and perhaps direction of the age differences found, the studies of different investigators become difficult to compare. Measures of constancy are sometimes couched in terms of mean amount of error (in absolute or percentage terms); sometimes in terms of the mean point of subjective equality (PSE); sometimes in terms of the function relating objective to perceived stimulus magnitude (as in the work of Leibowitz and his associates—cf. Leibowitz, Pollard, & Dickson, 1967; Zeigler & Leibowitz, 1957); and sometimes in terms not translatable into stimulus magnitude at all, as in studies using some form of a discrimination-learning or preferential-choice procedure (Bower, 1966; Frank, 1925; Misumi, 1951; Rapoport, 1969). On the other hand, where directly comparable measures and similar procedures have been used, the results obtained, though still affected by the particular targets, distances, stimulus conditions, and instructions used, do provide evidence of developmental trends which are at least commensurate in magnitude. For instance, if we compare the data from the studies by Cohen, Hershkowitz, and Chodak (1958), by Jenkin and Feallock (1960), by Lambercier (1946) and Piaget and Lambercier (1943, 1956) and by Rapoport (1967), we find reasonably good agreement on the overall pattern of age changes, and to an extent even on the magnitude of the means, especially once we separate the studies into those in which the standard was placed near and the variable far, and those which used the reverse arrangement. The two sets of data are shown graphically in Fig. 5-1a and b. It is to be noted that this comparability obtains in the face of differences in the distance of the stimuli (standard and variable were at 1 and 4 m from the subject in the Lambercier, and Piaget and Lambercier studies, at 2 and 6 m in the Rapoport and at 2 and 8 m in the Cohen *et al.*, and Jenkin and Feallock studies), in types of targets utilized, stimulus conditions, subject populations, etc.

On the other hand, these studies cover only a limited portion of the age range (there are no data below the age of 5, or after the young adult period) and are confined to data on *size*-constancy in a laboratory setting, based on the use of meaningless stimuli of simple form, compared over an essentially empty space. They are thus very limited in the information they provide concerning a modal developmental function for the development of constancy in a more general sense. Such a prototype function, if it is specifiable at all, would presumably be a composite of several different particular functions obtained across systematic variations along such variables as target distance, illumination, visual cues or information available to the subject, and above all across different perceptual dimensions, that is, size, brightness, and shape. There is some basis for cautious optimism that the contributions of the particular task variables will prove reducible to differences in the values of the parameters describing the developmental function (e.g., for high-cue conditions, a relatively flat age trend may be expected, asymptoting close to

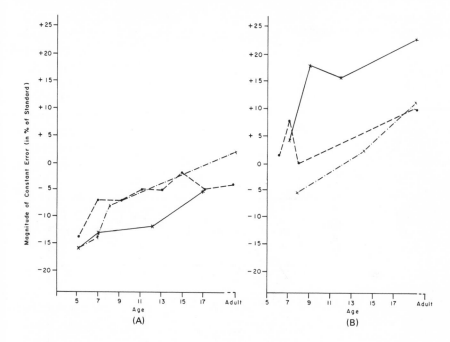

Fig. 5-1. Age-changes in size constancy found in different experiments, under two conditions of placement of the standard and variable stimuli. Condition A: Variable near, Standard far. Condition B: Standard near, Variable far.

veridicality, whereas for low-cue conditions the age trend will be steeper, and, at least in the case of size constancy, reach asymptote in the overconstancy range). Similarly, distance may be expected to be positively related to the slope of the developmental function and negatively related to its asymptote (cf. Wohlwill, 1963a, for evidence in support of some of these generalizations; see also Leibowitz, Pollard, & Dickson, 1967).

Note that the problem of dimensionalization in the case of constancy is relatively simple, since a rationally derivable measure, the Brunswik constancy-ratio (or its logarithmic equivalent, the Thouless ratio), exists for expressing the degree of constancy across different stimulus dimensions. Indeed, Brunswik (1956) has used his ratio to compare directly age changes in size, shape, and brightness constancy (cf. Fig. 5-2); unfortunately, it is doubtful that the task conditions were sufficiently well equated (e.g., in terms of the cues available to the child) to warrant such a comparison.

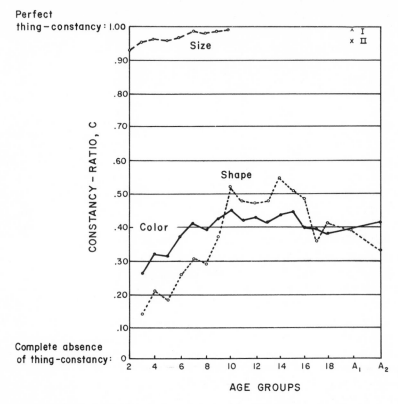

Fig. 5-2. Brunswik-ratios for size-, brightness- and shape constancy at different age levels. [From Brunswik (1956). Reprinted by permission of University of California Press.]

2. Logical Reasoning as a Developmental Variable

This variable, in contrast to the preceding one, defies any simple attempts to represent developmental change along a quantitative continuum. First, while constancy is, in principle, amenable to quantitative measurement in terms of an independently defined unit, there is no rationally definable unit of reasoning ability that could serve as the basis for the construction of a scale in this realm of development. It might be proposed that information-processing ability could be used as an operational definition of reasoning, which would prove quantifiable by resort to such indices as number of dimensions and items of information which the child can handle. The models suggested by McLaughlin (1963) and Pascual-Leone and Smith (1969) are indeed attempts to translate the development of thinking as conceived by

Piaget into information-processing terms. They do so, however, at a great sacrifice in the restrictiveness of their assumptions about what constitutes logical reasoning. Many of the behaviors which would be included under this rubric, including the majority of the problems discussed by Piaget and his associates—e.g., the formation of concepts of invariance (conservation), the ability to handle problems such as the lever, or systems of spatial co-ordinates, and to deal with probability concepts—would be excluded from consideration.

Quantification in this domain has not been lacking, of course. Measures of *speed* of problem-solving performance, and, most commonly, simple counts of numbers of items answered correctly have been used on a large scale in psychological testing. Yet, for several reasons, neither of these has proved very adequate to the developmentalist's task of charting the course of development. First, the units employed are suspect as measures of the under-lying variable—speed cannot be equated with ability (though it may be correlated with it), while adding up the number of correct responses is based on the fallacious assumption that each correct response measures an equiva-lent amount of the ability, regardless of the item answered.

In this sense the standard aptitude or ability test falls uncomfortably between two stools: One represented by a set of items selected to be all of equivalent difficulty (e.g., a set of simple addition problems), where number correct would amount to a measure of *rate* of performance; the other represented by a perfectly graded set of items, as in a Guttman scale, where number correct should be reproducible from the ordinal position of the highest item passed. Tests clearly fulfill neither of these conditions. (Recall the discussion in the preceding chapter of the problem of interdependence among responses to items.) It is undeniable that, in a purely pragmatic sense, test scores are useful predictive measures of ability. There is impressive evidence, furthermore, that there is little predictive gain from attempts to weight items differentially to allow for differences in difficulty level. Yet, given the uncertain status of test scores as equal-interval scaled measures of an individual's location on an assumed dimension of development, their usefulness for revealing details of the developmental function characterizing that dimension is subject to question.

There is a further, even more important, limitation of standardized tests in this particular context. It is impractical to attempt to construct a test that would differentiate among individuals over a very large range of ability or level of development on the variable being measured. It would be redundant in the extreme, and probably disastrous for the maintenance of attention and motivation, to require adolescents to respond to long sets of items intended to discriminate at the 6- or 7-year-old level, or vice versa. This means that for different portions of the variable different scales are required;

tests in the reasoning area such as the Thurstone Primary Mental Abilities (Thurstone & Thurstone, 1947, 1948, 1953), with its separate scales for ages 5–7, 7–11, and 11–17, as well as of course intelligence tests such as the Binet (which uses in effect a different scale for each age level), reflect this requirement. The problem of transforming such scores to yield a set of points along a single dimension (ruling out the intermediary of age scales, with their serious defects discussed in the preceding chapter) presents serious difficulties, which even as psychometrically sophisticated test constructors as the Thurstones do not seem to have resolved.

Last, quite apart from these practical problems of scale construction, there are more fundamental reasons for questioning the appropriateness of assimilating this domain to the mold of unidimensional, continuous scales of measurement. Not only is logical reasoning itself far from a unidimensional domain, as factor-analytic research has made abundantly clear, but the structure of the component dimensions appears to change over the course of development, reflecting changes of a qualitative order in the intellectual functioning of the child.

3. Aggressiveness as a Developmental Variable

In contrast to all of the preceding cases, the status of aggressiveness as representing a developmental dimension is itself in doubt. Intuitively it would seem that consistent developmental changes with respect to this variable would take the form of mode of expression of aggression rather than of systematic trends in amount conforming to some modal developmental function. The analysis of this developmental component may be assumed to be comparable to the study of the qualitative changes in the reasoning domain. As far as the intensive aspect of this variable is concerned, on the other hand, aggressiveness is probably to be considered as a differential variable, that is, one along which individual differences may be described, rather than a developmental one.

A definitive settlement of this issue would, however, presuppose the existence of a scale or set of scales along which aggressiveness can be assessed in terms that are commensurate over the length of the age continuum. This hardly seems a likely possibility; indeed, the experience of those who have studied this variable longitudinally with main interest in the question of stability (e.g., Kagan & Moss, 1962; Sears, 1961) offers little encouragement in this regard, at least so long as the variable is defined in the very nonspecific terms in which it has traditionally been studied on the part of child psychologists. This case is, in any event, primarily relevant to the study of differential aspects of development and, in that context to the issue of the stability of development; it will be discussed under that heading in a later part of this volume. It is mentioned here mainly to raise the issue of dimensionalization as it appears in developmental assessment in its most severe form.

The Search for Developmental Dimensions

The illustrations just presented provide a starting point for specifying a set of criteria to be satisfied in deciding on a behavioral dimension suitable for tracing the course of developmental changes. These include:

(*a*) Systematic shifts with age occur on the dimension (as established through prior research, or common observation). This is so obvious as to require no further comment. As we saw, it is on this basis that variables like aggressiveness, and similar bipolar personality traits, are ruled out of consideration (though we might want to redefine the variable as "mode of expression of aggression," in which case we would have a set of qualitative categories defining a nominally scaled variable).

(*b*) The dimension should be meaningful in terms of its reference to known or postulated developmental processes. This is obviously in part a subjective matter, but at the same time one subject to pragmatic forms of control (as seen in the case of the use of and subsequent deemphasis on asymptotal response rate as an index of probability-learning performance). Similarly, structurally linked measures of language development (e.g., percentage of free associations preserving identity of part of speech, as in Brown & Berko, 1960), can be expected to be more fruitful than purely descriptive measures such as vocabulary size.

(*c*) The dimension is defined in such terms as to yield measures based on a constant unit of measurement, or, alternatively: (*c'*) The responses defining the dimension constitute a homogeneous, unidimensional set, both within and across age levels. That is, unidimensionality must either be given us in terms of the measuring instrument utilized—as it is in any of the physical scales defined in terms of a standard unit—or we should have some a priori reason to have confidence in the validity of the unidimensionality assumption (though it will obviously remain subject to empirical verification, cf. Chapter VI). It is for this reason that we would distrust attempts to construct a developmental scale of logical reasoning ability, given the multifactorial nature of this domain, as well as the qualitative discontinuity which characterizes it.

(*d*) The dimension should be defined in general terms, sufficiently situation-independent to yield a valid as well as stable measure of developmental status. This is essential if we are to have an adequate bearing on the true basis for the developmental changes to be measured. For instance, if development on some hypothesized dimension Y takes a very different form under each of two conditions, A_1 and A_2, it is clear that we have failed to specify adequately what it is that is changing in the individual as he develops. The differential effect of the two conditions must itself be incorporated into the definition of the developmental variable.

It is the last of these criteria which is apt to present the greatest challenge, particularly where behavioral measures are chosen from the repertoire of the experimentalist, without regard to their developmental relevance. This problem merits more detailed consideration.

1. The Role of Situational Variables in the Search for Developmental Dimensions

It is useful to distinguish among three kinds of situations with respect to the manner in which situational factors relating to the stimuli, experimental conditions (e.g., instructions), etc., affect the definition of a developmental variable. These are, respectively:

(a) no interaction (situational variables account for significant variance, but do not interact with age);

(b) simple interaction (situational variables interact with age, but do not affect the direction or the form of the developmental function);

(c) complex interaction (direction and form of developmental function itself varies with situational conditions).

(a) *No Interaction.* The first of the above-mentioned cases is illustrated in Maccoby and Konrad's (1966) study of age trends in selective listening, in which kindergarten age, second-grade, and fourth-grade children listened to two simultaneously presented auditory messages (words), one spoken by a man, the other by a woman, and were asked to name the word spoken by one of them. The results are shown in Fig. 5-3a, for two different conditions of stimulus presentation: In one, the same message was presented to each ear, both of the voices being mixed in the input; in the other condition the two voices were split between the two ears.

It is clear from these data that the ability to listen selectively to one of two simultaneously presented messages not only shows marked improvement over this (relatively limited) age range, but that this improvement is equivalent in magnitude and form for the two conditions of presentation used. This finding is important, since it suggests that Broadbent's (1958) concept of filtering, which has inspired Maccoby's research in this area, is not central to the definition of the developmental change shown in these data.

A similar point emerges from the results of a subsequent study by Maccoby and Konrad (1967), comparing performance when the instruction as to

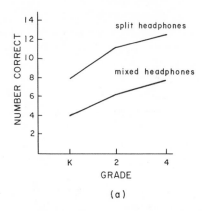 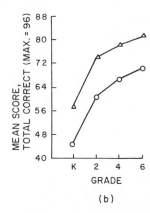

(a)   (b)

Fig. 5-3. Age trends in selective listening. (a) Data of Maccoby and Konrad (1966), comparing binaurally split versus binaurally mixed inputs of task and distracting stimuli. (b) Data of Maccoby and Konrad (1967), comparing pre- versus post-instructional sets. (△): Before signal; (○): After signal. [Reprinted by permission of The Society for Research in Child Development, Inc.]

which of the two voices the subject was to attend to was given preceding as opposed to following the message. The results are shown in Fig. 5-3b; again the age trends are directly parallel for the two conditions. Thus, another basis for the improvement in selective listening that might have been hypothesized is ruled out, namely, the ability to adopt an appropriate preparatory set.

Simultaneous investigation of the effects of age and experimental conditions, along the very inventive lines represented in this and other studies of Maccoby's research on selective attention, can play a most important role in transcending the limitations of ordinary age-group comparisons, so as to reveal the bases for some given age change in behavior more directly. In this respect, negative results with respect to interaction are as important as positive results, for, just as negative instances in a concept-formation or 20 questions type of task can speed up the process of finding the correct answer, so information as to what variables do not contribute to the course and extent of age changes aid in the eventual specification of their real basis and meaning.

From the perspective of our discussion, this type of research is of interest not just because it allows us to sharpen our interpretation of observed age differences, but because it leads to an improved definition of the dimension of age change we are dealing with. It is thus an essential first step in our programmatic approach to the study of developmental processes.

The question remains: If we are interested in arriving at a developmental dimension along which the course of development of individuals can be charted, how do we take account of the differences attributable to situational factors such as those illustrated in Fig. 5-3, even if they do not interact with age? Two possible solutions may be suggested, applying to two types of circumstances which correspond roughly to the differentiation between fixed and random effects in the analysis of variance.

In the case of the two studies of Maccoby and Konrad, since the overall level of the curves is clearly determined by the particular experimental condition, it would make sense to incorporate the conditions-variable as a parameter into the developmental function, either by representing it as a constant in any mathematical expression for that function that may be determined, or by "tagging" the function with the condition representing it. In either event the condition would, in effect, appear as a qualifier or determinant when attempting to locate a given individual along the dimension in question, though in the definition of this dimension we could disregard these situational variables.

On the other hand, where a set of different stimulus conditions is samples from among a number of alternative ones that might have been utilized (for instance, different stimulus domains, in the study of preference for complexity; different terrains or backgrounds in the study of constancy), if these fail to interact with age, they may be treated as constituting a homogeneous set with respect to the developmental dimension of interest. The results obtained for such a set can be averaged to yield a value for an individual's standing on the dimension that is presumably representative, at least in the sense of Brunswik's (1956) notion of ecological representativeness. Brunswik was, however, more interested in bringing out the *variation* in individual's responses under differences in situations comparable to the range within which his everyday adaptive behavior in the environment actually occurred. Our aim, on the contrary, is to abstract from this variation, to bring out the invariant course of development, averaged or combined over such a set of conditions.

(*b*) *Simple Interaction.*   Situational variables may interact with age for a variety of reasons. Perhaps the most common one is represented by the use of a base line or control condition, in which case the measure which the investigator is interested in becomes the difference between the base line value and some experimental condition. For instance, in measuring interference on the Stroop Color-Word test (cf. the discussion of this task in Chapter IV and Fig. 4-11), the time scores obtained under the interference condition must be considered in relation to the control values obtained in the absence of interference.

In cases such as this one it is apparent how an interaction between age and condition such as obtained in the case of Stroop test performance (cf.

Chapter IV) can be translated into a redefinition of the developmental dimension based on a measure of *differential* performance. The same point frequently emerges from situations in which interactions occur between particular conditions and age, but where the conditions studied, instead of involving a comparison of an experimental to a base line measure, play rather a coordinate role. The literature on perceptual development offers a number of interesting cases of this sort, two of which may serve for illustrative purposes.

The first of these examples actually involves comparisons across studies carried out by different experimenters, and thus does not afford direct tests of interaction in a statistical sense. It does, however, show the potential role of this type of evidence in bringing about a sharpened and frequently considerably revised identification of the developmental process at work. It derives from the body of research on the question whether the perceptual constancies increase with age (cf. Wohlwill, 1960a, 1963a). In a series of studies from Brunswik's laboratories referred to earlier (cf. Fig. 5-2), impressive developmental trends were uncovered, but these were challenged by Burzlaff (1931) and others, following a nativist Gestaltist interpretation of the constancy phenomenon, as an artifact of the experimental procedure favored by Brunswik and his associates, which did not permit the subject to view the variable stimulus in the context of an ordered series. Burzlaff demonstrated that under these latter conditions age changes virtually vanished. While this conclusion was subsequently thrown into doubt by Lambercier's (1946) convincing demonstration of the extent of central-tendency biases, varying with age, which arise under serial presentation of the variable, a comment made by Akishige (1937), based on the contrasting results obtained under the two attempted resolutions of the question may still be applicable. Surveying the contrast in the developmental evidence uncovered by Brunswik's forces, on the one hand, and Burzlaff and his camp on the other, and buttressing these results with further similar findings of his own, Akishige concluded that it may not be so much constancy per se that develops, but rather the ability to relate stimuli across temporal or spatial distances. Where the task facilitates this aspect of the constancy task, as it does when the variable appears as part of an ordered series, young children appear to be equivalent to adults in the extent of their approach to constancy.

Our second example comes from an unpublished M.A. thesis by Klein (1960), who studied age changes in performance on a task of intra- and intersensory integration of pattern information. He dealt with pairs of quasi-rectangular shapes, marked by jagged outlines replacing one of the long sides, the subject's task being to decide whether or not the two members of the pair would or would not interlock into a single form, i.e., as in a jigsaw puzzle. The task was administered under three conditions, one visual, one tactual, and one intersensory (the subject seeing one of the members of the pair while exploring the other tactually). Klein's original hypothesis was that the last-named condition would prove most difficult, and especially so for the youngest subjects; however, as Fig. 5-4 indicates, the result was quite different, the visual–tactual combination being in fact intermediate between the other two. In this case the interaction between age and conditions suggests that the relevant developmental variable is not that of intersensory interaction, but probably one of the integration of pattern perception from successively presented information, as demanded by tactual as opposed to visual exploration.

In both of these cases, then, the finding of an interaction between stimulus conditions and age points to a possible reinterpretation of the basis for the age changes observed under one of the conditions, and thus to a redefinition of the developmental dimension with which we are dealing. Obviously this will not be true of every instance of such interactions even when they are simple in form (i.e., limited to differences in slope of the developmental function), but it occurs frequently enough to recommend itself as a strategy for "purifying" behavioral dimensions for use in developmental research.

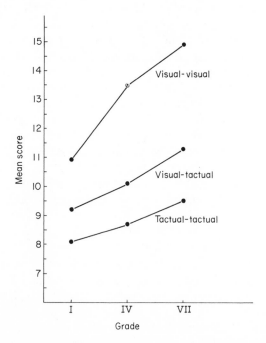

Fig. 5-4. Age changes in form–matching performance under visual, tactual and intersensory conditions of stimulus presentation. [From Klein 1960).]

(c) *Complex Interactions.*   For the sake of completeness, as well as to warn against the assumption that the indiscriminate use of the interaction design will necessarily yield revealing information concerning the processes underlying observed age changes, let us consider briefly the case in which significant interactions between an experimental variable and age occur, but in an irregular and inconsistent fashion. A good example is provided in the results of a study of the writer's, in which subjects at different ages made distance-bisection judgments from photographic slides (Wohlwill, 1965). The experimental variable was the density and regularity of the elements defining the texture of the stimulus field over which the bisections were made. The results are reproduced in Fig. 5-5. While there is some suggestion of a consistent interaction of texture density with age, the results for the regularity of patterning variable are simply too inconsistent to warrant interpretation. Faced with data of this kind, the main question would concern the relative magnitude of the experimental effect in comparison with the age differences. In this particular study, age changes were comparatively small (especially in comparison with the data from a very similar study carried out on the basis of a three-dimensional stimulus field, which showed much larger age differences, and lesser effects attributable to the stimulus field), so that one would be reluctant to use this task for the study of the development of space perception. On the other hand, where age trends are substantial, the finding of irregular interaction with an experi-

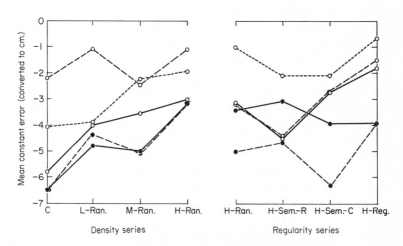

Fig. 5-5. Mean constant errors made in distance-bisection judgments from photographic slides, as a function of density and regularity of texture elements of stimulus fields and of Ss' grade level. (●———●): Grade I; (○———○): Grade IV; (●————●): Grade VIII; (○————○): Grade XI; (○------○): Adults. [From Wohlwill (1965).]

mental variable, even if it is significant, need not prevent the developmentalist from devising a representative index indicating the modal position of the
individual on the behavioral dimension, averaged over the conditions used,
or possibly over some plausible subset of these conditions.

2. THE PLACE OF THE INTERACTION PARADIGM IN
DEVELOPMENTAL RESEARCH

To relegate the role of the study of experimentally manipulated variables
in combination with age to that of a bulldozer, paving the way, as it were, for
the developmentalist to study age changes in depth, may seem to belittle
the potential contribution of this approach, not only to developmental
psychology, but to the experimentalist as well. It is undeniable that research
of this type has represented a fruitful mode of attack on a variety of problems.
Not only has it indicated the boundaries within which the laws of the experimentalist operate, to the extent that these are related to the individual's
developmental level—which, as we saw in Chapter I, has been argued to be
the major role the developmentalist can play vis-à-vis the experimentalist
(Russell, 1957)—but more positively it has proved valuable as a strategy for
revealing the operation of basic developmental and organismic processes.
Gollin (1965), in particular, has made a persuasive argument for this use of
the interaction research paradigm, illustrating its application both from his
own research on perceptual development and that of others, notably
Lashley, on differential performance as a function of differences in organismic state or neural functioning.

But there is nothing inconsistent with a recognition of the value of this
type of work in enlarging our understanding of behavioral processes in
general, and developmental changes in particular, and the use to which
we are proposing to put it; namely, to define the nature of the developmental
dimension underlying a particular measure. The point is that we require a
thorough understanding of what it is that develops, before we can hope to
undertake an intensive study of the mode of operation of developmental
processes, in the manner being proposed. We have noted repeatedly that
simple age-group comparisons will not provide us with this information,
the results being too ambiguous (i.e., too much subject to alternative interpretations). The age by conditions design is one way to increase the incisiveness of the developmental evidence; as we shall note presently, there are
others.

At the same time a mindless, purely pragmatic approach in the study of
experimental variables in interaction with age is to be distrusted, here as
elsewhere. The fact is that, unless there are effective ways to conceptualize
such interactions (ideally leading to the kind of redefinition of the developmental variable itself which we have already illustrated) they remain as

sterile facts, of interest neither to the experimentalist nor to the developmentalist. Certainly there is no basis for expecting each and every measure which the experimentalist has devised to prove of interest when studied developmentally, much less to recommend itself as a dimension along which to undertake intensive analyses of developmental changes. Only a sensitivity to the character of developmental processes can help the experimenter to discriminate between dimensions that are useful for this purpose, and those that are not.

3. THE CORRELATIONAL APPROACH TO THE DEFINITION OF

DEVELOPMENTAL DIMENSIONS

If the interaction paradigm is intended to direct us toward dimensions of development which can be considered as independent from particular situational conditions, a complementary task, relevant to criterion c of those noted earlier (the unidimensionality criterion) is to arrive at dimensions which are likewise generalizable over different response variables which are presumed to tap the same dimension. While this is in part a question of the homogeneity of the component measures, which is subject to empirical checks (cf. Chapter VI), it is also, to an extent, an aspect of the prior definition of the dimension.

There are some situations in which we may be led to a redefinition of of a dimension by finding measures assumed to index that dimension correlating highly with measures of a different kind. This is what seems to have happened for instance, in the case of Witkin's dimension of field-dependence, which in the more recent work by Witkin and his associates (Witkin, Dyk, Faterson, Goodenough, & Karp, 1962, pp. 46ff) has been subsumed under the concept of an analytic perceptual attitude, because of the correlation between the original measures of field dependence and measures such as the Gottschaldt embedded-figures task. Thus, just as probes manipulating certain experimental conditions are required to determine the range over which developmental changes remain invariant, so as to allow a proper definition of the dimension of development being studied, so a certain amount of correlational probing may likewise be necessary to determine the extent of the communality between the chosen criterial measure of that dimension and others presumed to measure different dimensions. This type of probe will provide a check on the appropriateness of the definition given to the dimension in question.

There is a further aspect to this definitional problem which likewise calls for a correlational attack. We frequently find ourselves confronted with a choice between two alternative measures of a given variable, without very firm grounds for deciding between them, except perhaps on the basis of practicality. The study of learning, with its often arbitrary resort to trial-to-criterion measures, as opposed to latency of response, or resistance to extinction, is a good example. But unless satisfactory intercorrelations among such measures can be established, the choice between them is not only arbitrary, but apt to bias the measure of the intended variable in such a way as to amount in effect to a redefinition of the variable. (Thus, in the measurement of conservation concepts—cf. Chapter IV—the resort to measures of "resistance to extinction," i.e., abandonment of the conservation principle in the face of apparent instances of its violation, may bring into play factors of suggestibility, etc. which may be quite independent of those entailed in the original learning of the principle.)

Conclusion

The discussion of the problem of dimensionalization in this chapter and the one to follow should at least serve as an antidote to the cavalier treatment of this problem on the part of developmental psychologists heretofore. If, as developmental psychologists, we are to come to grips with the study of change, it is imperative that we be able to identify clearly the variables along which the change occurs. The facile operationalism which has permeated the ordinary approach to this question is unlikely to prove adequate in the long run. While it may do for the purposes of detecting gross aspects of age changes as these emerge from age group comparisons, the identity of the variable actually undergoing change will remain subject to question, as long as the presumed variable of interest is assessed in terms of a single measure.

As was noted earlier, this is apt to constitute a particular problem where the dependent variable has been taken over bodily from the experimentalists' laboratory, where its operational definition may be perfectly adequate to the formulation and testing of experimental hypotheses or even theories, relating to variables under the experimenter's control. As soon as the same measures are applied to developmental study, however, the investigator ceases to have effective control over the processes determining age differences with respect to these measures, and accordingly the meaning of these measures becomes subject to ambiguity (as we saw in the case of the study of probability learning). Once the definition of the dimension over which age changes are to be traced is taken seriously, and the investigator starts concerning himself with establishing the dimensionality of his data both across tasks and across ages, there will be greater assurance that the resulting measures will be of value for the study of developmental processes. This will, however, require further detailed attention to the problems involved in constructing developmental scales, which form the subject matter of the chapter to follow.

CHAPTER VI

The Dimensionalization of Development (Continued): The Construction of Developmental Scales

Four Steps in the Construction of Developmental Scales

The general problem of constructing developmental dimensions can be specified in terms of a four-step sequence, as outlined in Table 6-1.

Three dimensions have been chosen for illustrative purposes, representing two variants of Case I of measurement scales (cf. Chapter IV), i.e., perceptual constancy and verbal ability, and preference for complexity, illustrating Case II. Let us examine the steps of this sequence individually.

1. CONSTRUCTION OF COMPONENT MEASURES

Once a developmental dimension with requisite characteristics for the study of developmental processes has been chosen and given adequate definition, the first step in the process of constructing a behavioral scale for assessing development on that dimension is straightforward enough. It consists merely in selecting or constructing a set of measuring instruments designed to index it across the total range over which the developmental changes are to be studied. If we start with a definition of the dimension referring to a basic construct which is of some degree of generality, so as to tie into a nomological network of interrelated behaviors, the problem then becomes one of tapping this network in a variety of places, in order to arrive at a stable as well as comprehensive assessment of the individual's standing on the dimension in question. For purposes of illustration, the following tasks and measuring devices may be suggested for each of the variables shown in Table 6-1.

Table 6-1
Schema for Construction of Developmental Scales

Step in scale construction	Case I	Case I bis	Case II
	Example: *Constancy*	**Example:** *Verbal ability*	**Example:** *Preference for complexity*
1. Construction or selection of measuring instruments for each component measure, maximizing stimulus or task invariance and response comparability	Tests of size, shape and brightness constancy based on constant or equivalent stimulus conditions and fixed psychophysical method	Tests of vocabulary and verbal fluency	Complexity scales for different types of stimuli (natural, artistic, nonsense shape) and/or different modalities (visual, auditory, tactual)
2. Collection of cross-sectional data over appropriate age span at closely spaced intervals			
3. Verifying homogeneity of component measures or subtests within and across age levels	Convergent and discriminant validation	Factor analysis	Monotonicity analysis
4. Converting to single, composite scale; determining scores to locate individuals on the variable	No conversion problem. Scores obtained from linear function of individual values (raw or weighted)	Conversion via "16-D" scale or similar method scores as in Case I	Conversion via superposition of component stimulus scales. Scores as in Case I (if interval scale).

Constancy. Measures of constancy of size, shape, and brightness are taken under conditions of comparable information. As a measure of constancy, the Brunswik or Thouless ratios are available; a preferable alternative might be the slope of the function relating matched size to distance, matched shape to angle, or matched brightness to illumination [following the approach of Holway & Boring (1941), as applied developmentally by Leibowitz and his associates, e.g., Leibowitz, Pollard, & Dickson (1967)].

Preference for Complexity. For this variable we need to construct a parallel set of scales, some of which will probably be at an ordinal level. They could include a variety of types of stimuli: irregular polygons varying in number of sides; works of nonrepresentational modern art and scenes from the physical environment scaled for complexity; tonal patterns varying in complexity in terms of number of elements, harmonic relations, rhythmic articulation, etc. Ideally, if responses on each scale were perfectly transitive, it should be possible to place the individual on the scale by the use of either noncumulative scalogram analysis (to be discussed later), or Coombs's unfolding technique (cf. Torgerson, 1958, pp. 403ff). A more realistic measure is to arrive at a scale value by averaging the scale values or ordinal positions of the stimuli chosen by the subject, as in Thurstone-type attitude scales or by the use of one of the standard scaling methods, such as paired comparisons or rankings.

Verbal Ability. For this variable a number of test instruments have already been developed, in some cases running down to the 2-year-old level. Meyers, Dingman, Orpet, Sitkei, and Watts's (1964) tests of "linguistic ability," comprising measures of receptive and expressive vocabulary and of verbal fluency (number of verbal responses to a set of pictures, or number of named objects falling into a given category), are available, as are more standard vocabulary and fluency tests developed for older children, such as those contained in the SRA Primary Mental Abilities tests devised by Thurstone and Thurstone (1947, 1948, 1953).

2. COLLECTION OF CROSS-SECTIONAL DATA OVER
    APPROPRIATE AGE SPAN

This phase of the dimensionalization task requires little comment; it is directed at providing the data from which the eventual developmental scale is constructed. The main point that needs some elaboration concerns the selection of the "appropriate" age span. The intent here is simply to ensure that the total age range over which the behavior in question can meaningfully be assessed is included in the scale. This is clearly a matter of proper test selection in Step 1. Thus, in the case of constancy, proper adaptation of standard psychophysical procedures will permit assessment on this variable down to fairly early infancy, while in the case of verbal fluency extension down at least to the preschool level should prove feasible. This will frequently mean that the functions thus generated will not be continuous, or the measures not be directly comparable over the different parts of the age span. The resulting problems will be considered in the discussion of Step 4.

3. VERIFYING HOMOGENEITY OF COMPONENT MEASURES

Within an age group, the question whether the measures collected for each variable do indeed represent a single, homogeneous dimension can be answered by recourse to diverse methods, the particular one indicated in a given situation depending on the nature of the measures at hand. Factor analysis suggests itself as one obvious approach, where a set of quantitative measures are available; under the hypothesis of homogeneity, a single factor would emerge, and the percentage of the total variance accounted for by this factor, or first principal component (if more than one factor were extracted), would serve as a convenient index of the homogeneity or uni-dimensionality of the set of scores. A variant of this method, which will be considered more fully in the following section on the scaling of qualitative data, is more generally applicable to this problem, since it makes no require-ments as to metric or even ordinally scaled measures. It is Bentler's (1971) monotonicity analysis, which is particularly well suited to the determination of unidimensionality, in data such as responses to sets of dichotomous items or sets of ordinally scaled responses.

Beyond the determination of homogeneity, however, it is equally impor-tant to ensure that the covariation of the responses to the set of tests is in fact attributable to the variable assumed to represent the common factor or underlying dimension, and, further, that this variable preserves its identity over the several age levels tested. In connection with the first of these points, it is useful to refer to the convergent and discriminant validation approach proposed by Campbell and Fiske (1959). These authors suggest that the validation of a measure of a trait proceeds by determining its correlation with other measures of the same trait obtained through different methods and comparing the extent of these correlations with those obtained by the use of the same method applied to the measurement of different traits. Their approach may be illustrated by reference to the case of the perceptual constancies, where the psychophysical method used must always be looked at as a potential contributor to, or even determinant of, observed age differences. For instance, where a method of serial presentation of the variable is used, age differences in the responses given on a constancy task are strongly affected by central-tendency effects diminishing with age (cf.

Lambercier, 1946). Thus one would expect measures of constancy obtained with this method to correlate more highly with measures of a perceptual illusion obtained via the same method than with measures of size constancy obtained via a different method, e.g., constant stimuli.

It should be observed that homogeneity should hold to an approximately equivalent extent across all age groups, if the measures are to prove useful for the purpose of constructing a composite developmental scale. In particular, if this homogeneity substantially decreases with age, it would point to the emergence of stimulus- or situation-specific factors requiring a redefinition of the variable being measured. The reverse age trend is equally possible. In this case, we would have the option either of selecting that measure or combination of measures for which homogeneity still obtained, or of considering the development of the variable as divided up into two or more discrete phases, and to investigate the development within each independently, homogeneity being assumed to hold within these limited time periods.

4. CONVERSION TO A SINGLE COMPOSITE SCALE

There is both a within- and a between-group aspect to the problem of how to arrive at a single, composite measure to locate an individual child on the variable being assessed, once the homogeneization task has been achieved. First, we need to find a suitable way of combining the scores on those of the measures which had, in the previous phase, been found to constitute a homogeneous set. While a simple arithmetic averaging process might seem to be the obvious answer, it has two drawbacks: It gives equal weighting to all of the scores, and it presupposes that they are directly comparable. The latter is a particularly serious limitation, since it will frequently be impossible to accomplish the purpose of situational sampling without introducing different measuring instruments. For instance, one measure of response to complexity may be based on a complexity scale utilizing the bit as a unit of measurement, while another may use simply numbers of sides, and a third may involve a rating scale.

Solutions to this problem will be of little value for the developmental psychologist unless they at the same time dispose of the between-group aspect of this problem, which refers to the requirement that the composite-score scale be directly comparable across age groups, in order that one may utilize it to assess the progress of a given child along the scale. Three general lines of approach may be suggested to accomplish this aim. The first is to transform means and variances of each scale so as to arrive at a common unit. This is in effect what Bayley (1956) has done in her construction of the "16D" scale, devised to chart the growth of intelligence where different tests are used at different ages, as described in Chapter IV. Apart from the specific limitations of Bayley's application of this method to data such as Stanford–Binet age scores, the method is not ideal from a scaling point of view, since it uses the equivalent of a within-group variance estimate (the SD of the 16-year-olds) as a scalar unit for measuring change across groups. As an approach to arriving at a composite score for children of any given age group, on the other hand, it is straightforward enough and has much to recommend it.

The second approach is via the multiple-regression equation. Given a set of variables X_1, X_2, ..., X_n (which we shall treat as variant measures of an underlying dimension X), the multiple-regression equation expressing the relationship of the combination of these measures with age can be used as a basis for deriving a composite measure $X_c = X_1 + X_2 + \cdots + X_n$. As a matter of fact, such a composite measure can readily be transformed into an "age"-type score, by simply adding to it a constant a, such that $\overline{X}' = \overline{X}_c + a = \overline{Y}$ = the mean age of all subjects utilized for the derivation of the composite scale. We would, in effect, be using the combination of measures to predict the subject's age, just as in any multiple-correlation situation. This measure would thus be directly analogous to the "age" measures cited in Chapter IV, such as skeletal and mental age. Herein lies the weakness of the method, however, since it would again force the means of scores into a linear relation with actual CA (an outcome built into the procedure by the linear-regression model utilized). The approach may still be of value, however, over segments of the age continuum over which such a linear pattern may be a reasonable approximation to the true state of affairs, as indicated by the shapes of the developmental functions for the separate measures.

The third approach is via factor scores. Following the homogeneity analyses referred to in the preceding section, all of the scores for all age groups would be subjected to a new factor analysis. The factor loadings from this analysis will be spuriously high, since scores on each test covary with age. However, the factor scores estimated from the results of this analysis could serve to locate an individual along a common scale. This approach has several further advantages. The several tests would be weighted in their relative contribution to the total score, in proportion to the extent to which each measured the common factor. Furthermore, at least for practical purposes, it would not be essential that all of the original measures be obtained on an equal-interval scale. Last, and most important, this procedure is the only one that provides a basis for translating scores obtained from different instruments used at different age levels onto a common scale. Obviously its application presupposes that we have established the identity of the factors representing the different measures of a variable employed at the different age levels.

The Dimensionalization of Qualitative Changes

The foregoing discussion has assumed for the most part that we are dealing with unitary developmental dimensions along which measurable changes occur over some significant portion of the period of development of the individual. Implicit in this assumption is the notion of a quantitative continuum; while the available responses might in fact constitute a qualitative, discrete set of categories, the presumption is that these are independently scalable, at least at an ordinal level, i.e., that they conform to Case II scales, as discussed in Chapter IV.

Under what circumstances will this presumption be reasonable when dealing with qualitatively defined responses? And what alternative models of development are indicated for the case in which an underlying continuum does not fit the data under consideration? In view of the stress which has been laid by a number of developmental psychologists on the prevalence of intrinsically qualitative changes, particularly in relation to stage-theoretical conceptions of development, these questions demand our attention, even though the methodological implications of the stage concept as such are more effectively deferred to a subsequent chapter. The major question with which we wish to concern ourselves at this point relates to the appropriateness of reconciling qualitatively defined sets of responses with a dimensional approach to the study of development, and the methods available for establishing the dimensional nature of such data.

1. TWO MODELS OF QUALITATIVE CHANGE: DIMENSIONAL AND NONDIMENSIONAL

Central in this context is the distinction already proposed in Chapter IV, between stimulus-defined and response-defined ordinal scales. So long as we are dealing with Case II-type data, where it is presumed that the behavioral categories can be scaled along a dimension by application of any of the standard stimulus-scaling procedures, or even on an a priori basis, there is clearly no problem. We may proceed with the dimensionalization task much as already outlined, except that if the responses cannot be scaled in terms of a metric (whether absolutely defined or relative to the scaling procedure utilized), some of the methods will require modification. When we are dealing with Case III-type data, on the other hand, the postulate of an underlying continuum ceases to apply, and alternative conceptions and methods become necessary.

Let us consider the first of these cases, i.e., performance on a set of tasks which has been independently scaled, or ordered, in terms of some assumed underlying dimension. Examples of these would include Schuessler and Strauss's (1950) and Strauss and Schuessler's (1951) work on the development of concepts of money, in which a set of items presumed to vary in level of abstraction was utilized; Nassefat's (1963) research in which items were scaled in terms of information-processing load involved in their mastery (cf. also Pascual-Leone & Smith, 1969); Lewis's (1963a) study of age changes in preferred level of adequacy in the representation of depth in drawings. All of these examples refer to readily statable dimensions along which development occurs. At the same time, questions of sequential progression, at least in the invariant-sequence sense, do not arise, since both the particular sequence observed and the extent of approach to sequential invariance are determined in essentially arbitrary fashion by the particular tasks or responses included for study (i.e., the particular points on the underlying continuum which the experimenter happens to have sampled). While it may still turn out to be an empirical fact that all, or nearly all, individuals pass through these points on the response scale in a regular, sequential fashion, the significance of such a finding is no greater than that attached to the observation that 42, 46, 51, 54, 57, and 61 inches represent an invariant sequence on the dimension of height.

In contrast, once we turn to Case III-type data, for which scalability is directly inferred from a set of response patterns, we are no longer dealing with the dimensionalization of development but rather with the determination of developmental sequences in a real sense. For example, the question, does the child pass through some particular sequence of responses during the course of his development, now becomes meaningful. The best illustration of this situation is provided by the various sequences of motor development studied by McGraw (1943), by Gesell (1954), by Shirley (1931a), and by others. Indeed, the concept of developmental sequences is most generally applicable in this realm of spontaneously observable behaviors; it becomes more difficult to apply consistently in the field of cognitive development, for instance, where we are dealing with elicited responses to a set of externally imposed tasks.

This distinction between observational and elicited response sequences brings up a closely related distinction which is important in the application of scalogram-analytic techniques in developmental research. The observationally determined motor sequences of infant development are prime examples of *disjunctive* scales, that is, sets of responses where each behavior, as it appears, displaces the preceding one. In the study of elicited responses to cognitive tasks, on the other hand, we almost invariably deal with *cumulative* scales, where lower-level responses are retained as the higher-level ones are acquired. Accordingly, we may differentiate between four types of situations, involving the combinations of Case II versus Case III and cumulative versus disjunctive. These four types, with illustrative item- or response-category sets for each, are shown in Table 6-2.

The difference between Case II and Case III, already emphasized in Chapter IV, is now seen in a new light. In Case II, we are dealing with arbitrarily chosen points on a predefined dimension. Other points on these dimensions might have been included, e.g., "Scrabble" might be fitted between levels *d* and *e* of the disjunctive scale; "Domestic Animal" between *a* and *b* of the Level of Abstraction Scale. In Case III, on the other hand, no dimension (apart from that of development itself) can be specified as underlying the sequences of responses indicated, and if any additional responses could be "squeezed" into the sequence, they would represent an actual gap in the sequence, and should be incorporated into it. In this connection we may refer back to the statement made in Chapter IV, with respect to Case III sets of response categories: "There is no possibility of obtaining anything except a monotonic relationship between the *Y* categories and the age variable." This conclusion follows from the determinate character of the response sets in Case III, and the fact that they are

TABLE 6-2
Examples of Qualitative Developmental Scales

	Case II (Independently scaled)	Case III (Response-defined)
Disjunctive	**Example:** *Preferred level of complexity in games* a. Chutes and ladders b. Dominoes c. Chinese checkers d. Monopoly e. Chess	**Example:** *Phases of responses in assumption of erect posture (McGraw, 1943)* a. Passivity b. Extensor-thrust c. Orthotonic phase d. Vertical posture e. Vertical-push
Cumulative	**Example:** *Level of abstraction in concept mastery* Concept of: a. Dog b. Animal c. Animate object d. Concrete noun e. Word	**Example:** *Stages of cognitive development* a. Sensorimotor b. Concrete operations c. Formal operations

presumed not to define any continuum that could be specified independently of age or development.

A look at empirical studies of developmental sequences using scalogram techniques discloses that in most cases the distinction between the two above-mentioned models has not been consistently observed. Items are frequently selected in a haphazard fashion, the nature of the underlying dimension being inferred after the fact (e.g., Weinstein, 1957). In other cases a combination of aspects of the two models is represented in a scale— as in the writer's own study of the development of the number concept (Wohlwill, 1960b), in which the hierarchy of items was based in part on assumed differences in level of abstraction and in part on the appearance of new cognitive structures, as assumed to be revealed by conservation responses.

Yet the distinction between Case II and Case III data is of significance in a variety of respects, transcending by far the realm of measurement. There are in fact basic differences in conception implied here, which have consequences not only for the dimensionalization question, our primary concern in this chapter, but for the interpretation and theoretical significance of data conforming to these two models. Let us consider some of the aspects of this difference.

(a) Determinate Character.   Case II data are properly treated as probabilistic; Case III as determinate. This follows from the arbitrary nature of the sampling of points along a dimension in Case II, as opposed to the fixed and univocally determined character of response sequences in Case III. For instance, in the typical Case II situation, it would be easily possible to select two items which occupied virtually the same place on the dimension. This would have the effect of lowering scalability, since it would be expected that subjects located in that region of the dimension could respond to either member of such pairs of items apart from the other. In contrast, in the case of true sequences of Case III, in which each response presupposes the acquisition of the previous one, there would in fact be no room for error, and deterministic models accordingly become more appropriate. This difference is depicted graphically in Fig. 6-1.

Note that the distinction between probabilistic and deterministic is intended to apply to the response patterns to adjacent items, rather than to the change in probability of response to any given item. As argued in the preceding chapter, it is quite likely that the acquisition of responses even in truly qualitative sequences is probabilistic in nature, and thus properly indicated by trace lines of the cumulative ogive, rather than discrete vertical jump type (cf. Fig. 4–6). But the relationship between any pair of items would only be univocally determined in the Case III type, that is, the trace

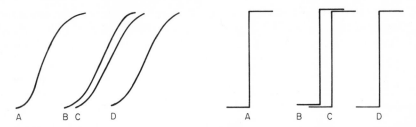

Fig. 6-1. Prototype trace lines for sets of four items (A, B, C, and D), showing probability of a response to each item on the part of subjects located at different points of the scale defined by the items. *Left*: Case-II data (probabilistic). *Right*: Case-III data (deterministic).

line for any response would not start rising until that of the previous one had reached asymptotal level.

(b) Mediation Assumption. For true developmental sequences, some form of mediation is generally assumed to hold for the relationship among successive responses [cf. Flavell & Wohlwill (1969) for a discussion of the possible types of such mediational chains]. No such mediation need be implied in Case II; all that is necessary is the postulate of some developmental process bringing about change on the dimension represented by the items.

(c) Criteria for Scalability. Detailed consideration will be given below to the application of scalogram technique and related analytic models in the study of development. At this point we may cite a distinction among alternative measures of reproducibility suggested by Milholland (1955). Measures based on the percentage of errors contained in the response patterns, such as the standard indices of reproducibility, are appropriate to Case II data, where the major issue is the extent to which the k stimuli or items are responded to as a unidimensional set. As for Case III data, on the other hand, the unit of analysis of main interest is the total sequence. Thus another of the indices suggested by Milholland is preferable in this instance, namely, the percentage of subjects whose response pattern conforms to one of the $k - 1$ scale types admissible according to the sequence.

(d) Developmental Models. The models of development represented by the Case II and Case III response scales are very different. In the former case, we are dealing with changes along a given dimension which may be presumed to be gradual and continuous, taking place in principle over a major portion of the developmental continuum, with different individuals developing at different rates and probably reaching different asymptotes.

In contrast, Case III sequences occur over a much narrower portion of the age span, with individuals differing in terms of the speed of their transversal of the sequence, and age of attainment at the endpoint of the sequence, rather than in terms of the terminal level attained.

In short, though the two types of data have been frequently considered in the same terms, they are in fact very different. This difference obviously extends to the analytic procedures indicated for each. The following treatment of scalogram analysis is written in the context of the dimensionalization problem, that is, considering this technique as a tool in the construction of developmental dimensions, appropriate to Case II data. Its application to Case III data, i.e., for the analysis of developmental sequences, will be taken up in the section to follow.

2. Scalogram Analysis and Alternative Solutions to the Developmental Scaling of Qualitative Responses Ordered along an Independently Defined Dimension (Case II)

Let us assume that we have a set of qualitatively differentiated items, selected to represent points along some continuum postulated by the investigator (e.g., concreteness-abstractness or complexity). We assume that these items have been satisfactorily scaled *qua* stimuli, at least up to an ordinal level, either on a priori grounds, or through ratings or rankings, or by applying one of the variety of stimulus-scaling or "judgment" methods considered by Torgerson (1958). All of these methods yield a metric scale for stimuli initially differentiated in qualitative or ordinal terms (e.g., methods of subjective estimates, differential sensitivity methods, and those based on Thurstone's judgment model, notably paired comparisons). There now remains a problem of establishing the homogeneity of responses to these items when used for developmental assessment, in other words, to locate an individual child along the dimension defined by the stimuli.

It might be asked, why not start out by using scalogram analysis or a similar "response" method (which Torgerson contrasts to the above-mentioned judgment methods), since these scale stimuli and subjects simultaneously. The answer is that this would leave us with Case III data; that is, the only definable dimension that would emerge would be that of the developmental status of the respondents, rather than an independent attribute of the stimuli. But the fact that we are starting with a set of prescaled stimuli does mean a change in emphasis in the determination of unidimensionality, as well as in the analytic techniques most appropriate to deal with the problem. First, the aim of the analysis is no longer to *uncover* a latent continuum represented by the items, but rather to verify the homogeneity of the *responses* to these items (i.e., to establish that the children at all ages do in fact respond to the stimuli as a unitary dimension). Since the stimuli are presumably scaled by adults, and since we assume that there is no independent objective criterion for defining their scale values, this question is of some pertinence. For instance, in order to locate children along an independently defined scale of complexity, we need to establish first whether in fact they respond consistently to this variable as defined. Thus, either of the functions shown in Fig. 6-2 would result in the individual's placement at the midpoint of the complexity scale, but we would attach significance only to pattern A, while we would interpret B as simply indicating a failure to respond to the complexity dimension. Admittedly, this question applies equally to objectively scaled stimulus dimensions (e.g., complexity measured in bits of information, or simply in terms of number of elements), but in that instance direct measures of the covariation of an individual's responses with the stimulus values become available. An interesting example is found in Oostlander's (1967) study of the size–weight illusion, in which an informational measure was applied to indicate the subject's differential use of the weight information at different age levels, for a series of standard stimuli varying in size and weight.

On the other hand, the fact that we do have an independently defined order for the items not only relegates the function of the scalogram analysis carried out on the data to a much more secondary role than it would have for Case III data, but suggests that consideration be given to alternative methods appropriate for verifying homogeneity of responses. Since adequate treatments of the problems of scalogram analysis are available, both as a general technique (Green, 1954; Torgerson, 1958) and in its develop-

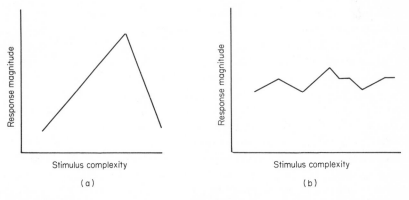

Fig. 6-2. Examples of two functions relating stimulus complexity to magnitude of response, resulting in assignment of subject to center of complexity scale. *Left*: Consistent response to complexity, peaking at intermediate level. *Right*: Lack of consistent response to complexity scale as defined.

mental applications (Kofsky, 1963; Wohlwill, 1960b), we will confine our-selves here to a brief discussion of the method, concentrating in particular on its limitations, and on the consequences of the a priori ordering of the items which we assume to be available for Case II data.

The Two Models of Scalogram Analysis: Cumulative and Disjunctive

The distinction between cumulative and disjunctive scales has been ex-plained previously; it corresponds to a differentiation between two models of scalogram analysis, of which the cumulative has seen by far more exten-sive development and application. The difference between them is best shown by indicating the ideal response matrices that would be obtained for each (Fig. 6-3).

1. THE CUMULATIVE CASE

Guttman's classical scalogram-analysis technique (Guttman, 1944; cf. also Green, 1954) was originally developed primarily with reference to the construction of attitude scales, where the intent was to arrive at a set of items representing variations in position along a single latent continuum, such that individuals' responses to the items would be determined exclusively by their own position on the same continuum. In recent years this technique' has been increasingly applied to the study of developmental changes, partic-ularly in the realm of cognitive development. The approach has a number of severe limitations, however; those most pertinent to Case II data are as follows:

(a) The Problem of Chance-Reproducibility. In any matrix of responses to a set of items which can be arranged in order of popularity or difficulty, a high degree of scalability, frequently reaching as much as .80 or even .85, can be expected by chance, simply as a function of the marginal totals (cf. Wohlwill, 1960b). This problem can be handled by reference to an index such as Green's index of consistency (Green, 1956), which evaluates the observed reproducibility in relation to the expected. Yet the small *effective* range of variation of observed reproducibility coefficients and the dubious subtractive procedure of Green's formula, $I = (Rep_o - Rep_C)/(1 - Rep_C)$, where Rep_o and Rep_C refer to the observed and chance reproducibility coef-ficients, respectively, create a difficult problem, particularly when a set of response matrices are to be compared in terms of their approach to perfect homogeneity (e.g., Nassefat, 1963).

Cumulative Pattern

Scale type	Items							
	A	B	C	D	E	F	G	H
VIII	+	+	+	+	+	+	+	+
VII	+	+	+	+	+	+	+	−
VI	+	+	+	+	+	+	−	−
V	+	+	+	+	+	−	−	−
IV	+	+	+	+	−	−	−	−
III	+	+	+	−	−	−	−	−
II	+	+	−	−	−	−	−	−
I	+	−	−	−	−	−	−	−

Disjunctive Pattern ($r = 2$)

Scale type	Items							
	A	B	C	D	E	F	G	H
I	+	+	−	−	−	−	−	−
II	−	+	+	−	−	−	−	−
III	−	−	+	+	−	−	−	−
IV	−	−	−	+	+	−	−	−
V	−	−	−	−	+	+	−	−
VI	−	−	−	−	−	+	+	−
VII	−	−	−	−	−	−	+	+

Fig. 6-3. Matrices of response patterns corresponding to cumulative and disjunctive models of scalogram analyses.

(b) The Role of Uniform Pass or Fail Patterns. The scalability of any response matrix can be arbitrarily enhanced by ensuring a sufficiently large number of cases of subjects responding to or passing either all or none of the items, which necessarily constitute perfect scale patterns. This is a relatively minor problem in the traditional field of application of scalogram-analysis, where such extreme would not be expected to occur more frequently than any other pattern; in fact, on the assumption of distribution of attitudes approaching normality, they should be relatively infrequent. In the case of developmental psychology, on the other hand, this is not necessarily the case, the critical problem being one of the age interval over which subjects are selected. To the extent that this interval exceeds the range of the scale sampled by the items, a piling up of cases in the two extreme response patterns is to be expected, resulting in a spuriously high degree of scalability. (To give a trivial example, if a set of items in the domain of arithmetic were to be given to children between the ages of 3 and 18, we could obviously expect such a piling up to occur.) While this problem is more severe in the case of the study of developmental sequences (Case III) which typically implicates only a limited portion of the age continuum, it is important to remain on the alert for it in all developmental applications of scalogram technique.

(c) The Determinacy of the Model. We have previously argued that the main issue arising with respect to Case II data, consisting of responses to a set of items representing arbitrarily selected points on an independently defined continuum, is the verification of the homogeneity of these responses (i.e., of the consistency of their covariation with stimulus changes along the continuum). This purpose, as pointed out earlier in the comparison of Case II and Case III models, does not square well with the determinacy built into scalogram-analytic techniques, which treat individual responses as changing through a series of stepwise increments as a function of the individual's own scale position, and which make no provision for error attached to such responses. Furthermore, scalogram analysis treats all distances among adjacent items as equivalent, at least in the sense that all are assumed to be beyond threshold relative to the individual's response system. Where the items have been scaled beforehand and the distances between them are thus known, methods should be applied which are both more efficient in their use of this information and more tolerant of error in their assessment of the homogeneity of the individual's responses.

(d) Homogeneity and Monotonicity Analysis. A number of variants of scalogram analysis are available; they have been effectively reviewed by White and Saltz (1957). Among these, particular mention should be made of Loevinger's (1947; 1948) technique of homogeneous tests, which differs

from Guttman's in taking response patterns to all possible pairs of items, rather than total response pattern to an item set, as its unit of analysis. Although less deterministic in conception than scalogram analysis and seemingly well suited to test construction in particular, since the procedure permits the assessment of the homogeneity for any given item with respect to the total set of items, it has seen little application in the literature.

A potentially more interesting approach as far as the developmentalist is concerned has been most recently proposed by Bentler (1971). It not only avoids the determinate character built into scalogram analysis and its derivatives, but provides a means for determining the dimensionality of the response space if it departs from unidimensionality. It is based on the definition of a monotonicity coefficient which is, in effect, a rank-order correlation coefficient, formulated as the ratio of the probability of concordant relationships to the probability of discordant relationships (concordance applies where *differences* between a pair of observations on ordinally scaled variables are of like sign, and discordance where such differences are opposite in sign).

Note that the "differences between observations" in this case are equivalent to differences between persons: The referent universe for these probabilities are differences in magnitude of response on a given variable for all possible pairs of *individuals* in a given sample. Translated to the case of binary responses to a set of items, the coefficient of monotonicity thus becomes a measure of the predominance of pairs of individuals in which one individual is superior to the other on both items (i.e., passes both while the other fails both) over pairs in which one individual is superior to the second on one item, and inferior to the second on the other item (i.e., passes item 1 and fails item 2, while the second shows the reverse pattern). Thus, in contrast to the ordinary ϕ coefficient, the unit of analysis is not the response pattern of a given individual to a pair of items, but rather the pattern *differences* in responses between all pairs of individuals over pairs of items.

The method is at a clear advantage over those considered previously, not only in bringing out the multidimensional structure of a response matrix, if one exists, but, more significantly, in not forcing a deterministic model on the behavior at all. Basically, it starts merely from the premise that one or more latent dimensions exist in terms of which a matrix of differences in an individual's responses to a set of items can most parsimoniously be accounted. This does not require the postulation of any direct functional relationship, hierarchical or otherwise, among the items (as in the case of a Guttman scale). Indeed, two items with nearly identical scale values on the major latent continuum would create no problems for Bentler's model, as it would for Guttman's. For this reason, it seems particularly appropriate for Case II data.

2. THE DISJUNCTIVE CASE[1]

This case applies in situations where, as the individual advances along the dimension defined by a set of response categories, he ceases to exhibit the responses which he had displayed previously—in contrast to the cumulative model, where it is assumed that all responses once acquired are retained as the individual advances along the scale (cf. Fig. 6-3).

With respect to Case II data, this model applies most cogently to data on preferences, interests, attitudes, and the like. In fact, Thurstone's classical method of attitude scaling, in which the scale positions of a set of items is determined from ratings made by a group of judges, could serve as the first step in the procedure required for the construction of disjunctive developmental scales. As in Thurstone's case, the items are then administered to the subject with instructions to choose those (e.g., those two or three items) with which he most closely agrees or which he most prefers. Thurstone did not concern himself with the scalability question, but it is readily attacked by examining the resulting response patterns in a manner closely analogous to the Guttman case. The problem of the measurement of reproducibility has been discussed by the writer (Wohlwill, 1963b), and more recently by Leik and Mathews (1968). Both entail a calculation of the relative frequency of errors in the matrix of response patterns, defining an error as any minus included between pluses in a pattern. Leik and Mathews's approach has the advantage of not requiring that all subjects respond to the same number of items (providing that they respond to at least two), which will be shown to be particularly useful in the case of developmental-sequence data. More important is that the index suggested by them does take chance reproducibility into account, although this problem is less serious for disjunctive data than it was for cumulative, since the relative frequency of response to each item is independent of scale position; thus, chance reproducibility will ordinarily remain relatively low.

The disjunctive model has thus far seen little application to empirical

---

[1]The use of the term "disjunctive" in the context of scaling models invites some confusion with the usage to which it has been put in the field of multidimensional scaling (e.g., Torgerson, 1958), where it refers to a response model in which a subject responds positively to an item if he exceeds its scale value on any one of the dimensions of the item space (as contrasted to both the conjunctive model, in which he would have to exceed the scale value for all dimensions, and the compensatory one, in which deviations from the item scale value on several dimensions summate algebraically). The reason for retaining the term in the present context, to designate what has previously been called the point or nonmonotone model of scaling, is that it best expresses the developmentally significant aspect of the model, where responses previously acquired drop out as new ones develop, as contrasted to the cumulative case.

data, either developmental or nondevelopmental. From the scaling stand-point, a problem that may have inhibited its wider use has been that involved in determining the item order to maximize scalability. In contrast to the cumulative case, the relative frequency of choices of an item is uncorrelated with its scale position. This problem is, of course, avoided when dealing with independently scaled sets of items, which developmental scales conforming to Case II are presumed to be. In this case we can proceed directly to the scalogram analysis to verify the unidimensionality of the responses to the items selected to sample the predefined continuum.

Let us note at this point a curious contradiction in the model, and in particular in the determinate character of the scalogram-analysis procedures used to evaluate scalability. We are dealing, to use Torgerson's (1958) term, with a "point" model of response, in the sense that any individual is assumed ideally to respond only to an item located exactly at the point on the latent continuum corresponding to his own scale position or at most to the single item closest to his position. Yet, in order to obtain response patterns which contain information as to scalability, it is necessary to ask each respondent to choose, or respond to a minimum of two items. (Any response pattern containing only a single + would necessarily be error free, i.e., scalable.) In effect, then, we need to conceive of an individual as responding to items within a certain range of his own scale position, though presumably with a response probability decreasing in either direction from that point. Thus, in contrast to the discontinuous tracelines envisaged ideally under the cumulative model (cf. Fig. 4-6), those for the disjunctive case must, in effect, be regarded as continuous, with response probabilities distributed around the individual's scale position according to some function such as the normal curve [cf. Thurstone's (1929) method of similar reactions, which postulates just such a distribution].

Alternative models to scalogram analysis are available for disjunctive or point-type data. Coombs's (1950) unfolding model applies in principle, pro-viding that it makes sense to ask each subject to rank all of the stimuli ac-cording to preference. The assumption, however, that individuals can discriminate the relative distances of stimuli from their own scale position when these stimuli may lie on opposite sides from that position becomes tenuous as these distances increase (e.g., a person who considers himself at the center of a radicalism–conservatism scale would be expected to have difficulty in deciding whether he prefers a statement representing the radical extreme to one representing the conservative extreme). This would be especially true for younger children. This problem can be alleviated by adapting Coombs's model to require rank ordering only among a subset of stimuli, the three preferred ones, for instance, as suggested by Torgerson. Even then, the model suffers from its deterministic bias, and analytic procedures for treatment of data conforming to it do not seem to have been worked out.[2]

The application of any of the foregoing models, and particularly of the disjunctive scalogram-analysis model, to developmental data raises an interesting substantive point: To what extent are we entitled to assume that the response probabilities for a given child are symmetrically distributed around his own scale position? That is, is a child as apt to respond to a stimulus located above his own modal position on a developmental scale as to one located below him? An alternative view would be that the child can only respond to stimuli up to his own position, thus generating a J-curve distribution falling off in a negatively oriented direction away from that position. The most plausible view is that the actual distribution is neither symmetrical nor J-shaped, but simply skewed, in other words, the probabilities fall off more rapidly above his own position than below.

The Use of Scalogram Analysis for the Study of Developmental Sequences (Case III Data)

For a number of reasons, the scalogram-analysis models just discussed, both for the cumulative and the disjunctive cases, are intrinsically more appropriate to the verification of developmental sequences, than to the determination of homogeneity or unidimensionality of a set of responses. Despite the original role of these models in the study of presumably continuous dimensions of attitude, the matrices of response patterns which are at the core of the model suggest the presence of a set of discrete responses, such as encountered in the study of developmental sequences, more than a sampling of points along a continuum.

On the other hand, as noted earlier in the comparison of the dimensionalization question for Case II and Case III data [cf. notably point (*d*) of that

---

[2]Coombs and Smith (1972) have developed a more general model of scaling for the disjunctive case, with particular reference to the study of developmental problems. Their model is a more general version of the disjunctive one as analyzed by Leik and Mathews, in the sense that acquisition patterns are differentiated from deletion patterns, and the possibility of an individual arriving at a point in a sequence (i.e., a particular pattern of manifested responses) via different routes is admitted. However, of most interest is the special case of the linear array, consisting of an acquisition and a deletion sequence combined into a single determinate pattern. This differs from the traditional disjunctive model insofar as a response may be deleted before it is replaced in a sequence, e.g.: A, AB, ABC, AB, ABD, BD, BDE, DE, B, BF, F. Here the conjunction of A and B is consistent with two different responses representing points on the scale above B, i.e., C and D, which would not be admissible under the Mosteller–Wohlwill or Leik and Mathews models. Coombs and Smith fail to provide any analytic procedures for the treatment of such data, and it seems doubtful that any but a longitudinal design would be able to handle data conforming to this model, which, it should be noted, remains as deterministic in its conception as Coombs's original unfolding model.

discussion], developmental sequences cannot be expected to span any very considerable portion of the age span. Their use as scales for the assessment of developmental change is limited to short-term studies of development over a narrowly defined age span, and thus departs from the treatment of developmental scaling presented up to now. This qualification notwithstanding, such sequences can still play an important role in the assessment of developmental progress, notably in the area of infancy (e.g., McGraw, 1943; Uzgiris & Hunt, 1966).

One issue to be faced at the outset is whether a given sequence is to be considered a cumulative or a disjunctive type. This problem did not arise in the same form in the application of scalogram methods to the construction of developmental dimensions; there the decision as to which of the two models was applicable could be based directly on the structure of the task, and the type of responses demanded of the individual. If the task was one of responding to as many items as a subject wished to endorse, or of trying to solve as many items as he was able to, it would fall into the cumulative type; if it was rather one of responding to a limited number of most preferred items, it would fall into the disjunctive. Basically, the differentiation is one between abilities and preferential-choice situations.

In the case of developmental sequences, however, the differentiation may not be as clear-cut. This is because most such sequences are determined via observational methods, that is, by noting which of a given set of behaviors an individual (typically an infant) actually displays, rather than those which he might be able to. Thus, in principle, it is possible to translate most disjunctive scales into cumulative simply by shifting from a focus on actual to one on potentially elicitable responses.

But this is by no means the complete answer to this question. First, there are some cases where earlier responses literally drop out once they are superseded by later ones, and thus could not enter into a cumulative scale. An example would be a sequence containing the incipient swimming movements observed in the neonate (cf. McGraw, 1943, pp. 31ff). Second, the differentiation between successive steps of an observational sequence is frequently such that the responses are graded on some qualitative scale, e.g., Phases G and H of the sequence of crawling and creeping, so that again a cumulative model is inapplicable, since the two response levels are mutually incompatible. For example, consider the following two items, as described by McGraw: "deliberate but unorganized progression," versus "organized progression." It would be patently impossible to score an infant as manifesting both of these simultaneously. Finally, notably in the study of motor development of infants it may simply make no sense to think in terms of potentially available responses: How would one elicit "beginning spinal extension" (Phase B in the sequence just mentioned) from an infant who was displaying the creeping posture (Phase F)?

Where, as is the case for the motor sequences of development, the response scale consist of a set of qualitatively differentiated response categories, we may agree that the disjunctive model provides a far more reasonable fit to the data than the cumulative. But not all developmental sequences, even in the study of infant development, are defined in such consistent terms, and as a result we sometimes find so-called sequences which are in fact a mixture of the two models. This is true in particular wherever the response categories are based in part on differences in the stimuli responded to, and in part on differences in the responses themselves. Take, for instance, the following set of items, taken from Griffith's (1954) scale of eye–hand coordination:

(a) Reaches for ring;
(b) Reaches for cube;
(c) Picks up cube;
(d) Reaches persistently;
(e) Reaches for second cube;
(f) Puts beads in box.

These items contain at least four separable types of relationships. That between (a) and (b) is empirically cumulative, i.e., if there is a consistent sequential pattern at all, presumably it is such that the infant initially reaches *only* for the ring, and subsequently reaches for both the ring *and* the cube. The relationship between (a) and (f) may be assumed to be empirically disjunctive, i.e., once infants have reached the point of putting beads into a box they are no longer observed reaching for a ring. The relationship between (b) and (d) is disjunctive also, but in a purely logical sense, i.e., (b) should really have been defined as "Reaches for cube, but fails to persist," so that it becomes incompatible with (d) and necessarily precedes it. Finally, the relationship between (b) and (e) is logically cumulative, in that it is impossible to do one without the other.

It is not surprising that, faced with the problem of scaling data such as these, Kohen-Raz (1967) should have avoided the issue of the type of scalogram model he was dealing with altogether. By opting for a procedure devised by Lingoes (1963), which confines itself to the determination of the preponderance of plus–minus to minus–plus patterns in the comparison of item pairs, he in effect adopted a cumulative model. At the same time, he limited himself to testing any given infant on items within a certain range of his own developmental level. A disjunctive relationship among items would necessarily depress the observed stability of the set as determined through Lingoes' method, since under a disjunctive model plus–minus and minus–plus patterns will occur with equal frequencies, and this may have happened in a number of instances in Kohen-Raz's study. At the same time, one suspects that in the actual scoring disjunctive relationships such as those between items (*b*) and (*d*) were translated into forced cumulative ones, by giving all subjects scored as "reaching persistently" credit for item (*b*) as well.

This hardly is a satisfactory procedure, yet the problem permeates the field of infant scales, becoming particularly acute in the realm of Piagetian scales, such as those developed by Escalona and Corman (1967) and by Uzgiris and Hunt (1966). Consistency of approach in this area would be best served by adopting the following guidelines:

(*a*) A clear-cut choice is made at the outset between the cumulative and the disjunctive model. In the field of infant testing, where it may be meaningless, if not impossible to administer all stimuli or tasks to all infants, or to determine the *availability* of all possible responses at all ages, this will typically mean a disjunctive scale. In the field of subsequent cognitive development, on the other hand, where we are generally dealing with elicited rather than emitted responses, a cumulative model will more frequently apply.

(*b*) If a disjunctive scale is indicated, differentiations among successive steps of the sequence are most effectively couched in terms of specific differentiable responses, keeping stimuli or task constant (e.g., "takes sidelong swipe at cube," versus "grasps cube firmly"). If differentiations based on stimuli must be incorporated into the scale, they can be so worded as to be turned into disjunctive categories, notably by resorting to measures of preference rather than ability. (For instance, if a rattle is picked up before a cube, it is probably also true that there is a shift in preference from the rattle to the cube when they are presented in pairs.)

(*c*) If a cumulative scale is indicated, differentiations among successive steps of the sequence are most effectively couched in terms of a graded series of stimuli or tasks, keeping responses either constant, or specified in such general terms as "passes" or "fails."

The prescription just offered for the construction of developmental scales suggests that developmental sequences are to be viewed either as sets of discrete, mutually incompatible responses exhibited in a constant stimulus situation (disjunctive case), or as hierarchically ordered generalized responses (e.g., skills or abilities) elicited by means of a variant set of tasks. Bearing in mind that we are not dealing here with responses to stimuli scalable along some independently definable dimension (e.g., preference for complexity), this does seem to encompass most if not all cases of true developmental sequences. One exception might be sequences of releasing stimuli or the like, e.g., a boy may show a disjunctive sequence of attachment responses to: (*a*) the mother; (*b*) the father; (*c*) the boy's peers; and (*d*) his sex partner. However, such sequences are rare, and of little value for developmental assessment, since they generally comprise too few steps, spread out over too long a portion of the age scale.

Once a consistent cumulative or disjunctive scale has been established, its approach to scalability, in the sequential uniformity rather than the dimensionality or homogeneity sense, is readily established by application of the above-mentioned scalogram-analytic methods, which as just noted fit the developmental sequence notion ideally. Alternatively the sequence can of course be established, or validated, directly by longitudinal study; this was in fact the way in which the various motor sequences of development were established. It may be worth reiterating, however, that, once established, such sequences play a very different role in further developmental study from the independently definable developmental scales considered in the earlier portions of this chapter. Their place in developmental assessment and in the descriptive study of developmental processes will be discussed in Chapter VIII.

Finally, the developmental sequence case has frequently been fused with the more general problem of developmental stages. The relationship is, in actuality, complex; certain developmental sequences, such as the motor sequences studied by McGraw, have validity in and of themselves, but have little relevance to the problem of stages, while others, such as Kofsky's sequence of classificatory development, are more closely bound up with the stage notion as used by Piaget. Most important, the study of developmental stages can and typically does proceed without the establishment of any but the most perfunctory sequences, which would have little value in and of themselves in developmental assessment. The stage problem thus transcends those of the construction of developmental dimensions and the specification of developmental sequences. It is much more closely bound up with questions of the changing patterning of behaviors evolving over a typically brief period of time, and appears to fit best into the more general treatment of the correlational analysis of development in Chapters IX and X.

PART III

MAJOR PARADIGMS OF
DEVELOPMENTAL RESEARCH

CHAPTER VII

Longitudinal versus Cross-Sectional
Methodology

It is little more than a truism to note that in the study of change over time (whether behavioral or any other type of change), the longitudinal approach is the most "natural" one; in the large majority of cases, in fact, its use is taken altogether for granted. Studies of learning and memory, adaptation and habituation, fatigue, as well as research on attitude change, and sociological research on institutional or population change has inevitably resorted to a repeated-measurements approach as the most logical one for obtaining the desired information. The only reservation in this respect derives from the possibility of contamination from the successive measures of behavior obtained, as illustrated in the research on memory for visual form, where the repeated-measurements design was shown to lead to artifactual results. The act of reproducing a previously seen form from memory at time t_1 itself influenced the way in which it was retained in memory subsequently, or at least reproduced at time t_2 (cf. Riley, 1962). This test–retest problem is one which has plagued longitudinal methodology in many areas of developmental psychology, and we shall need to examine it in some detail; yet, it is hardly the primary obstacle which has discouraged the wider use of the method.

The critical factor, of course, is the length of the human life-span, or more particularly the length of his period of development. Thus, animal researchers who have investigated developmental problems among inframammalian or lower mammalian forms have been much more inclined to obtain longitudinal data, and in some areas, such as the study of the effects of early experience, have been ready to undertake projects extending for several years to encompass as much as possible of the animal's total span of development.

At the human level, the sheer length of time that it takes for development to run its course has militated against the wider use of the longitudinal method, in two very different ways. The first of these has been widely discussed in the literature; there are the myriad practical problems of subject attrition, difficulty in maintaining interest on the part of the investigators, difficulty in obtaining facilities and financial support over extended lengths of time, etc. At the same time, a second factor has probably operated to reinforce the former, namely the very slow rate at which many of the changes—especially beyond middle childhood—are taking place, which may well havd contributed to the ready acceptance of the cross-sectional shortcut as a satisfactory approximation to direct information on behavioral change. Accordingly, it is hardly surprising that such longitudinal research as has been carried out with children has with few notable exceptions been confined to relatively limited sections of the period of development. It generally covers a period of 1 to 3 years, and tends to focus on the early portion of development—especially infancy—where major changes are visible over a matter of mere months.

In this respect, developmental psychology is in a peculiar position among the disciplines which are concerned with the study of *change*. In other fields in which the time span over which the change occurs has not permitted direct observation to be utilized, the historical approach has been resorted to as the favored method, and frequently the only one available to the investigator, as illustrated by the geological sciences, paleontology, archeology, and most obviously history itself. This approach corresponds to the retrospective approach in the study of behavioral development, which has been employed on occasion, and which we will discuss as a variant of the longitudinal method. The equivalent of the cross-sectional comparison approach, on the other hand, appears much less frequently in other disciplines, since it is applicable only where samples of objects, individuals, institutions, etc., representing differential "ages" or length of exposure to some condition or process, are available for comparison. Thus, a sociologist interested in long-term adaptation of migrants might compare recent arrivals to individuals who migrated *x* years previously. Similarly, the course of evolution of painting, or any of the other arts, can be studied by taking extant exemplars of each successive period and submitting them to a comparative analysis.[1] But over the run of phenomena included under the rubric

---

[1] The two examples just cited differ in a critical sense: In the case of the latter, we are presumably concerned with changes occurring over historical time in the original art works being compared, the works themselves remaining unchanged, whereas in the former case we would generally be interested in differences between earlier as opposed to more recent migrants as reflecting changes that have taken place during the interim. Yet there is an obvious source of confounding here, since different *generations* of migrants can be expected to differ, quite independently of their length of stay in their new environment, i.e., as a function of historical forces. This very ambiguity inherent in the cross-sectional approach has become a major issue for the developmental psychologist, as we will see presently.

of historical or developmental, this approach plays a relatively minor role, and if developmental psychology has relied on it so heavily, it is largely because of the fact that it appeared to fit readily into the paradigm of differential-comparative approaches, as discussed in Chapter II.

Cross-Sectional Designs: Shortcut or Short-Change?

In view of the obvious advantages of cross-sectional over longitudinal designs, it is important to achieve clarity at the outset as to the reasons one might have for rejecting the former, or preferring the latter to it. There are basically three quite different limitations of cross-sectional information. First, it is statistically inefficient, relative to the longitudinal—that is, data involving repeated measures of the same subjects provide a more powerful test of the significance of the time-related differences than those based on the comparison of independent samples drawn to represent the different points on the time dimension. The pertinence of this point actually is in inverse relation to the magnitude of the changes occurring with age. It does not require the reduced error variance afforded by longitudinal data to demonstrate at any desirable level of significance that children change with age in height, strength, vocabulary size, or mathematical ability. Yet, it is precisely for this kind of variable that we will find the shortcomings of cross-sectional data to be most acute. Conversely, the mere demonstration of statistically significant age changes would ordinarily not be considered adequate recompense for the investment entailed in resorting to the longitudinal method.

The second limitation of cross-sectional data is that they provide no direct information regarding change, at the level at which change does in fact operate: that of the individual. This limitation itself has two rather different aspects: First, the properties of developmental functions are based on *averaged* data, introducing distortion, to various degrees and of various kinds, into the resulting picture of the shape and characteristics of the developmental process; second, it precludes the possibility of answering questions concerning change in which the individual is taken as the unit of reference (i.e., correlations among measures obtained from the same individual at different times; analyses based on measures of change per se; relationships between events or conditions operating at one point in time and behavioral measures obtained at another, etc).

The third limitation concerns the difficulty of ensuring comparability of the populations from which the age groups are sampled, in respects other than age. This may appear to be a general problem of differential methodology, one susceptible to handling via the usual methods available to the investigator to control for the role of extraneous variables. There is, however, one particular source of confounding inherent in cross-sectional developmental designs, which has become increasingly of concern to workers in this field. This arises from the fact that individuals varying in age, when tested at a single point in calendar time, necessarily represent different generations of individuals, who at equivalent ages have been exposed to different environmental conditions associated with different periods of historical (i.e., calendar) time.

This issue, which surprisingly has only recently received attention and systematic treatment, turns out to cut across the cross-sectional versus longitudinal distinction. Whereas the first two limitations are advantageously considered as part of our examination of the characteristics of longitudinal data, the quantitative models available for their analysis, and the type of information for which longitudinal designs are either absolutely required or highly preferred. For this reason, it is convenient to start out with a generalized treatment of developmental designs, to bring out the problems involved in isolating the role of chronological age from other time- as opposed to age-related variables, as well as to show the insufficiency of the cross-sectional versus longitudinal dichotomy itself.

Two- versus Three-Factor Models in the Design of Developmental Research

Schaie's three-factor model. The first, and thus most systematic attempt to consider the alternative designs available to the investigator concerned with assessing the respective contributions of historical time and chronological age to developmental data is to be found in Schaie's (1965) paper in the *Psychological Bulletin.* In it Schaie proposed a set of three factors with which effects in developmental studies could be identified, that is, *cohort* effects, *time-of-measurement* effects, and *age* effects. The distinction between them and the diverse designs to which they give rise are most easily considered by means of Table 7–1, adapted from Wohlwill (1970b).

This table brings out the differences among the three major types of designs which Schaie has differentiated: the *cohort*-sequential, the *time*-sequential, and the *cross*-sequential. The first, represented by the cells forming the horizontally oriented parallelogram, corresponds to the longitudinal method as typically employed, repeated for several successive cohorts (i.e., samples of a population born in successive years). The second, represented by the cells forming the vertically oriented parallelogram, corresponds to the classical cross-sectional method, repeated in several successive years of testing. Finally, the third, represented by the cells contained within the central square, corresponds to Schaie's "time-lag" method, intended to identify differences related to historical time, or time-dependent environmental effects.

TABLE 7–1

Schema for Research Designs Corresponding to Schaie's (1965) Trifactorial Model of Developmental Studies[a]

Cohort (year of birth)	Time of measurement														
	1956	1957	1958	1959	1960	1961	1962	1963	1964	1965	1966	1967	1968	1969	1970
1946						15									
1947						14	15								
1948						13	14	15							
1949						12	13	14	15						
1950	6	7	8	9	10	11	12	13	14	15					
1951		6	7	8	9	10	11	12	13	14	15				
1952			6	7	8	9	10	11	12	13	14	15			
1953				6	7	8	9	10	11	12	13	14	15		
1954					6	7	8	9	10	11	12	13	14	15	
1955						6	7	8	9	10	11	12	13	14	15
1956							6	7	8	9					
1957								6	7	8					
1958									6	7					
1959										6					

[a] Entries represent ages corresponding to each combination of cohort and time of measurement.

Note.—In this table, *cohort-sequential* design is represented by the cells included within the vertical parallelogram; *time-sequential* design is represented by the cells included within the horizontal parallelogram; *cross-sequential* design is represented by the cells included within the square. [Reproduced from Wohlwill (1970b).]

TABLE 7-2

Information Obtainable from Schaie's Three Models

Model	Independent variables	Confounded effects[a]
Cohort-sequential	Age; cohorts	Age × Cohort interaction confounded with time[b]
Time-sequential	Age; time	Age × Time interaction confounded with Cohort
Cross-sequential	Cohort; time	Cohort × Time interaction cofounded with age

[a]For each model, the last-named term is assumed to represent a constant factor.

[b]"Time" refers to calendar time at which measurements are obtained.

The differences among the methods, and in the information yielded by each, are readily brought out by reference to Table 7–2, which lists the independent sources of variance for which each provides an estimate, along with the sources of confounding to which each is prey.

We thus see that each method yields independent estimates of two of the three factors distinguished by Schaie, while the third is confounded with their interaction. Note that, whereas the validity of the assumptions cannot in principle be determined from the data, but must rather be decided on a priori grounds, it is possible at least to check on their plausibility, by searching the data for the presence of *systematic* variations that could be attributable to the confounded factor. Thus, in the case of the cross-sequential method, comparing the values for the entries in each diagonal would provide a picture of differences that might be attributable to age (though it is apparent that a different number of such values would contribute to the estimate for each age level). If these are small, or unsystematic, it would seem reasonable to suppose the assumption to be tenable.

Let us examine more closely each of these methods, the situations in which each might be applicable, and the purposes for which it might practicably be applied. The *time-sequential method*, as already noted, corresponds to the classical cross-sectional method, repeated over successive times of measurement. It is ideally suited to provide a picture of age differences over any arbitrary age span within a limited period of time, while providing some correspondingly limited information on time-of-measurement effects. This approach is valid so long as the role of historical time is plausibly conceptualized in terms of effects operating at particular moments of historical time, but in a noncumulative fashion, that is, independently of true generational differences associated with year of birth. A good example is provided by data on physical growth obtained over the years of the depression, where a systematic trough appears for height and weight. These were, however, temporally localized effects, which failed to exert any long-term changes that might have been conceptualizable as true cohort differences (cf. Kodlin & Thompson, 1958). The same would be true with respect to measures of attitude (e.g., toward abortion, or toward war) that might undergo profound shifts from one point of historical time to another, but again acting in a temporally localized fashion.

Turning to the *cohort-sequential method*, it is indicated where age differences on which generational effects are suspected to be superimposed are of interest. It has the notable drawback, in comparison to the time-sequential method, of requiring a considerably longer period of time to provide information with respect to the alternate variable (in this case either age or cohort differences), as is obvious from a comparison of the vertical and horizontal parallelograms in Table 7–1. But in situations where true generational differences are of concern, whether of a genetic nature, or, more likely, attributable to the cumulative effect of environmental forces operating over the period under investigation, it is the indicated approach. Furthermore, while the longitudinal method is most closely identified with this design, it is by no means required by it. Indeed, the longitudinal versus cross-sectional question is orthogonal to the differences among the methods being considered. Thus, it is perfectly possible to draw independent samples to represent the successive age levels from each cohort, and under certain conditions (e.g., where large retest effects are expected, or where attrition due to loss of subjects from a longitudinal sample is large) there may be valid reasons for doing so. Conversely a repeated-measurements feature can readily be built into the time-sequential design, although, as Table 7–1 shows clearly, the number of successive tests administered would vary from one row (that is, cohort) to another.

As for the *cross-sequential* design, it is intended to provide information on time-lag phenomena, that is, shifts in behavior related to historical time, independent of age. It is thus particularly indicated for mature adults presumed not to be undergoing systematic age-related changes with respect to the behavior of interest. At the same time, it can provide information with respect to cohort differences that might be related to forces operating in the prior history of the individual which could have a bearing on that behavior. One example would be provided by the area of attitudes, e.g., on family limitation: There would undoubtedly be major shifts shown for any cohort over the interval 1965–1975; at the same time, one should expect differences in the opinions expressed by those who raised their own families during the depression, as opposed to those who raised theirs during the post-war period. (In this instance, age could be assumed to be a contaminating factor: The first group, being older by some 10 to 20 years than the second, would, on the one hand, be possibly more conservative, while on the other hand further removed from their own child-raising period; both of these factors could affect attitudes on the subject of family limitation expressed during the interval under study, but they would be inevitably confounded with cohort differences.)

1. TWO FACTORS OR THREE? THE BALTES–SCHAIE DEBATE.

The preceding example points up not only the question of the identity of the three factors postulated by Schaie, but of the merits of a three-factor model as such, as opposed to a two-factor framework, as proposed by Baltes (1968). Given that only two of the three factors are in fact independent, Baltes argues that a bifactor model is more parsimonious, and equally satisfactory. In his view, the only two factors worth differentiating are cohort and age; time-of-measurement is not regarded as meriting the status of an independent variable. Baltes, accordingly, espouses the cohort-sequential method as the one of most general usefulness in developmental research. (Since time-of-measurement effects are not considered as representing a valid independent variable, neither the time-sequential nor the cross-sequential models are applicable.[2])

Baltes further takes exception to Schaie's attempt to interpret the various factors in terms of the respective roles of maturational, genetic, general environmental and specific (i.e., time-dependent) environmental effects. Thus, Schaie suggests that true age differences be identified with maturational factors, cohort effects with genetic and general environmental factors, and time-of-measurement effects with specific environmental factors. Baltes regards such interpretations as unwarranted, both on intrinsic grounds (i.e., the impossibility of dissociating general environmental and maturational factors) and on the basis of the lack of independent status of these variables which has just been pointed out.

Schaie (1970), in reply, noted quite cogently that the lack of independence of the three factors is not in itself necessarily a valid basis for rejecting the trifactor model, so long as there are plausible bases for distinguishing among them conceptually. In his view, a place exists for each of the three designs among which he differentiated, each with its own realm of application. He

[2]It is worth noting that in his actual research Baltes has not in fact made use of this design, but instead has preferred what amounts to the time-sequential method in Schaie's terminology, but designated by the term "cross-sectional sequences" by Baltes, since it involves a set of cross-sectional comparisons repeated at successive times-of-measurement (cf. Baltes, 1968, and for applications of the design. Baltes & Reinert, 1969; Baltes, Baltes, & Reinert, 1970). While Baltes does not admit of the reality of the distinction between cohort and time-of-measurement effects, it is apparent from Table 7–1 as well as from Baltes' own representation of the design (Baltes, 1968, p. 158) that it does not afford a meaningful base for comparing cohorts.

might, in this context, have referred to the case of such interdependent sets of variables as temperature, pressure, and volume, or time, distance, and velocity, or, more appropriately yet, to the variables involved in the design of research on the effects of early experience—age at onset of experience, duration of experience, interval between termination of experience and start of testing, and age at test. The point is that the interdependence among a set of variables does not invalidate their separate identities as conceptually distinguishable variables.

Let us look for a moment at the case just cited, on the design of early-experience research, which will be taken up more fully in Chapter XI. It is apparent that only three of the four variables cited are independent variables, since $A_o + D + i = A_t$. (The symbols correspond to the four variables mentioned just previously.) Furthermore, there are dependencies even among any set of three of these variables; for instance, with respect to the set A_o, D, and A_t, $D \leq A_t - A_o$. Yet, conceptually these variables are distinguishable; an investigator starting from a critical-period hypothesis might focus on A_o and D as his independent variables, while one interested in the question of the reversibility of early experience effects might be more inclined to manipulate A_o and i.

Similarly, in the case of Schaie's three factors, granting that only two of the three are free to vary, the investigator may still choose the particular combination of the two most pertinent to his situation and formulation of the problem. For instance, in regard to the influence of TV-viewing on language development, a formulation in terms of cohort differences, via a cohort-sequential design, would seem to be appropriate: Children who grew up without benefit of TV would be expected to have a rather slower rate of verbal development, and possibly reach a lower asymptote, than those born since its advent. Note that difference in *rate* would be revealed in terms of an interaction between cohort and age, which, as noted earlier, was indistinguishable from a time-of-measurement effect. Yet logic, as well as parsimony, would dictate a formulation in terms of cohorts growing at different rates, rather than a particular time-of-measurement effect increasing verbal scores by some given quantity.

In contrast, take the case of the incidence of aggressive themes in children's stories or drawings obtained at different points in calendar time. This is presumably a situationally determined variable, though it too may be expected to reveal changes with age. Accordingly a formulation in terms of time-of-measurement effects, via a time-sequential design, becomes appropriate.

The question, in other words, is whether interactions between age and cohort represent true differences in developmental rate, or some other aspect of the developmental function (e.g., asymptotal level), or whether they are more parsimoniously attributable to time-of-measurement effects

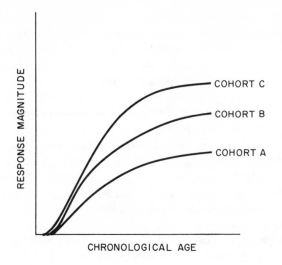

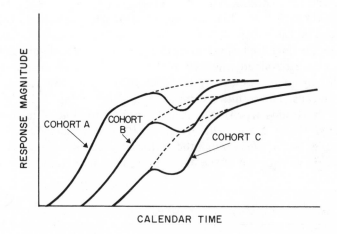

Fig. 7–1. (a) Prototype curves to illustrate cohort differences in developmental functions. (b) Prototype curves to illustrate time-of-measurement effects on developmental functions. [From Wohlwill (1970b).]

operating at specific points of calendar time to raise or lower performance in a patttern unrelated to the shape of the developmental function. The contrast is illustrated in Fig. 7–1, representing pure cases conforming to each model.

Admittedly, in any concrete case, it may frequently be difficult to decide between these alternative interpretations. While, in principle, statistical tests could be made by which to compare the relative magnitudes of systematic effects attributable to year of testing, as opposed to year of birth, the lack of comparability of the dependent measures required in each instance (i.e., mean raw scores in one case, versus indices of rate, or asymptotal level in the other) would make such a comparison hazardous. Possibly comparative trend analyses carried out by stratifying groups in terms of (a) time of measurement and (b) cohort would afford the best indication of which model offered a better fit. The problem, however, is in trying to apply this approach to data already collected. In most instances, the available data do not provide extensive series of measurements to trace development comparatively across cohorts. Most typically, the time-sequential design has been followed, explicitly or implicitly, that is, a cross-sectional study is repeated in several successive years. Under these circumstances only a more impressionistic kind of comparative analysis is possible; yet, even with such data organizing them in the two ways under consideration may reveal interesting differences that will allow one to choose between the alternative models.

Consider, for instance, the data on growth in weight of children between ages 6–7 and 12–13 obtained by Wolff (1940) during the years of the depression, 1933 through 1936, along with base line data for the period 1914–1920, reproduced in Table 7–3.

Despite the fact that these are cross-sectional data, highly suggestive differences are obtained when we plot them by year of measurement as opposed to by cohort, especially if we deal with increment values rather than absolute means. The results are shown graphically in Fig. 7–2. The irregularity of the trends when organized according to time-of-measurement effects (Fig. 7–2a) is apparent. By contrast, when arranged according to cohorts (Fig. 7–2b), even though the various intercohort comparisons cover only a restricted portion of the age continuum, the picture is much more

TABLE 7–3

Mean Weight of School Children in Hagerstown, Maryland[a]

| | Age (years) | | | | | | | |
Year	6–7	7–8	8–9	9–10	10–11	11–12	12–13	13–14
1921–27	47.6	51.6	56.9	62.6	68.4	75.2	82.7	92.6
1933	47.4	50.9	56.7	62.3	68.5	75.6	79.4	88.4
1934	47.2	50.6	55.4	61.9	68.6	74.8	81.0	86.7
1935	46.3	51.4	55.8	61.0	68.0	75.2	83.1	94.8
1936	46.8	50.6	56.4	61.3	66.8	74.6	84.0	94.2

[a] Reprinted from *Child Development*, 1940, **11**, by Wolff by permission of The Society for Research in Child Development, Inc.

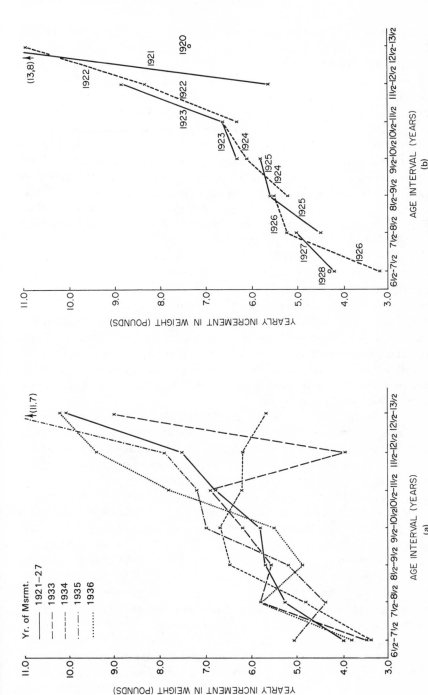

Fig. 7-2. Yearly increments in weight for children in Hagerstown study (data based on Wolff, 1940; cf. Table VII-3). (*a*) Data plotted with year of measurement as a parameter. (*b*) Date plotted with cohort (year of birth) as a parameter.

133

consistent. Note for instance, that in almost every case, that is, for each pair of cohorts for which values for adjacent age intervals are plotted, the curve for the earlier cohort crosses that for the later one. In other words, the earlier cohort generally shows a lower increment, initially, for any given age interval, relative to the later cohort; but in compensation a higher rate of increase during the succeeding interval suggests that the lowered nutritional status marking the earlier years of the Depression may in fact have been compensated for during the child's subsequent years. This interpretation is clearly at variance with Kodlin and Thompson's (1958) statement that Wolff ". . . observed a trough in the weight surface which was parallel to the age axis and coincided with the years of economic depression [pp. 28f]." As Table 7–3 shows, there is no consistent difference in the weight values arranged according to year of measurement; at best, the evidence for a "trough" is limited to the younger years.

To conclude this comparison between the time- and cohort-sequential methods, it should be apparent that the decision as to which of these two models in the study of age differences is the preferred one, far from amounting to a purely arbitrary choice of variables treated as independent, is in fact critical for both practical and theoretical purposes. From a practical standpoint, the cohort-sequential model requires a far greater investment of time than the time-sequential one, while, at a theoretical level, there is the considerable difference between effects acting to alter the shape of the developmental function and those involving rather a temporary perturbation superimposed on that function.

We should consider, finally, the place of the third of the designs proposed by Schaie, the cross-sequential. This one is, in principle, of limited value for the developmentalist, since it starts from the assumption that there are no true age changes, and that any observed effects may be explained in terms of either cohort differences or time-of-measurement effects, or their interaction. In fact, as Table 7–1 shows, comparisons among any set of rows, to obtain cohort differences, or any set of columns, to obtain time-of-measurement differences, are themselves dependent on the validity of the no-age-change assumption (for instance, the set of values for the 1950 cohort included within the square differs from that for the 1951 cohort in starting at age 11 rather than 10, and terminating at age 15, rather than 14). Admittedly, equivalent shortcomings attach to the previous two designs: The time-sequential presupposes an absence of cohort differences, since the different cohorts are not balanced across times-of-measurement (or age); and the cohort-sequential design presupposes an absence of time-of-measurement effects, since the different times of measurement are not balanced across cohorts (or age). But the net result is that the cross-sequential design is unlikely to recommend itself to the developmentalist, except for studies of

behavior change during maturity, considered to occur independent of processes of maturation or aging.[3]

Before proceeding with an examination of the way in which these various
designs have been applied by Schaie *et al.*, let us ask, first, what evidence
there is for the reality of changes attributable to generational and/or time-
of-measurement factors. It is, in fact, considerable, both for the course of
ontogenetic change and for aging, and points both to the operation of true
intercohort differences and of factors associated with particular times of
measurement. These are particularly well documented in the case of physical
growth, where both long-term secular changes (e.g., Tanner, 1961) and short-
term effects, such as those resulting from temporary dietary insufficiency or
the like, during the depression (cf. Kodlin & Thompson, 1958) or following
wartime conditions (Wolff, cited by Sanders, 1934, p. 187), have been
reported. Furthermore, whereas the effects just referred to apply to data on
ontogenetic development in height and weight, even more substantial effects
associated apparently with generational changes are to be found in studies
of aging, for such variables as strength and vital capacity, at least to judge
from the consistent discrepancies found between data from cross-sectional
and longitudinal studies (cf. Damon, 1965). These data do not permit a
systematic evaluation of the magnitude of such effects, since they are for
the most part confined to but a single time of measurement (in the case of
the cross-sectional studies) or a single cohort (in the longitudinal ones).
Nevertheless, the consistent attenuation or even elimination of the apparent
aging decrements to which the cross-sectional data had pointed when longitudinal series were examined, points to the inescapable conclusion that
major secular influences are operating.

In the case of behavioral data, the information at least with respect to
secular changes operating during the course of ontogenetic development is
much less clear-cut. There is the further problem of teasing out such effects
(when based on longitudinal data) from test–retest effects, in the typical
absence of control data obtained by drawing independent samples at successive age levels taken from the same cohort.[4] Baltes and Reinert (1969) report
data on intelligence-test performance where substantial intercohort differences were found within a 12-month period, but these were apparently
attributable to artifactual selection of subjects when age-groups were defined
in terms of grade in school (i.e., for children born within any given calendar

---

[3]Baltes and Nesselroade (1972) have applied the same design—and the same argument in
regard to the absence of true age-differences—to data on adolescent personality over the age
period from $12\frac{1}{2}$ to $17\frac{1}{2}$ years.

[4]Baltes (1968) has suggested the term "age sequence" in this connection, to designate designs involving measures at successive ages drawn from the same cohort, whether longitudinally or cross-sectionally.

year, those born in the last months of the year will, at an equivalent chronological age, be one grade ahead of those born in earlier portions of the year).
A subsequent factor-analytic study of adolescent personality by Baltes and
Nesselroade (1972), however, provides more suggestive evidence of true
secular changes, operating again over a period as brief as one year, which
appear to underly the discrepancies found between longitudinal and cross-
sectional results, which vary widely in extent from one factor to another.
There is, furthermore, some evidence of secular changes taking place over
considerably longer periods of historical time from replications of early
normative studies, such as Palermo and Jenkins's (1964) replication of
Woodrow and Lowell's (1916) study of word-associations, which point to
important secular shifts in this aspect of language behavior.

Most of the attention with respect to the issue of secular changes has,
however, focused on changes thought to occur as a function of aging, that is,
beyond maturity. The import, both practical and theoretical, of this question
is apparent: To the extent that the apparent changes with age which cross-
sectional data reveal can be shown to be a function of intercohort differences, our conception of and attitude toward the supposed decline in
intellectual functioning (along with other aspects of behavior) in later maturity and old age obviously requires radical revision.

Evidence pointing precisely in this direction has been accumulating for
some time, in the form of discrepancies between cross-sectional and longitudinal data. More incisive evidence, however, has come from research in
which the time-sequential approach has been followed, by taking a set of age
groups examined cross-sectionally at time t_1 and retesting them some years
later, at time t_2, to obtain an indication of longitudinal changes to which the
equivalent cross-sectional differences could be compared. The latter
approach, not surprisingly, is attributable chiefly to Schaie and Strother
(1968a,b; cf. also Schaie, 1970), who have obtained an impressive set of data
on changes in a variety of tests of intellectual, perceptual, psychomotor
ability, as well as a measure of educational aptitude and one of social responsibility, from 21 to 70 years, with each age-group being retested after a 7-
year interval. These data provide conclusive evidence on the reality of the
secular changes operating for some of these measures, and thus demonstrate
the distorted picture that is obtained from the cross-sectional evidence on
changes over maturity and old age. More important still, they allow one to
differentiate those measures for which true aging effects appear to be slight,
from those for which more substantial real changes occur. Interestingly
enough, the former turn out to be those, from among the Primary Mental
Abilities, which have been termed measures of "crystallized" intelligence
(e.g., spatial reasoning and verbal meaning), as opposed to measures of
"fluid" intelligence (e.g., psychomotor speed and word fluency), which have
been thought to have a biological component.

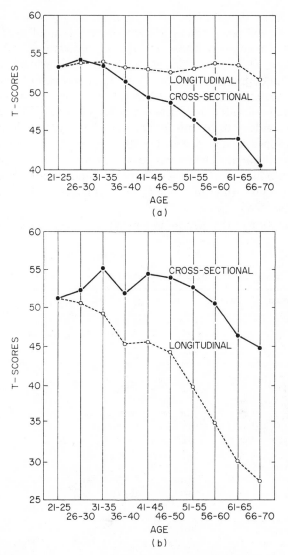

Fig. 7–3. Cross-sectional and (estimated) longitudinal age gradients for (a) spatial reasoning and (b) word fluency. [From Schaie & Strother (1968a).]

Let us examine two of Schaie and Strother's measures in more detail, to give us a better picture of the nature of their evidence on this question, and to serve as a basis for discussion of their approach to estimating "true" longitudinal trends. Figure 7–3 shows the data for measures of Spatial Reasoning and Verbal Fluency, selected to represent crystallized and fluid intelligence, respectively.

It will be noted, first, that the values for the space variable are consistently higher for the 1963 sample than for the 1956 sample, at all age levels except 26–30 years. In contrast, those for the word-fluency variable show the reverse pattern. This consistency, coupled with the consideration that these cross-sectional data represent a series of successive cohorts, might suggest that we are dealing here with true time-of-measurement effects, causing a systematic upward shift of performance on the space variable at the later test occasion, and a downward shift for the word-fluency variable, rather than a generational change. Yet Schaie (1970) proceeds to provide estimates of "true" cohort differences which would point to a steady rise in Spatial ability at age 23 (the only age level for which these estimates are carried out), while for word fluency a curious sinusoidal pattern emerges, as shown in the values given in Table 7–4.

An examination of the manner in which these estimates are obtained will

TABLE 7–4

Derivation of Estimates of Mean Word Fluency Scores at Age 23 for Different Cohorts

	Word fluency means[a]				Cohort[b]	
Age Group	1956	1963	Mean change	Mean yr of birth	5-yr change by cohort[c]	Estimated mean per cohort[c] at age 23
71–75	—	43.3	—	1890	−1.2	44.9
66–70	44.6	42.0	−2.6	1895	2.0	46.1
61–65	46.2	44.7	−1.5	1900	.4	48.1
56–60	50.5	46.7	−3.8	1905	− .2	48.5
51–55	52.6	48.0	−4.6	1910	−3.1	48.3
46–50	53.8	45.2	−8.6	1915	.1	45.2
41–45	54.3	50.2	−4.1	1920	.9	45.4
36–40	51.9	48.8	−3.1	1925	.7	46.3
31–35	55.2	51.9	−3.3	1930	.9	47.0
26–30	52.4	49.4	−3.0	1935	2.3	47.9
21–25	51.3	50.2	−1.1	1940	—	(50.2)

[a]From Schaie and Strother (1968a). Copyright by the American Psychological Association and reproduced by permission.

[b]Cohorts correspond to Age Groups for 1963 Data.

[c]Values obtained as follows: 1963 means converted to adjusted means for cohorts tested in 1956 (e.g., $[42.0 \times 3 + 43.3 \times 2]/5 = 42.52$ for Cohort born in 1893); Td_x (Mean change over 7-year interval for same cohort) obtained by averaging the resulting differences (e.g., $46.2 − 42.52$); $Td_x = −4.31$ subtracted from 1963–1956 difference (column 4) for each age group, and multiplied by 5/7, to yield an estimated generational shift attributable to inter-cohort differences; each of these are finally subtracted from the values for the preceding cohort (starting with the youngest), to yield the estimates in the last column. See text and Schaie (1970).

TABLE 7–5

Suggested Design Combining Cross-Sectional and Longitudinal Series

	Year of study				
	1st	2nd	3d	4th	5th
Cross-sectional	6 8 10 12 14	Cross-sectional	6 8 10 12 14	Cross-sectional	6 8 10 12 14
Longitudinal	6^a	7	8	9	10
Longitudinal	8^a	9	10	11	12
Longitudinal	10^a	11	12	13	14

Note.—Entries represent illustrative age groups for a 5-year study.

[a] For first-year measures, cross-sectional and longitudinal samples could coincide.

be instructive in showing the way in which Schaie's equations work in actual application. The values of Fig. 7–3 are rearranged to indicate the changes over the interval from 1956 to 1963 by cohort, instead of age group.[5] The mean shift for the 10 cohorts from 1956 to 1963 is then calculated (e.g., for word fluency it is $46.97 - 51.28 = -4.31$). By subtracting this value from the actual change from 1956 to 1963 for each age group, an estimate of the difference between successive cohorts is obtained, via the expression $Cd_i = Tld_{k \cdot m} - Td_{k \cdot xs}$, where Cd_i are estimated net differences between cohorts i and j; $Tld_{k \cdot m}$ is the difference between cohorts i and j at age m, and $Td_{k \cdot xs}$ is the net change from time k to time l averaged over all cohorts. Finally, the successive values of Cd_i are added to the value for the first cohort (i.e., the oldest), to obtain the estimates shown in the last column of Table 7–5, which details the whole procedure.

Schaie's procedure rests on several assumptions that should be noted. First, it is based on a strict additive model, where each estimate is obtained by analyzing observed data into a set of linearly related, orthogonal components. Second, the absolute values obtained via these equations have no meaning, since they are calculated by taking one of the extreme groups as a

[5] The actual procedure in the case of Schaie and Strother's data is complicated by the fact that a 5-year interval was used in defining the age groups, while the interval between test and retest was 7 years. This required converting all of the data concerning longitudinal changes over the latter period to a 5-year interval (cf. Schaie & Strother, 1968a, footnote 5. p. 272).

fixed base line and determining all estimates as differences from that base line. (For example, in Fig. 7–3 the starting points of the cross-sectional and longitudinal curves are forced to coincide, thus resulting in the particular divergent pattern of the curves shown; if some intermediate group was selected as a base line, the curves would have crossed instead.) Thus it is only the *relative* values of the estimates for successive groups that have a determinate meaning. Finally, and directly related to the first point, the model is a curiously static one, in the sense that there is no room for interactions among any of the component variables, as already noted. Nevertheless, particularly in the study of aging, it is undeniable that Schaie and Strother's analysis points to the importance of differentiating between changes related to chronological age and those related to either generational differences or effects associated with calendar time, and thus reinforces the dangers of inferences drawn from cross-sectional data alone.

Purposes of Longitudinal Data

Perhaps in the belief that the advocacy of longitudinal methodology in studying development needs no defense, its proponents have rarely been very explicit in specifying precisely what sort of information it was expected to yield, or in what situations it was either required or strongly preferred over the cross-sectional alternative. Given not only the considerable investment of time, commitment, budgetary support, etc., which it demands, but the objections which have been leveled against it because of the confounding of generational and time-of-testing effects and because of the pervasive problem of test–retest effects, it is particularly essential that we achieve clarity on this point.

We may distinguish among four kinds of information for which longitudinal data are either absolutely required, or substitutable only at a considerable sacrifice. They are, respectively: (1) to preserve information as to the shape of the developmental function; (2) to provide information on change and patterning of change; (3) to relate earlier behavior to later, and (4) to relate earlier conditions of life to subsequent behavior. Each of these, as we shall note, relates to a different aspect of developmental research, corresponding to particular chapters in this volume.

1. THE PRESERVATION OF INFORMATION AS TO SHAPE OF THE DEVELOPMENTAL FUNCTION

That averaging results in a loss of information is hardly more than a truism; the question to be asked is whether the information lost represents true information, or merely noise. This question takes on added significance when we are dealing, not with individual data points, but with sets of data determining a particular function. Take for instance, the function relating strength to age. If that function does conform to any determinate shape, it would obviously be revealed more clearly by taking the average values of *sets* of measures *taken from a single individual* at successive ages, rather than confining oneself to a single observation. That is, the averaging process would act to eliminate noise, i.e., random fluctuation around the true mean for a given age, from the data.

The situation becomes quite different when we average over individuals to obtain group means, as is done in any cross-sectional study. The information thus discarded pertains to relevant aspects of the question we are trying to answer, that is, the shape of the developmental function. Because of differences in individual rates of growth, etc., this question cannot be answered at the level of the group without abstracting from among the shared features of individual curves. If, on the other hand, a composite function is obtained by linking a set of means directly, the *possibility* for distortion in the characteristics of the function thus derived, relative to those that would be obtained from a set of individuals, becomes apparent.

The seriousness of this problem depends largely on the general nature of the developmental function. In the case of growth curves and exponential functions generally, averaging can lead to considerable distortion in the form of the resultant composite function. This point has been demonstrated convincingly by Merrill (1931) and Deming (1957) for the case of growth curves (cf. Chapter VIII, and Fig. 8–3 in particular); it has also been shown analytically by Sidman (1952) and Estes (1956), with particular reference to the study of learning curves. The latter has at the same time demonstrated that for nonexponential types of functions, notably the polynomial ($y = a + bx + cx^2 + dx^3 + \cdots$), the form of the individual curves is preserved in the averaged function. (See Chapter VIII for more detailed discussion of the matter.)

This is encouraging for behavioral scientists, since behavioral data are apt to be handled just as effectively by recourse to some type of polynomial function. Longitudinal data may nevertheless be distinctly preferable for certain purposes or in certain situations, particularly for developmental variables for which individual differences in rate, etc., are so pronounced as to render a group composite function, even though of the same *general* form as the individual components, of little value for analytic purposes. This point is pithily illustrated by reference to the classical curves obtained by Shuttleworth (1937) in the study of growth at adolescence, as shown in Fig. 7–4.

While we are dealing here again with a physical-growth variable, the point may be expected to apply equally to behavioral variables, such as vocabulary

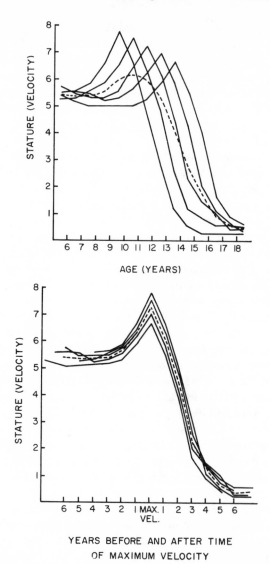

Fig. 7–4. Average annual increment in standing height of children in general, contrasted with generalized patterns based on nine groups of boys and 10 groups of girls, grouped by age of maximum growth. (——): Individual curves; (---): mean curve. [From Shuttleworth (1937), as redrawn by Tanner (1962).]

growth, motor development, etc. Here one would want to group individual functions into families in terms of some parameter of the developmental function such as rate or asymptotal level, in order to arrive at meaningful relationships to other situational or behavioral variables. As an example, while cross-sectional data may be sufficient to bring out the overall superiority of singletons over twins in language development, it would take longitudinal data, allowing the determination of growth rates for the individual child, to verify Gesell's (1939) postulate of "reciprocal neuromotor interweaving" with respect to the developmental relationship among the two aspects of behavior, for example, locomotion and sensorimotor coordination.

2. The Retrieval of Information on Amount or Patterning of Change

It has been generally assumed that where change, or properties of change, are themselves the object of interest, the longitudinal method is *de rigueur*. This assumption is probably traceable to the association of the study of change with the field of psychometrics, where the aim has been to study differential change among individuals, typically measured from a pretest given before the start of some educational program or experience to a posttest given following its termination. On the other hand, so long as gross amount of change for some *group* of individuals is the object of study, such change can be studied inferentially by the cross-sectional method, subject of course to the confounding with secular time discussed in the previous section. A good case in point from outside of developmental psychology is the study of people's adaptation to a new environment, via a comparison of individuals who have resided for different lengths of time in that environment. (Here again the problem of possible confounding with historic time is an obvious one.)

The problem for the developmentalist, however, is that many of the most interesting and important questions concerning developmental processes can only be answered on a per-individual basis, and therefore *do* require longitudinal data. Some of these questions relate to categories 3 and 4 to be discussed below; here we are concerned more particularly with aspects of the *patterning* of change, that is, the interrelationship among changes occurring in different behavioral domains, the study of which appears to be at the heart of the specification of the nature of developmental processes, as will be seen in much greater detail in Chapters IX and X. Basically the assumption is that the *timing* of change in one aspect of behavior may be functionally related to, or even set off outright, by changes occurring in another aspect. But as already noted, where there are large variations among individuals' developmental timetables, qualitatively and especially quantitatively, this results in the loss of essential information when the study of interpatterning is approached in a cross-sectional vein. (See the study by Wohlwill, Fusaro, & Devoe 1969, cited in Chapter X among other notable illustrations of this point.)

3. The Investigation of Relationships Between Early and Later Behavior

Here we are dealing with a problem which is by definition correlational, and thus predicated on information concerning individuals measured at different points in time. It corresponds in fact to the problem of the *stability* of behavior, i.e., that of the predictability of an individual's relative standing on behavior Y at time t_2 from his relative standing on behavior X at t_1, to which Chapter XII is devoted.

Note that by substituting situations for individuals as the unit of reference over which the correlation is determined, it becomes possible in principle to study this problem on a cross-sectional basis. Thus, one might intercorrelate the mean scores achieved on some standardized test administered city-wide by the first and sixth grades of all of the elementary schools of a district. This would in effect tell us something about the stability of the school and of its educational climate or quality across the 5-year period presumably represented in this study. But this surely is a different type of question, telling us about the development (or lack of it) of institutions, rather than individuals.

4. The Investigation of Relationships Between Antecedent Events and Later Behavior

A large number of questions posed by, or put to developmental psychologists concern functional relations between particular conditions or events occurring during the child's early experience (broadly defined) and subsequent behavior. Here the question becomes not so much that of a choice between longitudinal and cross-sectional methodology, as one between prospective and retrospective methods. This issue will be taken up further later; suffice it to note that the nature of the question posed requires information obtained from the same individual concerning at least two different points in time, namely the time at which the condition under investigation is (or was) in effect, and the time at which the child's behavior is assessed. But there are some situations in which the information concerning the conditions variable can be obtained at the same time as the behavioral measures are obtained. This matter will be discussed more fully later in this chapter, when we consider the merits of retrospective approaches as a shortcut to traditional longitudinal methodology.

Major Drawbacks of the Longitudinal Method

The many, diverse problems facing the longitudinal investigator, and the obstacles in his path have for the most part, received ample attention in the literature. (Anderson, 1954; Goldfarb, 1960; Jones, 1958; Kessen, 1960;

Kodlin & Thompson, 1958.) We will content ourselves, therefore, with a more selective examination of certain of these problems. They appear to be of four distinct types, though the first two are probably the ones that loom most seriously for the prospective longitudinal researcher.

1. PRACTICAL DIFFICULTIES

The fact that longitudinal research at the human level generally means long-term research creates a variety of problems which have yet to be satisfactorily resolved by developmentalists. For neither psychologically nor socioculturally is the research enterprise fitted to support and encourage research extending far into the future. The problems to be faced range from the primary one of financial support, to the impermanence of staff and facilities to the slow rate of return from investment of time, effort, and money.

This situation appears to be reflected in a major and significant shift in the planning and organization of longitudinal research. Back in the 1920s, a number of long-term longitudinal projects were initiated (cf. Kagan, 1964, for a review of the major ones) such as those at Fels, Harvard, Minnesota, and Berkeley. To a considerable extent, the behavioral data from these projects are limited by the lack of either developmental dimensions or developmental theory to guide their collection, resulting in the amassing of tons of personality-inventory type data, along with information from interviews with parents and the children themselves, generally obtained without any clear purpose in mind, nor without regard to the longitudinal character of the project. Along with such data, IQ test scores were uniformly obtained, which in turn has led to a proliferation of research on personality correlates of IQ, etc., largely because that was the only meaningful developmental measure available (though as discussed earlier, it is MA rather than IQ that represents the actual, though much less frequently utilized, developmental variable).

In apparent recognition of the difficulties of planning meaningful longitudinal research on a life-span basis, or even just to cover the period through late adolescence, the more recent emphasis has been rather on short-term projects in which children are followed up over a period of one, two, or three years, and a much more delimited and focused set of behaviors is studied. Examples of this trend include such studies as that by Almy, Chittenden, and Miller (1966) on Piagetian problems; the work of Emmerich (1964) and Martin (1964) on behavioral development over the course of nursery school; and the recent work of Kagan (1971) on the development of attentional processes in infancy.

The result has been a sharp increase in the incisiveness of information obtained with regard to the operation of developmental processes. Indeed it could be argued that, particularly in the case of behavioral development, few if any aspects of behavior are meaningfully investigated over a period exceeding 4 or 5 years. Conversely, by limiting himself to a shorter time period, the researcher finds a much more problem-focused type of longitudinal research emerging, which also promises to yield a much higher return on the investment, in terms of the gratification of the investigator as well as the advancement of his discipline. Yet the argument just suggested cannot be accepted as entirely valid; indeed, the advances which shortterm longitudinal research are making at present will undoubtedly themselves bring to the fore new problems demanding more long-term investigation, as insights into the operation of developmental processes multiply. But as we will see in the next section, compromises that may enable the developmental researcher to eat his cake in short-term fashion and still have it in the long-term sense, by an appropriate combination of longitudinal and cross-sectional methodologies are possible.

2. TEST–RETEST EFFECTS

One of the vexing problems facing longitudinal investigators is that of dealing with possible effects which may result from subjecting individuals to repeated tests or measures of some behavioral variable. The "uncertainty principle" which to some extent plagues all behavioral assessment—that is, the influence on the object of measurement of the act of measuring itself, or the experience of being examined, observed or tested—can become particularly severe where a relatively large number of observations is to be obtained from the same individual.

The obvious approach to determining the magnitude and direction of such effects consists in comparing longitudinal with cross-sectional data. Ideally, to ward against the possibility of time-of-testing effects, these cross-sectional data should be collected in the same years as the longitudinal ones, suggesting the advisability of a design consisting of three series: A cross-sectional obtained during the first year of a study, successive replications of the cross-sectional data in successive subsequent years, to provide indications of time-of-testing effects, and longitudinal follow-up measures of at least the youngest sample measured during the first year (cf. Table 7–5).

Even the more limited combination of a single longitudinal series matched to a cross-sectional series from the same cohort has been rarely employed—the Educational Testing Service Longitudinal Study (Educational Testing Service, 1968, 1969) representing a notable exception. More common are instances of cross-sectional data which have subsequently been expanded into longitudinal series by retesting of one or more of the original age groups at one or more subsequent times. The results do not, of course, allow us to tease out test–retest effects from time-of-measurement effects, but are nevertheless instructive in pointing to the frequent lack of comparability, not only of the means thus obtained, but even of the direction of developmental changes uncovered.

One of the earliest examples of this situation is the study by Walters (1942) on the Müller–Lyer illusion, which showed, on the basis of cross-sectional information, a very marked decrease in the strength of the illusion between ages 6 and 13 (in accordance with much other research on this question). When, however, the original 6-year and 9-year-old groups were retested 3 years later, both showed an *increase* over their previous mean values, an age change which thus ran diametrically counter to the cross-sectional findings.

It hardly seems plausible to suppose that over a 3-year interval the effect of being subjected to the Müller–Lyer figure would be so powerful as to counter the drop with age normally to be expected for this illusion, especially since effects of practice per se have generally been found to operate in the same direction as age changes, that is, to lead to decrements in the strength of the illusion. Walters tried, nevertheless, to account for her longitudinal findings in terms of test–retest effects, and indeed showed that a group retested after only 3 weeks likewise manifested an increase in illusion. There remains of course the alternative possibility, that the age differences shown in the cross-sectional data were attributable to generational or time-of-testing effects. But this interpretation receives little support from the many data obtained over a span of some 70 years, both previous to that study and subsequently, which do not indicate any secular changes such as could account for Walter's cross-sectional findings. The basis for her longitudinal results thus remains a mystery; possibly, they do indicate that the experience of just a single perceptual measurement can produce long-term change in the individual, unlikely as this may seem.

The problem is by no means a rare one, as illustrated in Holtzman's (1969) cross-cultural study of the development of American and Mexican school children. These were measured cross-sectionally over the interval from 6.7 to 14.7 years. At the time of the publication of the paper just referred to, retests of several of the groups after a period of 12 months were likewise available. Here a more consistent and more readily interpretable pattern emerged: On measures of cognitive performance (e.g., subtests of the WISC), the longitudinal means very closely matched the cross-sectional ones. For a variety of personality-measures, on the other hand, mostly derived from the Holtzman Inkblot test, the longitudinal trends were generally in a direction opposite to the cross-sectional ones, though in some cases the American and Mexican groups differed in this respect. The picture is shown in Fig. 7–5, which shows the results for (*a*) WISC Vocabulary; (*b*) Movement responses, and (*c*) Pathognomic Verbalization, the latter two being based on the Inkblot responses.

The possibility of an interaction between the magnitude and even direction of the test–retest effect with subject variables, indicated in Fig. 7–5c, is particularly troublesome. It suggests that a simple adjustment of longi-

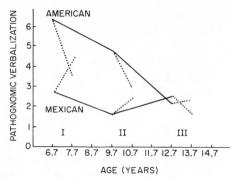

Fig. 7–5. Comparison between cross-sectional and longitudinal data on pathognomic verbalization on the Holtzman Inkblot test, at different age levels and for two cultural groups. [From Holtzman (1969).]

tudinal values for this effect, as determined from comparison with appropriate cross-sectional measures, could be highly misleading.

The Need for "Nonreactive Measures."   While a comparison between cross-sectionally and longitudinally obtained data—especially if both are drawn from the same cohort or set of cohorts—can provide information as to the likely role and magnitued of test–retest effects, the investigator finds himself in the embarrassing position of having to either discard or explain away the longitudinal data, if their trends run counter to the cross-sectional ones. A more effective strategy would be to follow Campbell's (1963) plea for the use of *nonreactive* measures, that is, measures that are minimally subject to test–retest effects. Though Campbell's suggestion is made with particular reference to the assessment of the role of specific experiental effects (in which context we shall return to it in Chapter XI), it is generalizable to the overall problem of test-retest effects. The reader's reaction to this recommendation may well be: "Easier said than done," yet, although the difficulties involved are very real, several avenues are available to the investigator in many situations which will enable him to alleviate the problem.

This leaves two further approaches to be discussed. One is Webb, Campbell, Schwartz, and Sechrest's (1966) "unobtrusive" measures, in which the individual is in effect measured without his being aware of it. Most of those considered by these authors turn out to be of the survey variety, but there are undoubtedly some, based on natural observation [e.g., playground behavior measures such as those by Patterson, Littman, & Bricker (1967) in their one-year longitudinal study of assertive behavior] which fit this category.

Finally, one time-honored way of keeping a response at time t_1, from influencing that given at time t_2 is to change the responses: the Alternate-

Forms approach known from the field of mental testing. If we take into account the fact that many of our measures, particularly in the field of abilities and cognitive development, rely in fact on an arbitrary sampling process for the selection of the test materials, there can be little objection to this procedure, provided we ensure that the two (or preferably more) alternate forms are in fact equivalent *at all ages*. For this purpose, a cross-sectional pilot study is strongly desirable. It may under some circumstances be used to provide the cross-sectional measures wanted at the start of the project, according to a time-sequential model. Note, however, that this approach does not ward against possible generalized effects of testing, that is, warm-up effects, or, for that matter, boredom or satiation effects, such as one might expect at the end of a lengthy series of longitudinal measures. (For a review of the evidence in this respect, with particular reference to intelligence test scores, cf. Anastasi and Foley, 1949, pp. 193ff. These authors place particular emphasis on the *qualitative* changes which have been shown in a variety of studies in regard to the meaning of a test score following repeated testing.)

Shortcuts to Longitudinal Data

The formidable obstacles inhibiting longitudinal research over an extended period of the child's development to maturity (and a fortiori through adulthood and into old age) have led to a variety of suggestions for easing the burden on the developmental investigator. We will consider three of these in particular.

1. THE "CONVERGENCE" METHOD

One compromise between the exclusive reliance on "instant" cross-sectional data and the time-consuming and obstacle-ridden longitudinal design is represented in the "convergence" method. In essence, this design consists simply of superimposing cross-sectionally a set of partially overlapping longitudinal series; or, to put it somewhat differently to take a set of cross-sectional samples and follow each age group over a number of years longitudinally, so as to allow one to verify from the longitudinal data the age trends initially obtained cross-sectionally.

This approach has been followed increasingly in developmental research of the past few years, notably in studies of perceptual and cognitive development (Cooper & London, 1971; Holtzman, 1969; Neimark & Lewis, 1968; Wohlwill, Devoe, & Fusaro, 1971). However, it would be inaccurate to treat it as a recent invention; in fact, we referred previously in this chapter to one study of rather more "ancient" vintage which used it: Walters's (1942) developmental study of the Müller–Lyer and Vertical–Horizontal illusions.

There was also noted one of the problems with the method: It assumes that either practice effects are negligible, in which case discrepancies encountered between longitudinal and cross-sectional trends can be analyzed in terms of time-of-testing (or cohort) differences, or conversely that the latter may be ignored, and discrepancies are attributable to test–retest effects. Note that these two types of processes might well operate to cancel each other out, thereby resulting in an essentially spurious correspondence between cross-sectional and longitudinal trends.

Reference to Table 7–1 reveals, furthermore, that the design under discussion actually corresponds to Schaie's cross-sequential model, intended to differentiate between cohort differences and time-of-testing effects, under the assumption of an *absence* of chronological age changes. In other words, it is validly used in developmental research only under the rather severe assumption that no secular trends whatever are operating, whether interpretable in terms of generational changes or effects operating at particular moments of historical time.

But even if we feel confident in the reasonableness of that assumption for the behavior under study, the critical question remains as to the usefulness of the longitudinal aspect of such mixed longitudinal cross-sectional data. To begin with, during the interval over which the subjects are followed up, we do have the opportunity to study change directly, and to answer questions relating to the determinants or correlates of such change, which longitudinal information alone can give us. Frequently this will, in fact, turn out to be the primary advantage of the longitudinal method. Instances of this use of the method will be illustrated at various points in subsequent chapters of this book.

One investigator, however, has gone further to suggest that the convergence design can be used to recover much of the information concerning shape and parameters of individual developmental functions which is lost in the cross-sectional method. Bell (1953) suggests that a composite function may be obtained from data collected according to this design, by determining the match between the data from age group A_{n+1} at its initial testing with those from age group A_n when the latter has reached the same age (cf. Fig. 7–6). This suggestion actually does not represent much of an advance over the straight cross-sectional approach, since it is predicated on the use of group data. Indeed, it is not apparent why a developmental function obtained in this way would be any different from an ordinary cross-sectional function. If the means for the ages at which the composite portions of the function are to be linked do in fact match, presumably the longitudinal means for the intervening ages should likewise be expected to match those that might have been obtained cross-sectionally.

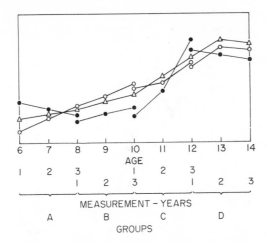

Fig. 7–6. Hypothetical growth curves for comparable and noncomparable groups. Δ: True curve; ○: Curves for comparable groups; ●: curves for noncomparable groups. [Reprinted from *Child Development*, 1953, **24**, by Bell by permission of The Society for Research in Child Development, Inc.]

Bell does in fact recognize the problem of the possible lack of correspondence between individual and group functions, and in a subsequent paper (Bell, 1954) shows how a more sophisticated version of his method might be applied to do justice to longitudinal information on a per-individual basis. He starts out with the assumption that individuals fall into distinct subgroups in terms of characteristic features of their developmental functions. Provided that there is some temporal overlap among successive age groups followed longitudinally, it should then be possible to match individuals in these groups in terms of some characteristic of their developmental function during this overlap period—most simply, the extent of their *change* over the interval.

He proceeds to illustrate the method by taking data from the Harvard Growth Study on growth in height in adolescent girls, over the period from 10.5 to 13.5 years, and dividing the total sample taken from this study into two subgroups, one for which data at ages 10.5, 11.5, and 12.5 years are used, the other for which data at ages 11.5, 12.5, and 13.5 are used; thus both groups share the 11.5- to 12.5-year interval. Bell proceeds to select those subjects from the second group who provided the best match to each subject from the first group, in terms of the value of D, derived from Cronbach and Gleser's measure of profile similarity, but used here simply to express difference in change from one age to the next (i.e., $D = d^2_{11.5} + d^2_{12.5}$), where d refers to the difference between the members of each pair at any given age.

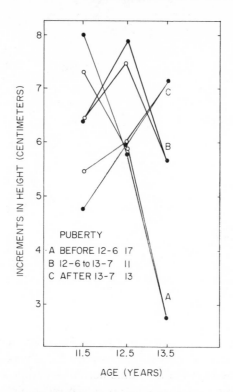

Fig. 7–7. Average annual increments in standing height for actual (●) and composite (○) growth records. [Reprinted from *Child Development*, 1954, **25**, by Bell by permission of The Society for Research in Child Development, Inc.]

The approach is illustrated in Fig. 7–7.[6] The most significant aspect of the results is that they indicate that the method preserves the information as to individual differences in growth-rate, related to age of attainment of puberty, as shown in the very different patterns of growth in the three groups separated (from information contained in the original data) according to this latter criterion.

It must be recognized that in this instance the degree of "acceleration" obtained via the convergence design is slight: Each group is measured over a 2-year period, to cover a total span of just 3 years. The question arises as to how effective matching over a similar interval of a year might be for arriving at a composite developmental function extending over a much longer period, for example, 10 years. Indeed, it is not even apparent how the method would be applied to arrive at such a function, that is, how several

[6] In this graph, the solid lines refer to the data from the original longitudinal study (stratified according to age at puberty), while the dotted lines represent data obtained by Bell's convergence method.

successive "splicings" of this sort might be obtained to result in a single synthetic longitudinal sequence. It appears rather that the method is restricted to a single such splice, that is, a total of just two groups, so that the gain over the traditional longitudinal method is limited to $k - o$, where k is the length of time over which each group is followed and o the interval of overlap between them. (For instance, a study might comprise one group tested at ages 6, 7, 8, 9, and 10, and another tested at ages 9, 10, 11, 12, and 13; the 7-year span is thus covered in 4 years, at a gain of $4 - 1 = 3$ years over complete longitudinal series.)

Furthermore, the method clearly places a considerable burden on the appropriateness of the matching procedure. In particular, the question arises as to how individuals in the second group representing approximately equivalent matches to an individual in the first group are to be discriminated, and, more important, what the prognostic validity of change over this interval for growth over the total age period under investigation actually is. Nevertheless, for data of sufficient reliability, conforming to a growth function, the approach deserves to be given a chance.

2. THE RETROSPECTIVE METHOD

Under certain conditions it may be possible to obtain longitudinal data retrospectively, that is, by searching for the requisite information in school records or other sources, so as to recover a longitudinal series of data extending over a possibly extended time period without investing more than the time necessary for locating and transcribing the information. In the field of physical growth, as well as of standardized ability and intelligence test scores, school records can frequently provide a fertile mine of such data, assuming that the investigator is successful in obtaining access to them. It goes without saying that the availability, extensiveness, and reliability of such information varies tremendously from one school system to another.

While few investigators would be happy with letting their research interests and plans be determined by the typically very limited information, particularly of a behavioral sort, that might be available in a given area, it is arguable whether data of this type that are in fact available have been exploited to their fullest extent. A good illustration is provided by the extensive longitudinal records which have been kept on the growth of children in Aberdeen, Scotland since about 1950 (cf. Tanner, Healy, Lockhart, Mackenzie, & Whitehouse, 1956), dealing with virtually all facets of the child's physical and behavioral development (though much of it is based on interview material). Admittedly, more routine records, such as those that might be obtained from a school system, for instance, would go beyond the much more systematic and presumably more trustworthy information available from the major longitudinal projects such as the Berkeley growth study and the Fels study. The vastly expanded resources for data storage and processing made possible by the advent of the computer should, however, encourage more widespread establishment of longitudinal data banks for the use of future developmental investigators.

Retrospective information of a particular sort has been used for some time in the study of effects of early experience and child-rearing practices. Here the investigator has typically been interested in relating data on some facet of the child's life in infancy or early childhood to some behavioral measures obtained at the time of the study. On occasion, the retrospectively obtained information has likewise included behavioral data, as in studies of behavioral stability and more generally of the relationship between early and subsequent behaviors. Here we are not dealing, then, with longitudinal series, and few of the problems of the longitudinal method are relevant, although special problems of sample selection and *ex post facto* control arise in this strategy. But these fall outside of the province of this chapter.

Where the retrospective method entails the use of recall data obtained from adults through personal interviews and the like, a host of further problems arise, having to do with the accuracy and reliability of such data. These have been cogently reviewed and discussed in the literature (e.g., Wenar & Coulter, 1962; Yarrow, Campbell, & Burton, 1970), but one finding reported by Yarrow *et al.* deserves particular mention. These investigators found that while retrospective reports in adolescence or adulthood generally show some degree of correlation with data recorded in the same individuals' childhood, there are frequently significant shifts in mean values, reflecting systematically biasing effects of memory. This point is of particular relevance to Baltes and Goulet's (1971) proposal to make use of the retrospective method as a general strategy for developmental research, to obviate the need for longitudinal data, while avoiding the problems of cross-sectional designs, notably those related to the confounding of age differences with cohort differences. These authors refer to the Yarrow *et al.* study, among others, in support of their argument; yet for their own purpose, concerned as they are with generating age functions, the biasing effects just referred to would severely impair the usefulness of such data. It is, furthermore, apparent that the kinds of measures to which recall data concerning child behavior would be necessarily limited—for example, rating-scale or three-point categorical data, or purely qualitative, open-ended responses—are quite unsuitable for the purpose of generating age functions. Given the relativized nature of most of these scales, such measures do not even permit valid inferences as to direction, much less magnitude of age changes. There is a serious problem of contamination, finally, if one were to rely on a single individual to make retrospective judgments of his standing on some behavioral variable at a series of different ages, which is in effect what Goulet and Baltes's proposal demands.

In brief, as a substitute for the longitudinal method for obtaining information on age changes in behavior the retrospective approach appears to be of very limited value, unless measures recorded contemporaneously are available. Where verbal reports involving recall-type information are employed—be these obtained through parents or other adults, or from the child himself at some later time—it has some limited applicability for the purpose of correlating experiential or behavioral aspects of the child's earlier life with some measure of contemporaneous behavior. But even here, where the recalled data do not refer to objective facts or events, the results are subject to a considerable degree of distortion.

3. THE SIMULATION OF AGE CHANGES

A kind of distant cousin of the retrospective method involves getting the subject to behave according to a particular age level either by asking him to do so explicitly (i.e., through role play) or through hypnotic suggestion. These are essentially variants of a simulation approach to the study of development, which as we shall note presently may take still other forms. The general principle of such an approach is to simulate the age changes that either have already occurred or may occur in the future by inducing a particular state in the organism, whether through mere verbal instructions, hypnosis, or possibly certain experimental procedures.

A particularly interesting example of this approach is to be found in a study by Parrish, Lundy, and Leibowitz (1969). Using the technique of hypnotic age regression, which had previously been employed in personality and clinical research (cf. Yates, 1961), these investigators were able to produce judgments on the part of their subjects which were comparable to those expected at the actual age levels to which they were regressed. This finding is all the more remarkable since the age trends for the two illusions run in opposite directions, that for the Ponzo increasing with age, while the Poggendorff decreases. These findings thus argue against a simple explanation in terms of a set effect designed to maximize the illusion such as presumably operated in the case of a control group (of only five subjects) which was given verbal suggestions comparable to those used with the hypnotized subjects. These subjects showed higher illusion effects under the regression instructions compared to base line conditions for *both* illusions.

The concept of hypnotic age *regression* brings up an interesting question, that is, whether this method, or other similar simulation approaches, can be used prospectively as well as retrospectively. Hypnotic suggestion does not seem to have been applied to attempts to produce behavior characteristic of an older subject; whether it is possible in principle to simulate maturing processes (i.e., adult-level responses in younger children) is an interesting theoretical question, as is the somewhat different one whether aging can be simulated. Verbal set *can* be employed in children to suggest a type of responding characteristic of adults, as well as the reverse—as demonstrated by Milgram and Goodglass (1961) in a study of word associations. These authors presented children from Grades 2 through 8 with a word association test in which the subject had to choose one of two response words to each stimulus word, one choice representing an abstract, the other a concrete response. Half of the test was administered under instructions to assume a "child role," the other half under instructions to assume an "adult role." Milgram and Goodglass found that from Grade 4 on there was a clear differentiation in the responses obtained under these two roles, in the expected direction, that is, more abstract choices under the adult set. The forced-choice nature of these responses should be borne in mind, however, in evaluating these results.

The interpretation of Milgram and Goodglass's results is far from clear, though we may grant the pertinence of their own explanation in terms of the development of role-taking ability. It might be noted that in terms of overt behavior children as young as nursery-school age demonstrate a high degree of ability to act *like* adults or persons of any age that they may have come in contact with. To that extent a developmental psychologist from Mars might even succeed in formulating some notions concerning the behavioral development of *Homo sapiens* terrestrialis by observing the house play of 4-year-olds.

Facetious though this suggestion might appear, it is pertinent to the attempt by Baltes and Goulet (1971) to elevate the place of retrospective and prospective simulation of age changes to the status of a technique for obtaining information on the course of behavioral development while avoiding the pitfalls of cross-sectional age-group comparison. In this context, they refer to a growing body of research on the *perception* of age differences on the part of individuals at different ages, for various aspects of behavior, and quote with approval the view of Thomae (1970) that "Perception of change rather than objective change is related to behavioral change [p. 4]." This view, applied to changes in maturity and old age, with respect to psychological adjustment to the menopause in women, to retirement, etc., may have some surface plausibility, as the popular saying "You are as old as you feel" attests. But it surely represents a dubious foundation on which to establish a generally viable approach to obtaining information on behavior change with age that might replace or even be effectively integrated with that obtained from direct measures of behavior at different ages. The field of social perception has provided all too ample evidence of the prevalence of stereotyping and other distortions and biases which permeate the perception of the behavior of others.[7]

There remains to be considered a final variant of the simulation approach, which involves the use of especially devised experimental conditions with adult subjects, designed to produce variation in performance that may be characterized in terms of developmental levels. The use of the microgenetic technique in perceptual research (e.g., Flavell & Draguns, 1957; Kragh, 1955) represents a prime example of this approach, as does other research carried out within the Wernerian framework (cf. Werner, 1957), notably Wapner's programmatic work on perception related to sensori-tonic theory (e.g., Wapner, 1964). If one accepts the Wernerian view of the concept of development as applicable to a wide variety of domains outside of the area of ontogenetic development, this approach involves less a simulation of age changes than a validation or extension of the principles that may have been established on the basis of age-comparative research concerning the operation of developmental processes. Once again, then, we are clearly not dealing here with an approach that is designed to provide us with a substitute for or shortcut to information on age changes.

We are forcibly led to conclude that no such substitute or shortcut does in fact exist, and that only by studying individuals at different ages, whether cross-sectionally or longitudinally, or through some combination of the two methods, can we hope to answer the questions that concern us as developmental psychologists.

---

[7] This point receives ample support from the literature on the perception of different age groups on the part of individuals at different ages (for a recent review, cf. McTavish, 1971). Ahammer and Baltes (1972) themselves appear to retreat somewhat from treating perceived age differences as a general strategy for studying age changes to the view that "... research on perceived age changes is interesting in its own right... for... a phenomenologically oriented developmental theory ... supplementing existing theoretical frameworks which are primarily based on actual [objective] age differences [p. 46]." With this theoretical argument we need not quarrel, nor with the authors' conclusion that "The present study... confirmed the proposition that the study of perceived age and/or generation differences is useful for the understanding of developmental phenomena [p. 50]."

CHAPTER VIII

The Descriptive Study of Developmental Change

In Chapter III we considered briefly the place of a descriptive analysis of the developmental function in the study of developmental processes. The argument, in brief, was that in any realm in which change is the subject of study, a purely descriptive analysis of the characteristics and attributes of these changes can provide us with important and, in some cases, indispensable information concerning the mode of operation of the developmental processes implicated in the changes. The case of dark adaptation was mentioned as illustrative of this point.

Since descriptive research does not rank high on the scale of values of most psychologists, and is frequently treated with outright scorn, some brief elaboration of this point is in order. Clearly we are not making a case here for the collection of isolated facts, or even of normative data on the types or mean amount of response on some variable exhibited by individuals at different ages, for instance, information of the sort which characterized much of the early work on language development, on emotional development, etc. (cf. Jersild, 1954; McCarthy, 1954). Rather, the argument is that whenever we obtain direct measures of change in behavior, we have information relating directly to a functional relationship, that is, reflecting the operation of the psychological processes producing the change (in our case, of the developmental processes) that are of interest to us. The difference may be conveyed by simply comparing the following two statements: "The average size of the vocabulary of the 3–year–old child is 900 words," versus "There is only slight improvement with age in adaptation to rotated visual feedback up to the age of 12 years, when it undergoes marked and rapid change through late adolescence." The first statement is utterly devoid of consequences, while the second at least tells us about the timing of the changes involved, and may offer us some clues as to their nature and origin.

Another way of putting the matter is that, whenever we *observe* the changes produced by development, we are recording the outcome of a natural process just as we do when we record the movement of a glacier, or the change in activity rate on an activity wheel over the course of the estrus cycle of the rat. The results will not be as neatly interpretable as they are where the experimenter manipulates particular variables to produce the changes, but we will need to have an accurate picture of them, so that we may know exactly what it is that we need to explain through further theory and experiment.

One concrete example may suffice at this point. It takes the form of a single graph (the proverbial picture that is worth a 1000 words) taken from a paper by Count (1947) on the relationship between brain- and body-weight in man. It gives convincing proof of the fact that neural growth cannot be encompassed within a single continuous process, but clearly is made up of at least three successive phases, corresponding, respectively, to the prenatal, the neonatal, and the postinfancy periods (cf. Fig. 8–1).

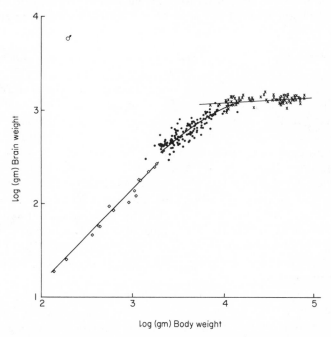

Fig. 8–1. Relationship between brain weight and body weight during development for females showing differentiation between fetal, postnatal and postinfancy periods. ×: Post-infantile; ●: transitional; ◇ fetal. [From Count (1947).]

The description of developmental change turns out to be most interesting when either quantitative data, conforming to Case I are available, or where we have qualitative data, conforming to Case III; the remaining two cases can be disposed of more briefly.

Charting the Course of Developmental Change along Scalar Dimensions

1. FORM OF THE DEVELOPMENTAL FUNCTION

The first and most general question to be asked about a quantitative developmental function is: What is its overall form? The answer to this question may vary all the way from simple indications of increase or decrease with age to elaborate attempts to specify the precise form of the function in mathematical terms. More precisely, three levels of analysis may be distinguished: (*a*) determination of presence and direction of developmental change; (*b*) determination of the general shape of the developmental function in terms of significant components of trend (trend analysis); and (*c*) specification of the mathematical form and parameters of the growth curve. Let us consider the kind of information each of these levels provides, and the value of longitudinal as opposed to cross-sectional data in each case.

a. Determination of Presence and Direction of Developmental Change. At this level, the only question of interest is simply: Is there a significant shift with age in the magnitude of some response, and if so, what is the direction of the shift? Probably better than 90% of so-called developmental research is restricted to this level, being so largely confined to the determination of the significance of the difference in the means of often arbitrarily selected age groups. Frequently such research is undertaken with the avowed intent of testing some developmental theory or hypothesis, but for reasons which were reviewed in Chapter II comparative data of this type are of very limited value for this purpose, since there are almost always an indefinitely large number of alternative interpretations for any observed age differences. This is true particularly where the age change is in the direction of an increase in amount, or of improvement relative to some fixed standard. Results of this type of study are thus best considered as purely descriptive, regardless of the investigator's purpose.

In many instances of this approach, the investigator confines himself to a comparison of two age groups (e.g., adults and children or 6-year-olds and 10-year-olds), thus eliminating the possibility of uncovering anything except monotonic age trends. Even where the number of age groups used is greater than two, age is still generally treated as a between-subjects factor in a standard analysis of variance model, frequently in combination with one or more within-subjects variables, or possibly between-groups treatment or other individual difference variables. This not only results in a progressively more inefficient test of the significance of the age differences as the number of age levels sampled increases (since in the ordinary analysis of variance each factor is treated as a nominally scaled variable), but it is wasteful of information concerning the overall form of the age changes, for example, the differentiation of linear from curvilinear, or monotonically increasing from inverted U-shaped changes. At best, comparisons among specified age group means following the overall analysis can bring out some of this detail, but only in piecemeal fashion.

It should be noted that, except for the attenuation of the confounding of secular time and chronological age referred to in the preceding chapter, there is little advantage to be derived from longitudinal as opposed to cross-sectional designs at this level of analysis. Longitudinal data do result in improved comparability of the subject-population across age levels (which is, however, offset by the possibility of selective dropout from any longitudinal sample); there are further statistical advantages accruing to any repeated-measurement design, which in turn must be weighed against the very real problems of test–retest effects operating in most psychological research (cf. Chapter VII). It might be observed, furthermore, that the developmentalist is rarely interested merely in establishing the statistical significance of age differences for a particular variable. By the same token, such differences can hardly be of much consequence for him if they are so statistically unreliable as to *require* a repeated-measurement design to be revealed.

b. Determination of Shape of Developmental Functions via Trend Analysis. In many instances, the interest and significance of developmental changes can be greatly enhanced by considering aspects of the gross shape of the developmental function. Consider, for example, the following three cases, illustrated in Fig. 8–2a, b, and c.

The first of these, Comalli, Wapner, and Werner's (1962) study of interference effects on the Stroop test was already referred to in Chapter IV. It is of interest, first, in the strong indication of a "regression" effect in middle and old age, in other words, a reversal of the ontogenetic trend toward decreasing interference with age. Leaving out of consideration, for the moment, the possibility of cohort differences and other artifacts of sampling procedures (i.e. differences in the populations from which the 40- and 70-year-old subjects were drawn), it is apparent that this reversal, or more generally the overall U-shaped form of the age function, may be of considerable theoretical interest, as is the question of how early this reversal sets in.

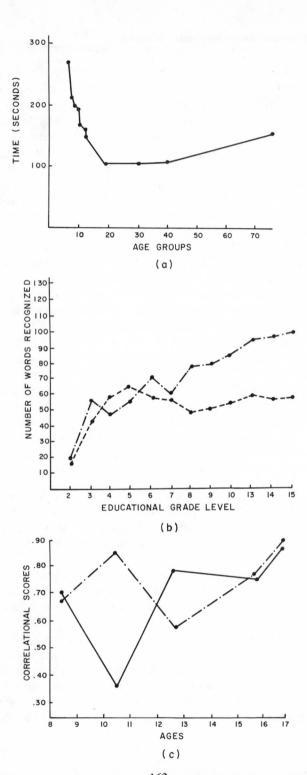

(a)

(b)

(c)

162

Is there a plateau starting in early adulthood and running through middle age, or (as a literal interpretation of the graph might lead one to believe) does interference increase again as soon as it has reached its minimum in late adolescence?

The second of the developmental functions shown in Fig. 8–2 was ob-tained by Forgays (1953); it indicates age changes in accuracy of tachisto-scopic recognition of words presented to the right and to the left of the fixation point. Of particular interest is the *drop* in accuracy for words pre-sented to the left of fixation during the middle school years. It provides suggestive evidence of the effects of the training of the visual receptor mechanisms (e.g., saccadic eye movements) through reading, favoring a right–left scanning process and accordingly creating a bias in favor of stimuli exposed to the right of fixation. Both the timing of the drop and the sub-sequent rise are noteworthy: the drop suggests that it is only after reading habits have become strongly overlearned that they affect word recognition, whereas the rise would seem to indicate that other processes improving with age (such as increased familiarity with words; improved ability to "guess" the identity of words on the basis of incompletely or imperfectly perceived sequences of letters) come to compensate for the biasing oculo-motor set.

Figure 8–2c, finally, is taken from a study by Ausubel, Schiff, and Gasser (1952) on developmental changes in accuracy of social perception based on sociometric data. The particular graph reproduced shows the results obtained for accuracy of each child's estimates of his same-sexed classmates' evaluation of him on a number of scales, expressed in terms of the correla-tion between his estimates and the mean ratings he actually received. Here the most intriguing aspect of the data is the drop in the accuracy of self-perception in preadolescence. The fact that this drop occurs earlier in girls than in boys strengthens an interpretation in terms of processes functionally

---

Fig. 8–2. Three examples of developmental functions, based on cross-sectional data. (a) Age differences in speed of naming colors on interference card (Card C) of Stroop test. [From Comalli, Wapner, & Werner (1962).] (b) Changes in tachistoscopic recognition of words presented to the right and to the left of fixation, as a function of grade level. (---): WR; (—·—): WL. [From Forgays (1953). Copyright by the American Psychological Association and reproduced by permission.] (c) Age differences in accuracy of social perception, as measured in terms of correlations between averaged sociometric ratings of each child within a class and the ratings children thought each of their classmates would receive from the class. (——): Girls' perception of girls' ratings; (—·—): Boys' perception of boys' ratings. [Reprinted from *Child Development*, 1952, **23**, by Ausubel, Schiff, & Gasser by permission of The Society for Research in Child Development, Inc.]

linked with the coming of adolescence as such. It may be recalled that in trying to account for this finding, the authors advanced the plausible suggestion that the criteria for the evaluation of others are changing at this time, and that there is a lag in the child's own recognition of this change, resulting in a lowered degree of veridicality in their view of others' responses to them. Obviously, this interpretation is little more than a hunch, and would require confirmation through further study specifically directed at the determinants of the drop in accuracy of self-perception. The point being made, however, is that the present data on the differential timing of this drop for the two sexes give us a clue as to where to look for an answer to this question.

The kind of detailed analysis of the shape of the developmental function required to provide trustworthy information concerning the several phenomena just referred to ideally calls for longitudinal study, both to bring out more sharply the form of the individual functions, without distortion through averaging, and to ward off artifacts of sampling from possibly disparate populations and cohorts.[1] Above all, however, it calls for an abandonment of the hypothesis-testing strategy embodied in statistical techniques such as the analysis of variance, in favor of one more attuned to the basically descriptive focus of such research. We would like, in other words, to be able to establish the true form of the function in order to determine the reality of the drop in the WL function in Fig. 8–2b, or to differentiate between a plateau, as opposed to a rising function over the period from 20 to 40 years in the Stroop effect in Fig. 8–2a. The technique indicated for this purpose is clearly that of trend analysis (Alexander, 1946; Grant, 1956), at least in the case of Fig. 8–2a and 2b; the data of Fig. 8–2c, being in the form of correlation coefficients for each grade, do not lend themselves to this type of statistical analysis.

In essence, trend analysis entails matching the empirical curve described by a set of means obtained for specified values of an independent variable (scaled on an interval scale) to several successive models representing polynomial equations of increasing degree. The observed values on the scaled variable are weighted by cross-multiplying them by sets of trend-coefficients, so as to bring into relief any tendency in the curve to follow trends corresponding to these polynomials. The total variance is then partitioned separately for each of these weighted sets of values, permitting an assessment

---

[1]This point is less applicable to the study of Ausubel, Schiff, and Gasser (1952) since one would hardly expect developmental functions obtained for correlation coefficients to be very determinate in character. This qualification is reinforced by the considerable dependence of these correlations on *variation* among the class members in their ratings of each child (i.e., if each classmate assigns the same rating to a given child, and the latter correctly guesses this to be the case, a correlation of zero would still result).

of the significance of the linear, quadratic, cubic, etc. components (up to the $k-1$th degree, for k points on the scaled variable) in terms of the ratio of the variance between the appropriately weighted means to the within-group variance. In the case of a repeated-measurement design, furthermore, the significance of each of these components of trend can be evaluated against the variance in the same *trends* between individuals, at a considerable increase in sensitivity.

The method is ideally suited for the analysis of developmental functions, in a number of respects. First, it does not start from any a priori model of the form of growth; rather it pulls out of the data whatever regularity is contained in them, to present in a purely pragmatic sense a composite picture of the form of the function expressed as a polynomial of the nth degree. This permits the investigator to determine whether a function is monotone or nonmonotonically increasing, linear, or curvilinear, etc. It further reveals whether temporary reversals such as that shown in the *WL* function of Fig. 8–2b represent real phenomena, rather than sampling fluctuation. In this case it would do so by showing whether the cubic component of trend was significant. While specific comparisons between means, following an overall simple analysis of variance, might be thought to accomplish the same purpose, the efficiency of the trend-analysis is clearly greater, relying less on *ex post facto* hunches suggested by the data. Above all, it is more systematic in providing a convenient expression for the form of the total function.

Of particular value is the power of the technique to uncover interactions between the age variable and some other independent variable, and express these as differences in trend. Thus the difference between the sexes in the rate of development of reading skills shown by Millard (1940), as well as the differences in the rate of perfection of intersensory discrimination for different combinations of modalities in Birch and Lefford's (1963) investigation would undoubtedly have shown up in trend-analyses of the data, either as differences in linear trend, or, particularly in Birch and Lefford's case, as differences in the highest component of trend (cf. Fig. 8–5). However certain limitations of the trend-analysis model need to be mentioned. A problem of a purely statistical nature concerns the homogeneity of variance assumption built into the technique, as a form of variance-analysis. There are undoubtedly many situations in which variances are far from homogeneous across age levels; in particular, for any variable starting from an effective absolute zero, means and variances can be expected to be correlated. The seriousness of violations of this assumption in the case of trend analysis have not, to this writer's knowledge, been specifically studied.

A more substantive limitation of the model in certain cases is that it, in effect, treats the data as though they are measured on a scale lacking an absolute zero. Arbitrary changes in the origin of the scale, by adding or subtracting a constant to every score, have no more effect on the results of a trend analysis than they would for any ordinary analysis of variance. Thus, expressing these in terms of a set of orthogonal components may be a fairly artificial and possibly misleading procedure.

This will be true all the more for data marked by a high degree of precision. For instance, when segments of the total growth curve for height are analyzed in this fashion, the results will be very much affected by measures taken following the cessation of growth. This is brought out in a reanalysis of the Harvard Growth study data on height by Wohlwill and Hall (unpublished). Taking longitudinal samples of boys and girls, the latter displayed a significant quintic (!) component, whereas the former showed only a significant cubic component. This was apparently attributable to the fact that measures were taken through the 17th year of age, which on the average was a year or more beyond the point at which girls reach their terminal height, while boys were still growing at this point. In order to fit the essentially horizontal part of the curve at the upper ages for the girls, quintic, septic, and nonic components were required to provide a fit to these highly reliable data. It is interesting to note that no such problem was encountered in a cross-sectional sample analysis of the same data, using independent samples representing ages 8–17 drawn from the published records of all of the cases included in the Harvard growth study (Dearborn, Rothney, & Shuttleworth, 1938). This is not surprising, but shows the considerably lower degree of sensitivity of the method when applied to cross-sectional data.

Admittedly, for most behavioral data which are not rigidly cumulative in the way that growth in height is, problems of this sort should not arise very frequently. Even here, however, the usefulness of cross-sectional data for trend analysis is limited by the lack of components of trend determined separately for each individual, which eliminates the possibility of evaluating the function described by the means against the variation in trends within individuals. As a result, the investigator's ability to discriminate between trends of different degree is severely curtailed, particularly where they increase or decrease monotonically with age.

c. Mathematical Specification of the Developmental Function. Under certain circumstances, we may be in a position to aim at a still higher degree of refinement, by attempting to determine the particular mathematical function providing a best fit to a set of developmental data. In the field of behavioral research, the area of mathematical learning theory provides perhaps the best example of such an approach, starting from a limited number of a priori assumptions concerning the learning process (e.g., Bush & Mosteller, 1955; Estes, 1950; Suppes & Ginsberg, 1963). Another area which has lent itself to mathematical function analysis is that of psychophysics, but with some exceptions, work in that area has been more descriptive in its approach, preferring to find the best fitting function corresponding to a given set of data, rather than starting with an a priori model.

For reasons which will be noted presently, in the study of development this degree of mathematical elaboration has been limited almost entirely to the field of physical growth. It was from this area that the study of mathematical growth curves received its impetus, so as to occupy at present a central place in biometric and anthropometric research.[2]

In this work, as in some of the behavioral work involving mathematical function analysis, we can distinguish between the model-testing and the empirical curve-fitting approach. Advocates of the former appear to be in a distinct minority. Among their foremost representatives, we may cite Bertalanffy (1951, 1960a), who starts from a conception of growth as involving a changing balance between anabolic (growth-enhancing) and catabolic (growth-inhibiting) processes. The exact form of the resulting function depends on several further assumptions about the forces controlling metabolic activity, which vary as between plants and animals, as well as among phylae. In its most general form, it may be expressed as $y = (1 - ce^{-kta})$, where y is the characteristic being measured, $c = (1 - y_a^1)$, k is a constant of growth, and a a parameter varying according to the dimensionality of the characteristic, that is, $a = 1$ for length; $a = 3$ for weight (cf. Bertalanffy, 1960a.). Bertalanffy's rational equations for growth may be contrasted to those developed by Weiss and Kavanau (1957), on the basis of a more complex model, postulating two types of substances: generative and differentiated, with growth being inhibited both through the progressive shift from generative to differentiated mass and through a negative feedback cycle in which the increase in the reproductive activity of the generative mass through catabolic "templates" is counteracted by an increase in the production of anabolic "antitemplates" (cf. Bertalanffy, 1960a, for a comparison of these two models).

The simplest and most straightforward treatment of rationally derived growth curves is given by Shock (1951), who distinguishes among four alternative models for cell growth: (*a*) linear proliferation of cells, with each cell producing catabolic substances at a constant rate; (*b*) linear proliferation of cells, with catabolic substances produced at a rate varying over time; (*c*) constant rate of proliferation, limited by available foodstuffs; and (*d*) exponentially proliferating cells, limited by available foodstuffs. From these four models Shock derives a prototype equation for each; those corresponding to the last two models are of particular interest, since they have been widely used on a purely empirical basis to describe growth for

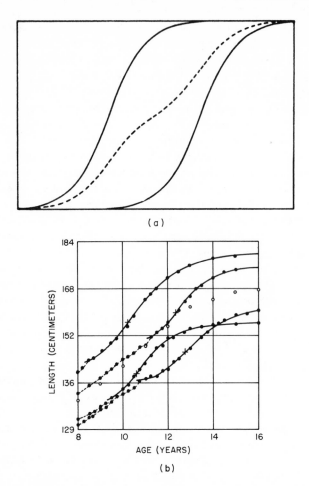

(a)

(b)

Fig. 8–3. Illustrations of logistic and Gompertz curves applied to the study of growth. (a) Two logistic curves, and the curve for their average. (——): Individual logistic; (– – –): Average curve. [Reprinted from *Human Biology* 1931, **3**, by M. Merrill by permission of the Wayne State University Press.] (b) Individual plots of growth in height, fitted to Gompertz curves. ○ Average. [Reprinted from *Human Biology* 1957, **29**, by J. Deming by permission of the Wayne State University Press.]

various animal and human body parts. They are, respectively, the logistic: $y = (1 - e^{-kt})$ which is familiar to mathematical learning theorists, and the Gompertz: $y = A \exp(be^{ct})$. The former is illustrated in Fig. 8-3a, taken from the work of Merrill (1931) on the growth of weight in rats; it serves to remind us anew of the necessity for longitudinal data in growth-curve analysis, already brought out in Chapter VII. The Gompertz curve is the adjoining graph, Fig. 8–3b, taken from Deming's (1957) study of growth in height in children.

It must be noted, however, that Shock, himself, emphasizes the limitations of these curves as theoretically meaningful representations of the growth process, as do other critics of rationally derived growth curves (e.g., Sholl, 1954; Waddington, 1950). Their objections derive from three considerations: The assumptions on which the curves are based were arbitrarily chosen from among a large variety of alternative possibilities; given, moreover, that the constants entering into the equations are uniquely determined, it is impossible to use any single set of data as a test of any particular model of growth. Second, irregularity and unreliability of measurements frequently make it difficult to decide among alternative best-fitting curves—cf. Gray's (1929) attempt to fit a set of observed data to both the logistic and the Gompertz, his conclusion being that either one provided as good a fit as the other. Last, and most important, for many aspects of growth, notably human growth in length, for instance, no single curve can be found to fit adequately the whole course of growth.

In a purely empirical sense, both the logistic and the Gompertz have been frequently applied in the study of human growth, the former by Brody (1945) and, in a more complicated version of the basic formula, by Jenss and Bayley (1937), while the latter has been applied by Dearborn and Rothney (1941), Courtis (1932), and Deming (1957), among others. In comparison to other possible growth curves, such as the simple exponential, $y = ae^{kt}$, or a curve cited by Israelsohn (1960) in connection with data from the Harpenden Growth study, $y = a + bt + c \log t$, the logistic and Gompertz curves have the considerable advantage of having an infection point, which appears to be more reasonable for describing the growth of quantities starting at zero and growing to some asymptotal value. The location of the inflection point can, furthermore, be used as one basis for distinguishing between them, the logistic (in its simplest version) being symmetrical, and thus reaching an inflection point at a value of y one-half of its terminal value, while the Gompertz is asymmetrical, with an inflection point at about one-third the terminal value of y. As already mentioned, however, neither of these two functions, nor any other single curve can be effectively fitted to the whole period of growth— a convincing argument itself for the operation of discontinuity in the growth process even for basic physical characteristics. It therefore becomes necessary to construct a composite curve consisting of several phases or cycles.

Count (1943) has made the most ambitious attempt to arrive at such a composite for growth in stature, using derivatives of the formula cited above, which Israelsohn (1960) refers to, $y = a + bx + c \log x$. This function itself is applied to the first phase, up to age 7; a simple variant of it, involving multiplication by a constant and addition of a constant, represents the second phase, up to about age 13; the final phase, however, involves a considerably more complex function, in which that of the second phase appears as an exponent, thus in effect transforming it into a logistic. Despite the rational arguments Count is able to marshall for the properties of this composite curve, and the surface plausibility of the three-phase process he suggests, for practical purposes, it is simpler to resort to another three-component curve, involving Jenss and Bayley's (1937) elaboration of the logistic ($y = c + dx - e^{a+bx}$) for the first phase (up through about 5 years); the simple logarithmic function just mentioned ($y = a + bx + c \log x$) for the second phase, up through the beginning of adolescence; and the Gompertz for the terminal phase (cf. Israelsohn, 1960).

If it does not appear possible at this time to base a choice of growth curves on a priori, theoretical considerations, we may well ask, what is their value? Their usefulness, even at a purely descriptive level, takes several different forms. First, given a prototype function, it becomes possible to differentiate among individuals or groups (e.g., the two sexes) in terms of the values of particular constants (e.g., Deming, 1957). Similarly, the study of interspecies differences in growth has been facilitated by recourse to mathematical functions (e.g., Brody, 1945; Stahl, 1962). Furthermore, Shock (1951) points to a number of variables whose role in the growth process has been conveniently expressed in terms of the parameters of growth curves, as in the study of effects of nutrition, hormones, and the like. It has served, in other words, as a means for expressing in simple, analytic form statements concerning differential growth among individuals and among species, and under different conditions.

Of particular interest is the use of mathematical growth curves in comparing growth for different body parts or functions, that is, in the study of differential growth. This aspect will be taken up more specifically in the chapter on correlational approaches, Chapter X, but it is instructive to refer to one example of this use of growth-curve methodology, by Weinbach (1938), both because it comes closer to the behavioral realm, and because it involves a comparison between an anatomical and a physiological function which, furthermore, is of some interest for psychologists. Weinbach obtained data for alpha rhythm observations and for brain weight, finding them to conform to a single function, of the type $M = M_m - M_m e^{-kt}$, as illustrated in Fig. 8–4.

As Shock (1951) rightly observes, the apparent similarly of the two graphs, and the fact that they could be fitted to the same function, is no proof of their interdependence, but the example does bring out the potential value of this kind of analytic approach to the description of growth.

What about the use of growth curves with behavioral data? Not too surprisingly, attempts to apply them have been few and far between. The reasons are obvious: first, few behavioral characteristics can be validly assimilated to the model of incremental growth. Second, we very rarely have the absolute units of measurement which are required to plot the course of

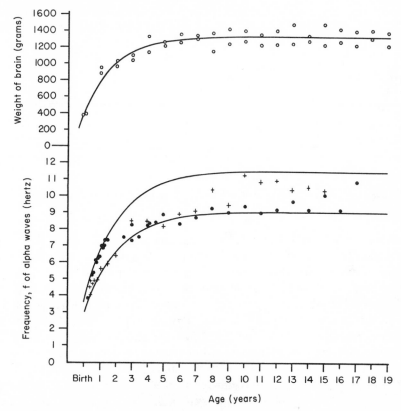

Fig. 8–4. Developmental curves for brain weight and alpha rhythm of the EEG. [From Weinbach (1938).]

development in the form of a growth curve, and to analyze the form of this curve in mathematical terms. Furthermore, as we saw in Chapter VII, growth curves of the type which have been discussed here are subject to serious distortion through averaging; accordingly, longitudinal data are necessary if we hope to apply them, yet with the exception of intelligence-test and ability data, there is virtually no extended longitudinal record of age changes with respect to quantitative behavioral dimensions in existence. Finally, it is apparent that unless the age changes under investigation are not only substantial in magnitude, but reliably and precisely measurable, we can hardly expect that a mathematical expression of the developmental function will yield dividends commensurate with the effort involved.

In this respect, it is instructive to examine two of the very rare cases in which an attempt has been made to fit growth curves to behavioral data. The first is a study by Weinbach (1940) in which the time taken by a single infant

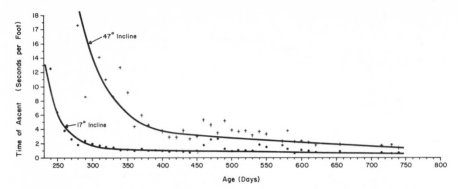

Fig. 8–5. Age changes in speed of climbing an inclined plane in infancy, for two conditions of angle of inclination. [From Weinbach (1940).]

to climb a 6-foot-long slide placed at varying angles between 0° (i.e., flat along the floor) and 47° was recorded on 42 occasions spaced for the most part at 10-day intervals between the ages of 8 and 24 months. It is interesting to compare two of the functions Weinbach obtained, one for a relatively easy inclination (17°), the other for the steepest (47°). They are given in Fig. 8–5.

The curves fitted to these data were derived simply be postulating some minimum asymptotal time toward which the child would converge and assuming that improvement in speed of climbing is a function of the difference between speed at any given age and that asymptotal value, i.e., $d/dt = k(\theta - \theta_m)$. This leads Weinbach to the function, $\theta = \theta_m + e^{k(t - t')}$, where θ_m is the asymptotal value, k is the rate of change of the function, t is age, and t' is a constant of integration, arbitrarily chosen so that for $t = t'$, $\theta = 2\theta_m$.

Weinbach's paper is of interest in several respects. The values of the constants in the above equation are of course derived entirely from the data; thus it appears to represent a case of pure empirical curve-fitting. Nevertheless the particular curve chosen is clearly only one of a variety of curves that might have been suggested, starting from different premises concerning the determinants of growth. Last, but not least, it provides a convenient analytical mode of representing the effect of the task variable, that is, angle of inclination, in terms of parameters of the developmental function, thus illustrating the points made in this regard in Chapter V. This is shown in Table 8–1, listing the major parameters as a function of angle-of-inclination.

Table 8–1 provides clear evidence (notably from the values of k and t') of the effect of increasing angle-of-inclination on slowing down the rate of improvement in this motor skill. It does not, of course, show the fact, equally salient from a look at Fig. 8–5, that the curve provides a much poorer fit to the data for the 47° inclination than for the 17° one. Weinbach's plots show, in fact, that the functions become increasingly irregular as the angle becomes

Table 8–1

Constants for Age Curves Fitted to Data on Speed of Climbing Inclines, for a Single Infant[1,2]

Incline	θ_m sec per foot	k per day	t' days	k_0/k ratio
0°	.67	.087	266	1.0
9.9°	1.00	.046	289	1.9
16.9°	1.00	.041	295	1.7
23.3°	1.17	.026	301	3.3
29.9°	1.33	.022	313	3.9
37.6°	2.33	.022	307	4.0
47.1°	2.50	.026	367	3.3

[1] Data from Weinbach (1940).
[2] Meaning of constants: θ_m is the minimum time of ascent; k is the velocity constant of growth; t' is the age when the time of ascent is twice the minimum time; and k_0/k indicates the number of days required to accomplish a development for each incline equivalent to one day of development of creeping on a flat surface.

steeper, despite the fact that each value plotted is actually a mean of five different values, so that the irregularities cannot be attributed to isolated aberrant measures.

Thus the attempt to represent this aspect of behavioral development through a simple growth function is apparently not valid beyond a certain level of difficulty or complexity of the task, quite likely because factors other than sheer motor ability (e.g., fear, motivation) may become predominant. For the easier inclinations, on the other hand, the curve-fitting effort is quite successful and effective. It illustrates the possibilities in this regard, where (*a*) longitudinal data are collected, and (*b*) a behavioral variable, such as time, is available that is both reliable and developmentally meaningful. Note, finally, that the "developmental function" here extends only up to the age of two. This is perfectly reasonable, given the particular nature of the behavioral variable involved. Indeed, one may suggest that this curve-fitting approach will be most apt to pay dividends in cases such as this one, where the major developmental change in response is compressed into a comparatively short interval.[3]

[3] It is apparent that Weinbach's curve confounds the effects of maturation and practice. Indeed, considering the short intervals between testings, many would be inclined to call this a learning curve rather than a developmental curve. In order to settle the question, it would be necessary to compare the rate of improvement in this curve with that obtained from averaged values of children tested only at a single age (cf. Chapter VII). Whereas undoubtedly some differences would be found, it seems safe to predict that a similar curve would result (though possibly less smooth, due to the cross-sectional nature of such data).

Our second example of the application of growth curve fitting to developmental data provides a sharp contrast with Weinbach's, being much more problematical in nature. It comes from an investigation by Birch and Lefford (1963) on the development of the ability to match forms presented across different sensory modalities. The intent of these authors was mainly to show that different intersensory form matching tasks (i.e., involving different combinations of modalities) were of unequal difficulty, or more precisely that they develop at different rates, in children between the ages of 5 and 11. Their basic results are shown in Fig. 8–6. (The terms "haptic" and "kinesthetic" refer, respectively, to a condition of active exploration of the stimulus

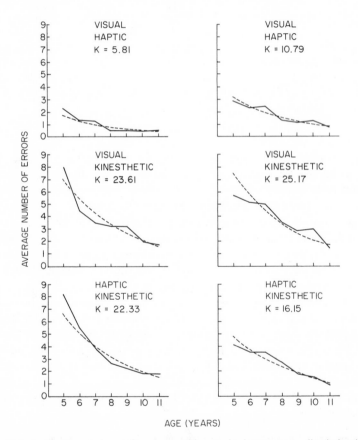

Fig. 8–6. Improvement in performance with age in intersensory discrimination, for objectively identical (left) and nonidentical (right) forms, and three conditions of intermodal matching. (——): observed; (– – –): theoretical. [Reprinted from *Monographs of the Society for Research in Child Development*, 1963, **28**, ser.no. 89, by Birch and Lefford by permission of The Society for Research in Child Development, Inc.]

outline, and to a condition in which the subject's arm was passively moved over a path describing the form of a particular stimulus.)

- The data consisted of mean numbers of errors made in making judgments of identity and difference for 72 pairings of the eight shapes used in the study, for each of the three conditions of intermodal matching. The developmental functions describing the mean errors at each age level between 5 and 11 years, cross-sectionally determined, were fitted to a simple exponential function, $y = ke^{cx}$ (misleadingly referred to as "the algebraic expression for growth"). Through a least-squares procedure, the constants of this function were determined, resulting in the equations given in Fig. 8–6 for each condition, and separated into the 16 pairings of identical stimuli and 56 pairings of nonidentical stimuli, since these yielded highly dissimilar results, as shown in Fig. 8–6. Since the values of the constant c varied very little from one function to another (the range was from $-.20$ to $-.29$), the authors assumed that this parameter was in fact fixed, and proceeded to assign the mean value of $-.243$ to it. The exponentials obtained by determining the best-fitting set of equations using this value for c are shown in Fig. 8–6, along with the curves representing these equations, that is, the dashed graphs in that figure. (The term "theoretical" for these graphs is a misnomer, since they were in fact determined by the data; even the choice of the prototype equation was suggested by the overall form of the graphs.)

While the values of the constant k describe the relative steepness of the developmental functions fairly faithfully, there is little reason to accept the proposed equation as having any intrinsic relevance to these data. First, the nature of the data, representing perfection functions, does not correspond to incremental growth, and the shape of the resulting functions is to a large extent an arbitrary consequence of the number and type of stimuli presented for judgment. Thus, the fact that all functions reach a lower asymptote by age 9 at somewhere between .5 and 2.0 errors has no meaning apart from the particular set of rather simple geometric shapes used in this study. Similarly, if a higher proportion of identical forms had been used instead of the arbitrarily chosen one of two-ninths (16 out of 72), the shapes of the "Identical Forms" functions would presumably have changed.

Furthermore, as noted in Chapter VII, cross-sectional data are not appropriately analyzed through exponential curves, owing to the distortion produced through averaging. This relates to the final point: Examination of Fig. 8–6 discloses some major discrepancies between the empirically determined function and the corresponding best-fitting exponential curve, for at least three of the six conditions (visual-kinesthetic and haptic-kinesthetic identical; visual-kinesthetic nonidentical). Yet Birch and Lefford report that chi-square tests show a probability of better than .99 of no significant difference between the observed and "theoretical" curves! Clearly this can only mean that the within age-group variation was so great that these tests became quite insensitive to major departures of the observed means from the values predicted from the exponential function. One suspects that a variety of mathematical functions, including a simple parabolic arc, or a logarithmic expression, would have fitted these data equally successfully.

The point of this extended criticism is obviously not to disparage Birch and Lefford's research, which stands quite impressively without this mathematical frosting on the cake. There is some indication that the authors have themselves become persuaded on this point, for in a follow-up study (Birch & Lefford, 1967) in which the same data are presented in comparison to some further developmental data on intersensory functioning, the growth curve-fitting model has been eschewed altogether. Rather, it is to show the limitations of such an approach, where the data that would make it appropriate are lacking. Given Birch and Lefford's data, as well as the hypotheses they were interested in testing, a much more effective and convincing approach would have been that of trend-analysis, which would presumably have revealed the differences in linear and possibly quadratic components of these curves under the various conditions. One problem that would admittedly have caused difficulty with these data would be heterogeneity of variance: The variance for the easiest condition, visual–haptic, undoubtedly is much lower than that for the other two; a negative relationship between variance and age is also to be expected for these data.

2. RATE OF CHANGE OF THE DEVELOPMENTAL FUNCTION

Whereas rate of change is but one particular aspect of a developmental function, it is of special interest in at least two respects. First, comparison of rates of change (or simply increments) at different portions of the age scale provides a particularly useful basis for determining the timing of the developmental processes implicated in the measured changes and spotting major discontinuities in the operation of these processes. Again the best example comes from the study of physical growth, namely the preadolescent growth spurt, which shows the discontinuity with particular sharpness in the rate of change function, that is, that relating increments in height to age. This is brought out in Shuttleworth's (1937) data from the Harvard growth study, as redrawn by Tanner (1962)—cf. Fig. 4–11b. That figure will remind us, incidentally, of the need for longitudinal data wherever the continuity or discontinuity in the rate of change of a function is the question at issue.

Since evidence of gross discontinuities of this kind for quantitative behavioral variables is more difficult to find, statements of changes in rate of development with age will generally be equivalent to statements about the general shape of the function, or about significant components of trend. Under some circumstances, however, special interest may attach to the timing of changes in rate, as in the study of psychological correlates of the differential rates of development between early and late maturing children.

Let us turn briefly to a second use of information concerning rate of change. It is frequently fruitful to look at differences in absolute standing between two groups (or individuals) at some point during their course of development as representing differences in *rates* of development, particularly where more than one point on the age variable is available, or where a common origin with respect to the behavioral variable in the two groups can be assumed. An example is shown in Day's (1932) comparison of the speech development of twins with that of singletons: The latter's yearly gains in length of response in the preschool period were double those of the twins. Similarly, Davis's (1937) demonstration that the difference between the two groups was considerably reduced during the elementary school years points to a subsequent acceleration of the speech development of the twins relative to that of the singletons.

In like fashion, measures of rate can be used to advantage to express the effects of special conditions of experience on development, as in the classical work on the effects of practice on early motor development, as well as in some of the Hebbian work on the effects of enrichment or deprivation of perceptual experience on behavioral development. As we shall bring out in our discussion of the study of the effects of experience in Chapter XI, the role of such experience is frequently expressed more adequately in terms of measures of rate, rather than of absolute differences at a particular point in time.

In regard to appropriate measures of rate of change, the ideal case is that in which it is possible to express a developmental function by means of a mathematical equation, since rate of change can then be determined by differentiating the equation. More generally, $\Delta X/\Delta t$, that is, the amount of change per unit of age, can be employed as a measure of rate. It has in fact found wide application in the study of physical growth (Dearborn & Rothney, 1941; Tanner, 1963), but its use assumes that the variable being measured is satisfactorily measured as an equal-interval scale, in other words, that equal differences can be treated as equivalent over the entire length of the scale. Where a quantity grows at a logarithmic or exponential rate (as is probably the case with respect to vocabulary development, for instance) the use of such increment or decrement scores is contingent on one's confidence in ruling out artifacts of the measuring instrument as the basis for the shape of the function, as well as shifts in the reliability of the measures over different portions of the scale.

3. AGE CORRESPONDING TO SPECIFIED POINTS OF THE DEVELOPMENTAL FUNCTION

Under certain circumstances the question at what age a specified point of the function is reached becomes of interest. This is true particularly with respect to the age at which growth ceases, that is, the age corresponding to the asymptotal level or maximum of the function. This question has been extensively debated in connection with the variable of intelligence, dating back at least to the early days of Thurstone (1925), who on the basis of his artificially constructed curve of intelligence decided there was no evidence of a slow-down of intellectual development even by late adolescence; Freeman and Flory (1937) came to a similar conclusion on the basis of their scale of mental ability.[4] Thurstone likewise raised the question of the origin of intelligence, as mentioned earlier in Chapter IV; it will be recalled that he found the zero point of the age function to correspond roughly to the age of conception. Conceivably, then, the absolute zero on the age scale should be located at the age of -9 months, rather than at birth. In the same vein, we may be interested in determining ages for the attainment of maximum growth, for the start of acceleration of growth (e.g., at adolescence), for the onset of decline (e.g., in old age), etc.

Note that in all of these examples age serves the function of a dependent variable, just as it is incorporated into the definition of the dependent variable in the case of the previously considered aspects of developmental functions such as shape and rate. This use of the age variable, which conforms to the approach to the conception of age formulated earlier in this book (cf. Chapter II) is shown with particular clarity where age of attainment to some specified value of a function is used as a criterial measure for differentiating groups. A good example is given in Fantz and Nevis's (1967) determination of the age at which infants first exhibit a systematic preference for the more complex of two stimuli, as a basis for comparing the perceptual development of institutionalized and home-raised infants. Paraskevopoulos and Hunt (1971) have similarly employed age of attainment of specified levels on various developmental scales as a criterion measure in comparing children raised in different institutional and home environments.

4. VALUES OF MAXIMA, MINIMA, AND TERMINAL LEVEL OF RESPONSE

At any of the determinate points of the developmental function mentioned in the previous paragraph, the level or magnitude of the response at-

[4]It might be observed that the question of the termination of development has preoccupied not only psychologists but biologists as well. For an interesting general treatment of the problem of determining whether an organism has reached adulthood, in the biological sense, see Van der Vaart (1953).

tained may become a useful parameter in terms of which to characterize an individual or group. This is true in particular with respect to terminal level of the response, which, representing the endpoint of the developmental function, can be interpreted without reference to the age level of the individual in whom it originated. For functions subject to aging effects, on the other hand, the maxima (or minima, as the case may be) reached at maturity would be the datum of major interest.

Here again the usefulness of these parameters is brought out to particular advantage when applied to assess group differences relating to experiential histories, conditions of rearing and the like. It permits us to express the effects of such variables in terms of differential attainment at maturity, rather than in terms of mean differences at some arbitrary point of the individual's development (cf. Chapter XI).

Descriptive Analysis with Respect to Qualitative Change

At the qualitative level, the equivalent of the comparison of age-group means to determine presence and direction of change, which was mentioned as the lowest form of descriptive analysis of quantitative data, is the determination of the incidence of responses of different types at each age level. This kind of information has played an important part in the classical developmental literature, notably in the areas of language (McCarthy, 1954), emotional development (Jersild, 1954), and the early research on cognitive development inspired by Piaget's work, relating to concepts of physical causality, moral judgment, etc. (cf. Russell, 1956). In a purely normative sense, it will undoubtedly continue to be of importance, in indicating dominant forms of behavior observed in children (as in inventories of fears, for example), and the major shifts with age occurring with respect to them.

Although the limitations of this type of data are similar to those cited for first-level quantitative analysis, namely the shortcomings inherent in age-group comparisons (lack of information about either the detailed characteristics of the age changes or the factors determining them), there are in the case of qualitative data fewer alternative possibilities for analyzing such data. Questions of the *form* of the developmental function are no longer applicable; they are replaced by the question of the invariant sequential patterning of a given set of qualitatively differentiated responses. That is, for such a set of responses the main descriptive task reduces to the specification of the sequence in which these behaviors appear during the course of development, together with the determination of how closely this sequence approaches to invariance over a sample of individual children. The methods for analyzing data with respect to this sequential-invariance question were considered at the end of the preceding chapter.

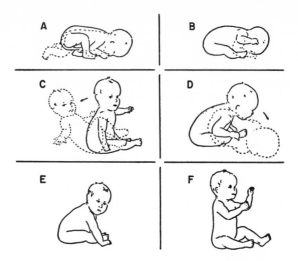

Fig. 8–7. Phases in the development of the sitting posture. [From McGraw (1943).]

One of the most impressive instances of the power of such descriptive sequential analysis is to be found in McGraw's (1943) work on sequences of motor development, with its painstakingly detailed specification of the patterns of movement and motor response displayed at successive phases of the development of the infant during the first year of life. Let us take one such sequence, concerning the development of the sitting posture, in its resistive aspect, that is, maintenance of the posture, which McGraw breaks up into six phases. These are illustrated in Fig. 8–7, and presented in abbreviated form below:

> "*Phase A, Newborn*: When the body of the newborn infant is pulled slightly beyond the right angle with respect to the surface, he exercises no appreciable resistance to gravitational force and falls forward so that his face rests on the surface near his feet. . . . Such behavior is under the dominance of subcortical nuclei.
>
> "*Phase B, Incipient Resistance*: Within a few weeks it has been observed that the infant shows a fleeting resistance against falling forward. As the axis of the body passes beyond the right angle, there may occur a few jerks back and forth, and when the infant finally falls forward until his face nears the surface, he is apt to express discomfort by crying. . . . This second phase. . . represents the beginning of an inhibitory influence upon subcortical functioning in the pelvic region.
>
> "*Phase C, Exaggerated Resistance*: Subsequently the resistance to falling forward becomes exaggerated, though the infant cannot maintain balance for any appreciable time. As soon as he is pulled into the sitting position he shows a tendency to push backward into the dorsal position. Sometimes the resistance is so marked that only with considerable pressure can the child be forced forward.
>
> "*Phase D, Trunkal Resistance*: In the subsequent phase the infant moves forward from the vertical position and remains for a few moments in a hyperflexed position,

though he does not flex so completely as in phase B. It is obvious that the trunk muscles are the ones most actively engaged in maintaining the posture. Even though the upper extremities may rest upon the underlying surface, they are not actively engaged in supporting the shoulders. Finally the child topples forward or sidewise.

"*Phase E, Sustained Resistance*: Further advancement toward the sitting posture is is clearly indicated when the child is able to maintain the leaning posture, since he supports himself on the extended upper extremities. The angle of flexion varies from time to time, and the length of time before falling over also gradually increases. As development proceeds, the angle of flexion widens and it is evident that the child depends less and less upon the supporting aid of the upper extremities.

"*Phase F, Independent Sitting*: Mature development in this activity has been defined as that stage in which the infant can maintain an erect sitting position on a flat surface, usually with one of the lower extremities flexed and abducted, while the other is fully extended in front of the body. The arms are free to engage in other movements. The position of the lower extremities provides a wider base and aids in the maintenance of equilibrium [McGraw, 1943, pp. 68–70]."

It is interesting to contrast this descriptive developmental sequence with the set of categories evolved by Parten and Newhall (1943) for the study of the development of social interaction in children during the preschool years. Based on their observations of behavior on the playground, these authors arrive at a set of six categories, as follows:

"*Unoccupied Behavior*: The child apparently is not playing at all, at least not in the usual sense, but occupies himself with watching anything which happens to be of momentary interest. When there is nothing exciting taking place, he plays with his own body, gets on and off chairs, just stands around, follows the teacher, or sits in one spot glancing around the room.

"*Solitary Play*: The child plays alone and independently with *toys that are different* from those used by the children within speaking distance and *makes no effort to get close to* or speak to the other children. His interest is centered upon his own activity, and he pursues it without reference to what others are doing.

"*Onlooker Behavior*: The child spends most of his time watching the others play. He often talks to the playing children, asks questions, or gives suggestions, but does not enter into the play himself. He stands or sits within speaking distance of the group so that he can see and hear all that is taking place. Thus he differs from the unoccupied child, who notices anything that happens to be exciting and is not especially interested in groups of children.

"*Parallel Play*: The child plays independently, but *the activity he chooses naturally brings him among other children*. He *plays with toys which are like those* which the children around him are using, but he plays with the toys as he sees fit and does not try to influence the activity of the children near him. Thus he plays *beside* rather than *with* the other children (cf. solitary play above).

"*Associative Play*: The child plays with other children. There are borrowing and lending of play material; following one another with trains and wagons; mild attempts to control which children may or may not play in the group. All engage in similar if not identical activity; there is no division of labor and no organization of activity. Each child acts as he wishes, does not subordinate his interests to the group.

"*Cooperative or Organized Supplementary Play*: The child plays in a group that is organized for the purpose of making some material product, of striving to attain some competitive goal, of dramatizing situations of adult or group life, or of playing formal games. There is a marked sense of belonging or not belonging to the group. The control of the group situation is in the hands of one or two members, who direct the activity of the others. The goal as well as the method of attaining it necessitates a division of labor, the taking of different roles by the various group members, and the organization of activity so that the efforts of one child are supplemented by those of another [Parten & Newhall, 1943, pp. 512–513, italics in the original]."

A close comparative examination of the preceding two sets of categories suggests the following: McGraw's, being obviously more molecular in its choice of behavioral units, is much closer to the raw data, as opposed to the degree of abstraction involved in the derivation of Parten and Newhall's molar behavioral categories. The latter accordingly arrive at what, to all intents and purposes, could be considered an independently scaled set of responses, that is, an ordinal scale of degree of social interaction. And yet, despite the continuity thus built into the social interaction categories themselves, the continuity of the developmental pattern, in the sense of the transformation of one behavior into the following, emerges much more sharply in the case of McGraw's categories of the maintenance of a sitting posture. This, one supposes, only reflects the fact that we are dealing here with a virtually invariant, built-in sequence, directly traceable (as McGraw convincingly traces it) to the forces at work in the neuromuscular maturation of the infant; whereas Parten and Newhall are dealing with behavior of a much more complex order, which would undoubtedly fall well short of scalability (if only because any given child would inevitably display a range of these types of social interaction behaviors at any age). But the net result is that the power of McGraw's descriptive analysis, in pointing directly to the developmental processes underlying this sequence, is well above Parten and Newhall's, who in effect provide no more than an instrument for assessing the type, and perhaps the degree of social interaction shown in the play of a child.

Lest the objection be made that this alleged advantage of McGraw's descriptive sequence derives entirely from its known neurophysiological substrate, let us note that the well-known sequences of sensorimotor development described by Piaget (1952b), for which no physiological basis could be specified at present, share fully in this power to convey the continuity of the stream of developmental change, that is, the ability to formulate each step as an outgrowth or transformation of the preceding one. Indeed, very much the same sort of comparison made above between McGraw's and Parten and Newhall's categories could be made between those which Piaget himself has given us for the analysis of the early cognitive development in infancy on the one hand, as opposed to the analysis of changes in such areas as causal reasoning and moral judgment on the other.

Along with the *form* of the developmental function, *rate of change* loses its original mathematical character for qualitative data; it retains meaning only as the amount of time taken to advance from one step or level of behavior to another. Comparisons of rates in this sense for different parts of the sequence have little meaning (e.g., one would not deduce, from the fact that the period of Piaget's sensorimotor intelligence runs its course in roughly half the time, or even less, of that of concrete operations, that cognitive development slows down following infancy). But such time values represent useful indices to compare speed of development in different individuals or groups.

In the same vein, *age of appearance* of particular types of behavior can represent a datum of interest, analogous to the age corresponding to particular points of the function, in the case of quantitative variables. As a matter of fact, information of this type has become common currency in talking about differences in the rate of development of individuals or groups with respect to certain phenomena of growth and physical development falling into the "phylogenetic" category, in McGraw's (1935) terminology, that is, those which form part of the universal experience of the developing child, presumably being genetically determined (see Campbell & Weech, 1941). Examples include age of onset of walking, toilet-training (at least in our society), menarche, etc. More recent work in infant development suggests a similar use of data on age of initial differentiation between mother and stranger, or age of formation of the "permanent object"; likewise there are indications that age of attainment of the conservations may soon be used as a datum in differentiating children in terms of the rate of their cognitive development.

Finally, as far as terminal level of development is concerned, it becomes of interest only in isolated instances, namely where groups or individuals vary in the portion of a particular developmental sequence which they traverse. For example, certain cultures or groups lacking formal schooling beyond childhood do not reach the stage of formal operations, as Piaget (Inhelder & Piaget, 1958) has described it, but might be categorized in terms of the highest level attained on some particular prototype task selected from those studied by Inhelder and Piaget. Similarly, Woodward's work on the stages of sensorimotor development observed in severely subnormal children up to 16 years of age (Woodward, 1959; Woodward & Stern, 1963) can be reinterpreted as a study of the terminal level of development attained by these children, if we assume—as seems reasonable, at least for the older among her subjects—that their development has been arrested at the level displayed in these studies.

QUALITATIVE DESCRIPTION AS A COMPLEMENT TO QUANTITATIVE
INFORMATION

One particular use of qualitative data on developmental change occurs as an adjunct to or elaboration of quantitative information. Here the intent is generally to enhance the meaning or establish the correct interpretation of the basis for some observed quantitative change. Used in this fashion, the qualitative data do not necessitate the postulation of a determinate developmental sequence, and can be effectively used on a cross-sectional basis, in conjunction with similar age-group comparison data of a quantitative type. However, when the qualitative data are interpreted as *explaining* the quantitative changes, questions of cause–effect relations arise which warrant closer scrutiny.

The major question to be faced in evaluating qualitative evidence used in this fashion is its relation to the criterial response measures which it is intended to elucidate. Here we may distinguish among four types of information.

a. Response-Pattern Analysis. In this case the responses analyzed are identical with those entering into the quantitative criterial measure, but they are classified in qualitative terms, to reveal patterns or strategies of response, or differences in response (e.g., types of errors) not taken into account in the quantitative measure. The best example is provided by the recent work on probability learning, notably the use by Weir (1964) and others of indices of response strategy (spatial response patterns; systematic reactions to reward versus nonreward, etc.) which succeeded in placing data on asymptotal response rate in a different light. Differentiations in terms of types of errors made on a concept formation task (e.g., Osler & Kofsky, 1966) or in terms of differential patterns of acquisition of the components of a task [e.g., Kempler's (1964) study of serial learning] fall into the same category. The essential feature of qualitative data of this kind is that they are based on the same behavior from which the quantitative measure is derived, so that questions of functional interrelationships between the two do not arise. The two sets are simply complementary aspects of the observed responses, and frequently (as in Weir's case) the qualitative measures of pattern come to supplant the quantitative, presumably because the age changes observed with respect to the former are more meaningful (in terms of other known facts about development), or easier to interpret.

b. Analysis of Overt Mediating Responses. In certain types of tasks, it is possible to record overt behaviors which, given the requirements of the task, can be assumed to play a mediating role in relation to the criterial measure of performance. This is true, in particular, of certain perceptual tasks in which orienting or exploratory behavior is recorded. A notable example is Vurpillot's (1968) study of children's ability to judge pairs of complex visual patterns as identical or different, in which records were obtained of the scanning patterns which the children displayed in exploring the stimuli. The measures of scanning recorded were themselves in part quantitative (e.g., number of different parts of each stimulus of a pair fixated), but these served as the basis for a qualitative categorization of the children into one of three scanning-"strategy" groups: searching for difference, searching for identity, and unsystematic. For the children in the first two groups (which included all but three children out of 60 above the age of 4 years) a clear relation was found between their scanning strategy and their differential performance on objectively identical and objectively different stimulus pairs. In the same vein, we may cite Abravanel's (1968) research on the development of intersensory discrimination performance, in which developmental changes in accuracy of performance were studied in correlation with the child's mode of handling and tactually exploring the stimuli he had to discriminate.

In cases of this type, where the observed mediating behavior is logically prior to the criterial response, causal inferences seem justified, providing it is psychologically plausible to suggest a functional relationship between them. Thus, while the two behaviors may still in principle be unrelated, if we do find them to be closely associated this can be taken as presumptive evidence for a causal link. Accordingly, the interpretation of the basis for the age changes in the criterial measure has been pushed back at least one step to a formulation in terms of some intervening mechanism.

The question may well be raised, what about verbal mediating responses? If we find differences, for example, in discrimination-learning performance, linked with differential verbalization of the stimuli or other aspects of the task during the course of its solution, would this not be just as presumptive evidence of a mediating link? There are several reasons for caution in this regard. First, reliance on spontaneous verbalization may be hazardous and unproductive, whereas under enforced verbalization the task is not only obviously altered, but variation in these mediating responses is effectively eliminated, thus resulting in a loss of their potential interest for the explanation of criterial-response variance.

Various empirical findings, furthermore, have brought into question the role actually played by verbal responses given by children during the course of a discrimination-learning or problem-solving task whether spontaneously emitted or elicited from them. Thus, Flavell, Beach, and Chinsky (1966) and Keeney, Cannizzo, and Flavell (1967) have shown convincingly in their work, involving the monitoring of the vocal production behavior during the course of a memory task, that children below about the age of 8 years give little evidence of engaging in any detectable verbalization such as might aid them in recalling in correct order short series of familiar stimuli presented previously, even though they know the appropriate verbal labels for them. The second of the above-mentioned studies indicated, moreover, that while children at this age could be trained to verbalize the stimuli, such responses were quickly extinguished once no longer demanded of them. We might point further to the curious finding by Kendler (1964), that verbalizations deliberately elicited from kindergarten-age children, far from mediating the instrumental response, frequently were in direct conflict with that response. Thus children who were made to verbalize the rule in a brightness discrimination-learning series during the training phase ("white wins, black loses"), kept right on verbalizing this rule intact during a transfer series in which their discrimination behavior had showed a reversal shift (e.g., choice of the black stimulus of each pair)!

Finally, the assumption that verbal responses mediate the criterial responses can be challenged on logical grounds, at least in a task such as discrimination learning problems, where it is just as plausible to argue that spontaneous verbal responses are a *result* of the achievement of the criterial behavior (i.e., a consistent response to the larger of two stimuli), or perhaps of the perceptual recognition of the relationship among the stimuli. This point applies with particular force to the role of verbalization in transposition, as in the classical study by Kuenne (1946) in which it was argued that the intervention of verbal labeling, that is, of verbal "control" over behavior, somehow changes the type of individual from one obeying simple S-R discrimination-learning and generalization principles to one responding on a very different basis, displaying essentially flat gradients of generalization. Kendler's (1963, 1965) interpretation of the apparent age shift in performance on discrimination-reversal problems places a similar, and similarly unwarranted causal burden on the role of verbalization.

For these several reasons, verbalization behavior is best regarded under the class of qualitative responses to be considered next, which may be correlated with the criterial response, but where causal mediation linkage is more uncertain than it is in the case of the orienting and exploration behavior referred to at the beginning of this section.

c.   Analysis of Correlated Qualitative Indices of Task Behavior.   In many situations, it is possible to record behavior exhibited by the subject during the course of his performance on a task which, while it does not play a direct mediating role in the sense of the behavior just referred to, does reveal qualitative differences in mode of approach to a task, in strategies of solution, or in attitude or set adopted toward it, so as to provide clues toward the interpretation of the age differences found with respect to the criterial response. An excellent example of this kind is provided by a study by Rand *et al.* (1963), on age differences in performance on the Stroop Color–Word interference test. By analyzing detailed taped records of all of the verbal behavior emitted by each subject during the course of his performance (which, as will be recalled, requires the subject to name the colors of a series of stimuli, when these stimuli are themselves words signifying colors incongruous with that of the ink in which they are printed), Rand *et al.* were able to specify different types of behaviors used by the subject in coping with this task, which played differential roles at different age levels. For instance, word-reading (i.e., naming the word rather than the color in which it is printed) increased from 6 to 9 years, and sharply decreased from 12 to 16 years; whereas inappropriate color responses other than word-reading, and contaminated responses (made up of combinations of colors, e.g., "brue," "breen,") decreased steadily with age. Inserted nonlinguistic utterances, on the other hand (emitting sounds such as "uh," "um," etc.) steadily increased with age. This kind of evidence led the authors to the conclusion that the marked decrease with age in the children's time-scores,[5] that is, their increased proficiency of performance, reflected an increase in the ability to maintain the task set in the face of a competing response-set.

A number of other examples of a similar sort could be given, sometimes taking the form of spontaneous verbalizations, for example, on discrimination-learning tasks, sometimes of affective responses to a task [e.g., Gellerman's (1931) study of adaptation to a double-alternation maze]. In this case, we can be less sure about the causal links involved, but the observed behaviors may nevertheless be used to provide plausible guesses as to the basis for observed age differences on the criterial behavior.

d. Analysis of Ex Post Facto Verbalizations. In many studies of discrimination-learning, problem-solving, concept-formation, and the like, the investigator elicits verbal responses from the subject at the end of the experiment which are designed to reveal the basis on which he responded, his understanding of a rule or principle, or the process by which he approached the task. These responses may vary all the way from a single word (e.g., in answer to a question such as "Which block always had the candy?") to lengthy protocols of open-ended responses given to postexperimental inquiries in which the subject is invited to explain his behavior during the task or his mode of attack on a problem.

---

[5]Here again, as in the very similar data of Comalli, Wapner, and Werner (1962), we face the question of the most appropriate way of expressing the age difference in the interference effect to which we referred in the discussion of the linearity problem in Chapter IV. Again, the use of ratios rather than differences (between the base line color-naming times and times on the interference task) would cause the age differences to vanish; in fact, this ratio is smallest (1.8) for the youngest group, maximal (2.9) at age 9, and intermediate in the two oldest groups.

Because of the *ex post facto* nature of these responses, the assumption that they provide information as to the processes used by the subject which determined his criterial responses is frequently questionable. Even the simple responses given at the end of a transposition or concept-formation experiment may frequently be unreliable indices of the basis for the subject's behavior during the course of the experiment—especially when the subject is a young child. On the one hand, failure to verbalize cannot be taken at face value as indicating a lack of availability of the concept or rule, or a failure of the child to respond on a conceptual basis. Just as surely, however, there is often reason to distrust such verbalizations given upon demand at the termination of the experimental session as actually explaining the child's behavior during the task. A quote from the above-cited study on the relationship between language and transposition by Kuenne (1946) may serve to illustrate this point: "The occurrence out loud of such verbal behavior in the learning or transposition series invariably was followed by transposition on the far test . . . In contrast, 43% of those who made such verbalizations only upon questioning at the conclusion of the experiment transposed on the far series with this consistency [pp. 487f]." Kuenne, with some plausibility, attributes the cases of the remaining 57% of the children who verbalized but failed to transpose consistently to what we would now call "mediation deficiency [Reese, 1962]." Yet, the point her findings bring out is a more general one, that is, that verbalizations given at the end of an experiment upon questioning by the investigator are a far from infallible guide to the basis for the child's behavior during the experiment.

These critical comments are not intended to dismiss the potential useful-ness of data of this type, provided the *post hoc* explanations given to interpret them are treated as hunches, to be followed up subsequently by more direct tests of the bases for children's responses, for example, by obtaining data falling into one of the three previously discussed types, and which are thus not subject to the limitations of *ex post facto* data when used to account for behavior given previously.

In conclusion, it is worth pointing out that there is no necessary corres-pondence between the quantitative–qualitative distinction and the process-achievement distinction (Werner, 1937) implied in the preceding discussion of the use of qualitative information to supplement quantitative data. That is, while developmental psychologists, as well as others concerned about the latter distinction have generally favored qualitative over quantitative data as somehow better attuned to the investigator's desire for information as to the psychological process underlying some observed behavioral end-product, it is entirely conceivable to have situations in which this relationship is reversed, that is, in which quantitative data are obtainable to provide process information related to a qualitatively defined end-product. An apt illustration is the use of visual fixation data in conjunction with the study of conservation responses (O'Bryan & Boersma, 1971), relating the number of times that the dominant perceptual dimension in a liquid-conservation problem was fixated to the level (preoperational, transitional, and operational) of the response given by the child.

CHAPTER IX
The Study of Developmental Stages

> *... discreteness of levels of thinking age by age was emphatically not found. Each type of thinking was found to extend over the entire age range studied, suggesting that causality does not develop in saltatory stages.*
> —WATSON, *1965, pp. 490f.*

The quote that appears above, taken from an account of Deutsche's (1937) well-known study on the development of causality in a standard child psychology text, was characteristic of American child psychologists' thinking about the problem of stages until relatively recently. The very concept appeared foreign to psychologists predominantly inclined to think in terms of discrete responses rather than constructs, and in the absence of a structural model of behavior the notion of discontinuity or qualitative change was difficult to accept.

The situation has changed markedly over the past decade, as the cognition revolution has taken hold, and stage concepts are met with greater tolerance, if not always understanding. Nor are they limited to the realm of Piagetian phenomena, though that is where the issue has been fought out, as well as thought through most intensively. Thus a perusal of McNeill's (1970) account of the structural-linguistics approach to the study of child language makes it plain that in that domain as well development is thought of as taking place in stages. This is hardly surprising, based as this approach is on Chomsky's structural model of language, which in its attack on developmental questions displays many features that are closely analogous to Piaget's system.

But it is the continuing concern over Piaget's system that has been responsible for the most concerted efforts to come to grips with the stage problem, at the level of broad philosophical and epistemological analysis, as well as of particulars of methodology. Suffice it to refer to some of the main discussions of the question up to the present: Kessen (1962), Wohlwill (1963c), Flavell and Wohlwill (1969), Pinard and Laurendeau (1969), Flavell (1970, 1971). These treatments have certainly advanced our thinking far beyond the avoidance of the issue reflected in the quote at the start of the chapter. But in a sense we might say that we are now deep into the woods, and it is by no means clear yet whether, let alone how, we shall find our way out of it.

A large part of the problem stems from the lack of agreement as to the meaning of stages, and as to the descriptive as opposed to explanatory status that should be accorded to it. Nor is this disagreement in discussions concerning stages rife only on the American scene, where the typical attitude toward the concept has been one of skepticism born as much of misunderstanding as of mistrust of the connotations of discontinuity and maturational basis that surround it. A perusal of a European symposium devoted to the topic (Osterrieth, 1956) discloses no more consensus, nor appreciably greater sensitivity to the issues involved.

The insertion of a chapter on stages in this particular place of our volume is intended to recognize at once the essentially descriptive manner in which the concept has been generally applied in the past, as it still is in many uses of the term, and the possibilities for strengthening it by applying it to account for systematic forms of *interpatterning* among sets of developing responses. Thus, when used in the latter sense, the methodology of stage research will be found to represent a special case of the correlational approach in the study of development, applied to qualitatively rather than quantitatively scaled data. Accordingly, this chapter and the following may in many respects be considered to represent parallel treatments of a common problem: interrelationships or communalities among developmental systems are undergoing change simultaneously. More specific points of contact between the two chapters will be noted at pertinent points.

Stage as a Horizontal-Structure Concept

STAGE VERSUS SEQUENCE

In a previous discussion of the stage concept, Flavell and Wohlwill (1969) noted that the stage concept attains maximal usefulness when it is used in reference to a *set* of behaviors intermediate in specificity between the case of an isolated response (e.g., crawling) and the case of a completely non-specific array of behaviors associated with a given age level, such as infancy or adolescence. Individual responses may still be subject to development in sequential fashion, as illustrated in the various motor sequences of behavior studied by McGraw (1943), Shirley (1931a), Gesell and Ames(1940) and others. Such developmental sequences have, in the past, been identified with, or at least assimilated to the concept of stages, mainly because they appeared to point to a set of qualitative changes in behavior. Fundamentally, however, they refer only to *dimensions* of development defined in terms of a set of discrete, nominally-scaled points, as discussed in Chapter VI. The stage concept, on the other hand, is most profitably reserved for nodal interrelationships among two or more qualitatively defined variables developing apace; conceptual links among these behavioral dimensions allow each stage to be defined in terms of a set of behaviors sharing some feature in common. In other words, "stage" is taken as a construct within a structurally defined system, having the property of unifying a set of behaviors. This is indeed the main benefit to be anticipated from its application to developmental data, and its main claim to any but a purely descriptive status.

In view of the frequently expressed skepticism concerning the need for or value of such a construct, it is worthwhile to attempt a more precise statement of this point, to guide us in the somewhat labyrinthine discussion of this problem to follow. The underlying assumption is that in certain areas of development, particularly in the cognitive realm, but not necessarily confined to it, there exist regulating mechanisms that modulate the course of the individual's development so as to ensure a degree of harmony and integration in his functioning over a variety of related behavioral dimensions. The mechanism might be thought of in part as a mediational generalization process, permitting acquisitions in one area, for example number conservation, to spread both to equivalent aspects of different concepts (e.g., conservation of length) and to different aspects of the same concept (e.g., cardinal–ordinal correspondence). The result is the formation of a broad structural network of interrelated concepts appearing, not all at once to be sure, but within a fairly narrowly delimited period, with further progress along any component concept or dimension being assumed to be deferred till the consolidation of this network—that is, the attainment of the "stage." Stage development thus provides for *relative* consistency of behavior, economy in the acquisition of new responses, and harmony and interrelatedness in the development of diverse concepts or skills across successive levels.

This is not of course the only way one might look at the stage concept, though it will turn out to be of heuristic value in the treatment of methodological issues in the study of stages to follow. But since the concept has been employed in such diverse ways, an overview of the major types of stage systems is called for at the outset. This overview will at the same time serve to enlarge the consideration of this topic beyond the all too confining limits of Piaget's system which, as noted previously, has virtually come to preempt the use of the term, and our thinking concerning it. The following uses of developmental stages will be taken up: Shirley's stages of motor development, Erikson's stages of personality development, Kohlberg's stages of moral judgment, Piaget's stages of sensorimotor development in infancy. Each of these can be represented graphically, to indicate the structural implications of stage as used by each of the investigators mentioned. Fig. 9–1 contains these schematic representations; their meaning and rationale will of course be clarified as each is discussed in turn, but they are presented here jointly to facilitate comparison among them, and to bring out the dimensions of horizontal and vertical structuredness in terms of which they may be differentiated.

a. Shirley's Motor Sequence. The common confusion between stages and sequences is well illustrated in the case of the well-known sequence of behaviors characteristic of the development of locomotion in infancy, as described by Shirley (1931a). Although frequently referred to as a sequence of *stages*, there is very little basis for doing so. The set of highly concrete, specific motor response patterns which Shirley described are no more than a series of qualitatively differentiated modes of motoric activity which appear in a predictable order during the course of the development of the infant (cf. Fig. 9–1, and Fig. 4–3). There is no more reason to label each of these responses as a "stage" than there is, for example, to apply that term to places on the itinerary of a bus line.

The readiness of writers—incidentally, on both sides of the fence as regards to acceptance or rejection of the stage concept—to fall prey to this lapse in semantic usage probably reflects the original association of the stage concept with qualitative change generally, along perhaps with the common use of the term to designate simply a delimited portion of a temporal process or sequence of events (e.g., "at this stage of the game"). It is to be noted, however, that the workers active in the flourishing field of the study of early motor development (Gesell, McGraw, Shirley) placed very little emphasis on this term as a scientific concept, relegating it apparently to a purely descriptive status, without any surplus meaning, or connotations of a structurally defined construct. Thus, while we do encounter the term in Gesell's popular writings, it is significantly absent from an early theoretical paper by him on motor development (Gesell, 1929). Similarly, Shirley uses the term loosely, and obviously interchangeably with "steps" in her description of the original "motor sequence" research (Shirley, 1931a), but again makes no use of it either in her theoretical paper on the sequential method (Shirley, 1931b) or in her review of motor development in infancy (Shirley, 1933). The same applies to McGraw (1943), who prefers the term "phase," which we shall encounter again in Erikson's system; in this case it suggests a lack of definition, in the

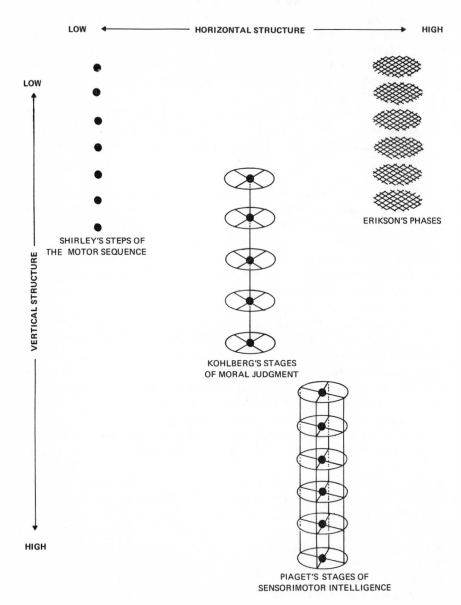

Fig. 9–1. Schematic representation of different systems of developmental stages, categorized in terms of the degree of elaboration of horizontal and vertical structure in the system.

temporal as well as the behavioral sense, which does not do justice to the sharply demarcated sequences which McGraw presents. Her sequences are in fact close cousins to Shirley's motor sequence, and would thus have similarly warranted the use of the term "steps." But it is equally apparent that McGraw did not intend any larger theoretical significance to be attached to her phases.

Note that the placement of Shirley's sequence on the upper left portion of Fig. 9–1, indicating absence of both horizontal and vertical structure, does not mean that the sequence is a purely random or fortuitous one. Undoubtedly, as Shirley (1931b) argues with some plausibility, there are sound reasons at the level of the maturation of the neurological mechanisms controlling these motor responses, for their appearance in the order observed. But the responses themselves bear no clear structural relationship one to the other—for example, "walk when led," "pull to stand by furniture," "climb stair steps," "stand alone."

This point leads to a reasonable question: What is the reason for the gap in the lower left-hand corner of Fig. 9–1? Are sequences devoid of horizontal structure *necessarily* also devoid of vertical structure? In principle, it is difficult to see why this should be so, but this writer was unable to find a convincing example fitting this particular category. Probably the nearest approach to it would be a sequence of responses such as those devised by proponents of the programmed learning approach to induce a given cognitive skill. The work of Gagné (1962, 1968) on the teaching of mathematical rules, and the learning of conservation, respectively, is a good case in point, but of course this work is conceived of entirely outside of the framework of developmental stages. Furthermore, Gagné (1970) himself insists that this approach provides for a degree of horizontal generalizability of the component skills, though as a general rule programmed learning at least of the linear, Skinnerian variety, has tended to neglect this aspect.

b. Erikson's Phases of Personality Development.   Erikson's (1959) developmental system represents in essence an elaboration of the stages of psychosexual development proposed by Freud, with a notable amplification at the adult end. Here again, there is a significant terminological equivocation, stages being used interchangeably with "phases," and the latter term being in fact preferred in the delineation of the specific features of each. "Phase" does indeed sound more appropriate to designate the very broad, not to say diffuse regions or zones of the life cycle which Erikson differentiates. As an examination of his "Worksheet of Developmental Phases" (see Table 9–1) even more than his epigenetic chart itself indicates, each phase refers to a constellation of emotions, feelings, and dispositions which do not have any direct reference to overt behavior patterns. Each phase seems intended to be

TABLE 9–1

Erikson's "Worksheet of Developmental Patterns"

	A Psychosocial crises	B Radius of significant relations	C Related elements of social order	D Psychosocial modalities	E Psychosexual stages
I	Trust versus Mistrust	Maternal person	Cosmic order	To get To give in return	Oral-respiratory, sensory-kinesthetic (incorporative modes).
II	Autonomy versus Shame, doubt	Parental persons	"Law and order"	To hold (on) To let (go)	Anal-urethral, muscular (retentive-eliminative)
III	Initiative versus Guilt	Basic family	Ideal prototypes	To make (= going after) To "make like" (= playing)	Infantile-genital, locomotor (intrusive, inclusive).
IV	Industry versus Inferiority	"Neighborhood," school	Technological elements	To make things (= completing) To make things together	"Latency."
V	Identity and repudiation versus Identity diffusion	Peer groups and outgroups; models of leadership	Ideological perspectives	To be oneself (or not to be) To share being oneself	Puberty.
VI	Intimacy and solidarity versus Isolation	partners in friendship, sex, competition, cooperation	Patterns of cooperation and competition	To lose and find oneself in another	Genitality.
VII	Generativity versus Self-absorption	Divided labor and shared household	Currents of education and tradition	To make be To take care of	
VIII	Integrity versus Disgust, despair	"Mankind" "My Kind"	Wisdom	To be, through having been To face not being	

SOURCE: Reprinted with permission from E. H. Erikson, "Identity and the Life Cycle: Selected Papers." *Psychological Issues* (Monograph), New York: International Universities Press, 1959, I:1.

useful mainly in describing commonly encountered sources and types of emotional conflict in the growing individual's personal and interpersonal life, and ordering these along the various segments of the life cycle.

Because of the very broadness and nonspecificity of Erikson's system, the question of the meaning and implications of his use of the stage concept hardly arises. Even the picture of a sharply differentiated series of levels conveyed by the schematic representation of the system in Fig. 9–1 is faulty; instead of a series of planes, a set of partially intersecting elliptoids, with fuzzily demarcated borders, would have been more appropriate. In any event, no ramifications of a structural nature emanate from this system, and it is difficult to discern any questions answerable in concrete terms that it would pose, except for the verification of the suggested thematic sequence of crises (or simply states), and perhaps the descriptive specification of the common modes of expression of these in different children, or for different interpersonal contexts.

This picture of Erikson's system, it should be noted, is vastly over-simplified. It fails to do justice to his attempt to incorporate interindividual variation in development, and abnormalities or disturbances in the normal developmental pattern in particular, in terms of a two-dimensional grid in which a horizontal dimension of behavioral *modes* is added to the vertical one of stages. The matrix is arranged so that normal development can be thought of as progress along the diagonal, while disturbances at any point may deflect the individual's further developmental course to off-diagonal cells, in a manner which Loevinger (1966b) considers analogous to the case of embryological development. The structural properties of this aspect of Erikson's system remain only sketchily and unsystematically worked out, and it is difficult even to determine to what extent the "binary fission" branching model which Van den Daele (1969) believes to be implied by Erikson's formulation does in fact represent his thinking in regard to alternative developmental channels. In any event, this is mainly a question of the form of deviations from the typical, or perhaps rather ideal sequence of stages; the latter does appear to conform to the succession of loosely structured behavioral layers just described.

c. Kohlberg's Stages of Moral Development.   On the basis of a structural cognitive theory of the development of moral judgment in children elaborated from Piaget's (1932) pioneer work in this area, Kohlberg (1969; see also Turiel, 1969) has postulated a set of six stages, representing successive modes of reasoning with respect to moral-conflict situations, which he argues conform to all of the criteria for the stage concept advanced by Piaget (1956, 1960), that is, sequentiality, hierarchical integration of lower into higher levels, gradual consolidation of stages in formation, structural whole character (unifying interrelated behaviors, concepts or skills) and equilibration. In the case of Kohlberg's stages, there is some empirical support for the sequential character of this scale, although it should be noted that we are dealing here with a disjunctive rather than a cumulative scale. Kohlberg's main way of circumventing this problem has been to obtain data on children's *comprehension* of responses representing the six levels, which he has shown to be indeed scalable in the Guttman sense. It would be of interest, nevertheless, to apply one of the disjunctive scaling methods to moral-judgment data, which would provide more direct evidence on this question. The fact, emphasized by Kohlberg, that children spread themselves over several adjacent stages in their responses to different parallel items, would make it easy to subject such data to analysis by either Wohlwill's (1963b) or Leik and Mathew's (1968) methods.

But once we turn to the structurization criterion, one wonders whether there is any systematic interrelationship between the responses to his set of moral judgment items that would warrant the use of the stage concept with respect to them. As pointed out already, sequentiality is not enough. But Kohlberg argues that there are both logical and empirical grounds for accepting this set of stages as structural wholes. On the logical side, he invokes the cognitive character of the underlying theory from which the system of scoring responses to the moral-conflict items is derived, and more specifically, the formal similarity among responses to different items belonging in the same stage. The empirical evidence is, unfortunately, less compelling.

Kohlberg relies, mainly, on an analysis of intrasubject variability in the levels scored for his responses to a standard set of five different moral judgment situations, using data both of his own and from a further study by Turiel (see Turiel, 1969, for the presentation and discussion of this evidence). Turiel states a five-step hypothesis concerning the changes to be expected in this variability (which he terms "stage mixture"), according to which variability starts low, increases during the period in which the lower stages are being structured, then decreases as they become consolidated, only to increase again markedly as the individual moves into the higher stages of moral judgment. Eventually, that is in adulthood, these become stabilized in turn, leading to a final level characterized by relatively low mixture.

In the absence of longitudinal data, the information is confined to mean variation scores found in different populations at various ages. Most of the data are obtained from three age groups, aged 10, 13, and 16 years, respectively; but data from a dissertation by Kramer (1968) on a more nearly continuous sampling of ages in the range from 14 to 26 years are also included. Turiel relies on a variation score which is essentially equivalent to the average absolute deviation from the mean, except that modal level is used in preference to the mean as the central tendency measure around which the variation is determined. These do conform to expectations, increasing with age from 10 to 16 years in children in the lower stages (I, II, and III in Kohlberg's scheme) and staying high in the same age range for those children who have reached the higher stages (IV, V, and VI). In older subjects (Kramer's group), they decrease again for those who are in the higher stages, but those still remaining in the lower stages remain relatively high, that is, fail to show the stabilization which Turiel had predicted should occur as that stage is achieved.[1] Furthermore, there is no evidence of such stabilization in the younger groups. In this respect, the procedure of dichotomizing the stages into lower versus higher seems suspect since it obscures essential information. Thus, at the lower stages one would look for Stage III subjects to start showing the drop in "stage-mixture" postulated by Turiel—assuming that within each of the two broad categories of low versus high stages, the individual stages are still intended to retain their meaning as representing points on the developmental scale of moral judgment.

The main weakness of the Kohlberg–Turiel approach to the structurization criterion resides, however, in the measure employed, which is of course simply a measure of behavioral variability lacking any structural significance, since it fails to deal with the *patterning* of responses. We shall have occasion later in this chapter to elaborate on this central point, and to show what sorts of measures and data-analysis strategies are called for to recover this type of information. But even prior to that treatment, it is worth dwelling on a major limitation of Kohlberg's system, which reduces the value of the stage concept as a heuristic tool of more than descriptive significance.

Kohlberg has in effect, like Shirley, constructed a *six-step sequence* of moral judgments. To be sure, these steps represent generalized modes of thinking, rather than discrete responses, and to that extent the use of the stage concept with reference to Kohlberg's system is justified, and profitable. Yet, while they remain clearly enough defined and their application narrowly enough circumscribed to have a determinate behavioral core, in comparison to the diffuseness of Erikson's much broader set of phases, there is no structural network that would tie together the sets of responses manifested at one level with those manifested at another. The situation is represented in Fig. 9–2. We see, then, that in this system "stage-mixture" is a function simply of the sampling of diverse contents, and thus reflects nothing more than behavior oscillation. Thus, it would be pointless to attempt to chart the interrelationship between a given child's development with respect to two or

[1]The situation is confused by the fact that two of the graphs bearing on this question, Fig. 5.2b and 5.6b of Turiel's paper, contain two different functions widely separated in absolute magnitude of variation scores, though ostensibly (i.e., in terms of the figure captions, as well as the legends identifying the groups) representing the same groups.

more of the items used by Kohlberg, since the interpatterning of the responses to them is of limited significance, except as an indication of the homogeneity of the item domain. In this respect his stages represent a rather more primitive, that is, more loosely structured construct, than Piaget's.

  d. Piaget's Stages of Sensorimotor Development. Considering the numerous discussions of Piaget's use of the stage concept in his work on the development of operational thought, there has been a surprising lack of interest in the application of this concept to his work on sensorimotor development in infancy. This neglect is all the more unfortunate, since the opportunity to trace and analyze the specifics of stages-in-formation should be optimal, at least in principle, for two reasons: First, because the process takes place over a more narrowly delimited set of differentiable series of responses—in contrast to the eight groupings differentiated by Piaget in his analysis of concrete operations, and the almost unlimited number of concrete tasks or situations in which any one of these could be studied. Second, because within each separable aspect of sensorimotor development there is a more clearly and finely differentiated sequence of steps on which to base an empirical study of the stage problem.

  Despite this fact, empirical analyses of this aspect of Piaget's theory have been very limited in number (in comparison either to the proliferating body of research on conservation and other concrete-operational concepts, or for that matter, to the mushrooming literature on behavioral development in infancy generally), and have been largely confined to attempts to construct scales for assessing cognitive development in infancy (Escalona & Corman, 1967; Uzgiris & Hunt, 1966) and to studies of the sequential character of the modes of response which Piaget has described (Miller, Cohen, & Hill, 1970; White, 1969).

  There is, admittedly, a question whether the six levels of response which Piaget has specified for several domains of behavior (general sensorimotor intelligence, formation of the permanent object, response to relations of time, space, and causality, and imitative behavior) do indeed conform to the criteria stipulated for the existence of stages. In particular, is there a structural basis to these behavior hierarchies, analogous to that underlying Piaget's formulation of concrete- and formal-operational thought, such that the developmental changes in the various realms can in fact be placed into one-for-one correspondence? Piaget (1954b) presents the material on object formation, time, space, and causality in terms of six-phase sequences which are intended to parallel those contained in the original volume on general sensorimotor intelligence (Piaget, 1952b), and his discussion of them suggests that he considers them all a part of one and the same process of structural change in the early cognitive development of the individual. Just as in his work on concrete operations, Piaget on repeated occasions makes cross-references from one of these several sequences to another, but he does not seem to lay as much stress on the equivalence in the ages at which corresponding levels of responses in different sequences are observed, or to insist on the necessary temporal synchrony of behaviors, as he does repeatedly throughout his work on concrete operations. In the present instance, such comparisons might have been all the more appropriate, given the fact that the same subjects—Piaget's own children—were the source for all of the observations; whereas in the concrete-operational work the children studies for one concept or operation typically came from a different group from those included in the study of the other concept to which cross reference is made. On the other hand, in some cases at least (e.g., the causality sequence) the discrepancies in the ages at which phenomena representing equivalent stages from different domains are observed are quite considerable, that is, horizontal "decalages" are the rule.

There is, as already noted, no study of infant development that is addressed to this question, possibly because the formidable problems of infant assessment would preclude obtaining the kind of consistent response records that one would require. White (1969) reports some deviations of the empirical from the theoretically expected (i.e., according to Piaget) *forms* of the behaviors subsumed under these stages, but this discrepancy applied mainly to one stage, where a greater variety of responses to the situation (object-in-hand) appeared than the schemata allowed for by Piaget. Miller, Cohen, and Hill (1970) have likewise questioned certain of Piaget's assertions concerning sequential emergence of particular responses—notably the assumption that response to invisible displacements necessarily follows that to visible ones—according to Miller *et al.*, this is true only for situations in which no object movement is involved. However, their study was actually designed as a replication of a very limited portion of Uzgiris and Hunt's (1966) investigation, involving just one of the latter's set of scales, that dealing with visual pursuit and object permanence. Thus Miller *et al.'s* results relate to the 15-item set drawn from that scale, rather than to Piaget's set of six stages. At the same time, their failure to confirm scalability for these items reflects in large measure their procedure of working with overlapping sets of eight items administered to infants in three narrowly defined age groups (6–8, 10–12, and 14–18 months old). It is not surprising to find less than perfect scalability when a set of items that clearly constitutes a very "dense" sampling of the dimension of infant cognitive development is tested over such a narrow age range.[2]

[2]The data of Miller *et al.* provide, incidentally, a convincing demonstration of the difficulty of "beating chance," when working with Green's index of consistency. The observed reproducibility coefficients for the three age groups included in this study range from .83 to .89; however, the corresponding chance reproducibility values are almost as high (.76 to .88), with the result that the values calculated for Green's index are all of negligible magnitude.

We do, however, have one study (Woodward, 1959) relating to Piaget's stages of sensorimotor development which contains data of more direct relevance to their structural aspect, in the sense of consistency of performance across different domains. It is, paradoxically, a study not of infants, but rather of severe cases of mental deficiency (the subjects were mostly categorized as idiots who, while varying in age between 7 and 16 years, had failed to achieve a basal age of two years on the Terman–Merrill scale). The very fact that Woodward was able to classify these subjects in terms of Piaget's sensorimotor stages, on the basis of their responses to several sets of tests taken from Piaget's observations is itself remarkable, attesting both to the extreme degree of these children's impairment and to the deep-seated character of these behaviors as true developmental bench marks.[3] But the feature of this study that is of main interest for us is that it provides information on the children's performance on several separable components of the development of sensorimotor intelligence—circular reactions, grasping or "problem solving" (involving responses to objects that could be made accessible to the child by the removal of a screen, or the use of a tool), and formation of the permanent object. Thus, the subject's assignment to stages of sensorimotor intelligence with respect to circular reactions was tabulated in relation to their stages for grasping and problem solving, though no clear rationale is given for combining these particular classes of behavior into one scale; the same was done for a composite measure of sensorimotor intelligence involving grasping (Stage II), secondary circular reactions (Stage III) and problem solving (Stages IV to VI), in association with stages in the formation of the permanent object.

Though these particular comparisons and the selection of items entering into them seem arbitrary, it is interesting to examine the outcome of these analyses, presented via contingency tables, that is, Tables 9–2a and 9–2b. They do show a rather strong association, particularly in the case of the latter, where 83% of the children fell into one of the diagonal cells (exact correspondence of stages).

If nothing else, information of this type points to a definite communality in the various behaviors classified as belonging to one and the same stage, which is precisely what the structural, or *"structure d'ensemble"* character of the stage notion emphasized by Piaget would lead one to predict. This kind of evidence has in fact been upheld as critical to the validation of

[3]The term "milestone" might have been fitting in this context, except for the fact that Loevinger (1966a) has used it to refer to her own phases of ego development that are explicitly designated as disjunctive, rather than cumulative. Piaget's stages appear to conform rather to the cumulative mode, though in actual testing the problem is at times unclear (cf. the discussion in Chapter VI).

TABLE 9–2

Cross-domain Comparisons for Stages of Motor-intelligence from Woodward's (1959)
Study of Severely Retarded Children

a. Circular Reactions Compared with Problem Solving or Grasping Behavior

		N in group	Circular reactions					
			Pri-mary II	Second-dary III	Derived Second-dary IV	Terti-ary V	Other manip-ula-tions (v)	No activ-ity
Did not grasp on sight	II-A	12	11	0	0	0	0	1
Grasped on sight	II-B	9	5	0	0	0	0	4
Handled objects	III	21	0	19	2	0	0	0
Screens (T. or O.)	IV	15	0	9	2	4	0	0
String or support	V	40	1	11	7	10	8	3
Totals		97	17	39	11	14	8	8

b. Comparison of Stages of Sensorimotor Intelligence and Object Concept Development

		Object concept stage					
		II	III	IV	V	VI	Totals
Stage of	II . . .	19	2	0	0	0	21
	III . . .	1	20	0	0	0	21
sensorimotor	IV . . .	0	8	0	6	1	15
intelligence	V . . .	0	0	0	39	1	40
	VI . . .	0	0	0	0	50	50
Totals . . .		20	30	0	45	52	147

Piaget's stage-theory, notably in the realm of concrete operations, with evidence being presented both pro (e.g., Braine, 1959) and con (e.g., Dodwell, 1963). We will return to this point in the following section, in which the study of stages of concrete-operational thought will be taken up in more detail, so as to bring out some of the reasons that have led most of those who have concerned themselves with this problem (Flavell & Wohlwill, 1969; Pinard & Laurendeau, 1969) to question the usefulness of this line of attack on the stage problem.

To anticipate one of the major criticisms of the reliance on contingency-table data on the degree of association between equivalent levels of response in different domains, it is predicated on a view of progression through a sequence of stages as a rigid, lock-step process which probably fails to do justice to the phenomena in the infancy realm as much as it does to those in the domain of concrete or formal operations. Not only is it a determinate model that does not make allowances for deviations from simple synchronous progression across two or more domains, due to a variety of situational or task- or domain-specific factors, but more fundamentally it represents a static conception of the problem that is out of keeping with the developmental character of stages (though possibly for this reason rather more successful when applied to a group of individuals such as Woodward's subjects, whose development appears to have been frozen in its tracks).

In other words, instead of an exclusive focus on behavioral relations within levels, coupled with examination of sequentiality across levels, a structural model of stage development must deal with the changing network of interrelationships among various channels subsumed under a given stage sequence, as depicted in the representation of Piaget's system of stages of sensorimotor development in Fig. 9–1. This system, as noted in the introductory comments in this section, appears to be in principle ideally suited to testing out the implications of the stage concept. In the absence of actual research on this question, the problem of teasing out the testable properties of the stage concept may be approached by reference to a set of alternative, hierarchically ordered models for handling data in this realm. These models will subsequently provide a convenient framework for a discussion of approaches to data analysis in this area, and to a consideration of the literature on this question devoted to the concrete-operational period.

Models for the Analysis of Developmental-Stage Data

We start by postulating a set of parallel developmental sequences C_1 to C_n, each of which consists of a series of k ordered responses, such that there is a determinate relationship among the responses in the same ordinal position in the various sequences. For example, in the case of sensorimotor development, we have the sets of phenomena or modes of response shown in Table 9–3; they are taken from the tables of contents of the two volumes in which the theory and observations on the development of sensorimotor intelligence are presented (Piaget, 1952b, 1954b). Note that there are a few instances of points in particular sequences that are left undefined, or merged with adjacent points. Furthermore, the specific behaviors that would be subsumed under each need of course to be defined in more concrete terms, and operationalized via the use of standardized assessment procedures

TABLE 9–3

Piaget's Stages of Sensorimotor Development in Five Domains of Behavior

	General sensorimotor intelligence	Object concept	Space	Causality	Time
Stage I	Reflexes	No special behavior related to vanished objects	Practical and heterogeneous groups	Contact between internal and external environment	Time itself and the practical series
Stage II	Primary circular reactions				
Stage III	Secondary circular reactions	Beginning of permanence	Coordination of practical groups; subjective groups	Magico-phenomenalistic causality	Subjective series
Stage IV	Coordination of secondary schemata	Active search for vanished object	Transition from subjective to objective groups	Elementary externalization and objectification of causality	Beginnings of objectification of time
Stage V	Tertiary circular reactions	Response to sequential displacements	Objective groups	Objectification and specialization of causality	Objective series
Stage VI	Invention of new means through mental combinations	Representation of invisible displacements	Representative groups	Representative causality	Representative series

such as used by Uzgiris and Hunt (1966), or Escalona and Corman (1967).[4] We are now in a position to elaborate a series of alternative models, in terms of the kind of temporal coordination envisaged (or observed) among corresponding steps of the several sequences. These are shown in Table 9–4,

[4]The sequences which Uzgiris and Hunt have determined for the various aspects of sensorimotor development might have served for this purpose, except for the fact that they are divided up into a rather large number of steps, to which one would not wish to accord the label "stage." In particular, the steps of the various sequences are not in any direct correspondence with one another, their number varying between 8 and 20, and *a fortiori* are not placed into a determinate relation to Piaget's own six-stage system. Presumably subsets of the steps of these sequences could be extracted from the total series to correspond to Piaget's schema, however.

TABLE 9–4

Models of Developmental Stages, Arranged in Order of Complexity of Interrelationship among Component Sequences

Model	Defining properties[a]	Major hypothesis	Implications for concept of stages
IA: Synchronous progression	$t(m_i) = t(n_i)$ for all i and all pairs (m,n)	Changes in level for all sequences occur in synchrony	Structural network tying together ordered sequences of responses at equivalent levels, with developmental progression occurring in unison in all sequences, linked in one rigid system
IIA: Horizontal decalage, convergent	$t(m_i) < t(n_i)$ for some pairs (m,n), with lag first increasing, then decreasing	Changes in level occur in synchrony, with exceptions for certain sequences, taking the form of staggered progression	Structural network integrating ordered sequences of responses at equivalent levels, with sequence-specific or extraneous factors resulting in temporary lags between systems at intermediary levels
IIB: Horizontal decalage, divergent	$t(m_i) < t(n_i)$ for some pairs (m,n), with lag progressively increasing	As in IIA above	As in IIA above, except that sequence-specific or extraneous factors have cumulative effect, with progressively widening gaps between sequences
III: Reciprocal interaction	$t(m_i) \neq t(n_i)$ for some pairs (m,n), with lag between them changing from positive to negative between $i = 1$ and $i = k$	Changes in level occur in synchrony, with exceptions for certain sequences, taking the form of intersecting developmental functions	Structural network integrating ordered sequences of responses at equivalent levels, with interdependence among particular sequences resulting in temporary perturbations in developmental timetable
IV: Disequilibration-stabilization	$t(m_i) = t(n_i)$ for selected values of i representing stage consolidation; $p[L(m)_t = L(n)_t]$ first decreases, then increases during intervals of t corresponding to values of i intermediate between the above	Attainment of levels of stage consolidation occurs synchronously for all sequences, separated by intermediary levels marked by behavior oscillation, irregular relationships among sequences	Structural network representing nodes at which ordered sequences of response become functionally integrated, with developmental progression occurring in fluid fashion between these nodes

$t(m_i)$ = time (age) of attainment i in sequence m.

$t(m_i) < t(n_i)$ means step i is attained earlier in sequence m than in sequence n.

$L(m)_t$ = level of sequence m shown at time t

the characteristic properties of each being given in semiformal terms; its implications for the stage concept, along with the particular hypotheses that would become of interest in reference to it, are also indicated briefly.

Three points concerning this table are to be 'noted. First, the several models delineated represent ideal types, arranged in a hierarchy of complexity of relationships among component sequences. It is likely that any empirical stage system will represent a mixed case, made up of combinations of features of different models. Thus, a particular pair of sequences may turn out to conform to a convergent type of horizontal "decalage," while another from the same set will exhibit a divergent pattern, and a third may conform to the reciprocal interaction pattern.

The second point is that, with the partial exception of Model IV, the defining properties are couched in terms of the age at which a given level is attained, following our previous discussion of age as a dependent variable, and the application of this use of age for extracting quantitative developmental function parameters from nominally or ordinally scaled behavioral variables. In practice, the continuous monitoring of the individual's status with respect to behavior sequences which would be required to arrive at reasonably precise measures of age of attainment may not be generally realizable. Nevertheless, this manner of expressing synchronous and lagged relations among sequences is convenient for our purposes.

The final point is that the schema of Table 9–4 assumes that all of the component sequences contain an identical number of steps or levels, each representing a separate stage in the structural network sense. In other words, the solid representing Piaget's sensorimotor stages in Fig. 9–1 is taken as a prototype for stage systems, with Models II-A, II-B, and III amounting to the introduction of tilt into the inclination of the planes representing each stage, relative to the central axis. As formulated here, the limitation applies equally to Model IV, which might be looked at as involving a set of planes similar to those of the preceding models, but with their angle of tilt being subject to random oscillations of variable amounts. We will show further on, however, how Model IV might be reformulated so as to circumvent this limitation.

Model I: Synchronous Development. This represents structural stage theory in its purest, and thus most simpleminded version. It stipulates that all of the various component sequences of the system develop apace in completely rigid fashion. Although this was indeed a current assumption behind some of the earlier tests of Piaget's system of concrete operations (reinforced by some of Piaget's own unqualified assertions as to the necessary temporal concomitance in the appearance of structurally equivalent modes of response), it has since proved altogether unrealistic and oversimplified

208   IX The Study of Developmental Stages

as an actual picture of the facts (cf. Flavell & Wohlwill, 1969; Flavell, 1970, 1971; Pinard & Laurendeau, 1969, for further discussion of the evidence on this point, and the reasons for the insufficiency of the model). It would undoubtedly prove equally unsatisfactory with regard to the sensorimotor stages. It might be noted that in practice this model becomes indistinguishable from the single vertical-axis model represented by Kohlberg's stages, as depicted in Fig. 9–1. That is, if all of the sequences turned out to progress in precisely synchronous fashion, one would in fact be dealing with but a single sequence, with alternative modes of expression at each level.

Model II-A: Horizontal "Decalages" (convergent). This model (along with its alternate form B, which has not previously been distinguished from it) has been most frequently suggested as representative of the true state of affairs, including Piaget himself in certain instances. The existence of "decalages"—temporal lags in the ages at which formally equivalent concepts are mastered—has generally been held as evidence damaging to Piaget's theory of stages. As long as an advance in the attainment of a stage in one domain over another is seen merely as a deviation from the expectation of synchrony, without any a priori basis for postulating it, it does constitute an apparent invalidation of the synchrony postulate embodied in the simple version of stage theory—albeit, let it be noted, a systematic rather than a random departure from it. Even if an a priori basis existed for predicting such a decalage, for instance, in terms of the relative difficulty or unfamiliarity of a task or situation, this prediction would generally originate in considerations from outside the stage theory itself, and to that extent require qualifying statements in that theory.

There is, however, another way of looking at the matter. To begin with, a single comparison between a particular pair of sequences S_i and S_j, limited to a single level k, may give a much exaggerated picture of deviation from concordance when taken in isolation. Interrelationships among the sequences should rather be considered for the various sequences at all levels jointly, if a fair picture of the situation is to be obtained. Thus, it might turn out that for a series of parallel tasks or situations, a satisfactory degree of concordance might obtain, despite the possible existence of certain decalages. A case in point may be represented by Lovell's (1961) study of different aspects of formal operations, where, despite certain variations in performance from one task to another, a considerable amount of concordance overall was yet observed.

In a more positive vein, the very existence of a systematic decalage—particularly in the convergent case—points at least to the possibility, if not likelihood of a functional interdependence between performance in two (or several) situations which is not necessarily out of keeping with a more sophisticated version of stage theory. What the presence of decalages suggests for the formulation and testing of a viable stage-theoretical model is that it must encompass time-lagged interrelationships along with synchronous progression, as alternative modes of interdependent development across domains. This assuredly complicates the picture, but need not be taken as a fatal mark against stage theory.

Model II-B: Horizontal "Decalages" (divergent). This variant from the preceding model is included here to point out that where the lag in the development of one sequence behind that of another progressively increases, the functional interdependence between them becomes correspondingly more difficult to affirm, and the hypothesized regulating function of the stage construct is thrown into question. The problem has rarely been studied over detailed enough sequences to allow a differentiation between the two alternatives; the case of the sensorimotor sequences should provide relevant information, but to date such correlative studies have not been done, with the exception of Woodward's. The latter's comparison between circular reactions and problem solving or grasping (cf. Table 9–2a) does in fact suggest a decalage of this divergent type, at least in the sense that the percentage of children who are at a lower stage for circular reactions than they are for problem solving or grasping steadily increases, from 35% at Stage II (i.e., on circular reactions) to 51% at Stage III and 64% at Stage IV. But, apart from the rather arbitrary sequence used here, combining grasping and problem solving responses, the question basically calls for longitudinal information to allow us to determine whether the lag of one sequence behind another changes within any given individual, that is, in terms of the age of onset of each level.

Model III: Reciprocal Interaction. It is conceivable that development in two or more domains proceeds according to a reciprocity pattern, such that progress in one initially follows, and subsequently overtakes that in the other(s). This might be the case where change from a lower to a higher stage in one domain involves overcoming some inhibitory or competing response tendency not present in the other; but once this resistance is overcome, development to the higher stage is relatively sudden, and could thus carry the equivalent higher-stage response in the other domain along with it. For instance, number conservation might initially lag behind the beginnings of seriation ability, since it involves overcoming an opposing response (i.e., the judgment of number in terms of length). But once the change has been set in motion, it could run its course more quickly, and by cementing the child's conceptual set in response to number would aid him in achieving the ordinal-cardinal correspondence demanded for the conceptualization of the number series at the level of concrete operations (Piaget, 1952a). In the realm of sensorimotor development, a similar relationship may conceivably exist between development in the general sensorimotor realm and that of the object concept, though for somewhat different reasons. The beginnings of the search for the vanished object at Stage III, involving as it does a memory or representational function, may lag behind the equivalent behavior shown in secondary circular reactions based on direct motor interaction with the object; but once the permanent object has been formed (i.e., Stage VI) it should be expected to aid the child in the "invention of new means" reflected in the novel use of tools at Stage VI of the general sensorimotor sequence.

Uzgiris and Hunt (1966) appear to look at the development of sensorimotor intelligence in the same vein, and even to have obtained some evidence favoring this model, which unfortunately is not given in their report. Herewith their conception of the developmental process:

> Development may be viewed as a branching process. The infant acquires numerous schemata through assimilation to—and accommodation of—the five ready-made schemata which he possesses at birth. Therefore, several series have similar starting points. Furthermore, development along the various series is probably to some extent interdependent. We do not yet know what the interrelationships are. One may guess that, up to a point, the rate of development may vary considerably along each of the series. However, at certain points the various series seem to come together, so that progress in one becomes the basis for progress in another. For instance, the infant has to develop the coordination between the schemata of vision and prehension in order to begin to grasp objects which, in turn, enables the infant to develop the variety of schemas that accommodation to numerous objects forces upon the schema of prehension. On the other hand, the grasping schema itself and the resulting interesting events which it enables the infant to obtain and to regain through secondary circular reactions both feed into his primordial feelings of intention and causality, contributing to development in Series II and IV. Or, as a second example, progress in the development of object permanence leads to search for objects which have disappeared along various trajectories and may be important for the construction of objective space. It is easy to agree with Piaget that the development of representation is a unifying theme for progress during the first two years of life [p. 11].

This model has some resemblance to Gesell's principle of "reciprocal interweaving" (Ames & Ilg, 1964; Gesell, 1939), except that the latter concept is intended to refer more specifically to motor responses that are opposites of one another (e.g., flexor versus extensor movements; right-versus left-hand actions), which according to Gesell succeed one another in leap-frog fashion, or form a developmental spiral. Such responses would not, of course, have any necessary association with developmental stages.

Model IV: Disequilibration–Stabilization. As we noted already in introducing the set of models and elucidating their formal presentation in Table 9–4, Model IV is in a number of respects discontinuous with the others. Of these, probably the most important is the substitution of a probabilistic formulation for the deterministic models represented by the preceding ones, and the resulting shift from age of attainment of a particular level of response to the probability of occurrence of a response at a given level. This loss in determinacy might seem to represent a fatal concession stripping the stage concept of one of its essential properties, and thus causing the whole shaky edifice of developmental stages to topple like a house of cards. Nevertheless such a loosening up of the model is essential if it is not only to provide a reasonably close fit to the data, but to do justice to the view of the developmental process sketched out by Piaget himself in his discussion of stages (Piaget, 1956).

The model postulates that sets of structurally interrelated sequences undergo development in such a way that the transitional periods between stages are marked by instability of behavior within sequences, and, consequently, by indeterminacy in the pattern of interrelationship among sequences. The picture shifts to one of increasing stability and intersequence consistency of response, as the individual attains a stage and it becomes consolidated across its various manifestations. A number of possible examples of this type from the domain of concrete operations will be discussed further. We are at present simply unable to make even a guess as to where, if at all, it might apply in the sensorimotor domain, though the notion itself of progressive stabilization is one which does not seem difficult to reconcile with infant behavior.

Let us go into the characteristics of this model in greater detail, elaborating on the specifications for it given in Table 9–4. The model envisages a subset of levels i representing nodal points at which all of the several component sequences come together; these nodal points represent most plausibly the achievement of a stage in stable, consolidated form. As the individual moves to the stage following, his behavior is thrown into disequilibrium, that is, marked by increasingly lower degrees of reliability, or consistency across items or stimuli. Correspondingly, there is an increasing likelihood that responses for any combination of sequences (m, n) will show a discrepancy in level. The probability of correspondence in level will increase again as the individual moves toward the following stage, and achieves stabilization at that stage. Two questions require clarification in this formulation.

The first relates to the probabilistic character of the model. What, precisely, does "probabilistic" refer to in this context? The model stipulates that the probability of a joint event, namely the co-occurrence of identical levels of behavior for sequences m and n, goes into a decline during the early phases of the transition from one stage to the next, and subsequently rises again. The problem is, how should such probabilities be conceived, let alone calculated? Even if one were able to decide on the meaning of the response probabilities within a given sequence, in terms of their relative frequency of occurrence, perhaps over a series of trials, or across a sampling of stimuli or situations, we would still not be able to specify the joint probability of two such responses from two different sequences, except under the limiting cases of complete independence or complete interdependence. However, note that the probability actually refers, not to the joint occurrence of two particular responses, but rather to the equality in level of whatever responses are exhibited for the two sequences. In other words, it would be possible empirically to obtain measures of the child's status with respect to each of a pair of sequences over repeated occasions, or a sampling of relevant items, and plot the distribution of *differences* between the response levels exhibited for the two sequences. It is this probability value that should follow the pattern of a decrease followed by an increase, approaching 1.0 as stage stabilization is attained, since by definition at that point the probabilities of responses at that stage for each sequence equals 1.0. This procedure will at the same time provide independent estimates of the separate probabilities of the responses in question, allowing one to establish directly the degree of their interdependence.

The alert reader may have spotted an apparent problem here, to wit: How do we ensure that this model remains distinct from the decalage models, that is, that in the interval in which the probability of level congruence declines no *systematic* discrepancy between response levels arises? It would be possible to build a specification to this effect into the defining characteristic of the model, simply by stipulating that the probabilities in question be symmetrically distributed around zero discrepancy, so that no directional asynchronous pattern could obtain a higher probability value than that for level equivalence. It seems preferable, however, to omit such a restriction, and to generalize the model to include asynchronous progressions, conceived of in probabilistic rather than deterministic terms. Model IV should thus be seen as incorporating all of the preceding ones, or at least to be combinable with them, while formulating both asynchrony and synchrony probabilistically.

This manner of conceiving Model IV has the considerable advantage, furthermore, of permitting us to reformulate it in different terms, so as to allow us to apply it to situations in which it is either not feasible or not meaningful to specify the probabilities of level equivalence. To this end, let us use response *variability* as a substitute for response *probability*. That is to say, if the probability of equivalence in level is very high, few alternative responses should be expected; in other words, variability is low. Conversely, a low probability of equivalence in levels implies either an approach to random distribution of response patterns, that is, high variability of response, or a systematic bias away from response equivalence, such as provided for by the decalage Models II and III. Thus we see that the variability criterion is in fact superior to the probability of level congruence criterion, since it permits us to differentiate between cases of departure from level congruence due to response uncertainty and those due to asynchrony, though as pointed out in the previous paragraph, these two are not mutually exclusive.

This leads us to the second question posed by the formulation of Model IV, whether in its original form or in the revised version we have just proposed. Model IV postulates that interrelated sequences converge in their development at specified nodal points, representing the consolidation of a stage. Let us leave in abeyance, for the moment, the question whether any stage ever reaches a state of complete consolidation and integration of component structures, at least in a developing child. This problem will be taken up at the conclusion of this chapter. For the time being, we will assume the existence of such nodes, and turn to the problem of identifying them with particular steps of different sequences, and aligning the latter so that corresponding levels are juxtaposed.

Ideally this alignment should be carried out on an a priori basis, by reference to the theory from which the empirical sequences being interrelated are derived, and which should in principle provide a determinate basis for placing equivalent levels for different sequences in direct correspondence, in terms of the type of structure represented in each. In practice, however, we find that even Piaget's theory only approximates to this ideal, at least in the sensorimotor intelligence realm. As noted earlier, the stages are specified in such general terms that their identification with particular forms of behavior within a given domain or sequence is by no means always unequivocal, and in some cases, as shown in Table 9–3, there may in fact be gaps in some sequences at particular levels. More serious, however, particularly in relation to the model under discussion, is the uncertainty whether each of the six stages of sensorimotor intelligence should in fact be accorded an equivalent status, in terms of their conformance to the various criteria for stages.

For our purposes, the criterion of greatest concern is that of consolidation; indeed, the model is formulated on the assumption that in this respect only a subset of the steps of each sequence correspond to a full-fledged stage. The same is suggested by the very descriptions given the various stages by Piaget himself, which are frequently couched in terms of "beginnings," "tendencies," or outright transitional forms. Thus, in his discussion of the stage problem, Piaget describes Stage 3 of sensorimotor intelligence, that is, "coordination of vision and prehension," in the following terms: "Beginning of coordination of qualitative spaces that up to then were heterogeneous, but without search for vanished objects; beginning of differentiation between means and ends but without prior ends in the acquisition of a new behavior [Piaget, 1956; author's translation]." The stress on "beginnings" in this statement of the stage is hardly consistent with a notion of consolidation, or for that matter with the notion of a broad integrative structural network tying together diverse responses.[5]

The Problem of Sequences of Unequal Length. The sequences developed by Uzgiris and Hunt (1966) for sensorimotor development, along with phenomena in the realm of concrete operations where the number of differentiable forms of response on the way to the achievement of the final level may similarly vary from one sequence to another, suggest the desirability of a model that would permit the analysis of intersequence relationships for sequences of unequal length.

One possibility, in situations of this sort, would be simply to prune the sequences so as to arrive at a set of equal length. This procedure involves discarding information, but the likelihood is that the larger the number of steps of a sequence the less differentiable adjacent steps become—as was borne out by the results of Miller, Cohen, and Hill's (1970) replication of Uzgiris and Hunt's (1966) work on the formation of the permanent object. The problem still remains of deciding on just which steps to discard or, alternatively, which ones to pool for a single probability value to characterize each level. In the case of Model IV, the problem could be met in essentially the same way as described earlier for the determination of the nodal stages; however, the very fact that we are presumably dealing here with transitional phases and probabilistic responses makes this process less reliable in the case of these intermediary steps. As for Models I–III, they require to begin with a univocal correspondence, term for term, among the steps of each sequence; thus they leave no room for handling this type of problem.

The alternative form of Model IV presented, based on a criterion of response variability, provides a more suitable means of handling this problem. The measure of variability, deviation around the modal category, can readily be calculated for either the rows or the columns of any $m \times n$ table, without requiring correspondence, term by term, between the two sets of response categories. The hypothesis central to the model would then state simply that response variability (or uncertainty) with respect to the categories of concept B, for subjects at any given level of concept A, first increases and subsequently decreases as the subjects move from initial to final level on A (or, alternatively, variability on A shows this pattern as a function of progress on B). Illustrative examples of the calculation and interpretation

[5]For further discussion of Piaget's concept of consolidation and its ambiguities, the reader is referred to the excellent treatment of Pinard and Laurendean (1969, pp. 129 ff).

of these measures, both for the corresponding- and noncorresponding levels case, will be given.

Prototype Response Matrices and Illustrative Examples for Each Model

In order to further clarify the distinctions among the models just outlined, and to illustrate the possibilities for differentiating among them via the calculation of some simple statistics based on the defining characteristics of each, let us examine, first, a set of prototype response matrices to characterize each of the models. We will then, proceed to some tables of fictitious data to represent these models, and to use them as a basis for the quantitative treatment of them. The response matrices are presented in Fig. 9–2, while the corresponding frequency tables follow in Table 9–5.

What these response matrices show is the diversity of combinations of responses admissible under each model under cross-sectional investigation,

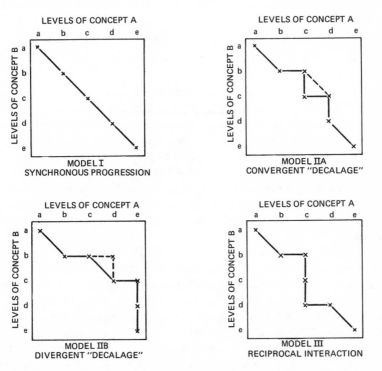

Fig. 9–2. Prototype bivariate response matrices conforming to the models of stages presented in Table 9–4. Each matrix is intended to represent the "permissible" patterns of combinations of levels for Concepts A and B; the lines linking the crosses show the developmental path(s) that a child would presumably follow if tested over a period of time.

TABLE 9–5

Three-way Matrices for Representing Development of Related Sequences

	C_1	C_2	$\dots$	C_9	
	$L_1 \dots L_K$	$L_1 \dots L_K$		$L_1 \dots L_K$	
S_1	$A(L_1 C_1 S_1)$			$A(L_K C_9 S_n)$	
S_2					Matrix A:
S_3					Ages of attainment of levels 1 to K
$\cdot$					for concepts 1 to 9 in subjects 1 to n.
$\cdot$					
$\cdot$					
S_n	$A(L_1 C_1 S_n)$			$A(L_K C_9 S_n)$	

	C_1	C_2	$\dots$	C_9	
	$T_1 \dots T_K$	$T_1 \dots T_K$		$T_1 \dots T_K$	
S_1	$L(T_1 C_1 S_n)$			$L(T_K C_9 S_1)$	
S_2					Matrix B:
S_3					Levels attained at times 1 to K
$\cdot$					for concepts 1 to 9 in subjects 1 to n.
$\cdot$					
$\cdot$					
S_n	$L(T_1 C_1 S_n)$			$L(T_K C_9 S_n)$	

and, by inference, the course of development across levels for any given subject if followed up longitudinally; the latter is indicated by the lines connecting the X's. Note that each matrix necessarily starts with the combination (a,a) and ends with (e,e); thus the apparent convergent pattern shown for Model II-B is but an artifact of the constraint that subjects will eventually reach the highest level for both of the concepts under comparison. The difference between that model and the convergent version, II-A, is thus to be looked for in the shapes of the two functions represented by the connecting line, up to the attainment of the most advanced level for concept A.

These response pattern matrices are similar to scalogram matrices in their deterministic mode of representing the course of developmental progress; no matrix is therefore included to cover Model IV. The latter is, however, represented in the illustrative frequency tables of Table 9–5, including examples of both the cases of correspondence and noncorrespondence of steps. Though these examples still constitute somewhat idealized versions of each model, designed to show how each may be differentiated from the others, they are at the same time intended to convey the nature of data such as might actually be obtained, and much as Woodward (1959) did in fact obtain in her aforementioned study of stages of sensorimotor development in severely retarded children (cf. Table 9–2).

In the columns to the right of each table and in the rows at the bottom of each table appear two sets of values: The mean level for one concept for each of the levels of the other (the liberty having been taken of representing them on an equal-interval scale), and the mean (absolute) deviation from the modal category (AD_{mo}), to permit a comparison of each of the models to Model IV which, as noted above, may be conceived of as incorporating all of the others.

It will be seen that the pattern of the row- and column-means provides one basis for differentiating among the models, that is, in terms of the best-fitting function for the means of the rows—linear for Model I, slightly concave for Model II-B, and concave changing to convex, intersecting the curve for Model I in the center, for Model III. A further feature to be noted for Model II-B, which differentiates it from Model II-A as well as from I and III, is in the pattern of the variability measure (AD_{mo}) for concept B, which progressively increases from the first to the last level. This trend reflects the plausible, if not inevitable tendency in the divergent case for the extent of the lag between the two concepts to be subject to increasing interindividual variation as the modal lag increases.

Ideally, a differentiation among these alternative models should of course be based on statistical tests for goodness of fit. This problem is complicated, however, by the status of these values as frequencies, rather than means for groups of subjects, which would allow for the application of trend analysis. Procedures are available for testing for *linearity* of trend in contingency tables with ordered categories (cf. Maxwell, 1961, Chapter VII), but these relegate all further trends to a residual category. They would thus not differentiate between Models II-A and II-B, though they would be adequate to compare either of these against Model I.

What about Model IV? As noted earlier, this represents in effect an extension of all of the others, based on a probabilistic conception of developmental change. Accordingly, it is not surprising to find the AD_{mo} measure failing to differentiate the particular pattern of frequencies used to illustrate the Model (Table 9–4a) from those of Model II-A: It is, in fact, quite consistent with the notion of a converging decalage to have variability maximized in the central portion of the table. At the same time, the frequencies in that table were chosen to illustrate a case of asynchrony which was far from deterministic, that is, included considerable variability. Note, however, that in the case of Model II-B, this pattern applies only to concept A; as already pointed out, for concept B we find a monotonically increasing trend of the AD_{mo} measure across levels, for the reasons already noted.

This discrepancy in the pattern of the AD_{mo}'s for the two concepts appears likewise in the case of Model III. There, it is concept B that shows a pattern in accordance with Model IV, while concept A is changing in bimodal fashion, consistent with the crossover between the two functions that characterizes this model. Only experience with actual data will indicate whether such divergent patterns for the AD_{mo}'s for the two concepts are an intrinsic feature of this model (as they do appear to be for Model II-A), or whether its appearance here represents an artifact of the fictitious set of frequencies chosen to illustrate the model.

It should be noted, in any event, that group frequency distributions of the type presented here will inevitably retain a certain equivocal character in several respects. First of all, the variability measures are necessarily subject to severe constraints at the end rows and columns, so that to some extent the pattern of the AD_{mo}'s defining Model IV may be artifactual. Second, the models as defined refer to within-individual patterns of development, studied over time, and can only very imperfectly and indirectly be verified through the cross-sectional tabulation of response patterns contained in the matrices of Table 9–5. Thus Model IV calls, at least, for supporting information on an intraindividual basis, whether in terms of the originally specified measures of response probability, or simply on response variability across occasions or tasks, or similar measures of instability or inconsistency. For all models, furthermore, the picture of the developmental patterns observed and their fit to any particular model would be greatly sharpened by longitudinal information that would show the path actually taken by a given subject in moving from one stage or nodal level to the next.

We shall see presently that this point applies even more forcefully to the type of evidence—typically limited to the ubiquitous 2 × 2 contingency table—that has thus far been collected on the synchrony question. Let us turn, then, to a critical examination of this body of literature, and of the analytic techniques employed in the study of stages, and suggest how they may be strengthened to bring out the type of information which our discussion thus far suggests we need in this area.

Approaches to Data Analysis in the Study of Stages

From our discussion, thus far, it should be obvious that according to the view of stages espoused here the investigation of developmental stages is in principle a multivariate enterprise, but because of the qualitative character of the dimensions in question, coupled with the intricacies of the developmental patterns applying to the formation of stages, the nature of their interrelationship is not adequately represented by current models of multivariate analysis such as factor or cluster analysis. In the most general terms, the investigation of stages involves, first, the specification of behavioral *nodes* defined via analogous responses on different dimensions, and second, the determination of the interpatterning among the changes in the levels of response exhibited for the various component dimensions or sequences over the transition from one node to the next. In order to see more clearly what is entailed in obtaining such information, let us look at the data matrices that one would generate in investigations of this type in their most complete form, in either of two possible versions. The first is a matrix of *ages of attainment* of successive levels, in accordance with the specification of defining characteristics for the various models presented previously. The second is a matrix of levels attained at successive testings. These are presented in Table 9–6.

Either of these matrices serve to bring out a problem which will return to plague us even more persistently in the following chapter on correlational models, that is, the fact that we are dealing with matrices extending into three dimensions. In the case of matrix A, the age entries are defined by combinations of subjects, concepts, and levels; whereas in the case of matrix B, the measures of level are defined by combinations of subjects, concepts, and ages (or times of testing). Thus, a complete handling of such data demands an extension of factor analysis into the third dimension, such as that developed by Tucker (1963), to be discussed in Chapter X. As we will note in that context, Tucker's model seems ideally calculated to unravel complex forms of interpatterning of developmental changes along several parallel channels. It is even possible that, when applied to age-of-attainment data, it could provide a ready means of operationalizing the stage concept, in terms of the emergence of general factors associated with particular levels. Unfortunately this possibility is likely to remain unrealized, not only because of the thus far very imperfectly developed state of three-way factor analysis, but also because of the patent difficulties of obtaining such age-of-attainment data in this behavioral realm, dependent as these are on a virtually continuous monitoring of the child's progress in the several conceptual domains which are being interrelated. Even if it were possible to administer, for, instance, monthly probes to assess the child's progress, the likely role of test-retest effects would render such data virtually meaningless.

Let us turn, then, to matrix B, which can serve as a generalized schema for the study of development along several qualitatively differentiated variables. As presented, it still requires resort to a three-dimensional model of analysis. Virtually all data on the stage problem that have been collected can be looked at, however, as involving cuts across this three-dimensional space, achieved by collapsing the three dimensions into two.

To anticipate, once more, the more thorough treatment of this matter in the chapter to follow, there are basically three ways in which such collapsing might be achieved. One, corresponding to P-technique (see Chapter X), is to restrict oneself to a single subject, and analyze the matrix of relationships among concepts across occasions of testing. Though factor-analytic

TABLE 9-6

Illustrative Bivariate Frequency Matrices for Different Models of Interdependence between Levels of Related Concepts

Model I: Synchronous progression

Levels of concept B	I	II	III	IV	V	Overall Mean	AD_{mo}
I	18	2	0	0	0	1.1	.10
II	2	16	2	0	0	2.0	.20
III	0	2	16	2	0	3.0	.20
IV	0	0	2	16	2	4.0	.20
V	0	0	0	2	18	4.9	.10
Overall Mean	1.1	2.0	3.0	4.0	4.9		
AD_{mo}	.10	.20	.20	.20	.10		

Levels of concept A

Model II: Decalage

Form A: Convergent decalage

Levels of concept B	I	II	III	IV	V	Overall Mean	AD_{mo}
I	18	2	0	0	0	1.1	.10
II	2	8	8	2	0	2.5	.80
III	0	2	8	8	2	3.5	.60
IV	0	0	2	16	2	4.0	.15
V	0	0	0	2	18	4.9	.10
Overall Mean	1.1	2.0	2.7	3.6	4.7		
AD_{mo}	.10	.40	.55	.70	.30		

Levels of concept A

Form B: Divergent decalage

Levels of concept B	I	II	III	IV	V	Overall Mean	AD_{mo}
I	18	2	0	0	0	1.1	.10
II	1	7	7	5	0	2.8	.80
III	0	0	2	9	9	4.4	.60
IV	0	0	0	3	17	4.8	.15
V	0	0	0	2	18	4.9	.10
Overall Mean	1.0	1.8	2.2	2.6	4.1		
AD_{mo}	.05	.22	.22	.63	.80		

Levels of concept A

Model III: Reciprocal interaction

Levels of concept B	I	II	III	IV	V	Overall Mean	AD_{mo}
I	18	2	0	0	0	1.1	.10
II	2	8	8	2	0	2.5	.70
III	0	2	16	2	0	3.0	.20
IV	0	2	8	8	2	3.5	.70
V	0	0	0	2	18	4.9	.10
Overall Mean	1.1	2.3	3.0	3.8	4.9		
AD_{mo}	.10	.40	.80	.40	.10		

Levels of concept A

Model IV: Disequilibration-Stabilization

Case A: Corresponding response levels

Level of concept B	I	II	III	IV	V	Overall Mean	AD_{mo}
I	18	2	0	0	0	1.1	.10
II	5	10	5	0	0	2.0	.50
III	2	4	8	4	2	3.0	1.20
IV	0	0	5	10	5	4.0	.50
V	0	0	0	2	18	4.9	.10
Overall Mean	1.4	2.1	3.0	3.9	4.6		
AD_{mo}	.55	.30	.50	.30	.55		

Levels of concept A

Case B: Noncorresponding levels

Levels of concept B	I	II	III	IV	V	Overall Mean	AD_{mo}
I	18	2	0	0	0	1.1	.10
II	5	10	5	0	0	2.0	.50
III	4	6	6	4	0	2.5	.90
IV	0	5	10	5	0	3.0	.50
V	0	0	2	18		3.9	.10
Overall Mean	1.5	2.6	3.4	4.5			
AD_{mo}	.44	.78	.78	.44			

Levels of concept A

approaches are apt to prove ill-suited to the discrete type of data which emerge from studies of developmental stages, an intensive analysis, on a per subject basis, of patterns of relationships across conceptual domains as these evolve during the period in which the transition from one stage to the next is taking place should yet prove of interest. Nevertheless, it is doubtful that results from such individual cases will be accorded much significance in the continuing debate over the stage problem.

The second way of collapsing our three-way matrix onto two dimensions corresponds to T-technique (cf. Chapter X) and consists of restricting oneself to a single response variable, intercorrelated across occasions of testing. Since we have already defined the stage problem as relating to the inter-patterning of responses, this solution is of no interest for us.

This leaves the third and most frequently employed solution, in which the age or test dimension is eliminated (thus corresponding to R-technique, cf. Chapter X). Thus, we have a matrix of subjects x concepts, which allows us to investigate the interpatterning of responses on a single occasion. Since our interest is in the changing mode of this interpatterning over time, this collapsing is again bought at a considerable price. It is possible, however, to recover some of this information by adding the age dimension on to the subject dimension, that is, via cross-sectional study of groups of subjects stratified by age. Alternatively, the procedure applied to the analysis of the contingency data of Table 9–5 is available. This involves, in effect, dividing up the collapsed subject x concepts matrix according to levels of the bivariate distribution, and looking at the congruence of the responses, or their variance, as a function of these levels, rather than assessing relationships for the matrix as a whole.

Since these cross-sectional approaches have represented and will undoubtedly continue to account for a very large share of studies on this problem, the consequences of this cross-sectional short cut warrant examination, in terms of its adequacy in providing the information which each of the models of stages delineated above calls for, the techniques available to obtain this information from such data, and the comparison of this design to either a limited (i.e., two occasions) or extended (several occasions) longitudinal design. These questions will be considered separately for each of the several models discussed earlier.

Model I. Verification of stage synchrony has most typically taken the form of contingency tables indicating the strength of the association of responses at equivalent levels for different domains supposed to be structurally interrelated. Well-known examples are provided by the investigations of Braine (1959) on the relationship between seriation and conservation of length; Smedslund (1964) on the relationship between conservation and transitivity; Shantz and Smock (1966) on the relationship between distance conservation and the understanding of spatial coordinates; Lunzer (1960) on interrelationships among various geometrical concepts, etc. In most cases, the data have been presented in the form of 2 × 2 contingency tables, with performance on each of the two concepts scaled on a pass-fail basis. In principle, the approach can be extended to $m \times n$ contingency tables, but in the domain of concrete operations, despite the common practice of classifying children's performance into three types or levels, studies of cross-domain association have generally been limited to dichotomous response categories. Dodwell's (1963) study of spatial concepts represents an exception in this regard, but perversely he limited his analysis of such associations to children who performed at the most advanced level on *one* of the items; thus, in effect, he obtained only one half of the contingency table for any given pair of items.

The previously cited results of Woodward (1959) (Table 9–2) illustrate nicely not only the extension of the approach to the $m \times n$ level case, but the essential questions which arise in practice in the use of this approach. First, just what should the criterion be by which synchrony is to be either established or rejected? With fallible data, we would not expect very often to find O's in the off-diagonal cells; yet, the model is fundamentally a deterministic one, in the same sense that the use of scalogram analysis to test for sequential patterning is. Thus, at the very least, one would look for considerably more than the mere establishment of statistical significance in the association between the responses to two domains, for example, via *chi*-square. The use of *phi* or in the $m \times n$ case, of the coefficient of contingency, C, suggests itself as one measure of the *strength* of association between two such sets of responses. It is surprising that it has not been used more, especially since the major alleged limitation of these measures, the dependence of the upper limit of *phi* and C on the distribution of marginal frequencies, is actually an asset in the assessment of synchrony. Table 9–7 shows this point clearly: With a concentration of all of the discrepant cases ((plus, minus) and (minus, plus) combinations) in one cell, a lower value of *phi* results than with these

TABLE 9–7

Contrasting Cases of Contingency Tables with Equal and Unequal Marginal Frequencies (Synchronous versus Asynchronous Patterns)

	+	−				+	−	
+	20	5	25		+	20	20	40
−	5	20	25		−	0	20	20
	25	25				20	40	
	$\phi = .76$					$\phi = .50$		

cases equally distributed in the two cells, but the former pattern actually represents the case of one response developing ahead of the other, in contrast to the latter, in which departures from synchrony are random. Thus, the real problem of criteria is not so much one of assessing the degree to which the synchrony postulate is met as one of differentiating between random and systematic departure from synchrony, that is, between borderline variants of Models I and II. We will return to this question shortly, in considering Model II.

Meanwhile, another look at Table 9–2 will bring out a more basic limitation of the contingency table as a source of information on synchrony of the acquisition of particular stage-related responses. Recall that Woodward's subjects were in fact mentally retarded children, well out of the normal infancy period. The data thus show what, for the majority of these children, represents undoubtedly the terminal stage of their development with respect to the skills being interrelated. They do not permit us to make any inference concerning the simultaneity of the child's *arrival* at the corresponding levels for the two domains.

This is, of course, an extreme case, owing to the peculiar status of these children representing, as already noted, a state of arrested development. Yet the problem applies, even if attenuated in degree, to all such contingency tables obtained via a single cross-sectional cut. At the very least, it can be argued that any such table will show an exaggerated picture of synchronous development—particularly in a 2 × 2 table—since subjects who may have arrived at the given level for one concept or domain ahead of the other but who have subsequently "evened the score" are not differentiable from those who did in fact move up to that level at the same time for both concepts. Given a sufficiently large sample, one would of course expect that, where asynchrony of attainment does in fact occur, the table will reveal this situation by "catching" some number of children who had advanced to the higher level for one concept but not the other. But the number of such cases of violation of synchrony will be a gross underestimate of the number who actually showed a similar asynchrony in their developmental pattern.

The problem fundamentally requires data on age of attainment, involving probes of the child's progress repeated at short intervals. But even in the absence of such near continuous monitoring, the use of a longitudinal design to provide information on synchrony versus asynchrony of *change* directly can result in a considerable increase in the power of the contingency-table approach. This is because it abstracts from correspondence in level at a single point in time, and thus allows us to discount those cases which fail to show a change within any given interval, and which therefore do not contribute information to the synchrony of attainment question, whereas those same cases, if analyzed cross-sectionally at either point in time, would be likely to inflate artificially the number of cases of correspondence. This is shown, for instance, in the longitudinal data of Benson (1966). Comparing the results for his items on number conservation (Test II-2,4) and on ordinal correspondence (Test III-1), examination of the contingency tables for each of his three tests separately shows between 50% and 60% of the responses falling along the diagonal cells of these 3 × 3 matrices, that is, showing equivalence in level. Yet the data on *changes* indicate that of the 35 children who showed a shift in level of response from either the first to the second or the second to the third test, only 8 (23%) changed on both tasks (in the same direction, i.e., counting occasional instances of regression as no change).[6]

One particular limitation of the coefficient of contingency as a measure of association between levels of response in $m \times n$ matrices should be noted. Based as it is directly on chi-square, that is $C = \sqrt{\chi^2/(N + \chi^2)}$, it is sensitive to departures from random distribution of any kind, without regard to the ordered status of the response categories (i.e., levels) for the two variables under study. By the same token, cases in off-diagonal cells have the same effect on depressing its value, regardless of how far off the diagonal they are, that is, how serious the extent of the deviation of the response patterns from strict correspondence of levels. Thus, where the levels of the variables exceed three, a measure of correlation which takes into account the ordinal or scalar values of the response levels would be preferred. Goodman and Kruskal (1954) have suggested one such coefficient, λ (cf. also Hays, 1965, p. 655f), as well as reviewing a variety of alternative approaches to the analysis of contingency tables (Goodman & Kruskal, 1959; cf. also Mosteller, 1968).

One final point concerns the desirability of obtaining measures that will reflect the extent of correspondence in level among k measures, rather than just two. Factor analysis, along with its variant, monotonicity analysis, is calculated to do so; the former will be considered in the chapter following (being of course intended for use with continuous data), while the latter has already been mentioned and explained in Chapter VI in connection with the dimensionalization of development. Note that the central question which the use of these techniques would be designed to answer is how strongly the various sets of response covary, that is, whether a single general factor accounts for a substantial portion of the covariance among them.

A rather simpler measure is available which accomplishes essentially the

---

[6]This analysis is based on the complete data given in Benson's Appendix B. The number-conservation data are taken from a combination of items two and four; where a child gave discrepant level responses to these two items, the lower level response was arbitrarily selected for this analysis, except that in rare cases where a child gave a Level A response to one item and a Level C response to the other, he was assigned to Level B.

same end, but is intended for use with data allowing subjects to be ranked. It is Kendall's coefficient of concordance, W (cf. Siegel, 1956); it has in fact been employed by Lovell (1961), to determine the extent of agreement in the assignment of subjects to levels for several tasks from the domain of logical reasoning, that is, Piaget's formal operations. Its use presupposes, however, that the responses for each task are scaled on a sufficiently fine scale of levels to allow for reasonably effective discrimination among subjects, so as to yield rankings that are not overloaded with ties. Whereas pragmatically, there is no limit to the number of ties that can be handled by the formula for W, the logic of the procedure would seem to be violated where the response scale is so coarse as to effectively preclude placing subjects in rank order with any consistency. Lovell was able to overcome this problem by using a nine-point scale of levels of reasoning, based in part on the subjects' explanations for their responses. Quite apart from the doubtful reliability of this particular classification, in the realm of concrete operations the possibilities for arriving at such a fine-grained diagnosis of levels of development appear to be limited.

Models II-A,B.   The contingency tables that have served to test the synchrony hypothesis are, as we have just seen, equally pertinent to the sequential progression case. The specification of an index to measure "goodness of fit" of a set of data to this model constitute something of a problem, however. Furthermore, once we generalize the situation to an $m \times n$ matrix, the differentiation between the two models A and B, though rarely considered in the literature, becomes critical.

The Diagnosis of Asynchrony in 2 × 2 and 3 × 3 Contingency Tables.   Starting with the popular 2 × 2 table, we note (Table 9–7) that the critical information is contained in the two diagonal cells, representing combinations of Level 1 for concept A and Level 2 for concept B. The other two cells in fact contribute information of relevance to the asynchrony question only in terms of the proportion of the total cases that are contained in those two cells. Prior investigators have contented themselves with simply noting the relative magnitudes of these frequencies in deciding between synchrony and asynchrony. A more precise index for this purpose would clearly be useful, particularly in comparing the extent of asynchrony in different tables. Such an index of asynchrony should reflect the preponderance of cases in one of the discrepant-level cells over the other, but at the same time take into account the relative frequency of such discrepant cases overall. A convenient index *alpha* that fulfills these desiderata is:

$$\alpha = \frac{\left(\dfrac{b + c}{2}\right)^2 - bc}{\dfrac{N}{4}(b + c)} \quad .$$

The rationale for this formula is roughly as follows: The numerator in the formula is a measure of asymmetry in the diagonal cells b and c; for $c = 0$ or $b = 0$ this value will be maximal, that is, $b^2/4$ or $c^2/4$, while for $b = c$ the numerator $= 2b^2/2 - b^2 = 0$. The expression in the numerator, in order to be interpretable as a ratio independent of absolute frequencies, needs to be divided by $(b + c)^2/2$, so as to result in a value of 1.0 for b or $c = 0$. In order to take account further of the relative proportion of asymmetry-relevant cases (cells b and c) in the total table, the resulting fraction is multiplied by the fraction $(b + c)/N$. After cancelling, the equation above for α results.

This expression for α has the advantage over alternative formulas that might have been devised (e.g., by recourse to the simple expression $b - c$ in the numerator) of being formally comparable to ϕ. Its effective range is rather restricted, however, since α attains to its maximum value of 1.0 only for the degenerative case in which $N = b$ or $N = c$. More generally, α_{max} (for tables in which either b or $c = 0$) $= b/N$. Thus α will, in practice, rarely exceed .50.

The formula is particularly well suited to the asynchrony of development problem, in that discrepant cases (cell b or c, whichever is smaller) have a marked effect on α; thus, for $a = d = 10$ and $b + c = 20$, α decreases very quickly from its maximum of 0.5 for $c = 0$ as c increases: for values of c from 1 to 5, $\alpha = .40, .32, .24, .18,$ and .12, respectively. The fact that with a 3:1 ratio (i.e., 15 versus 5) between the two asynchronous cells b and c, α equals only .12 might seem to point to a lack of sensitivity in this index, but this is precisely what one would look for in conformance with the basically determinate assumptions underlying Models II-A and II-B, according to which discrepant cases can only be attributed to error.

While *phi* and *alpha* are comparable only in a formal sense, that is, in terms of the ingredients of the respective formulas, and the latter will almost invariably be higher than the former, one might on purely pragmatic grounds stipulate the criterion of $2\alpha > \phi$ in deciding whether Model II (asynchrony) represents a better fit to the data than Model I (synchrony). Thus, considering again the limiting case in which $c = 0$, and assuming further that $a = d$, we find that for $b > .8a$, the criterion just mentioned will be satisfied. (For instance, for a table for which $a = b = d$; $c = 0$, $\phi = .50$, compared to $2\alpha = .75$; for a table in which $a = 2b = d$; $c = 0$, $\phi = .67$, versus $2\alpha = .40$.) What these values indicate is that, even in the "pure" case of errorless data ($c = 0$), the other discrepant-level diagonal cell, b, must contain about as many cases as either of the other two diagonal cells (or their average), in order for asymmetry to be satisfactorily demonstrated. This appears reasonable, since a large preponderance in the equivalent-level diagonal cells, a and d, would in itself constitute evidence against Model II, according to which one concept develops ahead of the other.

It should be remembered, on the other hand, that the relative frequencies in these cells are very much a function of the sampling of subjects, together with the speed with which the change from one level to the other actually takes place. Where the sample is chosen so as to include subjects well below and above the transition phase, we may get an artificially high proportion of subjects in the equivalent-level cells. Similarly, if the transition period is very brief, the probability of finding subjects in that period who might be expected to manifest a discrepant level response pattern will be correspondingly small. In either of these cases, then, the criterion enunciated above is apt not to be satisfied, that is, Model I will not be rejected. We already touched on this point in our consideration of Model I, where we noted that typically 2 × 2 contingency tables based on cross-sectional data provide a gross underestimate of the degree of asynchrony that may in fact apply to the development of two concepts. All of which only points to the real shortcomings of cross-sectional shortcuts for determining the actual course of developmental change.

Finally, considering briefly the extension of this analysis to the case of 3 × 3 contingency tables, we are immediately confronted with a difficulty, due to the fact that the index does not take the *direction* of asymmetry into account. Since the 3 × 3 table contains several possible cell frequency comparisons relevant to the asymmetry hypothesis (cf. Table 9–8 taken from the aforementioned data of Benson, 1966), an index would be required that integrates over the several sources of asymmetry present in the data. But any attempt to derive such an index from the formula for *alpha* given above runs up against the directionless character of the latter. For instance, if asymmetry goes in one direction for the contrast between cells *b* and *d*, and in another for that between *f* and *h*, this would actually be evidence in favor of Model III, rather than II, but a different type of index would be required

TABLE 9–8

Interrelationship between Levels of Performance on Number Conservation (Task A) and on Double Seriation (Task B) on Three Successive Tests[a]

		Generalized contingency tables Levels of task B			First test levels of task B			Second test levels of task B			Third test levels of task B		
		A	B	C	A	B	C	A	B	C	A	B	C
Levels	A	a	b	c	2	2	2	0	0	0	1	1	0
of	B	d	e	f	8	13	3	4	11	3	1	7	2
task A	C	g	h	i	0	2	3	2	8	6	1	9	13

[a] Arrows indicate direction of asynchrony. [Relationships between corner cells *c* and *g* are not included (data of Benson, 1966).]

to reveal it. Under these circumstances, one suspects that the most effective procedure would be to return to the approach of Table 9–7, that is, to obtain means for successive rows, scaling the three levels as though representing equal intervals, and determining the extent and direction of the departure of the three means from those predicted by the synchrony assumption.

Differentiating between Models II-A and II-B. It is apparent that on the basis of 2 × 2 contingency tables, it would be impossible to differentiate between these two versions of the decalage model, except insofar as the asynchrony should emerge more potently in the case of the latter, while the former would include proportionally more cases in the synchrony diagonal. For more direct evidence on the convergent as opposed to divergent character of decalages, however, one would need at the minimum a 4 × 4, and prefer-ably a 5 × 5 table, which could then be subjected to the procedures outlined above for the illustrative examples given in Table 9–5. With the exception of Woodward's (1959) data which were previously cited in this connection, no data appear to have been collected that would bear on this question.

The Meaning of Model II for k Sequences. While the synchrony assump-tion for Model I could in principle be tested for *k* sequences simultaneously, Model II applies necessarily to the interrelationship between individual pairs of sequences, taken two at a time (cf. the defining characteristics listed in Table 9–4). Thus, for any particular set, it may well turn out to be the case that a mixed model applies, with pairs of sequences distributed among the different models. (This point applies equally to Model III.)

Model III. This model, postulating as it does a cross over between the developmental functions for two concepts, is entirely dependent on the avail-ability of finely enough differentiated sequences to reveal its applicability to a particular set of data. A 5 × 5 table would seem to constitute the minimum requisite for this purpose, and the analysis would proceed as already shown. Once again, we lack actual data that bear on this model, although a relationship of the kind envisaged here was suggested by a devel-opmental pattern uncovered in research by Wohlwill, Fusaro, and Devoe (1969) on the interrelationship between level of conservation (based on responses to three different types of conservation tasks) and a measure of a continuous variable, proficiency in spontaneous measurement tasks. This evidence was, however, obtained on the basis of longitudinal information, using a procedure ("change-score" analysis) to be detailed in the following chapter. In brief, the results indicated that, over the lower segment of the Measurement scale, performance on measurement predicted *subsequent* changes in level of conservation. The latter changed, however, at a more rapid pace than measurement, and for the upper portion of the measurement scale the relationship appeared reversed, conservation being perfected ahead of measurement.

The Problem of Borderline Cases. The analysis presented earlier to illustrate the various models on the basis of the fictitious data of Table 9–5 did not provide us with any determinate criteria, let alone statistical tests, that would allow us to decide univocally among the applicable models in borderline cases. Greater refinement of the suggested quantitative indices and, above all, provision for appropriate statistical tests of goodness of fit, can be expected to improve on this situation. Yet the fact remains, as already mentioned in the context of the treatment of Table 9–5, that the developmental patterns hypothesized by these models refer to intraindividual change, and thus call for longitudinal information preferably couched in terms of age of attainment. This would be particularly true of Model III, with its relatively intricate interweaving of developmental functions; indeed, the data of Wohlwill, Fusaro, and Devoe just referred to, when looked at cross-sectionally, failed to reveal this pattern with any clarity.

Model IV. As observed repeatedly in the preceding discussion, Models I, II, and III are deterministic in character, implying either rigid one-for-one correspondence in the attainment of equivalent levels in different sequences (Model I), or systematic lags of diverse forms between such levels. The methodological approaches suggested for use in testing these models are consonant with this deterministic feature, as we have seen. Once we turn to Model IV, on the other hand, we depart from such deterministic conceptions of the developmental process involved in the acquisition of stages, and accordingly, require a new set of methodological tools to provide the type of information envisaged under this model. Basically we wish to supplement, if not replace, the search for synchronous as opposed to lagged response patterns with an examination of interrelationships among responses in probabilistic terms, along with a determination of the changing stability and consistency of these responses over the course of the establishment of a stage.

The analysis of patterns of response variability, as presented in connection with the data of Table 9–5 represents one approach for use with $m \times n$ contingency tables. Other ways of obtaining the information demanded by this model are available; they are exemplified par excellence in two studies by Nassefat (1963) and Uzgiris (1964).

Both of the these investigations share three important features, found all too rarely in Piagetian research. First, they include children over a rather extended age range (6 to 11 years in Uzgiris's study; 9 to 13 in Nassefat's) sufficient to reveal the process of stages in formation over their entire course. Second, they include a variety of tasks, each represented in several alternative forms. Uzgiris's study dealt with three types of conservation concepts (substance, weight, and volume); whereas Nassefat included concepts of probability, distance, and volume, understanding of spatial transformations, and verbal reasoning. Third, and most important, by incorporating the two features just mentioned into their design, these investigators were able to trace the changing form of the interrelationships among the various tasks over the course of the children's development. The desirability of this feature is not, of course, limited to the present model. In their complete statement, the previous models likewise call for such comparative information on response patterns at successive developmental levels (cf. their schematic representation in Fig. 9–2). The verification of Model III in particular is dependent on the collection of data of this kind, and it is plausible to attribute the lack of concrete evidence conforming to it to the shortcomings inherent in contingency tables or similar modes of correlational analysis performed on the total sample. But the studies of Uzgiris and Nassefat suggest precisely that once such comparative information on interpatterning at successive age levels is obtained, Model IV, rather than one of the simpler deterministic models, will turn out to conform most closely to the data.[7]

Briefly, Uzgiris found two trends in her data relevant to the present point: First, she found the correlations between the children's conservation scores for pairings of the four different materials in which each of the three conservation problems were presented changing with age in the manner indicated in Table 9–9. (At each age level six correlation coefficients were obtained, representing the six possible pairings of the four materials; the table presents the range and average value of these r's.)

While some might question the propriety of pooling the responses on substance, weight, and volume conservation to obtain one overall score (representing responses to 12 items, four for each concept), the conclusion seems justified that the changing intercorrelations among the scores for different materials reflect real changes taking place in the stability of conservation. The drops in the values of r, first at Grade 2, and subsequently in Grades 4 and 5, point to transitional periods during which conservation was becoming

[7]Note an important difference between the age-group comparative design of Uzgiris and Nassefat and that implied by the response-pattern matrices of Fig. 9–2 and Table 9–6. Both involve a collapsing of the original three-way matrix (Table 9–5) of levels-attained data onto two dimensions, but in different ways. Uzgiris and Nassefat simply substitute age for the time variable in matrix B of that table, and add it to the subject dimension as a stratifying variable. They thus transform a three-way correlation problem into a series of two-way problems. In the case of the bivariate frequency matrices of Table 9–6, on the other hand, the time variable has been discarded altogether, but by breaking up the total bivariate relationship pattern according to levels of the two concepts, the changing form of that relationship over time can be partially recovered though obviously not in the form of correlation coefficients.

TABLE 9-9

Intercorrelation of Conservation Responses across
Materials at Successive Age Levels[b]

Grade	Average correlation[a]	Range[a]
I	.82	.78 – .88
II	.67	.37 – .84
III	.77	.73 – .84
IV	.61	.47 – .73
V	.53	.31 – .77
VI	.66	.33 – .91

[a] Average r and range of r's based on six correlations at each age level, representing pairings of four different materials.

[b] Reprinted from *Child Development*, 1964, **35**, by Uzgiris by permission of The Society for Research in Child Development, Inc.

TABLE 9-10

Percentage of "Oscillating" Subjects on
Items of Substance (S), Weight (W), and
Volume (V) Conservation[a]

Grades	S	W	V
1st grade	11	11	4
2nd grade	15	12	0
3rd grade	5	20	0
4th grade	8	22	2
5th grade	5	14	4
6th grade	4	10	5

[a] Reprinted from *Child Development*, 1964, **35**, (based on Table 5) by Uzgiris by permission of The Society for Research in Child Development, Inc.

established with respect to substance and weight, respectively. (Conservation of volume did not exceed 30% even by Grade 6.)

This interpretation is strengthened by data on the relative incidence of cases of inconsistent responses across the three transformations administered for each combination of concept and materials, that is, cases in which a subject gave conservation responses to one or two of the three transformations. Such inconsistent responses were comparatively rare, never exceeding

1/4 of the subjects for any concept at any age level (i.e., in the large majority of cases, subjects conserved on either none or all three trials of a concept-materials combination). Yet, as shown in Table 9–10, the incidence of such inconsistent or oscillating responses is maximal in Grades 1 and 2 for substance conservation, and in Grades 3 and 4 for weight conservation, pointing further to these age intervals as transitional periods for the acquisition of these respective concepts. Note that the incidence of such inconsistent responses remains very low throughout in the case of volume conservation, showing (as the low incidence of children given credit for this concept had already suggested) that even the transitional period in the acquisition of this concept was still beyond the age range studied by Uzgiris.

Another way of looking at the same data is to classify the subjects according to patterns of response for substance and weight conservation, as Flavell and Wohlwill (1969) did in their reanalysis of Uzgiris's data to test a probabilistic formulation of the stage attainment process closely akin to our Model IV. This reanalysis showed that subjects with patterns of either zero or four conservation responses on both substance and weight had the fewest oscillations (means of .75 for the 0–0 group and .09 for the 4–4 group). In between oscillations were more frequent, being maximal in the group of subjects with a combination of one to three substance-conservation and zero to four weight-conservation responses (1.85 oscillations), and slightly lower (1.48) in subjects who had attained the former (four substance-conservation responses) but not the latter (zero to two weight-conservation responses). It might be noted that this picture is not entirely consistent with that postulated for Model IV, insofar as stabilization appeared to be reached for substance conservation while the subjects were clearly still transitional for weight. Here we have then a true picture of a decalage, rather than progression in parallel, and it is only by treating the stages separately for each concept, that is, admitting the attainment of substance-conservation and weight-conservation as different stages in the overall sequence, that the data could be reconciled with our model.

Turning now to an examination of Nassefat's study, we note that it differed in at least one important respect from Uzgiris's. Whereas the latter was concerned exclusively with the development of concepts falling into the concrete operations period as defined by Piaget,[8] Nassefat was interested

---

[8]This statement requires qualification, to the extent that the status of volume conservation as part of concrete-as opposed to formal-operational thought is in doubt. Piaget considers it to belong with the former, along with other forms of the conservation concept. Yet, quite apart from the marked lag found empirically between volume conservation and other concrete-operational concepts [note the low incidence of success on volume–conservation by Grade 6 in Uzgiris's study, which corresponds to the experience of other investigators, e.g., Elkind (1961), for this concept] there are sound logical reasons for classifying it under the rubric of

rather in tracing the transition from concrete operations to formal operations (cf. the age ranges included in the two studies). This meant that the transitional period between the attainment of successive stages could emerge more sharply from Nassefat's investigation.

Flavell and Wohlwill (1969) have provided a convenient précis of Nassefat's approach and major findings; suffice it to reproduce the major portion of their summary, and to elaborate upon it in certain directions.

[Nassefat] selected 150 *S*s in this age range, and administered to them a set of 48 items, falling into six domains, dealing with both concrete and formal operations (e.g. probability problems, problems involving the level principle, conservation of volume, and so on). For each item a number of different response categories were empirically set up into which the responses were classified; the number of such categories varied from a low of 2 (equivalent to Pass-Fail) to as many as 20. Each item was classified as *Concrete* (C) or *Formal* (F), in terms of the operations assumed to be required for adequate performance; roughly one-third of the items were, however, assigned to an *Intermediate* (I) category, based on ambiguities or inconsistencies in the responses actually given by the *S*s. The response categories for each item were subsequently combined, and further collapsed to form a four-point ordinal scale, representing different levels of performance in regard to the sorting out of relevant from irrelevant information, combined with failure versus success in the inferences that the child drew from the pertinent information.

The analysis of the data proceeded along a series of fronts. Having first demonstrated the validity of the ordinal response scale as a measure of developmental level attained on a given item (the *taus* for the association between response type and age level were for the most part highly significant), Nassefat turned to an analysis of the scalability of the data in the Guttman sense, based simply on dichotomous, Pass-Fail response measures. Scalability was assessed *separately* for each age level and for each of the three item categories (C, I, and F) in terms of both Green's index of consistency and Loevinger's index of homogeneity. Restricting ourselves to the former, we find consistency generally highest at the age level at which the discriminative power of each item category is maximal, i.e., at age nine for the C items, at age eleven for the I, at age twelve for the F. (Actually, the consistency of items in the F category never exceeds .25, apparently reflecting the fact that even at the oldest age level only a minority of *S*s passed them.)

The interesting feature of this scalogram analysis is that it is used, *not* for the usual purpose of establishing a developmental sequence (since the analysis is carried out separately for each age level), but rather to determine the degree of homogeneity, i.e. unitary dimensionality, characterizing a particular item domain. The assumption

---

Footnote (cont.)

formal operations. Volume–conservation, at least in the sense in which it has been most frequently conceived, that is, the conservation of amount of water displaced by solids equal in mass but different in shape, represents a two-step inferential process which entails at the very least a quantum shift in level of abstraction from any of the other conservations. This interpretation is further supported by the very different results obtained for conservation of *interior* volume, that is, of the room contained inside different structures made up of the same number of blocks; in this case, the age of attainment of conservation is roughly comparable to that for weight (cf. Lovell & Ogilvie, 1961).

is that the acquisition of the requisite mental structures is essential to bring out such dimensionality—just as, in measuring attitudes concerning a given topic, responses on a Guttman scale should prove scalable only for respondents who had formed a set of crystallized and articulated attitudes toward that topic. Nassefat regards this progressive homogenization of the item domain as one of the signs of the stabilization of the stage reached by the child; for the C items, this is already present at the youngest age level included in the study (nine years), since the process of acquisition of concrete operations is in general completed by that time; conversely, for the F items, it is clear that the homogenization is still far from complete at age thirteen, i.e. the stage of Formal Operations is still in process of elaboration at the oldest age level included [p. 96ff].[9]

This analysis was further supported by an examination of the age changes for the four types of responses, representing four levels of information processing, into which Nassefat classified the child's answers to each item. These age changes were plotted separately for each of the three types of items (Concrete, Intermediate, and Formal). Responses of types A and B showed a consistent decline with age for all items, and at the same time were most common for the Formal type items and least for the Concrete, as would be expected. The picture is reversed for responses of type D (the most advanced level), which increased with age, and were highest for Concrete, and lowest for Formal items. Most interesting is the picture for type C responses, which, as defined by Nassefat, involve correct abstraction of the essential information in the problem, but faulty processing of that information, that is, incorrect deductions or inferences. These responses showed an inverted V-shaped pattern for both Intermediate and Formal items, rising to a peak at age 10 for the former and age 11 for the latter; for the Concrete items they remained infrequent throughout.

It appears significant that type C responses are at a maximum at precisely those ages at which scalability (i.e., homogeneity) is at a minimum, for, as the developmental pattern itself indicates, these are legitimately considered as reflecting a transitional level on the way to the child's acquisition of a stage—though in this case we would be forced to elevate success on the class of Intermediary items to the status of a stage in itself. Lest it be objected that this conclusion is inconsistent with the apparent lack of clear evidence of the achievement of the Formal-operations stage within the age range that Nassefat investigated, it should be noted that type C responses actually level off at between 25% and 30% beyond their peak at age 11.

We come, finally, to Nassefat's data on the interrelationships among the responses to the different items. For each pair of items a contingency table was set up, showing the association between responses to the two items, based on the original set of 2 to 20 response types differentiated for each item; this was done separately for each age group. Rejecting the contingency coefficient, *C*, because of its failure to take the ordinal relations among the response categories into account, and being apparently unaware of Goodman and Kruskal's *gamma* that would have fitted this situation, Nassefat decided to assess association via Kendall's *tau*, that is, rank-ordering the subjects in terms of their responses to each item, and determining *tau* for these pairs of rankings.

Nassefat reports the percentage of *taus* found to be significant at the .10 (!) level at each age level, classified in terms of the combination of operational levels (C, I, or F) represented by each pair; the data for item-pairs belonging to the same level, which are of greatest interest for us, are shown in Fig. 9–3.[10]

The adoption of such a low level of significance, if not the application of *tau* itself to data of this type, which necessarily involved a very large number of ties, since the rankings were frequently based on as few as three or even

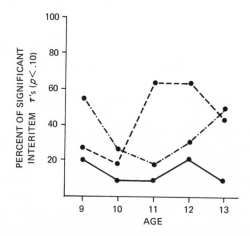

Fig. 9–3. Interitem associations (*tau*'s) at different age-levels among pairs of concrete, intermediate and formal items in Nassefat's (1963) study. For age 9 through 12, *N* = 10 item-pairs of concrete (——), 28 for intermediate (– – –), and 66 for formal items (–·–·–); for ages 13, *N* = 6, 21, and 66, respectively. [Data taken from Table 129, p. 178.]

[10]Figure 9–3, taken from Nassefat's Table 129, is preferred here to Nassefat's own graphic representation of these interitem relationship data in his Fig. 13, since the latter used a hybrid measure combining percentage of significant *taus* with incidence of "privileged associations"— cases in which more than two-thirds of all cases fell in a single cell, representing combinations of equivalent levels on both concepts. This obviously does not provide a measure of *association* between two variables, and thus is incommensurate with *tau*, though it might have been generalized to provide information on average *discrepancies* between the levels of response for each pair of items. The overall picture which Nassefat obtains via this combined index is not materially different from that of Fig. 9–3, in any case.

just two categories, suggests that these data should be treated with a certain amount of skepticism, all the more so given the very uneven absolute numbers on which these percentages are based. Yet the approach remains of interest, and as far as they go the data once more confirm the hypothesized lowering of consistency of performance during the transitional period—note the inverted-V shape for the Formal operations items, and the suggestion of a similar trend, but peaking earlier, for the Intermediate level ones.

Let us note in closing that Nassefat's design would have been well suited for a direct test of the adequacy of Model IV. His data would have permitted him to construct a sequence of levels attained within each of the domains included in his investigation, based on a combination of the Concrete-Intermediary-Formal classification and the four-point scale of information-extracting and processing established for each item. We would, thus, have had an opportunity to at least estimate the probabilities of each subject's dominant response levels, based on his responses to the several items for each domain, so as to verify, albeit from cross-sectional information, the trend postulated for the probabilities associated with equivalence in level for any pair of domains, in accordance with our Model IV. Alternatively, an extended contingency table could have been set up to test the data for their fit to Model IV, or any of the other models (cf. Table 9–5).

Conclusion: Stages—Mirage or Reality?

In the view of this writer, the usefulness of the stage concept remains an open question today, and its potential promise is as yet unfulfilled. This is because investigators have thus far failed to undertake the type of multivariate, yet fine-grained analysis of qualitative response patterns undergoing development that would be required to reveal the potential contribution of this concept. Since we have laid such stress on the regulating and unifying character of stages, it is appropriate that we terminate this discussion by considering briefly the view on this matter which Flavell has espoused at length. In his chapter on concept formation in the third edition of the *Manual of Child Psychology*, Flavell (1970) has argued forcefully that the demonstration of concurrence in the acquisition of two concepts is no guarantee of a functional link between them, and conversely that concepts or cognitive operations may have a structural interrelatedness character, and yet fail to appear in strict synchrony during the individual's development. The first of these points need not concern us here, not because it is not valid or important to consider, but because the synchrony postulate itself has not received very consistent support, as Flavell himself notes. Furthermore, to the extent that concurrence in the development of a whole "bundle" of cognitive skills postulated to be related via some common operation is demonstrable—particularly concurrence of the *changes* which they undergo—the assumption of their functional interdependence becomes reasonable, if not proven. (There are, furthermore, ways of testing for such functional links, e.g., via tests of the generalizability of the experimental induction of one concept to the acquisition of the others.)

Flavell's second point is more critical for our purposes. It has been considerably elaborated in a subsequent paper (Flavell, 1971), in which he has analyzed the meaning of structure and the synchrony question, along with other aspects of the stage problem in cognitive development at much greater length, but the essential point is effectively made in the earlier statement. The gist of it is that the binding together of a set of concepts, notions, rules, operations, etc., into a total structure (Piaget's *structures d'ensemble*) may be a characteristic of the end-product of the development of that structure, but need have no implications for the manner in which its components develop. Specifically, the synchrony postulate is rejected on both logical and empirical grounds. His analysis leads Flavell to suggest, in his own words, "the following, not entirely facetious proposition: If you really want to study a Piagetian concrete-operational structure in all its power and glory, choose an adolescent as your subject—or better yet a bright adult [p. 1040] !"

This view, for all its seeming surface plausibility, is clearly at variance with that of the present chapter. In fact, it would leave the stage concept paradoxically devoid of any developmental significance, since it would be merely a descriptive characterization of an ideal end-state, lacking in any implications for the process by which it comes into being during the course of the child's development. It may be countered in several ways. First, even if one were to grant that the structural cohesiveness of a stage does not become manifest except in its terminal form, and is achieved only when all development with respect to its component elements has ceased, it would still be true that each such stage is generally followed by further development toward higher-level stages. Flavell's suggestion, intriguing though it appears in principle, is thus not practicable: The late adolescent or adult, well into the elaboration of formal operations, does not afford us an adequate picture of concrete operations even in their mature form, any more than the six-year-old would with regard to the final stage of sensorimotor development. The same point is of course true *a fortiori* for more delimited stages, such as those of the sensorimotor intelligence period, which may have no more than a purely transitional status, but may yet lay claim to a structural entity and serve a unifying function.

More positively, stages do remain way stations, for the most part, rather than end points on the course of development, and give rise to specifically developmental phenomena during the period between the child's acquisition of one set of skills, concepts or operations, and the next set, such as observed during periods of transition and consolidation (cf. the studies by Uzgiris and Nassefat described previously). These phenomena are difficult to account for, and to investigate effectively, without postulating stages as a regulatory, harmonizing mechanism in the child's development.

The essential question to be asked in this connection is perhaps whether, for a set of parallel domains investigated in comparable terms (e.g., seriation, conservation, understanding of spatial coordinates, representation of water level in a tilted jar, etc.), acquisition of these concepts and skills stabilizes before further advances are made for any of these domains, that is, in the direction of formal operations. This would be the sense in which one could speak of nodal points, tying interrelated cognitive skills together. There would, inevitably, be a gradual converging toward this point from the several directions (note that, in our representations of Models II-A and IV, some children are assumed to reach Level V for concept A while still on Level III for concept B, and all models include some such cases combining V on A with IV on B; this pattern is in accord with Flavell's emphasis on the typically staggered order of arrival at a final stage for different concepts). But essentially complete stabilization for all interrelated concepts would be required, before the disequilibration process marking the movement toward the following stage could begin.

It is likely that, when looked at in this way, the scope of applicability of a stage will be more narrowly circumscribed than Piaget's theory suggests. It may be that nodal stages are formed in a unitary way not across all concrete operations, but only specific subsets of them, whether defined in terms of specific concepts, as Pinard and Laurendeau (1969) believe, or in terms of particular groupings, as this writer has previously suggested (Wohlwill, 1966a). But this would still leave room for considerable power for this postulated unifying character of the stage concept; for instance, if a stage is specific to a particular dimension such as length, one would still predict such diverse skills or concepts as conservation, transitivity, seriation, and conceptualization of distance to form part of the child's conceptualization of this dimension. Similarly, if defined in terms of a grouping such as multiplication of relations, it would comprise double seriation, representation of points in a coordinate system, understanding of the principle of compensatory relations between weight and distance in the lever, etc. And let us not forget, finally, the potential applicability of the present framework to realms other than that of the school-age child's thought processes—notably that of sensorimotor intelligence, where the opportunity to observe the alteration between nodal points and intermediary, transitional states of instability has as yet hardly been explored.

In fairness to Flavell, his main quarrel is with the synchrony postulate, rather than with the stage concept as such. Yet one is left with the impression—particularly from his subsequent paper (Flavell, 1971)—that, in part because of the unsatisfactory status of the synchrony criterion and the character of a fully perfected stage as an ideal to which the child only approaches asymptotically, the stage concept itself may well be dispensed with, at least as a concept of value to the developmentalist. It would seem, however, that Flavell has allowed himself to be misled by the pervasiveness of asynchrony in the acquisition of concepts into a position from which the development of supposedly related concepts occurs in an essentially indeterminate fashion, with only gross correspondence of chronological periods remaining as a hopelessly watered-down restatement of the synchrony principle. As a result, Flavell has chosen to emphasize the sequential aspect of the development of concepts, and provided us (Flavell, 1972) with a systematic and invaluable analysis of the diverse forms which such sequences may take, and of the diverse functional bases for them. In the context of the stage problem, this analysis would undoubtedly be useful in trying to account for some of the systematic decalages found in the field of concept development. It is aimed, however, at a rather molecular level of analysis, focused on the interdependence between two isolated responses, and thus it is of limited value for the purpose of creating order out of the by no means totally chaotic patterns of relations appearing in the development of sets of several analogous concepts or skills related via a common operation.

This brings us to the final point, that despite the undeniable fact of asynchrony, a considerable degree of order and regularity—or, to put it another way, of constraints on the forms which the interrelationship of developing elements of a structure may take—still obtains. It is to handle these that the models for the analysis of stages, and Model IV, in particular has been proposed. Suffice it to end by pointing out, once again, that our predilection for the cross-sectional shortcut has undoubtedly given us a very misleading picture in this respect, underestimating the complex interdependencies that may in fact exist among skills or concepts in process of development.

CHAPTER X

Correlational Methods in the Study of Developmental Change

A good case could be made for the proposition that correlational analysis, however denigrated in certain quarters, is the method par excellence for developmental study. First, it represents a viable middle ground between the essentially sterile age-group comparison approach and other more sophisticated variants of descriptive-level models of analysis on the one hand, and the highly problematical experimental approach to the study of developmental change on the other. As we shall find in the following chapter, the latter is beset with problems of both a practical and an intrinsic order that severely restrict its applicability, at least at the human level.

There is a further, ultimately more telling reason why correlational methodology deserves to assume a much more elevated place in the armamentarium of the developmentalist than it does at present. This is simply that behavioral development does not take place in isolated packages or along neatly separated, independent tracks, but along a variety of fronts in close interaction with one another. Note that this feature not only demands correlational, or more appropriately multivariate methodologies, but at the same time methods transcending most of our present correlational techniques, designed as they are to extract information as to intervariable relationships and behavioral patterning for an essentially static system, that is, at a single point in time. Fortunately, the multivariate study of change has begun to undergo vigorous development in recent years (Cattell, 1966b; Harris, 1963b), and models are being developed which promise to be tailored very effectively to the needs of the developmentalist.

The major portion of this chapter will be devoted to the presentation and discussion of these models at a preformal level, and in a manner which may strike the mathematically sophisticated as intuitive at best. Hopefully, the treatment will at least succeed in indicating not only the way in which the focus on change imposes a need for more elaborate and specialized techniques than those current in the field of correlational analysis, but at the same time, the vastly richer yield from the application of those techniques for the developmentalist in the search for information on the processes governing change. For, just as at the descriptive level, there is a vast difference between a statement of an isolated, normative datum, applying to a single cross-section of the developmental continuum and a statement of the form or characteristics of a developmental function, there is also a basic difference between the study of the intercorrelation between variables on a single occasion and the study of the patterning of changes for a set of variables over a portion of the span of development.

Finally, the reader will hardly need to be reminded that multivariate modes of analysis were already introduced in Chapters V and VI, in connection with the isolation of developmental dimensions. In a very real sense that problem should be seen as continuous with the one to be handled in this chapter, that of the interrelationships among *different* variables over the course of development, since in the course of work on the task of dimensionalizing development change information of the latter type will almost inevitably emerge. The major difference—and it is an important one—relates to the investigator's aim, and correlatively to the narrowness or breadth of the net he casts out in his choice of measures to be interrelated.

Five Levels of Elaboration in the Multivariate Study of Age Changes

The task of working change-process information into the extant multivariate methodologies can be solved at several distinct levels, ranging from the lowest, where the matter is in effect solved by eschewing the developmental components of the problem altogether to the highest, where selected parameters of a developmental function are taken as the data entering into the correlation matrix. Since these levels provide the basis for the organization of this chapter, it may be helpful to give a brief overview of them at this point in the form of a table (Table 10-1), before turning to their examination in more detail.

1. DATA FOR ALL AGES COMBINED INTO A SINGLE CORRELATIONAL OR FACTORIAL ANALYSIS

Let us begin with the simplest case imaginable: An investigator undertakes to study the interrelationship between two behavioral variables in individuals varying in age, in order to be able to assert that the development of these variables has a common base, or possibly even to account for the changes

Table 10–1

Five Levels of Analysis in the Correlational Study of Development

Level	Type of analysis	Major kinds of intervariable patterning information provided with respect to:	
		Groups	Individuals
A	Joint correlational analysis of pooled cross-sectional data	Magnitude of correlation between two variables (e.g., with age partialled out.) Overall factorial structure; contribution of age to total correlation matrix	None
B	Separate within-age group correlational analyses of cross-sectional sets of data, compared across age levels	Comparative picture of age-group differences in magnitudes of correlations, factorial structure, magnitude of first principal component, etc.	None
C	Analysis of interrelationships for longitudinal data sets obtained on two occasions for a set of individuals	Patterns and factors of change (over two occasions); stability of factors across occasions. Cross-lagged correlations	Relative magnitude of change on different variables
D	Analysis of longitudinal series of data obtained on an extended set of occasions, (a) for a single individual, (b) for a single test, (c) for multiple individuals and tests	(a) None (b) None (c) Emergence and disappearance of factors; change in constellation of factors; etc. Time-lagged relationships	(a) Interrelationships among set of variables over course of development; (b) none; (c) differential progress with respect to factors
E	Correlative analysis of developmental functions obtained from longitudinal records on a set of individuals	Relationships among parameters of developmental functions for several variables	Idiosyncratic interpatterning of variables across development

observed in one of the variables in terms of changes occurring in the other. An instructive illustration of this case, and of the latter of the two intentions just cited, comes from the study by Feffer and Gourevitch (1960) on the development of social-role perception in children, which was referred to briefly in the introduction to Chapter III.

The authors started from the hypothesis that age differences in performance on a role-taking task are attributable to changes in the child's cognitive functioning; more particularly his increasing ability to decentrate (to shift his focus from one aspect of the situation to another). Accordingly, they gave children between 6 and 13 years a set of Piagetian class-inclusion and conservation tasks, assumed to measure decentration, along with a role-taking task. Not surprisingly, both the Piagetian and the role-taking task measures were strongly related to age. In order to examine the relationship between the two measures independent of age, the children at each age level were divided into subgroups above and below the median on the two sets of scores, and a *chi*-square value was then determined for the association between the two variables for all children combined.[1]

The procedure used raises two questions, each of which presents a dilemma. The first is the strength of the correlation that one should accept as demonstrating a functional relationship between the two variables. Statistical significance hardly seems to be what is wanted here; at the least, one would look for some measure of the strength of the relationship (e.g., the magnitude of r, or perhaps r^2) between the two variables, in order to assess the validity of the original hypothesis.

The second dilemma is a more troublesome one. Since the intent here is to relate age differences in one variable to age differences in another variable supposed to be acting as a determinant of the former, does the procedure of partialling out the role of age not amount to throwing out the baby with the bathwater? To the extent that the partialling-out process leaves a residual of individual variation that is not only independent of CA but of development as such, the procedure appears to be self-defeating. For it is conceivable that the factors mediating a relationship between two variables within an age level may be quite different from those involved in the concomitant developmental changes taking place with respect to them.

It should be noted further that the procedure used by Feffer and Gourevitch presupposes that the extent and mode of the interrelationship between the variables remains invariant, or nearly so, across age levels, where substantial changes occur in this respect the determination of a single value to express the intercorrelation across age is hardly very meaningful.

Once we turn to a factor-analytic model, the picture changes somewhat insofar as the role of age is concerned. For now age no longer needs to be partialled out; to the extent that there is any general tendency for all or most scores to change with age, a principal factor identifiable with that variable

---

[1]The results provide a statistical curiosity, insofar as the strength of the relationship between the two variables is reportedly almost the same, whether age is partialled out or not. (The values of χ^2 are 5.54 and 6.01, respectively, for $df = 1$.) What has happened apparently is that subjects falling at the median on either variable have been eliminated, causing a loss of 10 subjects for the analysis involving the pooled within-age group median splits, and leaving a residual of subjects in whom the relationship is revealed in somewhat spuriously pure form.

will emerge, leaving other more specifically content-related factors which
will in fact retain some developmental component, namely that portion
attributable to change with respect to the variables identified with the
factors. However, in order to bring out this type of information we would
require a factor-analytic model suited to the situation. The most effective
one is probably a method such as the centroid or principal axes, with
rotation to oblique structure, and extraction of second-order factors. By
including age as an artificial variable in the correlation matrix, it becomes
relatively easy to verify the hypothesized status of the second-order factors
as specific-developmental. If these second-order factors show substantial
loadings for the age variable, this would point to patterns of development
common to particular subsets of variables, over and above the general
covariation of all variables with age presumably reflected in the first primary
factor.

A variety of objections can be, and have been raised against oblique structure rotation, and more particularly against the extraction of second-order
factors (cf. Nunnally, 1967). Apart from the indeterminacy of the solutions
resulting from such rotations there is a real possibility, at least for ability
type variables, that the contribution of age to the total variance will be such
as to obscure the picture with respect to the residual interrelationships (cf.
Cattell, 1963). This may be the reason why cross-sectional studies of factorial
structure, such as those based on the differentiation hypothesis of the development of intelligence, have most typically opted for the approach to be
discussed in the following section, involving individual correlational or
factor analysis for each age level separately.

A somewhat different approach to this same problem has been used by
Lee (1971), who was interested (much as were Feffer and Gourevitch) in
verifying the assumed cognitive basis for developmental changes occurring
in one aspect of interpersonal relations, namely in the area of moral judgment. She administered measures of level of moral judgment, based on
Piaget's (1932) original work, to children between ages 5 and 17, along with
several measures of cognitive development, taken from Piaget's more recent
work on concrete and formal operations, involving conservation and spatial
reasoning tasks. Lee proceeded to obtain evidence on the interdependency
between these two domains by determining the correlations between
measures of each of the moral levels separately (i.e., frequency of response
falling into each of the four moral reasoning categories stipulated by Piaget)
and each of three cognitive components. The latter measures represent
factor scores for three factors, a general, a concrete, and a formal factor,
respectively, which emerged from a factor analysis of the cognitive task data.
These correlations were performed both with and without age partialled out.
This procedure differs in an important respect from Feffer and Gourevitch's,

Table 10-2

Intercorrelations between Cognitive Factor Scores and Level of Moral Judgment and Age.

Cognitive factors	Authority	Authority reciprocity	Reciprocity	Societal	Chronological age
		Moral levels			
General	−.70* (−.57*)	−.36* (−.10)	.26* (.26)	.61* (.40*)	.79*
Concrete	−.52* (−.55*)	.14 —	.19 —	.06 —	.11
Formal	−.09 —	−.32* (−.19)	−.01 —	.60* (.50*)	.42*
Age	−.51*	−.39*	.13	.50*	

*Significant at $p < .01$.

Note: Values in parentheses represent partial correlations with age as the control variable. Where zero-order correlations were nonsignificant, partial correlations were not determined. [From Lee, 1971.]

insofar as the measures being correlated refer to discrete response categories which display differing patterns of change over age. The situation is shown in Table 10-2, which shows the correlations, with and without age partialled out. We note, first, a very high correlation between the general factor and age, and a moderate one between the formal factor and age, while the concrete factor is not significantly age related. This pattern becomes understandable when we examine the relations of each of the factors with the moral judgment levels. Thus we find a change in the inter-relationship between concrete-operational reasoning and moral judgment from substantially negative, for the lowest level, to essentially zero, for the highest, while formal reasoning shifts from nearly zero to substantially positive. The general factor, finally, changes from highly negative to highly positive.

This pattern is, of course, precisely what one would expect, given the gradual supplanting of one level of moral reasoning by the next, and of concrete by formal reasoning, with the general factor in evidence at all levels. The relationship is obviously still strongly age dependent; indeed, one suspects that if one substituted measures of skeletal age, number of permanent teeth erupted and adrenal hormone secretion for Lee's three cognitive components one might arrive at a very similar pattern. Here, of course, is where the partial correlations with age removed become important; the fact that those measures that were substantially intercorrelated in the zero-order analysis retain their relationship (even if somewhat reduced in magnitude) with age partialled out indicates the functional interdependence between these responses. Admittedly the picture would have been much more incisive with longitudinal data showing the interdependence of the changes in these two domains. At the same time, Lee is in a much stronger position than were Feffer and Gourevitch, not only because her relationships are so much stronger than just barely significant, even with age controlled, but also because each of her measures is itself period specific, that is, indicates strength of response associated with a particular level, rather than level of attainment on a developmental continuum. Thus Lee manages to preserve the developmental focus of her correlational analysis even while partialling out age, by dealing, not with a single correlation between two measures, but with patterns of correlations for a set of measures of qualitatively defined but ordinally scaled developmental levels.

We may refer in passing to a further, corroborative analysis between development in the two realms, based on similarity of the "transition" functions for particular tasks from the cognitive realm, compared to different levels of moral reasoning. The strongest parallelism (of three pairs that are reported) was found between formal operations and the "societal order" level of moral judgment. But the procedure employed to generate these functions, involving the plotting of biserial correlations between progressively summed age groups (i.e., shifting the cutting-off point for the definition of the two groups being intercorrelated progressively up the age scale), is obscure in its import, not to say bizarre.

A much simpler procedure was likewise employed by Lee, in this case to compare the interdependence between particular tasks of the cognitive battery, simply by plotting the age functions for specific pairs of such tasks. Despite the fact that means for cross-sectionally defined age groups are utilized here, the high degree of correspondence between some of the functions, notably between mass and liquid conservation, and between balance-task and shadow-projection task scores, does suggest a definite common basis to the developmental changes for these tasks, beyond a simple general aging factor. Basically, however, this approach is equivalent, though at a much less refined level, that to be taken up in section 5, dealing with the analysis of relationships among parameters of developmental functions.

2.   COMPARATIVE STUDY OF RELATIONSHIPS WITHIN INDIVIDUAL AGE GROUPS

Rather than combining the data from all age groups, only to partial out the effect of the age variable in the end, an alternative and for certain purposes more informative procedure is to analyze the relationship between the variables of interest for each age level studied individually. This was the procedure followed by Wolfe (1963) in a study that is formally very similar to Feffer and Gourevitch's. It does not, of course, provide any information on possible common origins for the observed age changes on the variables being intercorrelated, but at least it allows one to trace changes with age in the interrelationship between the variables themselves. Wolfe's study did not in fact uncover any very consistent evidence of such changes, but he restricted himself to children between the ages of 13 and 17, where it would be surprising to find marked changes occurring in the interpatterning of cognitively loaded variables.

Note that this type of research, using an age-group comparison strategy, has much in common with that discussed in Chapter VIII under the heading of Descriptive Research, and could legitimately have been included in that context. This would only have required extending the framework of that discussion to include a consideration of correlation coefficients and factorial loadings as the data for a comparative study. There is, however, one quite significant respect in which this latter type of study does differ from that considered in the earlier chapter: Of necessity, it refers to a characteristic of a group, rather than of an individual; in fact, it tells us something about the variables we have isolated and measured at the different age levels, but nothing about an individual's development along these variables.

This particular strategy has, however, gained some prominence from its application to one problem in particular, namely the study of age changes in the interrelationship between mental abilities or components of intelligence. This problem has been of interest in relation to the hypothesis of the age-differentiation of intelligence originally proposed by Garrett (1946). As Reinert (1970) shows in a recent review, the state of the evidence in regard to this hypothesis is quite equivocal. But this fact is of less concern for our purposes than the variety of methodological problems which arise in this type of study. At the risk of a temporary detour from our main concern in this chapter with the examination of the patterning of developmental change, let us briefly discuss the most important of these problems. They can be treated under three main headings: comparability of subject populations; comparability of form of score distributions, and (in the case of factor-analytic studies) comparability of factorial patterns.

The first of these is the most obvious, and most widely recognized. Comparability of subject populations with respect to characteristics other than age, or variables intrinsically related to it, is of course always an issue in any comparative study of different age groups. Selection can, however, be a special problem in correlational research, to the extent that it affects variability of the measures being correlated, as is almost inevitably the case, for instance, when data from an adult group of college students are compared to those obtained from an unselected public school population. Thus the case that Garrett tried to make for the differentiation hypothesis is greatly weakened by his failure to recognize this problem in citing evidence of this kind, that is, comparing the magnitudes of the correlations uncovered in different investigations of school-age children on the one hand and college adults on the other.

The matter of the comparability of the distribution of the measures being intercorrelated at the different age levels is considerably more complex. To begin with, to the extent that a linear-regression model is used in comparing correlations or factor loadings at different age levels, avoidance of very marked departure from normality, and of large discrepancies in the form of the distribution for the variables being intercorrelated is of some importance if the resultant correlation coefficients or factor loadings are to have a determinate meaning (e.g., Carroll, 1961). Thus, to the extent that these distributions change markedly over age, comparability of the correlations may be impaired. Indeed, Ferguson (1941) has given a convincing demonstration of the effect of heterogeneity of score distributions (i.e., difficulty level of tests) in depressing the size of the intercorrelation between them—a point which had already been established by Hertzman (1936). In the present context the significance of this point derives from the very real possibility that, if the tests in a battery are of comparable difficulty at one age level, this may not hold true for an older group, if the abilities being measured develop at different rates.

But even if differential rate of development is not involved, there is a more general problem relating to the dependence of the magnitude of a correlation on difficulty level as such, quite apart from heterogeneity with respect to difficulty. In other words, two tests being intercorrelated may be of equivalent difficulty, but if that difficulty changes across age—as it is almost bound to do whenever the same test is applied to different age groups—an artificial shift in the magnitude of their intercorrelation will result, an increase in difficulty being associated with a decrease in the correlation. This point is brought out in a study by Curtis (1949), specifically aimed at showing the influence of difficulty level on the relative magnitude of the general factor which results when data from a single set of ability tests administered to different age groups are factor analyzed.

Specifically, Curtis constructed two batteries of 10 tests each, of a numerical, spatial and verbal kind. These two batteries differed only in the level of difficulty of the tests, being constructed so as to make the tests on Form I at age 9 comparable in difficulty to Form II at age 12 (which means of course that Form II was relatively hard for the 9-year-olds and Form I relatively easy at age 12). Correlation matrices were obtained which were by no means comparable for the two forms at either age level, the easier form producing rather larger correlations. Accordingly, factorization of these matrices by the bifactor method yielded a general factor which accounted for 40% and 45% of the variance on Form I (at ages 9 and 12, respectively), but only for 34% and 39% of the variance on Form II. The contributions of the group factors were correspondingly higher on Form II than on Form I. Furthermore, comparison of Form I at age 9 with Form II at age 12 showed that there was no appreciable difference between the two age groups in the contribution of the general factor. On the other hand, comparing the two age groups on either Form I or Form II separately would give a misleading picture of a substantial *increase* in the contribution of the general factor with age, due apparently mainly to the decrease in difficulty of the material.

The problems connected with test difficulty and more generally with test-score distributions cease to apply, obviously, once the tests or measuring scales used at the different age levels are themselves permitted to vary, as is frequently necessary in order to obtain valid measures of a single variable at different ages. Here a new problem arises, however, which has to do with the comparability of factors obtained from different correlation matrices. In the particular case of the test of the hypothesis of the differentiation of mental abilities, what would be wanted is mainly a factor-analytic method that has the property of maximizing general factor variance and does so according to a univocally specifiable solution. In this respect the principal axis solution (Harman, 1960) appears to be the most advantageous, but it has seen little application in this domain, even though developments in computer programming have largely eliminated its major drawback which had previously discouraged its use, that is, the laboriousness of this method. Those that have been most wisely used, on the other hand, such as the centroid method, are much less well suited to this particular problem, since the factorial structure is neither unique, nor such as to yield a maximally saturated first factor. Even the bifactor method of Holzinger (cf. Harman, 1960) or Burt's (1941) bipolar method, both of which yield a heavily weighted first factor, fail to provide the kind of determinate solution that is needed for a direct comparison between the percentage of variance contributed by that factor in different groups, which is the criterion most commonly used in tests of the differentiation hypothesis.

A more extended discussion of the problems pertaining to the comparison of factor matrices in developmental research will be found in Baltes and Nesselroade (1970), who point to developments in this field for evaluating the degree of factor invariance or factor similarity, for instance, via methods of rotation of axes designed to maximize the similarity in the pattern of factor loadings of the same or equivalent tests on corresponding factors. This approach is to be contrasted with a different strategy, that of determining a separate factor matrix for each age group, based on a criterion of rotation such as simple structure, or a Varimax solution. Assuming that corresponding factors in the several matrices are identifiable, it is possible to arrive at a measure of the comparability of the factorial structure, in several ways. Perhaps the most satisfactory is that proposed by Pinneau and New-house (1964), who suggest intercorrelating the *factor scores* for the subjects in each group with those obtained for the same subjects by using the factor loadings from the matrix of the comparison group, and vice versa, the comparison of the two resultant correlations serving as an indication of factorial similarity or invariance.

Yet it is important to point out that factorial invariance or stability is not really the question the developmentalist is apt to be most interested in—except in the context of the more general problem of the stability of behavioral measures across age, which will be taken up in Chapter XII. Beyond this question, the value of comparative factor analysis as a tool in the study of developmental processes is rather limited, since it shares all the shortcomings of the cross-sectional comparison paradigm noted previously. It is at base an enterprise at a purely descriptive level, and at best may provide some information, for example, in regard to changes in general-factor variance, in number of factors, or in the identity of factors, from which a rough picture of age differences in structure for some behavioral domain from the field of abilities, personality traits and the like may emerge (cf. Black, 1965). But this picture remains a static one, conveying little about the nature of the processes governing the changes.

3. CORRELATIONAL ANALYSIS FOR LONGITUDINAL MEASURES ON TWO OCCASIONS

The simplest and most obvious way of obtaining information concerning interrelationships among two or more variables in process of development is to measure them at two selected points in time, and to intercorrelate the resultant change scores. This procedure, while yielding direct information concerning change, has two major drawbacks. First, it requires an essentially arbitrary cut across the span of development at only two points. Second, it is subject to the multiple problems and difficulties associated with the statistical treatment of change scores. Let us examine each of these in turn.

The major problem relating to the first of the above-mentioned limitations may be expressed as the imposition of a linear straitjacket on developmental change. It is readily seen that intercorrelating difference scores between sets of measures obtained on two occasions makes sense only providing the changes in the interval are approximately linear. Granted, in a purely pragmatic sense, it can be argued that it does not matter what happens to the individuals in between, for instance, in evaluating gains made as a result of some experience or special training program with respect to two or more measures of ability. But generally in intercorrelating such measures of gain, we are concerned with generalizations about psychological processes which underlie the gains made on these several variables. And from that point of view, it certainly does make a difference whether these variables are changing in parallel over the interval, or whether one changes ahead of the other, that is, at a substantially faster rate, or possibly even in a pattern directly opposite to that of the other (cf. Fig. 10–1).

As Fig. 10–1 shows, the problem raised by the assumption of linear change over the interval chosen is directly related to that arising through the arbitrary selection of two points on the developmental continuum over which the change is measured: Clearly, it is only in the linear case that the segment of the continuum chosen can be relied upon to provide a valid picture of the

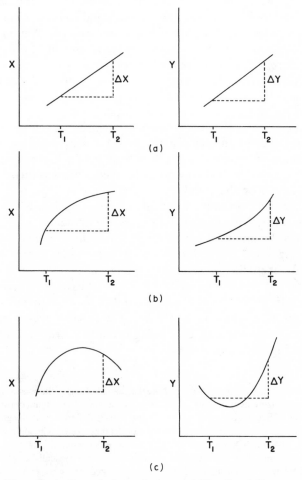

Fig. 10–1. Three illustrations of change in two variables, X and Y, over a time interval, $T_1 - T_2$, showing how linear difference measures may obscure the form of the relationship between the variables over the course of the interval.

interrelationship between the two variables over the total course of development. Admittedly situations resembling the last of the three cases depicted would rarely be encountered in the study of development, at least in this extreme form, though if we extend this study to include changes during aging, the example may be less farfetched than it looks. There are, furthermore, certain biological variables for which relations of this sort might apply, for instance, between lymphoid-endocrine and genital-tissue growth [cf. Scammon (1930)].

The second objection to the use of change scores derives from statistical considerations, which become apparent once we follow the psychometrician's lead and look at a subject's observed standing on some quantitative scale as a composite of a true score and an error score.[2] Among the more compelling discussions of the problems in the treatment of change scores, we may cite Bereiter's (1963). He distinguishes among three dilemmas, that is, more or less unpalatable alternatives confronting the investigator. These he designates as the dilemmas of under–versus overcorrection, unreliability versus invalidity, and physicalism–subjectivism.

The first of these is the most widely recognized one; it arises because there is bound to be a spurious negative correlation between initial and gain scores, assuming that errors on the initial and the final scores are uncorrelated. In this case an individual whose observed score was raised above his true score by error on the initial test would, on the average, be expected to show a smaller gain than another individual whose initial observed score was depressed by error. This situation thus gives rise to the necessity, or at least desirability (in the minds of most though not all differential psychologists) for introducing some correction in correlating change scores with some other variable (including, presumably, change on another variable, though Bereiter does not address himself to this special case), or alternatively to find some substitute for them. The most typical solution is to replace $r_{X_1 - X_2, W}$ by the partial correlation r_{X, WX_1} (W being a variable whose correlation with gain in X is of interest), care being taken to correct for unreliability in X_1 in so doing (cf. Lord, 1958).

---

[2]Generally speaking, developmental psychologists have been as disinterested in considerations of error of measurement, as well as similar concepts from the domain of psychometrics, as have their experimentalist cousins. Here, we find a good illustration of the gap separating "the two disciplines of academic psychology," as detailed so convincingly by Cronbach (1957)—cf. Ch. II—which has its counterpart in the psychometrist's lack of concern for development problems. For instance, the concept of error is typically treated as a fixed characteristic of a test , independent of the testee, when everything we know about children would suggest that changes in reliability with age—as found, for instance, on tests of infant intelligence (Werner & Bayley, 1966) and even on the Stanford–Binet (McNemar, 1942), reflect as much on the testees as on the tests themselves.

The second of the problems cited by Bereiter represents a dilemma in a truer sense, since the investigator is confronted with a choice between alternatives which, in most cases, are equally unattractive. It concerns a basic shortcoming of change scores, namely, their relatively low reliability. As Bereiter notes, this reliability is in inverse proportion to the correlation between initial and final scores, so that in order to maximize the reliability of the change scores, one needs to work with variables showing a minimal degree of correlation across occasions of testing. This requirement may be relatively tolerable in the study of *states* rather than *traits*, in other words, temporal changes in behavior occasioned by particular situational or personal factors; conceivably Cattell's (1963, 1966b) preference for working with change scores in the face of this situation is based on his interest in the investigation of states (as well as traits).[3] For the developmental psychologist, on the other hand, the requirement is quite severely restrictive. In the absence of some fairly substantial correlation of a measure over the interval in which change is being studied, the stability of the trait or characteristic in question would be in doubt, that is, one would no longer feel confident that the variable along which the change was being measured did in fact retain its psychological identity.

Bereiter himself appears less concerned over this question; he suggests rather that the real issue is the investigator's interest in change per se, or the meaningfulness of dealing with measures of change as a primary dependent variable. As he puts it:

> It would appear that the critical question is not whether a test measures the same thing at time one and time two. The critical question is whether, taking into account whatever we know about the meanings of scores at time one and time two, individual differences in change on the test are of any interest to us [p. 13].

As Bereiter notes, there are undoubtedly cases, as in the study of attitude change, for instance, where the answer to the last question is affirmative. On the other hand, among his examples of cases in which he considers an interest in change as such to be misplaced he cogently includes a developmental situation, that is, change in performance on an arithmetic test over a period of several years. Here Bereiter argues that over such an extended

---

[3]Cattell's disposition to ignore the problem of the correlation between initial and change scores and his reluctance to adjust or correct them for such correlation may have a similar basis in his state-theoretical frame of reference from which he approaches the treatment of change scores. When changes in temporary states are the object of study, the distinction between true and error components is apt to become rather elusive—cf. Cattell's statement: "If we could remove the correlation due to error alone without removing whatever may be due to systematic, real score relations, this would be attractive [1966b, p. 375]!"

interval the factors determining the change would be so difficult to unravel that little psychological significance could be attached to the shift in level of performance from the first test to the retest.

As for the third of Bereiter's dilemmas, it has in effect been anticipated already in our previous discussion. The physicalism–subjectivism dilemma amounts to a philosophical issue: Do we conceive our scale to have reference to an objective, physically verifiable dimension, whose units are known, or at least knowable, or do we settle for a subjective definition of a variable of change as such, which our measures (e.g., ratings of amount of change on some personality trait) assess directly? This issue has obvious implications for the question of the validity of the measure: Bereiter is disposed to take this for granted for subjective measures, while questioning it under the physicalist assumption, on the grounds that there is no assurance that the difference on our scale of measurement is equivalent to the extent of change on the underlying psychological dimension. The physicalism–subjectivism distinction is similarly relevant to the closely related question of the linearity of our scale, or the invariance of our units of measurement along the scale, which needs to be assumed in working with difference scores.

Despite its concern with change as such, the subjectivist alternative envisaged by Bereiter is not a very useful one for the developmentalist, since it proposes to study change in a disembodied sense, that is, without reference to the level of development already attained by the individual. In fact, we touch here on a further fundamental objection to the use of measures of change in a developmental context. That is, that any set of difference scores obtained for two separate ages represents nothing more than an arbitrary cut taken across the span of development (as already noted in connection with the linearity question). Indeed, one might well argue that the most meaningful change scores are the raw scores themselves, to the extent that they represent sheer amount of development since birth—at least for variables for which a magnitude of zero at birth (or possibly rather at conception) may be assumed. This is not to urge that we revert to the static, single-occasion correlational study considered under Section 2, but rather that we work with more complete developmental series, which will permit sets of successive measures on two or more variables to be interrelated in a much more effective fashion and to illuminate processes of development much more compellingly than the use of difference scores obtained at two occasions could possibly hope to do. The techniques at our disposal for accomplishing this end will be taken up under Sections 4 and 5.

For these various reasons then, the procedure of intercorrelating difference or gain scores to determine common developmental trends is not recommended, and has in fact been rarely used. We may still wish to work with residual gain scores, by applying a procedure such as Tucker, Damarin, and Messick's (1966) "base-free" measures of change, which involves separating the true gain into an independent component and one that is determined by initial level. Yet Cattell's (1963, 1966b) caution against eliminating entirely the contribution of initial level to gain deserves recognition, particularly by the developmentalist, since there may well be an intrinsic reason (i.e., one having nothing to do with regression effects, and possibly going in a direction opposed to such effects) for change to be related to the individual's position on a scale at the outset.

The main point in intercorrelating data on change, in any event, is that a much more complete and valid picture of the interrelationship is obtained by retaining the information as to initial level on the variables being intercorrelated, along with the change measures. This is brought out convincingly in Harris's (1962) discussion of the analysis of change. Harris first differentiates among several different expressions for measuring change, based on the use of raw scores, deviation scores, standard scores, and finally, residual gain scores, these last being analogous to Tucker *et al.*'s above-mentioned "base-free" measures, except that the distinction between observed and true scores is not made; in other words, error of measurement is ignored. All of these measures create their problems for the developmentalist, which we have already discussed with respect to raw and residual-gain scores. As for the use of deviation or standard scores, the process of relativizing scores in this fashion translates change into shift in an individual's standing relative to his group, which is of much less interest for developmental variables, though it may be of value in the study of the development of individual differences in behavior. The more interesting aspect of Harris's analysis, however, is his formulation of the multivariate analysis of change in terms of a supermatrix, made up of a set of four matrices which may be designated as

$$\begin{array}{cc} R_{22} & R_{21} \\ R_{12} & R_{11} \end{array} .$$

Regardless of what particular function of $Y_1 - Y_2$ is used—that is, raw gain, standard or deviation scores, or residual gain scores—a set of matrices of the above type is obtained, made up of the intercorrelation of the initial and of the final measures (R_{11} and R_{22}, respectively), and the cross correlation of the initial with the final measures (R_{12} and its transpose, R_{21}). There are several different ways of analyzing such "supermatrices." (We will assume, from this point on, that we have a set of k measures for each matrix; in the limiting bivariate case, all of the relevant information would be contained in the three pairs of correlations, $r_{X_1Y_1}$ and $r_{X_2Y_2}$; $r_{X_1X_2}$ and $r_{Y_1Y_2}$; and $r_{X_1Y_2}$ and $r_{X_2Y_1}$. We will discuss this case further in the text.)

The approach favored by Harris (1962, 1963a) is that of canonical factor analysis, which was originally designed for situations in which a set of predictor variables is to be related to a set of criterial variables, constituting thus an extension of the multiple correlation problem. This "parentage" appears to be responsible for the fact that, as applied to the study of change, the canonical factor analysis starts from the matrix of standardized scores, the standardization being carried out separately for each occasion. Thus, the procedure sacrifices information as to changes in *level*, to bring out more clearly changes in the interrelationships among the variables.

The procedure involves factoring the R_{11} and R_{22} matrices together, yielding a single set of factors for the two occasions on which the loadings of each variable can be compared. Furthermore, the differences themselves can be factor analyzed, either by using the standard scores themselves, or by recourse to the (standardized) residual difference scores, in which the correlation across occasions has been removed. Harris (1963a) illustrates the procedure by reference to a set of data representing five of the Primary Mental Abilities (PMA) tests administered to children in grade 8 and again in grade 11. Despite the small N (49 boys and 61 girls) Harris follows the authors of the original study (Meyer & Bendig, 1961) in carrying out separate analyses for the two sexes, leaving one to wonder about the reliability of the results reported, not only with respect to sex differences (e.g., for girls, one of the tests—word fluency—loads on two separate factors in the two grades, while this is not found true for boys), but with respect to the age changes in the loadings of tests on factors more generally. Nevertheless, the example indicates the type of information which this procedure provides, notably in regard to major shifts from one occasion to another in the loadings of particular tests on particular factors. These are, however, difficult to summarize or interpret, due to an unfortunate feature of the procedure, namely the fact that it yields too many factors. There are only six variables entering into the factor analysis (the five PMA tests just mentioned, plus an additional achievement measure included in grade 11), which are treated as 11 separate measures. These are factored into seven separate factors for the R_{11} and R_{22} matrices, as well as for the $F_1 - F_2$ difference-score matrix. This profusion of factors tends to distribute loadings for each of the five PMA variables over the factor matrix, making such occasional shifts as do occur in the loadings from grade 8 to grade 11 difficult to interpret. The same applies to the results for the difference-score matrix, which in any event has relatively few loadings of any magnitude. Thus, of the seven factors of this matrix, five show no loadings as large as .30. In other words, there are at most two change factors derivable from this set of data, which are, however, inconsistent over the two sexes.

It is worth reminding ourselves that the canonical-correlation approach, at least as formulated by Harris, looks at change only in a relativized sense;

it is thus of greater interest for determining to what extent a particular scale provides consistent measures of individual differences with respect to an ability or trait over age, than for isolating dimensions of change per se. It may thus be useful as an adjunct procedure in validating developmental scales (Chapter VI), but less so in using them to yield information about development. Note also that, since the procedure results in a single, fixed set of factors for both age levels, it in effect presupposes factorial invariance to exist.

Cattell (1966b) proposes a somewhat different approach to dealing with supermatrix data obtained from observations on a set of variables at two different points in time. To begin with, he recommends the use of "joint c-a scaled scores" (i.e., "change-absolute normalized"), these being obtained by standardizing all scores on both occasions together. This has the notable advantage of preserving information as to change in level, though it places a large burden on the assumption of linearity, that is, of equality of the intervals on the scale. He then suggests factoring the scores for each occasion separately, and to rotate axes so as to achieve optimal alignment of the factors from each matrix. The degree of correspondence achievable by this means would constitute, in a sense, a measure of the invariance of factorial structure over the occasions; but by the same token, since the factors finally determined for each matrix are specifically chosen to minimize discrepancies in loading patterns across occasions, the latter could not be used to draw inferences as to specific changes for particular variables or factors.

Like Harris, however, Cattell proceeds to the extraction of a further set of factors representing the *differences* between the two sets of occasions, based on the $R_1 R_2$ matrix and its transpose, and more specifically on that portion of the cross-occasion covariance which is not contained in the intra-occasion matrices. Cattell's procedure also appears to share the shortcoming observed for Harris's, that is, it results potentially in too many difference factors (since each pair of initial and final measures might, through the variance specific to that test, define a factor specific to those two measures). But to the extent that particular clusters of variables did tend to change in unison, they should be expected to define true change factors that would be of direct interest for the developmentalist. Herein we see both the considerable gain from the test–retest feature over the cross-sectional comparison of factor structure (Level 2), and the advantage over Harris's approach, which removes all information as to level from the analysis.

Unfortunately Cattell does not provide either the details of his method, or any illustrative example, so that its usefulness in practice remains to be tested. It should be mentioned, further, that Cattell himself prefers an alternative approach, that is, to analyze the matrix of difference scores directly. As we noted earlier, he is not convinced by the arguments against the use of change scores, based on the correlation between change and initial level, which he argues is in part an intrinsic rather than artifactual aspect of change. He is, on the other hand, forced to give recognition to the problem of the lack of reliability of difference scores, which alone would militate against this approach.[4]

Derivatives of the Multivariate Analysis of Change over Two Occasions: Cross-lagged Correlation and Change-Pattern Analysis. It may be noticed that neither Cattell's nor Harris's model appears to make very effective use of that part of the information in the R_{12} matrix that involves relationships between one variable on the first occasion and a *different* variable on the second. Within the framework of factor analysis, such relationships would probably be submerged by the more potent correlations obtaining across occasions for identical tests, which would be likely to define the factors to the exclusion of the relationships just referred to. Nevertheless, for certain purposes, the developmentalist may find relationships of this kind to be of considerable interest to him.

We will confine ourselves mainly to considering the technique of cross-lagged correlation, devised for single pairs of variables each measured on two occasions, rather than an extended set of variables presumed for a factor analysis (Campbell, 1963; Campbell & Stanley, 1963; Pelz & Andrews, 1964; Yee & Gage, 1968). The procedure is aimed at unraveling the *direction* of causal chains in situations in which experimental manipulation may not be a feasible approach. Accordingly, it has been of particular interest to sociologists, but developmental psychologists might similarly find it of value, as in looking at the relationships between parental socialization practices and child behavior, where, as Bell (1968) has forcefully argued, the identification of the causal and consequent variables is by no means unequivocal.

The approach involves comparing the magnitudes of the cross-lagged correlations for the two variables in question, that is, $r_{X_1Y_2}$ with that of $r_{X_2Y_1}$. To take the example just referred to, for instance, the question might be the following: Is severity of parental discipline at age 2 more highly cor-

---

[4]Cattell further mentions a third way in which double matrices made up of sets of test scores obtained over two occasions may be treated, that is, by factor analyzing the two matrices separately. In this connection, he shows that, where the two sets of data are obtained longitudinally, the difference factors that would be obtained by factor analyzing the difference-score matrix are mathematically derivable from the factors obtained from the matrices for each occasion; thus, insofar as the information about change is concerned, the two methods are in fact equivalent. The extraction of change-score factors from the two single-occasion factor matrices presupposes, however, that the latter are of the same rank (i.e., contain the same number of factors), and that it is possible to put individual factors from one matrix unequivocally into correspondence with those of the other.

related with aggressiveness of the child at age 4 than severity of discipline at age 4 is with aggressiveness at age 2? The formulation of child psychologists such as Sears (e.g., Sears. *et al.*, 1953) according to which parental behavior represents an antecedent of child behavior, would require the answer to the above question to be in the affirmative; should the relationship be reversed, on the other hand, the inference would be that child behavior may in part determine that of the parents. Finally, if the two correlations were of the same order of magnitude, the most reasonable deduction would probably be that each of the two variables both affects and is affected by the other, reciprocally.

Whereas the example just stated is in effect extraneous to the subject of this chapter, insofar as it concerns a correlation between child behavior and a situational factor, one might readily extend the model to cover interrelationships among different behaviors; for instance, size judgments and distance judgments, or measures of social versus cognitive egocentrism, which are thought to be in functional relationship to one another, but where the direction of a functional mediation of one by the other, if any, is uncertain.

Two points have been raised in criticism against the use of this method. Rozelle and Campbell (1969) raise a question of the logic involved in the interpretation of the difference in the lagged cross correlations, maintaining that the model invoked is an overly simplified one. In particular, should the correlations turn out to be opposite in sign, they argue that interpretation of causal chaining would be problematical. The example they give, based on a study of relationships between grades and absences in foreign language courses in high school over a year's period, seems unconvincing, since the two correlations they cite are so small (.08 and $-.063$) as to be of little interest for making any kind of an inference with respect to causal linkage, even if as claimed, the difference between these two values is highly significant statistically.

Rozelle and Campbell are particularly worried about cases in which the two cross-lagged correlations turn out to be opposite in sign—and for good reason. Consider the example they cite, from the paper by Pelz and Andrews (1964), who report coefficients of association (*gamma*) between intention (I) to buy a TV set and actual purchase (P) of it. Here $\gamma_{I,P_2} = .75$, as compared to $\gamma_{I,P_1} = -.57$. What this result shows is neither a strongly directional cause–effect relationship from I to P, as inferred by Pelz and Andrews, nor an ambiguous, either-or situation with respect to direction of causality, as Rozelle and Campbell imply; but rather a two-way causal chain, with intention positively related to purchase, and purchase in turn negatively affecting intention. This is of course a rather special, though in many ways interesting case, since we are dealing here with a relationship between a continuously changing variable and a dichotomous, on–off process. The two are inter-related according to a negative feedback loop, such that Y remains in one state until X reaches a threshold value, whereas the change in Y at that point presumably causes a reverse discontinuous change in X—a relationship comparable to that between the amount of paper in a waste paper basket and the decision to empty it.

The example just given is an instructive one, in pointing to the inadequacies of one-way conceptions of causality. Surely the major finding of interest in these data resides in the opposing signs of the two correlations, rather than the relatively slight difference in (absolute) magnitude between them, since it indicates the action of a closed feedback loop, rather than a simple unidirectional causal chain.

Such closed loops are, however, less likely to operate in the case of developmental changes; as has repeatedly been noted (e.g., Bertalanffy, 1960b), the earmark of a system under development is that it is an open rather than a closed one. Thus we should expect in general to find like-signed cross correlations operating in a positive-feedback relation, that is, the two variables mutually influencing one another. But again, the uncovering of such reciprocal relationships would seem to transcend in significance the question of which appears to be more of a causal agent than the other.

This brings us to the second caveat in the use of cross-lagged correlation, noted by Bohrnstedt (1969), and more incidentally by Pelz and Andrews (1964). This is that cross-lagged correlations are in part confounded by the correlations of each variable with itself from the first to the second occasion. For instance, Pelz and Andrews cite data on the correlation between height and weight in children (boys, $N = 100$) measured at yearly intervals between 6 and 11 years. They hoped to use these as a test of the workability of this method to tease out causal relations, on the assumption that an increase in height would necessarily have to be accompanied by an increase in weight, whereas the converse would not be true. The full set of intercorrelations (synchronous cross correlations, lagged self-correlations, and cross-lagged correlations) are shown in Table 10–3, along with the partial cross-lagged correlations, with initial level on the second occasion variable partialled out.

These results provide testimony to the fact that, in situations where there is a high degree of stability in the variables entering into the cross-lagged correlations over the interval in question (as shown in the self-correlations), the directional differences in the cross-lagged r's may virtually vanish, however plausible they may be on a priori grounds. But these differences are recoverable, once the effect of initial level on the variable being predicted is partialled out (though curiously only the comparisons involving intervals starting at age 6 yield significant differences between the two partial r's).

Table 10–3

*Synchronous, Self- and Cross-lagged Correlations between Height and Weight,
from Longitudinal Data for 100 Boys between Ages 6 and 11[a]*

Age at measurement		Cross correlations		Lagged self-correlations		Cross-lagged correlations		Cross-lagged partial correlations	
First	Second	H_1W_1	H_2W_2	H_1H_2	W_1W_2	H_1W_2	H_2W_1	$H_1W_2.W_1$	$W_1H_2.H_1$
6	7	.79	.80	.96	.94	.79	.76	.25	.02
6	8	.79	.75	.93	.90	.77	.72	.22	−.07
6	11	.79	.72	.89	.83	.71	.67	.15	−.11
7	8	.80	.75	.95	.94	.75	.75	.01	−.06
7	11	.80	.72	.90	.88	.68	.70	−.06	−.06
8	11	.75	.72	.94	.90	.69	.69	.04	−.08

[a]Data of B. O. Hughes, reported in Pelz and Andrews. Detecting causal priorities in panel study data. *American Sociological Review*, 1964, **29**, 836–848.

What Pelz and Andrews fail to note—and even Bohrnstedt only hints at the matter, in his very brief dismissal of the cross-lagged correlation method—is that, given the strong dependence of these correlations on the self-correlations over time for the two variables, a substantial difference in stability between them is bound to yield a spurious differential in the cross correlations, and thus a misleading picture of directionality in the cause–effect relations.

All in all, it has become increasingly clear that major difficulties of a statistical, and above all of a logical order arise in attempts to use the cross-lagged correlation approach for the purpose of answering questions concerning direction of causality. An excellent brief discussion of this aspect of the problem has been contributed by Howard and Krause (1970). At this point, suffice it to note that the power of this approach can obviously be enhanced by allowing it to operate over more than two occasions. Sandell (1971) has, in fact, argued in a brief note that adding a third observation to the first two allows the investigator, under certain circumstances, to resolve certain of the ambiguities in the interpretation of cross-lagged correlations. Sandell's reasoning is, however, predicated on the assumption that whatever causal forces may be operating over the first two occasions will be dissipated by the time the third one is reached. This appears to be an altogether arbitrary assumption, whose validity is wholly dependent on the experimenter's good or bad judgment in his choice of interval between occasions. More generally, Pelz and Andrews have demonstrated quite convincingly the extent to which the results obtained are a function of the investigator's success in pinpointing the time interval which optimizes the differential in the cross-lagged correlations.

Generally speaking, to be sure, correlations do become attenuated, the greater the gap of time separating the occasions at which the measures were obtained. Nevertheless, the possibility for delayed action relations, or "slowed-up causal sequences," as Rozelle and Campbell call them must be borne in mind. This is true especially for developing systems which certainly do not change in a completely rigid fashion, that is, in complete synchrony over all parts, but where a more elastic model allowing for functional relationships operating across a time gap would seem to be required. To reiterate, we would generally want more than two observations, to ensure that we have given an opportunity for any slowed-up casual sequences that may be operating to reveal themselves. But where such multiple series of observations are available, more efficient methods may be applicable to handle nonsynchronous interdependencies between variables (cf. the Level 4 models, to be taken up in the following section).

There remains a variant of the above-mentioned correlational techniques to be considered; it is appropriate in situations where one of the variables entering into a supposed relation with a second is measured on a qualitative, or at least discrete scale. This method is that of change-pattern analysis (Wohlwill, Fusaro, & Devoe, 1969; Wohlwill, Devoe, & Fusaro, 1971). It consists of equating subjects with respect to their level of initial performance on Y, and correlating the change (dY) in Y found to take place over a given interval with level of initial performance on X, in order to determine whether X may in any sense constitute a predictor of the occurrence of change in Y. It is readily seen that this approach is equivalent to correlating dY with X, partialling out the contribution of Y_1 to the correlation with gain in Y. Whereas in general, it might seem preferable to allow Y_1 to vary freely, and neutralize its effects through partial correlation, the procedure being suggested here is appropriate whenever Y is defined in qualitative terms, or in terms of a few discrete steps, as in relating a child's movement toward a new stage to the extent of his previous development with respect to a variable thought to be a functional mediator of that movement.

This procedure is illustrated in the previously mentioned work of the writer's where the interest was in relating the changes observed to take place in children with respect to their performance on a set of conservation items to the level of their performance on a set of measurement items on the initial test. This question was of interest since it bears on the hypothesis that the attainment of conservation is in fact a by-product of other processes occuring in the child over the period during which changes in conservation responses are observed to take place, these changes having the effect of providing the child with experience in conceptualizing quantitative dimensions in appropriate terms. Measurement and related activities involving comparing, counting, and seriating were considered to serve this function;

Table 10–4

Measurement vs. Conservation Change Pattern

Conservation change pattern	First to second test change analysis Mean measurement score			First to third test change analysis Mean measurement score		
	1st Test	2nd Test	N	1st Test	3rd Test	N
I–III	3.38	4.88	8	3.78	5.83	9
I–II	2.40	2.20	5	1.89	4.50	9
I–I	1.43	2.26	29	1.53	3.87	19
	$p < .01$			$p < .05$ (I–III vs I–I)		
II–III	4.28	4.94	9	4.10	6.35	10
II–II or II–I	2.71	4.14	7	2.63	3.50	4
	$p < .05$			$p < .05$		

accordingly, a group of children was followed up over an 18-month period and tested on three occasions over this interval to assess their level of development with respect to (*a*) the set of measurement tasks, and (*b*) the conservation items, performance on the latter being trichotomized into a three level scale, in view of the strong bimodality of the distribution of these responses referred to earlier (cf. Chapter IV). The results are summarized in Table 10–4, in which groups of children representing differing patterns of change on conservation over the first two occasions are contrasted in terms of their performance on measurement over the same occasions. Chief interest for our present purposes centers on the differences on Test 1 on the measurement variable for groups equated on conservation on that test, but showing differential patterns of change in conservation from Test 1 to Test 2 and Test 3, such as Groups I–II and I–III versus Group I–I; similarly Groups II–III versus Groups II–II and II–I. (It was necessary to combine certain of the change patterns into one category, because of the small number of children represented by some of the individual patterns.)

Although the above-mentioned comparisons showed the difference between the groups on the initial measurement scores to be significant, caution is necessary in interpreting these particular data, since differences in grade level are associated with the different conservation-change pattern groups—that is, the I–I group was predominantly made up of kindergarten children. (See Wohlwill, Fusaro, & Devoe, 1969, for a more extended discussion of this problem.) Yet the approach commends itself as a relatively straightforward one in order to extract information of functional relationships of this type that may operate in a delayed manner. Obviously a good deal would depend on the investigator's success in finding the test–retest interval that brings out these relations most clearly; this is primarily a question of determining the interval within which some intermediate proportion (e.g., one-half) of the children show shifts in their level of performance on the discontinuous variable. To that extent, the problem is more readily handled than in the case of cross-lagged correlations with continuously varying measures; here, as noted previously, the determination of the particular time gap across which the delayed effect is maximally operative may require that measures on both variables be obtained repeatedly, and at frequent intervals.

4. ANALYSIS OF BI- OR MULTIVARIATE LONGITUDINAL DATA SERIES

The correlational model as such is basically a static one, having been developed in order to measure relationships among variables at a given point in time. If we are to bring time-related changes in response into the picture, we have to adapt the model to encompass these, or else to deal with derived measures which themselves express characteristics of the temporal change as the raw scores entering into the correlation matrix. This last approach has in effect been considered in the discussion of change-score methodology in the preceding section; where the measures are based, not on differences between two occasions, but on some function of a series of data, more elaborate, as well as informative approaches are called for, which will be taken up in the section to follow.

There are several different ways, however, for applying the correlational model to advantage to time-series data. To begin with, let us refer to Cattell's extended model of multivariate analysis, which treats correlational and factorial analyses carried out over any two of the three axes of this covariation chart (Cattell, 1946; see also Cattell, 1966a, pp. 68ff).[5] As is well known to any but the most hidebound anticorrelational psychologists, Cattell differentiates among three sources of variation that may be used as a basis for intercorrelating two variables: individuals, responses (or tests) and occasions (or conditions). Thus Cattell arrives at six types of correlations, made up of the three combinations of pairs of the above and their transpose variants, as seen in Fig. 10–2.

The important point to note, in the developmental context of our presentation, is that the occasions axis may enter either as a source of variation,

---

[5]Since its original formulation Cattell's three-dimensional schema has been expanded into a 10-dimensional Basic Data Relation Matrix (BDRM) (Cattell, 1966a). For our purposes, however, this elaboration adds little of significance, and in fact, only succeeds in detracting from the treatment of change over occasions as one of the alternative sources of variation for the generation of correlation matrices that is of particular interest to the developmentalist.

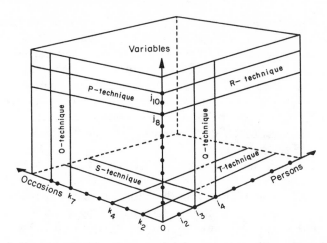

Fig. 10–2. Cattell's covariation chart (from Cattell, 1957, p. 494).

with either responses or individuals being intercorrelated (P and S technique, respectively) or as the referent of the correlation itself, taken across either responses or individuals (O and T techniques, respectively). Staying within the framework of two-dimensional correlational or factor analytic techniques, therefore, we may treat data representing age series for two or more variables in any of four ways: by limiting ourselves to one individual, and determining for him the covariation of responses over age among a set of tests (P technique) or the covariation of responses over tests among a set of ages (O technique); similarly, by limiting ourselves to one test, and determining for that test the covariation of responses over individuals among a set of ages (T technique), or the covariation of responses over age among a set of individuals (S technique).

A matter of some importance comes up at this point, namely the conception of the occasions axis, or more generally of the status of time, implied in Cattell's formulation, and its relevance for the developmentalist. Indeed, a controversy has arisen on this very point, between the "Catellian" and the "Holtzmanian" conception of time (Cattell, 1963, p. 180). The former equates time to occasions, sampled as a nonordered set from some presumed universe of discrete points in time, whereas the latter represents the more orthodox conception of time as a unidirectional continuum along which observations may be taken. It is not surprising that very different approaches are entailed by these two conceptions; thus to Cattell's P-technique corresponds that of time-series analysis which Holtzman (1963) has similarly applied to the study of a single individual's patterning of responses across age. Both of these models start from the same kind of data, but treat them in ways that are necessarily as disparate as the conceptions of the time variable underlying them.

Cattell's P-technique. Suppose we obtained measures of verbal and mathematical ability for a single child over a reasonable large number of occasions, between the ages of 4 and 18, for instance. The magnitude of this correlation is, presumably, an index of the extent to which these two abilities covary over age, that is, to which their development is intercorrelated. If we now move from a bi- to a multivariate situation, by obtaining scores on a larger set of variables, we would expect to arrive at a set of factors representing the dimensions of change underlying the observed developmental changes for the several tests.

The problem that immediately arises is the one that already plagued us in the corelational analysis of cross-sectionally obtained data (Level 1), namely, the role of age. That is, in this situation, age is bound to define a general factor which is apt to account for a heavy proportion of the common variance. If the variables entering into the analysis are subject to substantial changes with age, little room may be left for further factors to emerge that would provide more particular information on the association among developmental changes for particular subsets of variables, and thus point to the operation of more specific developmental processes at work.

Cattell tends to take a laissez-faire attitude in this regard. For him, developmental data are not, in principle, different from those that might be obtained from an adult tested over a set of occasions, over which the measures would be expected to show unsystematic fluctuation. It is readily apparent that in this latter case, *P*-technique will reveal the existing patterns of interrelationships among the variables that would cause them to vary jointly as a function of changes in condition or state from one occasion to another. Conceivably, furthermore, if the variables were all of a similar sort, a general factor could likewise emerge from such a correlation matrix, which would have no necessary relation to the time dimension (the day-to-day or occasion-to-occasion variations might have been quite irregular), but only indicate some factor which performance on all of the tests has in common, and which was subject to variation across occasions—for example, level of motivation or alertness.

Cattell suggests that we treat age in the same way as we would treat any other set of occasions, that is, according to his conception of time which, as we have seen, is regarded as a directionless variable. In his own words: "Our object is really to *sample the environment*. If this has any reference to time, it is only in the sense of time as a distance, not direction [Cattell, 1963, p. 175]." It does not seem likely that this view will prove acceptable to the developmentalist, nor gain adherents for the use of *P*-technique in developmental research. For the fact is that it is no more suited to the investigation of time-dependent phenomena than analysis of variance: Both of them treat age as a random, or at least as a nominally scaled variate. As Cattell himself observes, the information as to the temporal ordering of the data is lost in the factor analysis: "Suppose we have scores for all tests on one occasion punched on one IBM card" (i.e., yielding a deck of n cards for the n occasions); "If now, unknown to the experimenter, someone shuffles the IBM cards (or the secretary drops them on the stairs),. . . the 'organic' correlations among the variables will ... be completely unaltered by this shuffling [Cattell, 1963 p. 180f]!'"

Despite the foregoing considerations, P-technique is not without its value in developmental analysis, in comparing the factorial structure and composition of age × test matrices for different individuals undergoing development. Such characteristics or attributes of this matrix as its rank, the contribution of age as a second-order factor (assuming an oblique-structure rotation) and the angles of inclination for the various resultant axes (i.e., the intercorrelation among the factors) should indicate characteristic aspects of the individual's development with respect to the domains tapped by the tests (though to this writer's knowledge, it has not as yet been used for this purpose). This use would presuppose, furthermore, that the age factor was not so powerful as to absorb an undue proportion of the total variance, preventing other clearly defined factors from emerging, and that those factors that did emerge were identical for the individuals compared, by one of the accepted criteria of factor matching.

It should be noted, further, that the lack of a directional time dimension in the determination of the factors does not prevent one from putting them to use, as it were, for strictly developmental purposes: The course of a given child's development can in fact be conveniently charted in terms of the change in his *scores* on the factor over time.

In the paper under discussion, Cattell compared P-technique with incremental R-technique, which involves the factor analysis of a matrix of difference scores obtained from measures of n individuals on K tests over two occasions (an approach discussed earlier, under Level 3). He contents himself in the main with noting the general correspondence between the findings obtained from the two approaches (as well as from traditional R-technique) in the studies of adult personality from his own laboratory, where P-technique has been used to study variations in states, for example, across day-to-day fluctuations. At the same time, he points to the relative disadvantages of the incremental R-technique discussed previously (the limitation to two occasions; the problem of whether or nor to partial out the effect of initial status), and the compensating drawback of P-technique, that is, its limitation to a single individual. Curiously, he fails to mention an obvious variant of the latter, which has in fact been used in at least one developmental study (whereas P-technique itself does not seem to have been aplied to developmental problems as yet). This is incremental P-technique, in other words, *P*-technique applied to a set of successive difference scores obtained for changes in response over a number of occasions and tests for a single individual. Tyler (1954) has applied this method to a set of physical-growth measures for a boy obtained at half-year intervals between the ages of 11 and 18 years.[6] The results are primarily of illustrative interest—they suggest that for the particular measures included (there were 12 in all, representing standard anthropometric data, including strength of grip) growth for this boy was not a uniform process, since only half of the variables loaded significantly on the first factor. The latter was identifiable, as might be expected, as a general growth factor, including tissue mass and skeletal growth; two further factors tending to bimodality emerged, but each included only a single significant loading. The pattern of loadings for the second factor suggested that it might be identified with growth in width (as opposed to height, which was strongly represented in the first); the identity of the third factor remained unclear.

These results are less than startling, but they should serve to bring out the potential usefulness of the method in answering questions concerning the homogeneous as opposed to heterogeneous character of development, with respect to the primary mental abilities, or a set of perceptual measures, for instance. At the same time one major problem needs to be overcome in applying it, which it shares with longitudinal data generally: the need for a large number of administrations of the same test (or equivalent forms of the same). As a matter of fact, in this respect Tyler's analysis is sadly deficient, including as it does just 15 observations, whereas Cattell (1963) points to a minimum of 100 as necessary for the application of the technique, just as in *R*-technique a sample size of that order of magnitude is generally regarded as necessary. Even assuming that a sufficient number of equivalent forms can be constructed to guard against effects of perseveration, familiarity and other test–retest effects—as Cattell suggests might be accomplished by constructing sets of 20 or so variants of each test, which are administered in a cycle over a set of 100 or 200 occasions, for example, at daily intervals in the study of state-related fluctuations (cf. Moran, 1959)—the practical problem of carrying out longitudinal research involving such a large number of repeated measurements represents a very severe limitation on the usefulness of the approach. Nor can we resort, in the present instance, to one approach Cattell has devised to alleviate this problem: The use of chain *P*-technique, whereby the requisite total number of occasions is obtained by stringing together data from a number of subjects. Since this is only possible by

---

[6]Tyler actually does not use the term "incremental *P*-technique," preferring to regard his study as an application of *P*-technique to data on *rates* of growth. In thus interpreting increment as rate, he is of course assuming linearity of change.

"ipsatizing" each individual's scores, in other words, standardizing them over the set of occasions tested for each subject, information as to level inevitably is sacrificed, thus ordinarily eliminating it from consideration for the developmental psychologist.[7]

Cattell's T-technique. In contrast to *P*-technique, *T*-technique is not, properly speaking, a multivariate technique at all, at least in the sense of providing information concerning covariation among different *response* variables. In compensation, it allows for the examination of temporal patterns, for a single response measure, but for a sample of individuals. For in *T*-technique it is the occasions, rather than the test which are intercorrelated over a set of individuals. Interest therefore centers on communalities among the occasions. In view of Cattell's primary interest in relationships among response variables, as well as his conception of occasions as essentially a random variate, it is not surprising that this technique has seen little if any application in his laboratories, though it would seem to have some relevance for the investigation of cyclical phenomena. For instance, if measures of alertness obtained at different periods of the day and night are obtained over a series of days, one would expect factors for particular times of the day, that is, early morning, late morning, midafternoon, dinner-time, evening and night time to emerge, since a group of individuals would generally show a high level of alterness on late morning testing, and a low level on night time testings.

The number of factors that would result is clearly very much determined by the spacing of the occasions; for instance, if measures were only taken twice a day, no more than two factors would be expected, unless there were longer cycles operating with, perhaps, periods of a week or a month. In a developmental context, however, a different issue arises, relating to the effect of the dimension of temporal proximity or distance represented by the set of occasions. For such a set will inevitably form a simplex, in Guttman's sense, that is, the correlation matrix will be such that correlations will be maximal nearest the diagonal (that is, among adjoining occasions) and fall away systematically as the distance between the variables along the time (or any other) dimension increases.

---

[7] A different approach to the treatment of data of this type, making use of analysis of variance, has been taken by Kerlinger (1954). His procedure involves the use of growth age for a single child, to test the hypothesis of heterogeneity of growth versus its alternative, homogeneity (i.e., the null-hypothesis). Apart from the limited information concerning the patterning of growth yielded by this technique, the results obtained are in part a function of initial differences in level of development among the various dimensions of growth tested. Furthermore, it is not possible to distinguish between truly homogeneous growth and a type of growth that is rather irregular, resulting in the failure to reject the null-hypothesis due to enhancement of variance. This approach appears thus to be of limited usefulness.

This point was brought out by Cronbach (1967) in a critique of what probably remains the lone application of the technique to developmental data, namely Hofstätter's (1954) factor analysis of longitudinal data on mental growth from the Berkeley Growth Study. For this analysis Hofstätter took MA data (or their equivalents for the period of infancy) for children between the ages of 2 months and $17\frac{1}{2}$ years, and subjected the resulting correlation matrix to a factor analysis, which yielded three factors, which he identified as (a) sensorimotor alertness (infancy), (b) persistence or rigidity (early childhood), and (c) "g," or verbal-conceptual intelligence (later childhood and adolescence). This result was thought to reflect parallel discontinuities in the course of intellectual development, appearing in fact to bear out the reality of the stages in the development of intelligence postulated by Piaget. (As a matter of fact, the three periods corresponding to Hofstätter's factors do not correspond to Piaget's stages; the second one is roughly equivalent to the period of "intuitive thought," which represents a preparatory substage in the development of concrete operations, whereas the major differentiation between concrete and formal operations stipulated by Piaget is not recovered in this analysis. Nor was there any reason to expect it to be, given the nature and make-up of the intelligence-test data used for it.)

Cronbach considers this result to be a pure artifact of the simplex character of the correlation matrix, which inevitably forces a pattern of factors and factor loadings such as Hofstätter found on the data. In support of this point, Cronbach refactored the same correlation matrix using a principal-component instead of the centroid method employed by Hofstätter, essaying both a three- and a four-factor solution. In addition, he reanalyzed the data omitting, first, the two earliest tests, and second, the two latest. The results are reproduced in Fig. 10–3.

Cronbach's main point is that any correlation matrix conforming to a simplex will necessarily result in three or four factors whose loadings will increase and decrease with age according to the functions shown in Fig. 10–3, and that there is nothing determinate in the points at which these factors peak or crossover, since these can be markedly altered by changing either the method of factor analysis, or the ages included in the analysis. Actually, neither of these criticisms appears especially relevant to the limitations of factor analysis applied to simplex-type correlation matrices, since for any factor-analytic problem the results could be expected to vary as a function of the method of rotation employed, or the particular measures (in this case, occasions) included in the matrix, at least insofar as the pattern of resultant factor-loading patterns are concerned. The more basic point, however, which Cronbach hints at but somehow manages to obscure in his paper is the fact that the factor-analytic model is fundamentally unsuited to data

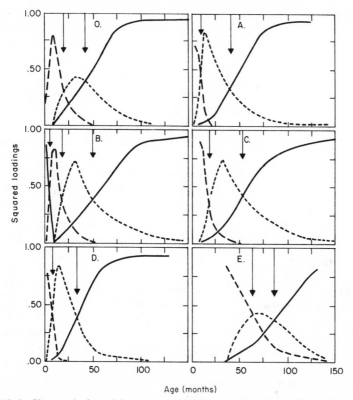

Age (months)

Fig. 10–3. Changes in factorial structure of intelligence, according to Hofstätter's analysis of Bayley data by T-technique (graph O), and four reanalyses of the same data by Cronbach (graphs A to D; see text for explanation). Graph E is based on data from Fels study. [Reprinted from *Child Development*, 1968, **38**, by Cronbach by permission of The Society for Research in Child Development, Inc.]

conforming to a simplex, because of the determination of the correlations by the single dimension of proximity (i.e., decreasing as an inverse function of the temporal interval separating them).[8] The situation is roughly comparable to that considered in the previous chapter, concerning the appropriateness of correlational or associational measures for data conforming to a scalogram pattern, in this case of the disjunctive type.

[8]In the strictest sense, the concept of a simplex implies a linear decrease in correlations falling away from the diagonal. The unequal age intervals included in Hofstätter's analysis make it difficult to test this question. Yet the evidence of a sharp drop in correlation, e.g., in the columns for both 5 and 8 months, from the 14- to 21-month row of the matrix, is hard to reconcile with the idea of a simplex, and suggests rather a real qualitative change, reflected similarly in the sharp rise of Factor II over this interval (Fig. 10–3a). The difference in the *tests* employed at these age levels must, however, be borne in mind (cf. text).

The same point appears to hold where the T-technique matrix is applied to data conforming to a cumulative pattern, analogous to the cumulative model of scalogram analysis. This will be the case wherever raw measures of growth in bodily dimensions, or in ability, vocabulary, etc. are used, so that in intercorrelating measures taken at successive age levels one is in effect dealing with part-whole correlations. This was not the case in Hofstätter's data, since he used standardized scores at each age level. An example of the sort of result to be expected when cumulative data are factor analyzed by T-technique is provided by Tucker's (1966) analysis of learning-curve data, involving a number of correct responses on a probability-learning task over a series of 21 blocks of 20 trials each (in the original publication, the blocks are themselves termed "trials," which invites confusion). Four different versions of the task (involving different pay-off ratios) were administered to 24 subjects each; when factor analyzed, the matrix yielded a pattern of loadings of trials on the factors which was markedly different from that shown in Fig. X–3, from Hofstätter's analysis. In Tucker's case, the first factor increased steadily and monotonically over trials: For two of the four task conditions, involving two-choice problems, this remained the only factor, whereas the other two conditions, involving four- and five-choice problems, yielded, respectively, three and two factors, the additional factors in each case likewise increasing monotonically over trials, but with loadings far below those of the first factor. This result is hardly unexpected; it shows mainly the gradual development of task mastery (or, in this case, perhaps more appropriately of a stable asymptotal response rate) over the course of learning. Again, even though the cumulative or part-whole character of the data meant some deviation from a simplex pattern in the correlation matrix, the factor-analytic model still is of dubious value when applied to data of this kind.[9] It seems, then, that T-technique is not an approach to be relied upon in any situation in which directional change in behavior over time occurs.

It might be noted, in regard to Hofstätter's analysis, that it would have been inappropriate in any case, if only because the measures entering into the analysis were not based on a single, constant scale. Thus the effect of

[9]Guttman and Guttman (1965) come to the same conclusion in their presentation of examples of matrices of intercorrelations of physical-growth measures obtained at a single point in time, some of which conform to the simplex model, involving noninclusive measures whose relationship is determined by a proximity dimension (e.g., breadth of shoulder, chest, hip, and hand), and some of which depart from it, involving partially inclusive measures, as when height and length of leg, arm, foot, and hand are intercorrelated. They likewise report data on intercorrelations of height measures over different ages, which again violate the simplex structure, at least at the two oldest levels, presumably because of the part-whole nature of the data.

the age-of-testing dimension was confounded with that of the response variable being tapped. In fact, we may presume that the factors found from the analysis reflect discontinuities in the tests used at least as much as in the intellectual development of the children tested. (The two are, of course, related: It is precisely because of the lack of comparability of "intelligence" in infancy with that in older children that very different kinds of tests are indicated to assess it.)

It is worth pausing to consider the question why the above shortcomings of *T*-technique do not similarly apply to *P*-technique. The answer is, of course, that the latter intercorrelates tests, rather than occasions. Presumably its little used transpose, *O*-technique, *would* be subject to the same objections cited against *T*-technique; by the same token, the transpose of the latter, *S*-technique, though apparently never employed, would be immune to them. In this technique, it is the individuals who are intercorrelated over a set of occasions; we would thus emerge with a typology of subjects based on the pattern of their developmental changes, just as *Q*-technique gives us a typology of subjects based on the pattern of their responses to different tests. The *S*-technique might thus be of value in isolating dimensions of individual differences in development (a topic to be discussed in Chapter XII), but it does not inform us about development per se.

Time Series Analysis. The same feature of a *T*-technique correlation matrix that forces it into a simplex, as we have just seen, raises problems for *P*-technique in another sense. The feature being referred to is the auto-correlation among the measures over time. As already noted, Cattell treats occasions as a random variate, and lets time emerge as a factor from the factor analysis. To the extent that there is dependence among successive observations, the applicability or usefulness of the factor analytic model is open to question. Apart from the effect of this dependence on the available degrees of freedom in *P*-technique (cf. Cattell, 1963; Holtzman, 1963), there is the more basic question, considered above, whether it is legitimate to treat a set of occasions as a random variate, particularly in a developmental context. A further substantive drawback to *P*-technique where autocorrelation among successive measures obtains is its failure to take cross-lagged correlations into account—the information in the matrix concerning relationships among variables across a gap in time is simply ignored.

P-technique, in other words, assumes at base a static model of behavior or rather one in which fluctuations may occur, but either randomly, or in a rigid fashion. Time-series analysis, on the other hand, provides us with information, both concerning time-related trends in the data for individual variables, and for time-lagged correlations among variables. It is particularly suited for the investigation of cyclical or recurrent trends, and partly for that reason much of the development and application of this technique has come from the study of econometrics, for instance, business cycles, where temporal lags between two indices, such as wages and prices, are common. Other applications come from the side of physiology, where cyclical processes are of course equally prevalent. Holtzman (1963) has provided a useful introduction to this method for behavioral scientists, utilizing illustrations of both physiological and behavioral measures taken from a single patient daily over a large number of days (245).

The major aim of the technique is twofold: first, to extract information concerning autocorrelation for a single variable, by intercorrelating the measures for n-lagged occasions (i.e., times separated by an interval of n tests), so as to yield a function showing changes in the magnitude and direction of the correlation as this interval increases. Of particular interest for the developmental application of the technique is its power to abstract cyclical or oscillatory trends from a general trend that may be superimposed on them, as illustrated by Sholl (1954), with reference to a longitudinal series of height measurements.

Note that we are dealing here with the analysis of single time series, which might well have been included in Chapter VIII, as a further approach to the description of developmental functions, where longitudinal data are available. Of greater relevance in the present context are the methods for the analysis of *multiple* time series, as discussed by Holtzman. The basic procedure is simply to intercorrelate the variables of interest across successive time lags, e.g., X_o with $Y_1, Y_2, Y_3 \ldots Y_n$; similarly for Y_o. This procedure, applied to the several measures mentioned earlier which Holtzman had obtained from the schizophrenic patient did not in fact reveal any very striking correlations, such as would have suggested a delayed effect of one measure on another, though there is a tendency for the perceptual speed measure to show increasingly larger negative correlations with a word-association relatedness measure as the lag increases from zero to four days.

In contrast to autocorrelation procedures designed to provide information concerning cyclical or rhythmic fluctuations of a function, which depend on a large number of successive observations being taken, multiple-time series analysis can be carried out with just a small number of longitudinal measures on two or more variables—as few as two, in fact; we already considered in the previous section the rationale and basic ingredients of the approach. The generalization to n observations is straightforward; the aim presumably would be to uncover the lag yielding the most clear-cut picture of the relationship among the set of variables, which is precisely what commends them to the developmental psychologist. On the other hand, it may be assumed that where a time lag in the interaction between two variables, or two systems in development, does exist (i.e., where the synchronous correlation is not the maximal one), the lag will be reasonably short, so as to require no more than a few measures, taken at fairly closely spaced intervals, to reveal itself. This optimal lag can itself be expected to vary with age, that is, to be a function of the speed of developmental processes, but even in later childhood or adolescene one would rarely expect it to exceed one or at most two years.

What evidence, if any, do we have of the operation of such time-lagged relationships? Very little, admittedly, thus far at least. But this is in large part because of the paucity of longitudinal data, and the failure of developmental psychologists to be on the lookout for such relationships even when they have the requisite data. Illustrative incidental evidence of this sort from the author's study of cognitive development was cited in the previous section. We might likewise mention the study of Ausubel, Schiff, and Gasser (1952) referred to in our review of the social perception work, as well as at the start of Chapter VIII, which suggests that a gap of this very sort is operating between the shift occurring in adolescence in the criteria which the child uses to evaluate others, and his perception of how others evaluate him. Presumably, according to their hypothesis, longitudinal data on criteria use should have revealed that the correlation between the child's use of certain dimensions, for example, femininity, or appearance, in evaluating others and his use of the same dimensions in his perception of others' evaluation of him was higher cross-lagged (perhaps by as much as two years, see Ausubel *et al.*'s data, or Fig. 8–2c) than that determined synchronously.[10]

This example suggests the possibility that cross-lagged relationships might be particularly likely to occur during a period of instability or transition, where two normally related processes may temporarily separate. Conceivably, the relationship between height and weight might provide evidence of this sort, though it is important to be mindful of Pelz and Andrews' (1964) warning cited in the last section, that where there is a high degree of autocorrelation for the variables, their contribution to the cross correlation should be removed, if it is to appear with any clarity.

Three-Way Factor-Analytic Models.   In view of the fact that we are dealing at base with a three dimensional problem, namely, the covariation among a set of m variables in n individuals over k occasions, it is apparent that none of the approaches that were considered are adequate to the task. What we need is a set of multivariate procedures that will permit us to look at interrelationships among these three dimensions simultaneously. Alternatively,

[10]Ausubel *et al.* did not actually obtain data of this kind, and the correlations they obtained as indices of accuracy of self-perception are not suitable for this purpose, since they represent correlations between the subject's own ratings and the modal ratings of the subject by his classmates; thus they cannot be obtained on a lagged basis.

we may try to collapse the three-dimensional matrix into a two-dimensional one, by intercorrelating or factor analyzing, not the original set of raw scores, but a set of measures derived from the developmental function for each variable, which express some characteristic of its change over age. The last-mentioned approach will be taken up in the section to follow; at this point we will examine briefly the current status of multivariate technology (or is it an art?) as applied to the three-dimensional case.

Only three models to handle this case are known to the author, and none of them has as yet seen much application, so that their value and their limitations remain to be determined. One of these, represented by a brief paper by Evans (1967) is only imperfectly worked through, and lacking in empirical application to actual data; though it represents an interesting attempt to isolate general and specific growth factors directly, we will not consider it further, and turn instead to the remaining two by Jöreskog (1969) and Tucker (1963).

First, let us consider Jöreskog's model for factoring multitest-multi-occasion matrices. Without going into great detail concerning the method employed, we will note that Jöreskog's approach treats the occasions dimension as coordinate with, that is, parallel rather than orthogonal to, the test-variable dimension. This does not mean, of course, that the factors that emerge from each may not be orthogonal to one another (there is obviously no such thing in factor analytic space as a set of parallel axes, though, as it happens, Jöreskog has chosen an oblique axes rotation for the example to be presented), but rather that Jöreskog in effect collapses his three dimensions into the usual two, simply adding room within the plane to accomodate the factors thus emerging. Accordingly, his generalized model provides for three kinds of factors: general, occasion-specific, and test-specific. More specific models are outlined to correspond to particular combinations of these; for instance, the investigator might postulate the existence of occasion-specific and test-specific factors in a given set of data, without any general factor.

For illustrative purposes Jöreskog chose a set of data which he thought might fit the case just mentioned, i.e., the combination of test- and occasion-specific factors. The data were those of Hilton and Myers (1967) consisting of longitudinal measures of performance on achievement tests in math, science, social studies, and reading, along with verbal and mathematical aptitude scores, obtained in grades 5, 7, 9, and 11. The results of his analysis in terms of factor loadings are shown in Table 10–5.

The zero values in this table are determined by the particular properties of the model chosen, that is, the V- and Q-factors, being occasion–specific, should have nonzero loadings only at age levels corresponding to the occasion defined by the factors; conversely, the test-specific S-factors should show loadings at all occasions but only on the particular test defined by the

TABLE 10-5

Factor Analysis of Growth Data by Jöreskog's Model BC (Occasion- and Test-Specific Factors)[a]
N = 703

Grade t	Test i	Occasion-specific factors								Test-specific factors						θ_{ti}
		V_5	V_7	V_9	V_{11}	Q_5	Q_7	Q_9	Q_{11}	S_1	S_2	S_3	S_4	S_5	S_6	
5	Math	0*				.91				.07						.42
	Sci	.63				.29					.17					.42
	SS	.59				.36						.14				.35
	Read	.93				0*							.04			.37
	Scat V	.89				0*								.26		.34
	Scat Q	0*				.86									.22	.47
7	Math		0*				.90			.05						.43
	Sci		.58				.30				.27					.46
	SS		.75				.18					.15				.40
	Read		.90				0*						.15			.42
	Scat V		.91				0*							.32		.26
	Scat Q		0*				.86								.25	.44
9	Math			0*				.94		.34						.00
	Sci			.58				.30			.30					.44
	SS			.73				.22				.04				.40
	Read			.91				0*					.24			.37
	Scat V			.92				0*						.25		.31
	Scat Q			0*				.85							.35	.37
11	Math				0*				.87	.10						.48
	Sci				.63				.23		.26					.51
	SS				.73				.20			.19				.40
	Read				.89				0*				.20			.45
	Scat V				.93				0*					.15		.35
	Scat Q				0*				.91						.25	.33

[a]From Jöreskog (1969), original data from Hilton and Myers (1967).
*Parameters specified by hypothesis.

factor. In addition, the hypothesis that reading and Scat verbal tests would have zero loadings on the occasion–specific quantitative factors, and that math achievement and Scat math aptitude would similarly have zero loadings on the occasion–specific verbal factors was built into the model, that is, ages were rotated so as to result in zero loadings for these variables on the factors mentioned.

This analysis reveals several different kinds of information relating to the development of ability in the areas tested. First, the occasion–specific variance on the individual tests is essentially invariant over grade levels, and effectively accounted for by the verbal and quantitative factors extracted. Rather larger changes over grade level are found in the test-specific factors, though it is difficult to encompass them within any simple general principle, since they follow no very obvious pattern. (Jöreskog suggests that the changing pattern for the math achievement factor shows the changing nature of the test, i.e., from computation to reasoning, but this would not account for the drop in loading from grade 9 to grade 11.)

An interesting feature of Jöreskog's model is that it allows him to express the "innovation" occurring with respect to each of the occasion–specific factors at any given occasion, in terms of the extent to which the corresponding factor scores are determined by, that is, predictable from the equivalent scores at the previous occasions. In the case of the factors shown in Table 10–5, the regression coefficients in question vary between .90 and .96; thus there is very little "innovation," or change from one grade level to the next in the factorial composition of the tests, which was already shown in the near invariance of the factor loadings.

Jöreskog's model should prove useful for detecting major qualitative shifts in the factorial composition of tests (or, conversely, in the nature of the factors emerging from a given set of tests at different age levels), and does so without confronting the investigator with the vexing problems of factor matching which the cross-sectional (Level 2) comparative analysis of factorial structure entails. Herein seems to lie the major gain for Jöreskog from the longitudinal feature of his model. On the other hand, Jöreskog's differentiation between occasion-factors and test-specific factors must be read with caution. The former are, as a matter of fact, highly correlated across occasions (a feature of the factorial structure brought out by the oblique-rotation solution applied to the data), which accounts for the fact that the test loadings on the "occasion-specific" factors are virtually invariant over age; the test-specific factors, on the other hand, represent residual variance and actually fluctuate markedly from one age to another. It would, indeed, have been surprising if developmental data of this sort would have yielded truly "occasion-specific" factors. The notion itself, though it might have some interest for the study of temporally localized phenomena, for example, mood states, effects of drugs, etc., appears in principle antithetical to the developmentalist's interest in tracing the interrelationship among particular developmental processes over age.

In contrast to Jöreskog's model, which, as we have seen, lays out occasions and test factors side by side, Tucker's (1963) three-way factor-analytic model keeps these two dimensions, or factor spaces, conceptually separate, and makes it possible to examine their interaction, that is, the evolution of factors over different segments of the time dimension. In its most general sense, it provides a means for handling any type of data representable via a three-way matrix; for instance, it has been applied to data obtained via the multitrait-multimethod approach to the validation of psychological constructs developed by Campbell and Fiske (1959), to which reference was made in Chapter VI. Thus, a set of personality variables might be assessed through several parallel methods, for example, ratings of different types of raters. Tucker's manner of analyzing such matrices provides for a set of factors corresponding to each of the two major modes of the matrix (traits and methods, in this instance), and further for a "core box" which shows the interaction between the two, in other words, the differential expression of each of the factors for one mode across those of the other. The model is thus in more than a superficial sense analogous to that of the analysis of variance, though it is obviously of a very much higher order of complexity, and thus places considerable demands on the development of appropriate analytic techniques, notably in regard to factor rotation, and to communality estimation.

While one supposes that computer programs have been, or are being developed to handle the analysis of data conforming to this model, at this writing applications of it remain scattered (cf. Tucker, 1967; Levin, 1965), and—with the exception of Tucker's (1963) purely fictitious example—untried in the study of developmental questions. It has, however, been applied to the analysis of multivariate learning data (Tucker, 1967), which represents, of course, a case formally equivalent to the developmental one, in that one of the modes (i.e., trials) is analogous to that of age.

In order to illustrate the kind of information one may expect to obtain via this model, consider Tables 10–6 and 10–7, the former showing the basic structure of the model, the latter the resulting factor loadings and other information based on Tucker's fictitious set of data.

Table 10–6 indicates the three resulting factorial matrices, that is, matrix A, describing the 12 individuals i in terms of the four individual factors m; B, describing the nine traits j in terms of three trait factors p, and C, describing the five occasions k in terms of the two occasion factors q. In addition it shows the "core box" G, showing the interrelationship among the three sets of factors. (The numerical entries in this figure are coefficients proportional to factor loadings.)

It is the last of these matrices that is of greatest interest for us, since it permits us to trace changes over occasions both in the factorial structure of the trait variables, and, via factor score estimation procedures, in the course of development of the factors themselves. This is shown in Table 10–7 and in particular in the last two items of that table, the variable factor scores and correlations. It should be noted that the factor analytic procedure used by Tucker involved the assumption that matrix B, expressing the relation-

TABLE 10-6 *Intrinsic Structure for Tucker's Three-Way Factor Analytic Model*[a]

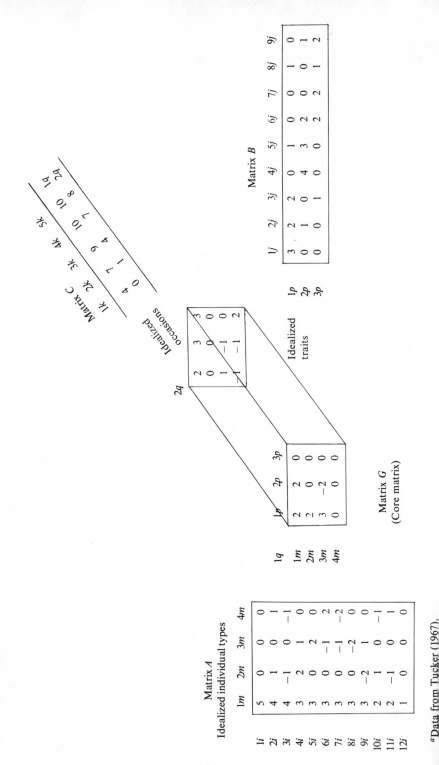

[a]Data from Tucker (1967).

280

TABLE 10-7

Internal Matrices for Occasions (k) and Variable Factors (p).[a]

Occasions		1k			2k			3k			4k			5k		
Variable factors		1p	2p	3p	1p	2p	3p	1p	2p	3p	1p	2p	3p	1p	2p	3p
Variable factor core matrices for occasions	1m	8	8	0	16	17	3	26	30	12	34	41	21	36	44	24
	2m	8	0	0	14	0	0	18	0	0	20	0	0	20	0	0
	3m	12	-8	0	22	-15	0	31	-22	0	37	-27	0	38	-28	0
	4m	0	0	0	-1	-1	2	-4	-4	8	-7	-7	14	-8	-8	16
Mean cross-products for variable factor scores	1p	848	544	0	3241	2391	478	8061	7134	3088	13378	12990	7042	14868	14840	8512
	2p	544	704	0	2391	3116	508	7134	9500	3568	12990	17588	8512	14840	20208	10432
	3p	0	0	0	478	508	94	3088	3568	1504	7042	8512	4606	8512	10432	6016
Variable factor covariances	1p	272	-32	0	937	-57	46	1977	114	280	2974	444	616	3204	584	736
	2p	-32	128	0	-57	515	49	114	1400	328	444	2459	763	584	2784	928
	3p	0	0	0	46	49	13	280	328	208	616	763	637	736	928	832
Variable factor scores	Mean	24	24	0	48	51	9	78	90	36	102	123	63	108	132	72
	σ	16.5	11.3	0	30.6	22.7	3.6	44.5	37.4	14.4	54.5	49.6	25.2	52.8	56.6	28.8
Variable factor correlations	1p	1.00	-.17	—	1.00	-.08	.42	1.00	.07	.44	1.00	.16	.45	1.00	.20	.61
	2p	-.17	1.00	—	-.08	1.00	.60	.07	1.00	.61	.16	1.00	.61	.20	1.00	.61
	3p	—	—	—	.42	.60	1.00	.44	.61	1.00	.45	.61	1.00	.61	.61	1.00

[a]Data from Tucker (1967).

281

ship between values on the nine observed traits and the three idealized trait factors, remained fixed over occasions; information concerning the interaction of traits with occasions is thus thrown into the core box, where it is expressed in terms of changes in the intercorrelation among factors, and in the mean factor scores.

From this fictitious analysis one would be able to arrive at several con-clusions. First, factor $3p$ is totally absent on the first occasion, its contribu-tion (in terms of factor-score means) rising at first slowly, then more rapidly, whereas the first two factors develop earlier; all three change little over the last interval, that is, between occasions $4k$ and $5k$. Of further interest is the interrelationship between the various factors, $1p$ and $2p$ changing from slightly negative to slightly positive, while both of them show a more sub-stantial but nearly constant correlation with factor $3p$ (beyond occasion $1k$, where this factor did not as yet appear).

As in the case of Jöreskog's model, the longitudinal aspect of Tucker's ensures the definition of a set of factors that are invariant over occasions, but in contrast to the latter, the provision for the core box, containing the interrelationship between the occasions- and traits-factors, affords a much more succinct picture of the developmental evolution of the trait factors. Unfortunately, what is true of the latter is not generalizable to the idealized individual factors, relating to the different types of persons. It would have been valuable to be able to use the model to isolate different patterns of development characterizing different types of individuals. However, because of the communalities problem, it is not possible to estimate factor scores for individuals on the individual type factors.

As already mentioned, the three-way model has been applied to the analy-sis of learning data, to pull out information concerning the number of definable factors relating to the trials dimension (based on data by Parker & Fleishman, 1960), and the differential expression of the measure factors (based on the different response measures used, that is, three types of errors, plus time on target) across trials. Here the core box analysis, furthermore, reveals some interesting three-way interactions among individual-type factors, measure factors and trial factors, such that certain individuals showed peaking with respect to each of the component measure-factors at different portions of the learning curve. An analogous case from the developmental side, which should be realizable with appropriate longi-tudinal data on mental abilities, would be the demonstration that certain kinds of children show a relatively precocious development with respect to the numerical factor, whereas others, developing more normally with respect to this factor, may show relatively late development for the spatial factor, etc. The model, in other words, appears ideally calculated to tease out some of the intricacies in the development of multidimensional aspects of behavior, for instance, in the realms of personality, abilities, perceptual skills, etc. This feature should commend it particularly to the attention of those interested in integrating developmental and differential study, a problem to be taken up in Chapter XII.

5. CORRELATIONAL ANALYSIS OF DEVELOPMENTAL FUNCTION
PARAMETERS FOR SEVERAL VARIABLES

Undoubtedly the most direct approach to studying functional relationships among several variables undergoing development is to apply traditional modes of correlational or factor-analytic techniques, not to the raw scores obtained for each variable at successive ages, but to particular functions of those scores expressing some property of the developmental curve that is considered to be of interest. In other words, the developmental information in the data is compressed into particular indices, representing parameters of the developmental function.

As a matter of fact the multivariate analysis of change scores (Level 3) represents a special case of this approach, since it makes use of a derived measure obtained from the original set of data, which has the effect of removing the time or age dimension from the factorial matrix. For the present purposes, let us generalize the approach to encompass functions of the original data other than simple linear-difference scores between two arbitrarily chosen occasions. In the ideal case, mathematical functions are obtained for every subject for each variable, and corresponding parameters of each, such as rate of change, acceleration or deceleration, asymptotal level, etc., are in turn intercorrelated or factor analyzed. This procedure has the real advantage over any of the procedures discussed thus far that different individuals are compared, not in terms of their status at particular occasions, but more directly in terms of corresponding characteristics of their developmental functions. It can thus encompass interdependencies among aspects of development operating over extended periods of time.

This writer is not aware of any studies in which this approach has been utilized, that is, in which parameters for different functions obtained from a set of individuals have been intercorrelated. The necessity for fitting individual curves and determining parameters for each separately may have acted as an inhibitory influence against this type of work, although in areas such as motor development, for instance, this approach would seem to have much to offer, particularly in determining interrelationships among functions developing over different age periods. For example, is the growth factor implicated in the development of climbing behavior, as studied by Weinbach (1940) (cf. Chap VIII, pp. 171f) related to the earlier development of crawling, e.g., in terms of the rate of change of the developmental function for each? It would not be difficult to suggest aspects of behavioral development for which this question would be equally meaningful: For instance, is the rate of development of infant intelligence related to that found for the development of verbal intelligence in early and middle childhood? This would seem to be a more meaningful question than the determination of stability coefficients, indicating the correlation between intelligence-test scores at some given age in infancy and another age in later childhood, and may in fact provide a very different picture as regards to the stability of the development of intelligence than that obtained thus far.

An interesting attempt to apply the approach being suggested to developmental parameters of a rather special kind is worth citing. As has been noted previously, one perfectly legitimate parameter of a developmental function, at least for certain dimensions of development, takes the form of the *ages* at which particular points of the function, or particular qualitatively defined physical or behavioral "landmarks" are attained. Indeed, the possibility for thus using age in assessing development was one of the prime arguments in favor of the definition of age as properly belonging on the dependent side. In certain situations, then, it may be informative to look at the interrelationship among different aspects of development in terms of the correlation among ages at which particular points or steps of the developmental function are attained, so as to obtain a picture of consistencies in the overall timetable of development underlying the changes observed with respect to those aspects. This is precisely what Nicolson and Hanley (1953) have done for a series of indices of physiological maturity, including measures of successive phases of sexual development (breasts for girls, pubic hair and genitalia for boys), indices of skeletal development (in terms of the ages at which particular skeletal ages were attained) and indices of general somatic growth (age at maximum height, and corresponding to attainment of particular percentages of mature height). On this basis, they obtained correlation matrices comprising 14 measures for girls and 11 for boys (the samples being taken from the Berkeley Growth Study), which were then factor analyzed to yield a general growth factor, from which a rate-of-maturation index for each subject could be determined, via a multiple-regression equation (equivalent in effect to the calculation of factor scores for the general factor).

How much does this line of attack have to offer for the behaviorally minded developmentalist? On this point Nicolson and Hanley offer only a set of incidental findings, which admittedly are less than encouraging. They report correlations between age of walking, and age of attainment of several of their physical and physiological growth markers, but these turn out to be consistently negligible and nonsignificant. There are, however, data to indicate that, over a shorter period, age of walking is related to the acquisition of other skills, not only in the motor realm, where Bayley (1935) reports a correlation of .65 with motor performance at 36 months, but even in mental development, where the corresponding value is still a respectable (and significant) .40.

Allometry. In the case of growth-curve type data, a different method has been used to interrelate different measures undergoing change during development. This is to express one as a mathematical function of the other. It has been applied particularly to the study of growth gradients, that is, of the relative growth for different parts of the body, which has been given the name of allometry. A basic "allometric formula" was suggested by its originator, Huxley, to express the relationship between the growth of a part and that of the whole, which has the form $y = bx^k$, or in its logarithmic form, $\log y = \log b + k \log x$. The latter expression shows that if the allometric relation holds, a plot of the logarithmic values of the dimensions being interrelated will be linear in form.

Work based on this hypothesized relationship has been subjected to a number of criticisms, discussed at length by Reeve and Huxley (1945), and more briefly by Hersh (1955), among others. The reliability, and even more the interpretation of k is frequently uncertain, and the extent to which empirical data conform to the relationship is a matter of debate. A further difficulty of a logical order is that it is impossible for parts of an organ and the organ as a whole *both* to show an allometric form of growth in relation to the size of the body unless growth of the organ is completely homogeneous among all its parts. Thus the question of the units or the scale of body parts within which the relationship applies arises.

For the developmental psychologist, the validity of the allometric formula is of less interest than the rationale underlying the approach. Certainly no one would expect to be able to reduce the interrelationship between two behavioral dimensions to such a simple expression, even assuming that growth functions of an incremental sort, as illustrated by active and passive measures of vocabulary, for example, were being interrelated. (As a matter of fact, even for physical variables most of the applications of allometry have been limited to the study of animal forms.) The main reason for calling attention to the subject at all is simply to emphasize the point that the study of the *magnitude* of the interrelationship between two variables, expressed via the correlation coefficient, does not exhaust the questions to be asked concerning the interaction between them, and that there may be cases in which the *form* of the relationship between them is more revealing.

Conclusion: The Place of Correlational Analysis in the Study
of the Patterning of Developmental Change

At the outset we launched this chapter with the statement that the correlational approach was possibly the method best calculated to provide the developmentalist with the information he required. This statement warrants closer scrutiny at this point, to bring out the merits of the correlation coefficient and of the techniques based on it—notably factor analysis—for this purpose, and to consider briefly certain alternative modes of analysis not as yet mentioned.

The correlation coefficient, however useful as a succinct index of strength and direction of the interrelationship between two variables, has several features which affects its usefulness in bringing out information concerning the interpatterning of developmental trends for sets of variables. Let us consider three of them in particular: (a) the linear mold into which the data are cast; (b) the loss of information as to level; and (c) the dependence of the results on both the extent of the variability in the data and the manner in which variation is introduced into the measures.

a. The Question of Linearity. The fact that the form of the regression of many variables on age departs markedly from linearity does not, in itself, necessarily mean that linearity will be violated in correlating two variables changing with age with one another. In fact, if both were precisely identical functions of age (no matter how nonlinear), the correlation between them would, of course, be perfectly linear. But where the two age functions differ substantially between themselves, and at least one of them departs markedly. from linearity, this is bound to distort the value of the correlation coefficient obtained for their interrelationship.

A particular instance of this sort is represented by the intercorrelation of two error functions, such as the intersensory discrimination curves obtained by Birch and Lefford (1963)—cf. Chap. VIII, specifically Fig. 8–6. In situations of this sort, transformations of the data (possibly logarithmic) are probably indicated, before calculating correlations from them. We will, however, forego more extended consideration of this issue, since it has been admirably discussed elsewhere (e.g., Cattell, 1966b), and since for most pragmatic purposes, barring U- or inverted-U-shaped relationships between variables, the relation between behavioral variables is generally not so high as to cause one to prefer a nonlinear to a linear model. The same applies *a fortiori* to the case of factor-analytic procedures, which are built on the assumption of linearity, not only through the use of the correlation coefficient itself, but through the basic factor-analytic equation, which expresses factors as linear combinations of the individual's scores on the set of tests multiplied by some chosen set of weights. While nonlinear models of factor analysis are available (McDonald, 1962), for practical purposes the gain achieved in adopting them appears to be negligible.

b. The Abstraction from Score Levels.   Correlations are of course dimension-free measures, that is, in the course of calculating them, all information concerning both means and variances in the original distributions becomes lost. While this is an obviously advantageous property (without it we would of course be unable to study the interrelationship among variables based on different scales, or the consistency of behavior across age levels, etc.) it is at the same time a limiting feature, since it considers only the extent of covariation among the measures, rather than aspects of the relative magnitude of the measures, for instance, which are an equally important aspect of the interpatterning among variables. Thus it seems as important to find out that passive vocabulary develops ahead of active vocabulary, as that the two covary to some specified extent over a set of individuals (cf. the foregoing brief consideration of allometry).

One way that correlational analysis of developmental dimensions can be extended to provide a parametric picture of developmental change is via the results of a factor analysis, yielding sets of estimates of factor scores through which an individual's standing with respect to a factor may be described. In other words, given that a set of tests (e.g., of perceptual illusions) appear to define a common factor (e.g., of assimilation tendency) we may express the level he has attained with respect to that factor in terms of his score on that factor, estimated by means of a multiple regression equation. His score on each component test is equated to a linear combination of the cross products of the loadings of that test on the set of factors extracted, multiplied by the corresponding scores of the individual on the factor (cf. Nunnally, 1967, p. 358f and Nesselroade, 1970, for more extended treatment of the problems relating to the estimation of factor scores, the latter paper having particular reference to developmental applications).

As applied to developmental situations, the procedure presupposes that the factor itself is invariant over age, that is, manifests an approximately constant set of loadings at the different age levels (cf. Baltes & Nesselroade, 1970). The most effective method of ensuring this is to rotate the factors from each age group to a common factor space, based on similarity-maximizing criteria. Providing the procedure is successful, and accomplished while preserving the original differences in level as they are for Cattell's (1966b) "joint c-a scaled scores," discussed above (cf. Cattell, 1968; Horst, 1965, for more extended treatments of this problem), we are in effect in a position to express the progress of the individual's development with respect to the factor in terms of the resultant factor scores. A particularly important feature of this approach is that it allows us to do so for subjects not included in the original factor analysis (though presumably representing the same population), since any individual's estimated factor score is simply a function of the observed scores for each of the tests showing significant loadings on the factor, and the loadings of the tests on the factor, which are presumed to be known from the original analysis, and to remain unchanged.

   c. *The Sources of Variability in the Intercorrelation of Developmental Dimensions.* It is a truism that correlation is dependent on variance. The extent to which correlation is affected by a relative absence of variabilility in the data has been generally recognized, under the heading of the problem of restriction of range, though its opposite, the exaggeration of correlations as a function of unusually large range has not received a proportionate amount of attention. The relevance of this point for developmental study is that, since variance frequently changes with age, increasing for growth functions and decreasing for error functions, concomitant artifactual changes in correlation are to be expected.

   Of more consequence, however, is the matter of the source of variance in correlational studies of development. Almost invariably this source resides in interindividual differences. A good case could be made, however, for the position that tests, or more generally stimuli, represent a better choice of source of variance as applied to developmental research, or, to take the factor-analytic equivalent that P- or Q-technique are preferable to R-technique.

   The problem with measuring variation across individuals is that when we are dealing with true developmental, as opposed to differential variables, individual differences within an age group represent in fact differences in the subject's standing on the developmental dimension. In other words, the variation is actually attributable to, or interpretable in terms of differences in *rates* of development, so that by capitalizing on individual variation within an age group we are actually catching the individuals at varying points of the developmental function. If we now wish to make statements concerning changes in correlation with age, for instance, it is apparent that we have a problem of confounding.

   Under certain circumstances, this problem can be avoided by following the approach mentioned in the previous section, that is, using, not response magnitudes, but ages of attainment of specified levels of response as the data to be correlated, as in the study by Nicolson and Hanley (1953). Under this approach, comparing correlations for different age groups is no longer a meaningful question, but the point is that we do not need to rely on such comparison to assess the interrelationship between our variables across development, since the use of the age measures has the developmental information built into them.

CHAPTER XI

The Experimental Manipulation of Developmental Change

The place of the experimental method in developmental psychology, and the meaning of this approach as applied to the study of developmental problems, was considered briefly in the introductory chapters (I and II), notably in connection with the treatment of the status of developmental psychology as an experimental as opposed to a differential discipline. Thus, we noted Russell's (1957) decidedly limited conception of the place of experimentation in developmental research, which he saw primarily as a tool placed in the service of the investigation of general behavioral problems; we saw others, such as Ausubel (1958), questioning the applicability of the experimental method in the study of developmental problems as such.

Few developmental psychologists today would align themselves with either of these views, one suspects, but as yet there is little agreement as to just what is meant by the experimental study of behavioral development. It is useful to differentiate among four research paradigms that might be subsumed under this rubric, though only the last two of these will turn out to be of relevance to the main theme of this chapter, namely, the application of the experimental method to produce, simulate, or interfere with developmental change under laboratory conditions.

Four Paradigms of Experimental–Developmental Research

PARADIGM 1: EXPERIMENTAL RESEARCH ON NONDEVELOPMENTAL PROBLEMS

As noted in our overview in Chapter I of the dominant influences in the field today, there is a large body of research of an experimental nature which, for one reason or another, happens to use children for its subjects, but deals with problems that have no intrinsic relevance to the developmentalist. This paradigm—illustrated in research on such questions as stimulus compounding (Spiker, 1963), effects of reward versus nonreward (Endsley, 1968), etc.—is included here mainly for the sake of completeness. There are some experimental child psychologists unwilling to concede to developmental problems any characteristics that would distinguish them from general behavioral problems, and who might thus deny that there is a real difference between this type of research and the others to be cited; it is of little interest for our purposes, since it raises no questions that have not been adequately covered in general treatments of experimental methodology.

PARADIGM 2: EXPERIMENTAL NONDEVELOPMENTAL RESEARCH ON
DEVELOPMENTAL PROBLEMS

There is a considerable amount of experimental research which deals with problems which either emanate from the province of the developmental psychologist, or which have turned out to be of relevance to him, but which are not directed at the developmental aspects of these problems, or at least at accounting for or simulating the developmental changes which take place with regard to them. This type of research is illustrated in studies of young children's response to form orientation such as Wohlwill and Wiener's (1964) and Sekuler and Rosenblith's (1964), as well as much of the work on reversal–nonreversal shifts (Kendler, 1963) and probability learning (Goulet & Goodwin, 1970).

Though this paradigm still does not qualify as an experimental approach to the study of development per se, it is of direct concern to the developmentalist by virtue of the problems investigated, and may frequently have important implications for accounts of the developmental aspects of the problem—as in studies such as House and Zeaman's (1962), pointing to an attentional rather than a verbal-mediational basis for the reversal-shift phenomenon. At the same time, the extrapolation of the role of experimental variables to account for developmental changes must be viewed with caution, as illustrated in the early history of developmental research on probability learning (e.g., Stevenson & Zigler, 1958);

One important variant of this paradigm involves the manipulation of experimental conditions in interaction with age. This type of study, which has attained considerable popularity in recent years, can clearly contribute in important ways to the specification or isolation of determinants of developmental change, and has already been discussed in Chapter V, in the context of the problem of specifying developmental dimensions in the face of interaction between task or condition variables and age. There is no need to repeat the treatment of this paradigm presented there; suffice it to note that while this type of study may qualify as developmental in the descriptive sense of investigating behavior comparatively at different age levels, it still does not involve a direct experimental attack on the observed developmental changes, and thus is quite different in conception from the two paradigms to follow. More to the point, perhaps, this research strategy again is essentially straightforward as regards the application of the experimental method, except for the problems that may arise in conceptualizing the interaction between the experimental variable and age (assuming that such an interaction appears) which were already mentioned in the previous discussion.

PARADIGM 3: THE SIMULATION OF DEVELOPMENTAL CHANGE IN THE LABORATORY

This particular paradigm is probably most closely identified with the Skinnerian approach to child-developmental research to which repeated reference was made in Chapters I and II. It is appropriate to consider it in greater detail here, but before doing so it should be placed in proper perspective, by noting that it has been employed both before the advent of the Skinnerians and more recently by psychologists of quite diverse theoretical persuasions, working only from the shared premise that controlled experience administered to children at a given age can produce behavior more commonly found in children at a later age. The further assumption that that experience in some sense reproduces or mimics the action of developmental processes, so that the experiential conditions can be interpreted as an explanation for the observed change, is frequently at least implicit in such research, though by no means invariably so; at times, the intent appears mainly to demonstrate how the course of developmental change can be accelerated through suitable training.

The alert reader will recognize in the generalized description of this paradigm just presented that it fits the case of a model of research which has attained much popularity in recent years. This is the work in which investigators pick a particular type of concept (typically one taken from the work of Piaget) exhibiting a consistent process of transition or change from one mode of response to a different one over a certain period of the child's development, and devise conditions of training to attempt to induce that concept in children not previously mastering it. This type of study has attained particular prominence in the case of concepts of conservation, and warrants careful analysis in that context. For a number of reasons, however, this analysis is more profitably reserved for a later section of this chapter, following upon the discussion of our fourth paradigm.

The Experimental Analysis of Behavior Change via the Model of Operant Conditioning. The essentials of this approach, in terms of the underlying rationale and assumptions, as well as the methodology, have been eloquently detailed by its major spokesmen, for example, Baer (1970); Bijou and Baer (1961, 1963); Bijou (1968); Gewirtz (1969); and Staats and Staats (1963). In their view—as already discussed briefly in Chapter II—any change in behavior observed to occur over age will, upon closer analysis, turn out to be the product of a history of specific interactions between the child and his environment. To quote Bijou and Baer (1963):

> We take a specific view of the nature of "development." A psychological organism as such is in interaction with its stimulus environment. These interactions usually change in the course of experience. The change constitutes a development of the organism, and will be understood only when the conditions necessary to produce the change have been demonstrated. . . . A developmental analysis would proceed by investigating the stimuli controlling this pattern of change. Perhaps it would be found that a caretaker emits syllabic speech on occasions of reinforcement and that syllabic sounds thereby become secondarily reinforcing; hence, behaviors by the infant with his own vocal apparatus that produce those sounds, or sounds like them, grow stronger. A demonstration of this would provide a developmental analysis, in that it would specify the events that produce the change. The essence of development in this sense is the ongoing *sequence of interactions* between behavior and environment, each part of the sequence contributing to the effect of the next interaction in the sequence [p. 198; italics in original].

Bijou and Baer do not, of course, claim that in any given case in which development of a response is observed to occur it will be possible to determine precisely the sequence of these interactions that is producing the change, let alone to recover this information retrospectively. Their belief that every instance of such behavioral change is, in principle, traceable to such a sequence of specific events leads them, however, to the suggestion that it should prove feasible to program the individual's history of sequenced interactions with stimuli so as to bring about such change experimentally—that is, to simulate the change in the laboratory, or by studying the individual child over a period of time under suitably controlled conditions. Here is how Bijou and Baer (1963) formulate the strategy of this type of study:

> (1) Select a form or class of behavior that seems essential to the performance of some everyday task, or one that is simply interesting to the development of behavior. (2) Describe the behavior in detail and in objective terms, i.e., establish a reliable set of clearly specified criteria. (3) On the basis of available information, prepare a sequence of materials and establish a procedure aimed at enabling the individual to perform such a task. (4) Find children who cannot perform as required (even though they possess the obvious biological equipment) or who perform it poorly and give them training on the sequence. (5) If the training does not enable them to perform according to specifications, modify the sequence in a systematic manner until it does.
>   Such an experimental history would not be expected to coincide with the way children of comparable age learn the same task in their everyday experiences in the

home, school, and play groups, since (1) the same criterion performance could, in all probability, be learned by other sequences, and (2) interactions in everyday living which interfere, decelerate, and negate such learning are experimentally eliminated. It would, however, provide *one* account of the variables of which such behavior is a function [p. 203].

By and large, Bijou and Baer, along with other child psychologists operating within the same framework, have concentrated on the analysis of social behavior, notably the infant's or child's responses to his mother or other adult caretaker, as well as the role of social reinforcement in controlling the child's behavior (cf. Gewirtz, 1969). There have, however, been occasional attempts to apply the approach to what we would term basic developmental phenomena, such as perceptual and cognitive functions, as well as, of course, to more applied concerns, for example, the development of reading skills (Staats, Minke, Finley, Wolfe, & Brooks, 1964). For our purposes perhaps the most interesting, as well as pertinent example is contained in the paper by Bijou and Baer (1963) cited previously, in which a study is described in which children between 3 and 6 years of age were given

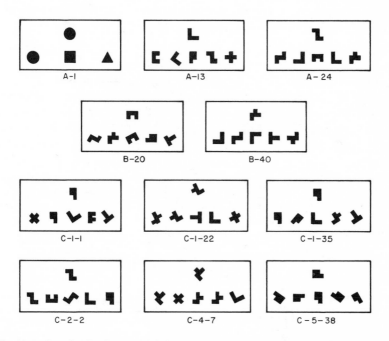

Fig. 11–1. Sample stimulus materials from Elementary (A), Intermediate (B), and Advanced (C) sets utilized in Bijou and Baer's (1963) study of mirror-image discrimination learning through programmed sequence of stimuli. (Top shape of each slide represents sample, to be matched to one of five choice stimuli below.)

systematic experience designed to achieve mirror-image discrimination. It is worth describing briefly, to illustrate the main features of this approach, and to serve as a basis for a critical appraisal of its place in the experimental study of development.

The procedure involved the presentation of graded sets of nonsense shapes in the form of slides in a matching-from-sample task with five alternatives; a correction procedure was used, that is, slides on which the subject responded to one of the four incorrect choice stimuli were exposed on the following trial, until he made the correct choice. Furthermore, following any slide on which an error was made, the sequence reverted (after the correct response was made) to the preceding slide in the series. The series involved an Elementary set, in which the correct choice matched the sample in orientation (cf. Fig. 11–1, A); an Intermediate set, in which differences in orientation were introduced between the correct choice stimulus and the sample (Fig. 11–1, B); and an Advanced set, in which following what appears to be largely a review series (see drawings I–1 through I–29 in Fig. 11–1, C), the discrimination of a choice stimulus from its mirror image was required.

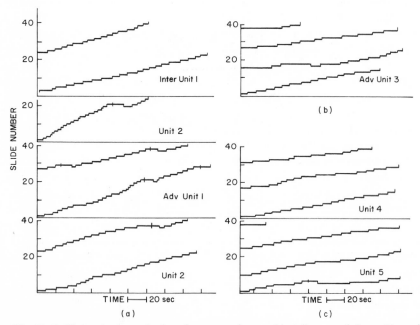

Fig. 11–2. Illustrative record of performance of one subject (boy, aged 5 yrs. 11 mos.) (a) Session 1; (b) Session 2; (c) Session 3. The ordinate indicates the number of the slide in each set to which the subject has advanced at each point in time of the training session. [From Bijou and Baer's (1963) study of mirror-image discrimination learning].

Results are not presented in detail, and it is not clear how many of the 100 children were able to advance to the last unit of the final set without error. Instead, the record for a single child is presented (Fig. 11–2), in the form of cumulative record curves, showing his rate of progress over time, as well as the frequency of errors (reflected in reversals in the curve, such as at Slide 20 of Unit 1 of the Advanced set, where the record shows a drop to the previous slide, in accordance with the procedure following errors mentioned above).

Let us assume that the majority of children, even from the younger portion of the age range sampled, showed success on this series comparable to this nearly 6 year-old. What, precisely, has this study accomplished? In a positive sense, it has demonstrated that children as young as 3 years old perhaps *can* be taught to make mirror-image discriminations, when given an effectively programmed sequence of stimuli for discrimination training. This demonstration would be valuable from a practical standpoint, for instance, in launching a program of reading at the preschool level. On a more theoretical plane, it is significant in showing that a perceptual skill such as mirror-image discrimination is susceptible to cultivation through intensive practice of the kind given here. More particularly the changes normally to be expected to take place over a period of several years can be reproduced within a relatively short period of time in the laboratory, thus ruling out a strict maturational account of this developmental change (though it is doubtful that anyone would have wished to defend such a view).

There is no gainsaying the reality and magnitude of the accomplishment of this study—again, provided that the procedure was in fact as successful as implied in the report of the study which, in the absence of any data for the group as a whole, must remain a moot question. But if we are to evaluate this as an approach to the experimental analysis of developmental change, we must pose several questions of this research.

To begin with, how plausible is the constructed-history approach, as used here, as a simulator of the developmental changes reflected in the improvement with age in the discrimination of mirror images? This is essentially the question of the sufficient as opposed to necessary character of the causal account given here of these developmental changes—a point to which we will return at greater length in the consideration of the conservation-training research. The point is: During the course of the child's everyday experience during which these changes are occurring is it reasonable to suppose that he is in fact encountering the type of differential reinforcement to permit him to achieve consistent differentiation of mirror images? While an answer to this question in the negative is by no means a foregone conclusion—since it is conceivable that this discrimination does not become stabilized before the child learns to read, where he is forced to learn such discriminations—we are simply left in the dark as to the answer from research of this type.

This is clearly a critical point, and deserves to be pursued further. It has not, of course, been ignored by the advocates of the "constructed history" approach, as shown in the previous quote from Bijou and Baer (1963). In a subsequent paper, Baer (1970) again addressed himself to this same question, and in characteristically pithy terms. As a participant in an APA Symposium on "The Concept of Learning with Implications for Research Strategy," he espoused the view that developmental psychologists could profitably forego the use of age as a variable in their research. He recommended a strategy of devising suitable training procedures under controlled conditions, that would produce a behavior in a child at age x which according to the study of age differences did not typically appear till age y. By way of illustration he referred to an experiment by Jeffrey (1958), in which it was shown that 4-year-old children could be taught to discriminate left from right, or more precisely to discriminate among two figures that were left–right reversals of one another. This was a task that appeared beyond their ability when differential verbal labels were to be learned to the two figures, though 7-year-olds had little difficulty learning such a discrimination. However, by substituting differential motor responses (reaching to the right for one figure and to the left for the other), Jeffrey was able to demonstrate that 4-year-olds could similarly exhibit the capacity to make left–right discriminations. To quote Baer (1970):

> What I want to emphasize is that by the end of the study, the four-year-olds apparently had *developed*. They were not older than at the beginning, but their Jack and Jill learning behavior had become functionally like that of seven-year-olds. Jeffrey may well have shown us an effective developmental mechanism. The first part of his study had suggested that if a four-year-old who cannot solve the left–right problem is simply allowed to grow three years older, he will probably be able to solve it then. What is it that happens during those years? Obviously, various processes of development go on, but the demonstration of an age difference is not thereby the demonstration of one or more of these developmental processes. On the other hand, the second and third parts of Jeffrey's study point to exactly an environmental process which *can* produce that delightful ability of a seven-year-old to tell his Jack from his Jill.
>
> It may be asked: is that what happens during the three years? Do four-year-olds begin to discriminate motor responses to stimuli differing on various left–right dimensions, such that about three years later the Jack and Jill problem will be one they can easily mediate with some already existing part of their repertoire? I don't know, of course. What Jeffrey's study tells us is that such a mechanism is a demonstrated possibility. It is not merely logical; it is feasible.
>
> In my opinion, Jeffrey's design is the essence of development research: it describes a *possible process* of development. In my opinion, it is the process of development, not merely the *outcome* of development, which should be our subject matter [p. 240; italics in original].

In response to Baer's argument, we might observe, first, that Jeffrey taught his 4-year-olds a skill vastly different from that which he initially found in his 7-year-olds: To learn to make a *directional* motor response, with the direction of movement correlated with the direction in which each of the two figures to be discriminated were pointing, is surely not equivalent to learning to attach differential verbal labels to these same stimuli. Thus, Baer's claim that "What Jeffrey's study tells us is that such a mechanism is a demonstrated possibility," is unwarranted, if "such" is intended to refer to the role of the motor responses as mediators of the eventual differential verbal response: No such mechanism can be deduced from Jeffrey's study.

But let us suppose that Jeffrey had in fact succeeded, on the basis of the motor discrimination, to train the 4-year-olds to attach the desired "Jack and Jill" responses to the two stimuli—a procedure which, curiously enough, reverses the postulated role of verbal labels in facilitating other (e.g., motor) discriminations, as in the predifferentiation literature (Ellis, 1965). Baer tends to dismiss as irrelevant the question of the correspondence between the process which the experimenter had shown to be effective in the laboratory and that which had in fact been operating during the years between 4 and 7 to change the child's discrimination ability. To quote him once more "Seven-year-olds are an essentially mysterious group; we do not know what process gives them their ability to make left-right discriminations. Hence the developmental aspects of the study, as I see them, are restricted to the actual study, in which age was *not* a variable [Baer, 1970, p. 241]."

Few developmentalists would be satisfied with such an answer, no more than were Gollin (1970) and Sutton-Smith (1970) in their replies to Baer as part of the aforementioned symposium. Surely the fact that it is possible to produce American adolescents who can exhibit a degree of French-speaking ability, by rather laborious drill involving a mixture of paired-associate training, learning of grammatic rules, and other tricks of the trade would not be considered a contribution to our understanding of the French child's original learning of his language. (The fact that we are dealing here with the acquisition of a skill by an older group equivalent to that normally observed at an *earlier* age, should not affect the argument, since Baer is unwilling to assign any valid role to age at all.) As a matter of fact, in this realm we can point to the application of Baer's strategy in reverse: By making sound guesses as to the way in which a young child acquires language naturally, the language instructor has been able to devise conditions which facilitate the learning of a foreign language in older children or adults (cf. the Berlitz method).

Baer's dissatisfaction with the straightforward age-group comparison approach to the study of developmental change is understandable and in effect shared by the present writer, as earlier portions of this book should have made clear. Nevertheless the strategy he suggests simply sidesteps what to the developmentalist is the real question, that is, the "mystery" of the change in behavior observed to take place wherever an age difference is uncovered. We have pointed to some partial approaches to the solution of such mysteries via correlational methods in the previous chapter, and will examine more direct experimental approaches differing from Bijou and Baer's simulation strategy presently. Before doing so, let us mention more briefly two other important limitations of that strategy.

One concerns the effect which the training has on the developmental changes that would be expected to take place with respect to this aspect of behavior, that is, on the developmental function per se. This is a question, first, of the permanence of the improvement shown. Indeed, if it is a product of differential reinforcement, in the manner envisaged by Bijou and Baer, one should expect a regression to the earlier level of performance following the cessation of the learning experience. Here we find one major respect in which the effects of limited learning based on an S-R reinforcement model differ from the stable and generally irreversible changes observed during development. (Again, the question is difficult to answer in the present instance, where continued reading experience may be required to maintain improved mirror-image discrimination.)

Furthermore, how parsimonious is the constructed experience paradigm as a model of developmental change? Note, first, that the programming of the experience is undertaken in an essentially pragmatic fashion. The sequencing of the stimuli is based, not on any particular hypotheses concerning the developmental processes that are implicated in the changes observed in this realm, or even on a systematic analysis of the hierarchies of responses required—as in Gagné's (1968) model of the attainment of conservation, for instance—but rather on the basis of successive approximation, utilizing previously collected records to pinpoint common sources of difficulty and refine the procedure. Bijou and Baer's (1963) account of their mirror-image discrimination work gives explicit recognition to this pragmatic line of attack, as does Baer's (1970) more detailed description of an attempt by one of his students to train a young boy with severe reading difficulties to discriminate letters.

Speaking more generally, the approach entails a piecemeal account of behavioral development which would require, it seems, the treatment of every conceivable type of skill or response in isolation from all others, except to the extent that principles of response generalization or specific transfer of training might prove applicable. Herein lies probably the clearest distinction between the field of learning and that of development—when dealing with the latter, it is simply not very fruitful to reduce experience to isolated programmed sequences of stimuli, nor to define behavior in terms of similarly restricted sets of particularized responses. In this respect, it should be noted, the laboratory simulation paradigm, especially in its Skinnerian version, differs markedly from that to be taken up next, exemplified in research on the effects of early experience.

PARADIGM 4: EXPERIMENTAL CONTROL OF EXPERIENCE

The type of research to be considered under this last rubric is in many ways continuous with the previous category. It differs, however, in two major respects. First, the individual's experience, and the behavior to be related to it, are defined in much broader terms than the "constructed-history" approach of Bijou *et al*. would allow for. Instead of exposing rigidly programmed sequences of discrete stimuli to which completely determinate responses are given, the work to be considered (best exemplified by the research on the effects or early experience of Hebb and his associates, and that inspired by it) deals with the effects of pervasive conditions of experience over an extended segment of the organism's period of development. Here the behaviors of interest are not only defined in broader and frequently multivariate terms, but studied typically at some later period in time, following the termination of the experiential conditions. This in itself marks a sharp departure from the approach considered under the preceding paradigm. The rationale, furthermore, involves not the simulation of development, but rather a deliberate attempt to modify its course, whether in a positive or a negative direction. Symptomatic of this difference in conception is the routine provision of "normal" control groups to serve as a basis for comparison in evaluating the effects of the experience—a feature which could be considered expendable in the Skinnerian operant-analysis approach.

It is this type of work that brings up the most interesting and challenging questions for a developmental psychologist, and the problems of design and scientific method to which it gives rise deserve more explicit and extended discussion than the paradigms previously considered.

Major Problems in the Design of Research on the Effects of Controlled Experience

Representative of the discussions of laboratory research on the effects of experience on development is King's (1958) review of the early animal research on this problem. He lists seven parameters to be considered in this type of research: (*a*) the age of the animal when the experience is given, (*b*) age at the time of the test, (*c*) the duration or quantity of the experience, (*d*) the type or quality of the experience, (*e*) the type of the performance task required of the adult animal, (f) the method for testing persistence of the effects, and (g) the relation of the experience to the genetic background of the animal. The first three variables are of particular interest for a general discussion of the design of experimental-developmental research.

Conceptually there is no question that these first three variables are separate determinants of the effects of early experience. The first, that is, the age at which the experience is administered (or more precisely the age of the subject at the time of the initiation of the experience) relates to the critical period concept, as well as to such notions as primary versus secondary learning (Hebb, 1949), Thompson's (1966) three-zone model of differential learning effects, etc. The second variable, age at the time of test, relates most directly to the question of the permanent as opposed to temporary character of the effects, which is of obvious relevance to the way in which the role of the experience on the organism's development is conceptualized. The third variable, finally, the length of the time interval over which the experience remains in effect, presumably acts to determine the magnitude of the effects, as well as bearing again on the critical-period concept. According to the strict interpretation of this notion experiential effects operate in a temporally localized fashion, so that duration per se should play a relatively minor role—except perhaps to ensure that the critical age is covered by the period during which the experience is operative.

But let us now examine these three variables in relation to one another. First, are they susceptible to *independent* manipulation? Let us label the values of the variable, age at onset of experience, $A_1, A_2, \ldots A_n$; the values of the age-at-testing variable $T_1, T_2, \ldots T_n$ and the period of duration of the experience $D_1, D_2, \ldots D_n$. It immediately appears that any two of these three are independent, but given any two, the third can vary only within definite limits. For instance, given any combination of values of A_i and D_i, $T > A_i + D_i$ (clearly, the test cannot occur before the end of the experimental period— or can it? See below).

As a concrete illustration of this point, if rats were given experience starting at either 15 or 60 days, and for either 20 or 40 days, we wind up with periods for the experience lasting from 15 to 35, 15 to 55, 60 to 80 and 60 to 100 days, respectively. Thus, assuming that testing is not to take place till the end of the experimental period, there is very little room left for varying the time-of-testing variable, if one assumes that rats have effectively reached the end of their growth period by 90 to 100 days.

Two further, and fundamentally more serious problems present themselves here. First, even to the extent that we can vary time of testing, a further factor enters the picture which is rigidly determined by the other three, though it may quite possibly itself directly control the magnitude of observed effects. This is the interval between the end of the experience period and the administration of the test. Thus, one would presume that of two animals tested at 100 days, the one where experience ended at 90 would show greater effects of that experience than the one whose experience ended at 45 days, not because later experience was more important, but simply because there was less time for its effects to dissipate. (Admittedly in the case of a highly localized early-experience phenomenon, such as imprinting, this principle would be overridden.) There is a real question, then, as to the proper identification of the variables determining our effects, which may not correspond to the manner in which we choose to define them.

The second problem with the independent-variable view of design in this area is that the organism is undergoing development during this period, and that development is not a linear process. In other words, it is fallacious, not to say absurd, to compare the effects for rats of 20 days' experience given from 10 to 30 days, with the same duration administered from 70 to 90 days. This point becomes even more obvious, once we extend the time scale beyond the point of the cessation of growth or development, e.g., by substituting "180" for "70" in the example just given, so that the experience would fall entirely outside of the developmental period.

We are clearly at an impasse here, which has been bequeathed to us by our predilection for imposing the orthogonal-variable design on developmental situations, where the variables do not fit such a design. (A similar point was made in Chapter II, with respect to attempts to vary CA and MA according to an orthogonal design.) How can we extricate ourselves from this predicament?

What is needed here is a redefinition of the variables in developmental-function terms. Let us distinguish, first, between two cases: The first, defined by situations in which the dependent variable of interest is present to a measurable degree at the time of onset of the period of special experience; the second, by situations in which this is not the case. The relevance of this distinction will become clearer once we turn to the consideration of the effects-of-pretesting issue.

In the first case it is apparent, first, that variable T, time of testing, ceases to be a meaningful independent variable, once the developmental function itself is the criterial dependent variable. The point is illustrated in Fig. 11–3. Section A shows the case of experiential effects during period E becoming increasingly marked over the course of *subsequent* development, whereas Section B shows the more common case of effects becoming attenuated during later development. Rather than conceptualizing time of testing as an independent variable determining the magnitude of the experiential effect, the latter is expressed in terms of the slope or some other corresponding parameter of rate of the developmental function.

This leaves only the former variables A and D, which may be retained,

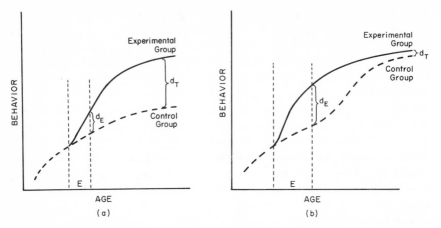

Fig. 11–3. Two hypothetical cases of effects of experience on development, showing alteration of developmental function. E = duration of period of special experience; d_E = enhancement of behavior at end of experimental treatment; d_T = residual differential in behavior at
maturity.

though looked at in slightly altered terms. Since the experiential effects are
conceived of as determinants of the parameters of the developmental function, $R = f(x)$, it is reasonable to treat A and $A + D$, that is, the time of
onset and of termination of the experience, as the variables determining
the magnitude and form of these effects. This formulation gives recognition,
furthermore, to the obvious but generally ignored fact that the effects are
presumably operative during the course of the experience itself, even
though we may be unwilling or unable to carry out tests of these effects
during that period. In other words, A by itself acts to determine the effect
of a given experience on the developmental function, with $A + D$ determining the alteration of the function subsequent to the termination of the experience.

Section B corresponds to that involved in much of the Hebbian research
on early experience, where the behavioral effects of the experience are in
principle not measurable at the time of the onset of the experience, and on
occasion not till some time following its termination [cf. Hunt's (1941) classical study of the effects of food deprivation in infancy on adult hoarding].
Here time of testing may still be dispensed with as an independent variable,
providing that we again express the effects of the experience in terms of the
parameters of the developmental function, taken from whatever point of the
life-cycle the latter becomes measurable. In regard to the other two variables, on the other hand, since the function by definition has a value of zero
at A and possibly at $A + D$ as well, it may be more meaningful to define these

in terms of age of onset and duration, respectively, that is, as variables independent of the developmental function itself.

Two main points are noteworthy in connection with this proposed reformulation. First, in studies in which a developmental variable is studied in relation to some experimentally manipulated condition of experience, the effects are meaningful only in relation to some "normal" control condition, defining the expected developmental function in the absence of the experience. This in and of itself sets the experimental study of development apart from the study of learning, in which a no-learning control condition would ordinarily be expendable. Second, the development of the behavior should ideally be monitored all along the course of the period of development over which it is measurable, including that of the experience itself, where possible, and in any case, at repeated points beyond the point of termination of the latter—unless the experience extends to maturity. While this ideal may not always be realizable (due to a variety of factors, of both a practical and intrinsic nature—notably the difficult problem of test-retest effects), it should at least be borne in mind as implicitly demanded in research of this type, so that effects of experience may be conceptualized, not in terms of the level of behavior observed at a single, often arbitrarily chosen point in time, but rather in the context of the total developmental function. We will return to this point presently, in examining the need for follow-up data in studying the effects of experience.

To Pretest or Not to Pretest. An issue has been raised by Solomon and Lessac (1968) which serves to illustrate some of the pitfalls into which a facile application of principles devised for the study of learning phenomena in the laboratory to the experimental investigation of the role of experience on the development of behavior can fall. Solomon and Lessac start out, cogently enough, by noting that research in this domain (e.g., on the effects of sensory restriction) is frequently hampered by the absence of a base line measure preceding the onset of the experience. Without such a measure it may not be possible to distinguish between effects that interfere with or retard the development of some behavioral variable normally to be expected and those involving an actual deterioration of behavior relative to the organism's status prior to the administration of the experience.

The incorporation of pretests on the criterial measures of behavior for both experimental and control groups at the time of onset of the experimental treatment, as advocated by these authors, represents, without a doubt, an essential feature for studies on the effects of special experience in development—providing, as Solomon and Lessac note, that the behavior in question is meaningfully testable at that time. The authors insist, however, on the use of four groups in research of this type, two of which are pretested, whereas the other two are not. Quite apart from the doubling of research effort and expense which this prescription entails, there is a serious question whether the addition of groups without pretests is either necessary or even helpful. As we will see, designs of the type that Solomon and Lessac espouse to study the effects of experience on development, borrowed as they are from the experimental study of such nondevelopmental phenomena as attitude change or transfer of training, may in fact not be suitable to answer the questions posed by developmental research.

The point of the four-group design which Solomon and Lessac recommend is to assess change from pre- to posttest, while controlling for the effects of the pretest itself. Thus, they suggest using the pretest means for the pretested groups as an estimate of the assumed pretest values of the non-pretested experimental and control groups, so as to provide measures of change over the pre- to posttest interval for the two conditions, uncontaminated by the effect of the administration of the pretest. These mean change measures could then be compared to those actually found for the pretested groups, in order to obtain an indication of the magnitude of test–retest effects, and of their interaction with the experimental condition.

One might suppose that unless the investigator is specifically interested in the influence on posttest performance of the pretest itself, at least one of the four groups in Solomon and Lessac's design could be dispensed with, namely, Group I, the pretested experimental group. Thus, of the seven outcomes which they list as "most interesting" and which the four-group design allows one to differentiate, the first five involve only Groups II and IV (the nonpretested experimental and control groups), plus the pretest measures for Group III (pretested control), to provide the values required for the estimated change measures for Groups II and IV. (The last two outcomes cited refer to possible effects of the pretests.) Exclusive reliance on these estimated values places, of course, a considerable burden on the comparability of the three samples used, although in animal research this problem may be alleviated by the use of the split-litter technique. In human research, on the other hand, the price paid by foregoing the use of the individual as his own baseline and, equally important, by eliminating the possibility of matching control groups and experimental groups on the basis of pretest performance, is a considerable one.

This brings up an objection of a purely statistical nature to the comparisons which Solomon and Lessac propose: It is very doubtful whether comparing mean posttest performance for Groups II and IV (no pretests) with the pretest values estimated for them from the results for Groups I and III is equivalent to comparing the change from pre- to posttest for the latter two groups, for two reasons. First, the individual serves as his own control in case of Groups I and III, whereas for the others the estimates are based on

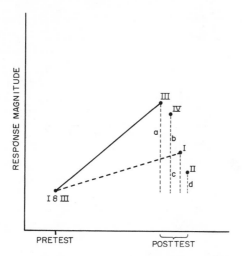

Fig. 11–4. Schematic representation of experimental and pretesting effects deducible from Solomon and Lessac's (1968) four-group design (see text).

group comparisons. Second, any procedure of matching groups on their pretest scores, such as one would want to undertake in assigning subjects to Groups I and III, would render statistical tests based on them noncomparable to the scores in the other two groups; that is, within-group variability would be affected.

There is, however, a much more fundamental objection to the application of designs of this sort in developmental research. The reasoning behind them presupposes, in effect, a static model of behavior, in which the control group serves mainly to control for warm-up, test–retest, and similar effects. It implies, furthermore, a purely linear conception of developmental change. The picture is shown graphically in Fig. 11–4, representing a hypothetical "impoverishing" situation. From this graph it is possible to deduce the following: The net decrement in response R attributable to the treatment is $b - d$. The difference in gain for the two pretested groups attributable to the treatment is $a - c$. The effect of taking the pretest interacted with the experimental treatment, enhancing the gain of the experimental group by $c - d$, while for the control group it only increased it by $a - b$.

This model contrasts sharply with that of the developmental function view, which looks at the effects of an experimental treatment or experience, not at a single point, but on the overall course of development. That is, the part played by the experimental treatment can be properly evaluated only by placing initial and terminal level in the context of the total function representing the development of the response or capacity in question. Figure 11–5 illustrates some of the possible ways in which a hypothetical

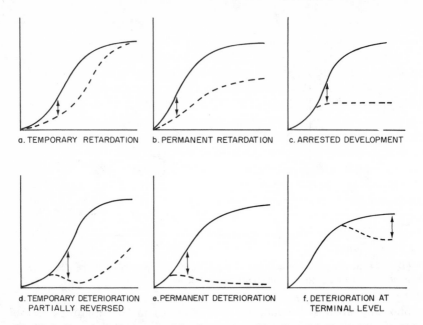

a. TEMPORARY RETARDATION   b. PERMANENT RETARDATION   c. ARRESTED DEVELOPMENT

d. TEMPORARY DETERIORATION   e. PERMANENT DETERIORATION   f. DETERIORATION AT
PARTIALLY REVERSED   TERMINAL LEVEL

Fig. 11–5. Hypothetical patterns of development resulting from the effects of "impoverishing" experience. Solid curves represent standard normal growth pattern; dashed curves represent course of development under conditions of special experience. Arrows indicate uniform amount of decrement at end of experimental treatment (assumed to start at point of divergence between solid and dashed functions).

impoverishing condition might act to inhibit development: The first three would correspond to the retardation case, as Solomon and Lessac define it in terms of a reduction in normal increment of response at the end of the period of treatment, whereas the last three represent the deterioration case, as defined by absolute decrement of response.

The point of these graphs, the top three of which could readily be exemplified in the empirical literature, is to show that the effects of a condition on development are not meaningfully described in terms of mean increments or decrements at one point in time. Ideally, repeated measures are called for, not only immediately before and after the period of special experience, but at subsequent points, so that the long-term effects of the experience can be gauged. Even where this is not feasible, individual longitudinal pre- and posttest measures are required, so that the amount of change for a given individual over the interval of the treatment can be related to the portion of the total developmental function covered by this interval, which at a minimum would mean to his level of performance on the pretest. The group-averaging procedure, and the linear differential model built into Solomon and Lessac's proposals, fail to do justice to the nature of developmental data in this respect.

But what about the effects of a pretest on subsequent posttest performance which are, after all, at the heart of Solomon and Lessac's espousal of a four-group design? In the study which serves to provide their argument with an empirical foundation, Lessac and Solomon (1969) provide us with what little evidence we have on the possible operation of the effects in question. The study is noteworthy for its use of a whole series of parallel measures of behavior, to determine the effects of raising dogs under conditions of isolation, from the age of 12 weeks to 64 weeks (i.e., for a period of one year). Table 11–1 shows the measures used in this study, and the means for the 12-week pretest for the pretested experimental and control groups, and for the 64-week posttest for all four groups, along with a brief statement of the nature of the effect in each case.

Of the 10 measures, half do show a difference between the pretested and nonpretested groups, which in some cases was significant, even with the small number of animals. This might seem to bear out the cogency of Solomon and Lessac's proposal, all the more since in some of the cases the results did indeed point to an "inoculating" effect from the pretest against the deleterious role of the isolation experience (cf. measures 7, 8, and 9, in particular). Upon closer examination, however, an interesting point is revealed in these data: Only 3 of the 10 measures show any consistent developmental change over the period in question—as shown in the comparisons between the pretest for the pretested controls and the posttest for the nonpretested controls. These are measures 3 (running time on the Umweg test), 9 (amount of shock taken on nonavoidance trials during shuttle-box learning), and 10 (discriminative transfer). And of these, only the second showed any effect of pretesting. In other words, the problem appeared to be limited largely to cases (e.g., measures 7 and 8) in which changes observed from pre- to posttest appear to represent effects of practice or possibly adaptation to the testing situation, rather than true developmental changes. In these cases exposure to the pretest did apparently serve to counteract the otherwise marked impairment of behavior that the nonpretested experimental animals displayed. On the other hand, in the case of one measure, #2, the effect was the reverse: The performance of the experimental pretested animals deteriorated sharply from pre- to posttest, to a much greater extent than was true for the nonpretested experimentals. There is no easy way to account for this reversal, nor, for that matter, for the "positive inoculation" effects found on the other measures.

We must grant, however, that the seemingly adevelopmental character of most of the measures would not have become apparent without the use of the nonpretested control group, since in a number of cases substantial

TABLE 11-1. Summary of Data of Lessac and Solomon (1969) on Effects of Early Isolation Experience, to Show Effects of Pretesting[a]

Measure	Experimental groups			Control groups			Summary of effects
	Pretested		Nonpretested posttest	Pretested		Nonpretested posttest	
	pretest	posttest		pretest	posttest		
1. Mean running times on straight alley test (sec)	2.88	3.25	6.41	2.35	2.04	2.68	Pretested experimental group superior
2. Mean running times, first trial reversal (sec)	10.7	148.2	35.3	5.8	5.8	5.9	Pretested experimental group shows greater adverse effect
3. Mean running times, Umweg test trials 1–5 (sec)	54.7	129.7	126.8	49.8	13.8	10.2	No effect of pretesting
4. Mean running times Umweg test, trials 6–10 (sec)	5.5	137.2	140.7	4.9	7.8	11.1	No effect of pretesting
5. Shock threshold (flexion) (milliamp)	.79	.79	.96	.80	.90	.83	No effect of pretesting
6. Shock threshold (yelps) (ma)	2.67	2.92	2.79	2.85	2.80	3.00	No effect of pretesting
7. Shuttle box avoidance training (trials to crit.)	42.2	26.7	70.0	29.0	23.2	38.8	Pretested groups superior (especially Exp)
8. Shuttle box (median latency, first ten trials)	13.10	13.96	51.37	13.52	3.72	11.32	Pretested groups superior (especially Exp)
9. Shuttle box (mean sec of shock taken on nonavoidance trials)	16.59	14.96	43.86	15.14	1.10	9.22	Pretested groups superior
10. Discriminative transfer (Mann–Whitney scores)	3.33	24.33	31.50	12.00	7.60	6.83	No effect of pretesting

[a]From Lessac and Solomon (1969). Copyright by the American Psychological Association and reproduced by permission.

changes from pre- to posttest did in fact take place for the other, pretested animals. What is the answer, then, to Solomon and Lessac's analysis of the problem? Obviously we are face to face here with the more general problem created by repeated testing in longitudinal research, which derives from the psychological equivalent of the uncertainty principle: The inescapable dilemma arising from the fact that any measurement of a characteristic of an object introduces a change in state of that object which will be reflected in the value obtained from the measurement. Indeed, if we extend Solomon and Lessac's argument to its logical conclusion, we would have to enlarge their design to include two further groups, given neither pre- nor posttests! The answer to this dilemma is surely not to ignore the problem, but neither is it to attempt by devious ways to circumvent it, at the expense of the very information about behavior change which we are interested in obtaining.

In the chapter on longitudinal methodology (Chapter VII) we discussed some of the approaches open to the developmental investigator in this situation, via the construction of behavioral measures specifically designed to minimize test–retest effects, and by recourse to relatively *nonreactive* measures (cf. Campbell & Stanley, 1963). We also referred, in that discussion, to the desirability of supplementing longitudinal by cross-sectionally obtained measures, to obtain some indication of the nature and magnitude of test–retest effects. These correspond of course to Solomon and Lessac's nonpretested control group, multiplied, however, by the number of points on the age continuum at which observations are made—or some subset of these. But at least the necessity for dual sets of experimental subjects would be obviated under this design.

Admittedly there will always remain a possibility of an interaction between a given pretest and a particular experiential condition, but in general it would seem hardly worth the investigator's expenditure of time, effort, and expense involved in following Solomon and Lessac's prescription for controlling for such interaction, especially since, as we have noted, little information of interest in the study of developmental change can be extracted from the types of cross-sectional group-mean comparisons which that design provides. Here, as in other respects, developmental research entails dealing with questions of rates and patterns of behavior change which cannot be readily encompassed into the traditional designs of the experimental psychologist, based upon an essentially linear model of response increments or decrements expressing the magnitude of experimental variables at a single point in time.

Campbell's Time-Series Designs.   Although originally intended for the educational researcher, Campbell and Stanley's (1963) comprehensive analysis of experimental designs is of direct relevance for the developmental psychologist, as they systematically evaluate the merits of each design in terms of its success in controlling for the role of maturation, historical change, and test–retest effects, among other factors. Furthermore, two among their "quasi-experimental" designs turn out to be of particular pertinence to the present discussion, as they are based on the use of time series, or, more simply, repeated measures bracketing the experimental treatment on both sides. (Campbell and Stanley's use of the term "time series" does not imply resort to time-series statistics, which would be irrelevant in this context, as well as requiring many more measures than one would generally wish to obtain in this type of study.) The two designs in question are, respectively, the "Time-Series Experiment" (Design 7) and the "Multiple Time-Series Experiment" (Design 14). They differ only in the inclusion of a control group as part of the latter design.

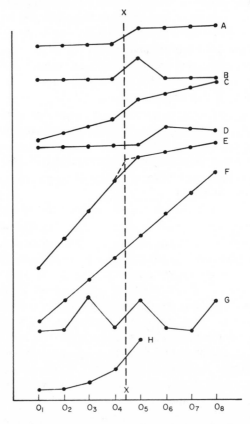

Fig. 11–6. Some possible outcome patterns from the introduction of an experimental variable at point X into a time series of measurements, O_1–O_8. [From Campbell & Stanley, 1963.]

Let us start with the former, by reproducing the graph devised by the authors to represent some of the alternative outcomes of such an experiment (Fig. 11–6). Two points are of particular interest for us here. First, not one but a series of pretest measures is obtained, to "catch" the trend of change in the behavior over time that the measure under study is subject to, independent of the experimental treatment. This feature of the design is obviously of even greater importance for the developmentalist than for the educational researcher; more frequent incorporation of such a series of pretests would help to sensitize the investigator to the way in which the effects of his experimental conditions are in fact superimposed on an ongoing process of developmental change. Obviously, in the study of the effects of early experience on development (e.g., the Hebbian research), there would generally be no opportunity for even a single measure prior to the institution of the treatment. On the other hand, in research on the effects of special training on the development of particular perceptual skills, concepts, etc., the interest of the findings could be considerably enhanced by resort to this type of design. And, of course, the design similarly brings home the value of a series of posttests, to gauge the permanence, or lack of it, of the experimental treatments (e.g., Case *A* versus Case *B* in Fig. 11–3).

A further point comes from the realization that in situations of this kind, inferences concerning the effect of the experimental treatment may be permissible even in the absence of a control group. To the extent, that is, that the treatment creates a sharp change in the time trend of the measures observed up to the onset of X, the treatment may plausibly be held responsible for that alteration (as in Cases *A*, *B*, *C*, and *D*, and more arguably, *E*). By the same token, it is seen to be ineffective in Case *F*, and most probably in *G* and *H* as well. To be sure, these conclusions would always be made with greater confidence in the presence of comparable control-group data (i.e., the use of the multiple time-series experiment); the latter, furthermore, would provide essential information for the developmental psychologist concerning the long-term effects of the treatment. But the fact that change of rate or discontinuity in trend constitutes prima facie evidence of the effects of experimental treatments is nevertheless significant, showing the extent to which developmental situations involving ongoing change depart from the static model of experimentation on which Solomon and Lessac's analysis is predicated.

The Case of Qualitative Response Variables. The preceding discussion has dealt entirely with situations involving the effects of experience on changes in the quantitative amount of some behavioral variable, as in the study of physical growth—e.g., of effects of supplemental nutrition, administered over a limited period of time, on height. This not only is a highly restrictive model, but leaves out of account some particularly knotty problems that arise in this area, where we are dealing with either qualitative variables, or shifts from one dimension of behavior to another.

A good example is provided by Melzack's (1954) study of the effects of perceptual isolation on the subsequent emotional behavior of dogs; more particularly, their response in the face of pain-emitting stimuli. This was part of a larger investigation, in which dogs were placed under conditions of varying degrees of sensory restriction for the first 7 to 10 months of their life. A set of tests of the effects of this experience was given approximately one month following its termination, covering diverse aspects of the dogs' behavioral development (cf. below), including problem solving, social competition, and emotional behavior. For the latter, the animals were confronted with umbrellas opening in front of them, bear skulls, and the like. The three main forms of behavior displayed by the experimental and control animals (home raised pets) were excitement, avoidance, and no emotional response; as Table 11–2 shows, however, avoidance was by far the most frequent response in the control group, whereas the experimentals responded predominantly with undifferentiated (and nonadaptive) excitement. The full significance of this finding did not, however, emerge until the retest one year later, which disclosed that the experimental animals had now developed an effective avoidance response—thus showing that there had been no permanent impairment in their adaptive behavior—but that, at the same time, the controls had advanced to a new form of behavior, that is,

TABLE 11–2

Mean Number of Different Types of Response to Pain-emitting Stimuli in Isolated (Exp.) and Pet-raised (Cont.) Dogs.

Type of response	Posttest I[a] Exp.	Cont.	Posttest II[a] Exp.	Cont.
Excitement	3.9	.5	1.6	.2
Avoidance	1.9	5.5	4.0	3.5
Aggression	0	0	0	2.2
No emotional response	1.3	.8	1.3	1.2

[a] Posttests I and II were administered 3–5 weeks and 10–12 months after the termination of the isolation period, respectively. [From Melzack (1954). Copyright by the American Psychological Association and reproduced by permission.]

aggression toward the object. Such a response was not observed at all in the experimental animals, indicating that the original deprivation experience had indeed resulted in an overall retardation of the normal developmental process, at least for this aspect of behavior. (Unfortunately the other behavior systems, i.e., problem solving, and social interaction, which was included in the original tests of the effects of restriction, were not included in the follow-up tests.)

This study is an excellent example of the contribution which a design incorporating follow-up tests to evaluate the effects of early experience can make in enlarging our view of the modification of development as a result of such experience. It was cited in part as an example of effects of early experience studied in terms of qualitatively defined behavioral variables. The importance of taking account of the qualitative forms of behavior is particularly acute in the study of the effects of early experience, where effects may be found, not only at points of development temporally removed from the period during which the experience was in operation, but for that very reason on aspects of behavior for which no relationship to the manipulated experience had been anticipated.

Probably the best-known example of this point comes from Harlow's work with mother-surrogate-raised monkeys (e.g., Harlow, Harlow, Dodsworth, & Arling, 1966) where the true meaning of the surrogate experience, as well as of the difference between the two types of surrogates did not become apparent until the animals had reached mating age. Thus, the experiments had originally been designed to reveal the role of "mother-love," as it is expressed in the type of body contact afforded by the terry-cloth surrogate, on normal behavioral development in infancy, and showed a seemingly normal pattern of behavior on the part of the terry-cloth-raised animals in contrast to the wire-mesh animals. Yet, the eventual failure of both groups of monkeys to develop functional mating behavior and concomitant deficiency in maternal behavior upon maturity points to major residual effects of the absence of the true mother in infancy (as well as of the subjects' peers) which apparently remained hidden during the animals' early development.

In summary, then, the design of studies on the effects of early experience must make provision for both follow-up study, and the detection of effects with respect to qualitatively, as well as quantitatively differentiated behavioral variables: First, changes in *form* of behavior are one of the earmarks of the operation of developmental processes, and second, given the potential breadth and persistence of the action of experiential effects, these may reveal themselves with respect to aspects of behavior of very diverse kinds, and appearing at different points of the life span.

Problems of Control and Behavior Monitoring in
Early Experience Research

Discussions of methodology and design in the study of effects of early experience, such as King's (1958) and Solomon and Lessac's (1968) have left out of account what would seem to be the most important element in such research, namely the problems of the selection, definition, and control of appropriate experiential variables. In particular, little effort has been made to achieve any degree of control over, or even monitoring of the organism's behavior during the time that the experiential conditions are in effect. In fact, as this writer has argued elsewhere (Wohlwill, 1973), it is not even always clear whether the concept of "experience" is to be regarded as an aspect of the stimulus environment impinging on the individual or of his behavior, even though this is a theoretical issue of no little consequence. For instance, it sets apart Hebb and his followers, who have laid exclusive stress on *sensory* experience, from those, ranging from Held and his associates to Piaget, who in one way or another regard the role of the overt behavior in which the individual engages during the course of his early experience as critical. But the fact remains that rarely have the proper controls been made that would allow us to decide this question—a limitation that is as true of the Hebbian work as it is of the research at the human level, by White (1971), for instance, inspired by a combination of Heldian and Piagetian notions.

Just what sort of controls are indicated here? The problem is more easily resolved in the case of attempts to establish the role of overt responses during early experience, where the organism's sensory experience must be equated. The well-known study of Held and Hein (1963) provides one example of an eminently successful approach to this problem, by arranging the experimental situation so as to guarantee equivalence of perceptual experience for experimental and control groups while eliminating motor response on the part of the former. This was achieved by placing pairs of experimental and control subjects in tandem in a carousel type of apparatus, the former being placed in harnesses which deprived them of the possibility of active locomotion whereas at the same time they were subjected to identical amounts of motion around the carousel by the movements of the control animals to whom they were linked by their apparatus.

In the converse case of research on the effects of sensory experience per se, the problem of dissociating the effects of the exposure to stimulation from that of the behavior which that stimulus environment would be expected to elicit has generally not been recognized. To be sure, we do have studies comparing the relative efficacy of perceptual enrichment with and without motor experience—for example, by presenting the "enriching" stimulation, visible from the cages, to a group of caged animals, and comparing their subsequent behavior with that of a group of animals raised in a "free environment" (i.e., large boxes, cf. Hymovitch, 1952). While the results of this work do appear to give support to the primacy of perceptual experience postulated by Hebb, they are thrown into question by subsequent conflicting findings from the work of Forgays and Forgays (1952), and of Forgus (1954, 1955). But more to the point, for our purposes, is that we still cannot be confident that motor experience was in fact eliminated as an effective variable in the case of the caged animals. For instance, it appears likely that during the course of the period of exposure to the special stimulus experience the caged animals would have made many approach movements to these stimuli in their own cages, that is, by mounting or jumping against the wire-mesh enclosure. Although such movements obviously would not have given them direct contact with the stimuli outside, their role in enhancing general development cannot be ruled out, particularly in the light of the work of Held *et al.* on the role of reafferent feedback from movement per se. Certainly, in comparison with the caged nonenriched controls, the enriched animals would be expected to have engaged in more motor activity inside their cages.

This problem becomes much more serious in the case of deprivation experiments. Consider the typical Hebbian experiment in which one group of animals is brought up in the dark, and compared to a control group given ordinary visual stimulation. The question of what the effect of being reared in the dark is on the animals' motor activity seems never to have been considered. Yet, it is apparent that depriving a caged animal of visual contact with any stimulus object in its environment over a prolonged period of early experience should result in a considerable reduction in the extent of the animal's motor activity, both in a general sense, and more particularly in interaction with a particular stimulus (e.g., the food-box).

The general point applies with equal force to research on the effects of exposure to particular stimuli during an animal's rearing period in facilitating discrimination-learning problems given at maturity involving those stimuli. A series of studies of this kind was undertaken by E. Gibson and her co-workers (cf. Gibson, 1969 for a review). Here again the assumption was that sheer exposure to these stimuli would prove beneficial, but no observations were made of the frequency or type of motor response the animals made to the stimuli during the exposure period. The importance of this point in this context was demonstrated by Kerpelman (1965), who showed that this predifferentiation effect appeared to depend on the stimuli being present over the food compartment during the animal's feeding period, when it presumably became the focus of attention as a part of the stimulus situation during which eating took place. (Even here, however, Kerpelman contented himself with controlling the time and place of presentation of the discriminanda, without recording overt responses to them made by the animals.)

There are two morals to be drawn from this discussion, one obvious and essentially trivial, the other less so. The first is that in experimental research on effects of early perceptual experience, adequate controls are needed to distinguish between the respective roles of exposure to a certain type of stimulation (or deprivation of same) per se and of motor responses made to stimuli. Ultimately, the only fully adequate means of assessing the possible role played by such responses is to immobilize the animals through chemical means.

The second moral, much more to the point for the developmentalist, may in part conflict with the first. It is that, to the extent that it may be either impractical or undesirable to impose the kind of restraints on the subjects' behavior during the period of special experience that a doctrine of strict control would entail, there is a much more informative approach open to the investigator, namely, to monitor the animals' behavior during the period of experience, so as to obtain a more accurate record of the latter's effect on the individual's concurrent motor responses.

To this writer's knowledge this recommendation has not been followed in any of the work on the effects of early experience, though it is difficult to believe that in some of this research, such as that at McGill University on dogs, which extended over a period of close to a year, the experimenters did not at least make incidental observations of the behavioral development of their animals as the experimental period wore on. Its pertinence is much broader, in fact, than the specific question of the contribution of sensory versus motoric experience in Hebbian type research. Consider the work of Harlow and his associates referred to previously, which disclosed that the absence of the natural mother in the early experience of Rhesus monkeys rendered them quite unfit for normal mating and maternal behavior when mature. This research does not permit us to say very much about how this deficiency came about, and what the chain linking it to the absence of the mother is (if, indeed, this *was* the factor responsible at all). For the fact is that we have no information whatsoever on the nature of the animals' intervening experience, which may well have differed in particular ways from that expected of a monkey raised by his natural mother.[1]

[1] Harlow *et al.* do present evidence to show that it is the combined deprivation of the natural mother and the infants' peers that is critical in producing the adverse effects on mating and maternal behavior in maturity. They further postulate that the problem is one of ineffectual development under the isolation conditions of the monkeys' normal aggressive behavior, though the link between this deficiency and the incapacity for copulation is not further explicated.

The Problem of Causal Inference in Experimental
Studies of Development

Consider the following phenomenon—admittedly based on nonexperimental evidence, and for that matter evidence not even of a behavioral, but rather a biological nature. Yet it serves to bring out an interesting paradox which faces the behavioral investigator in this realm as well. The phenomenon is depicted in Fig. 11–7, representing the growth in height of a girl who had been afflicted with Cushing's syndrome, involving a suppression of the growth process due to an excessive secretion of cortisol, prior to and

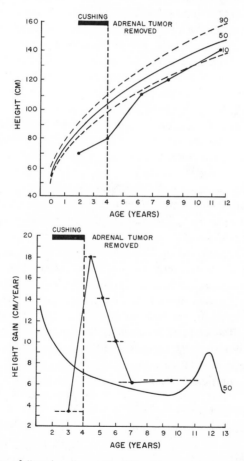

Fig. 11–7. A case of "catch-up" growth, following removal of adrenal tumor in a girl suffering from Cushing's syndrome. (From Prader, Tanner, & von Harnack, 1963).

subsequent to excision of the adrenal tumor. This and similar cases have been described and discussed by Tanner (1963) as exemplifying the nature of "catch-up growth," in other words, the manner in which physical growth recovers from a temporary period of inhibition of normal growth, so as to lead to a terminal level (which Tanner terms the individual's "target size") which is equivalent to that which would have been predicted for the person if there was no interruption in the normal growth process.

For the present discussion we may ignore the point, though it is a critical one for Tanner's hypothesis, that the predicted "target size" turns out to be based merely on gross group averages, rather than on any extrapolation of the individual's terminal height from a knowledge of his growth prior to the onset of the illness. The question that is worth examining for our purposes concerns the interpretation to be placed on the speed-up of growth following the termination of the inhibiting condition or agent. The necessary eliciting conditions for it are (a) the prior period of inhibition, due to disease, anorexia (i.e., prolonged refusal to eat), or temporary malnutrition, and (b) the termination of that period, with the restitution of normal conditions for growth. But what, then, is the "cause" for the speed-up in growth (relative to that of a normal child over an equivalent age period)? It would be preposterous to assign to the disease or other inhibiting force itself the status of a causal agent here; yet the alternative, of assigning the cause to the purely negatively defined entity, that is, termination of the disease, hardly appears any more satisfactory. (Note that the issue is not of explaining the mere resumption of normal growth, which would not require any special causal agent, but rather why these children should be growing at a *faster* rate than normal.)

The paradox appears to be traceable to the particular developmental character of the phenomenon, and thus to have more general implications for experimental research in which intervention is made in the normal course of development. It arises, more specifically, from the fact that the inhibiting force (in the growth example) is superimposed on an ongoing developmental process, and its effects can only be understood in relation to that process, so that simple cause-and-effect accounts limited to the action of the externally imposed condition are inadequate to the situation. We are, in other words, dealing with a complex set of forces interacting with one another, which appear to call for their own mode of causal analysis, and by extension of scientific method and inference.

Note that this formulation does not commit one in any sense to a vitalistic or teleological view of development processes. In certain areas of development, such as embryology and perhaps even physical growth, at least as analyzed by both Tanner and Bertalanffy (1968), with their stress on the equifinality of developmental processes, it may indeed be difficult to avoid recourse to vitalistic-sounding concepts. But there are other purely physical forces, such as those involved in homeostatic mechanisms, which create just as great difficulties for a traditional causal account as do developmental processes—as seen in such phenomena as the oscillating pattern of servo-mechanistic processes, zeroing in on a target or equilibrium state.

Necessary versus Sufficient Causes in Development.   Once we grant the existence of "normal developmental processes," that is, acting independently of particular specifiable external agents or conditions, there follows a much more far-reaching consequence. That is that we can only hope to isolate necessary, rather than sufficient causes, i.e., those without which we can assert development does not take place, rather than those *thanks to which* it does take place. This would suggest, in other words, that the basic tool in the experimental study of development is the deprivation study, rather than the enrichment or special experience study. This will come as no news to the experimental embryologist, who has rarely been tempted to explain developmental forces by accelerating them. It may, however, be a source of embarrassment to some developmental psychologists who have hoped to account for certain developmental processes by arranging a situation in which a given process would in fact be exhibited ahead of its normally expected time of appearance. More generally, the principle just enunciated, if valid, must inevitably hamstring the experimental study of development at the human level, given the ethical objections against experimentation on humans involving deprivation or restriction, and especially humans in process of development. (We have had no dearth of research on sensory deprivation at the adult level, despite the known, though admittedly temporary adverse effects frequently produced by that condition.)

To examine the validity as well as implications of the assertion concerning the primacy of the development-inhibitory over the development-facilitatory approach in the search for explanatory constructs or mechanisms, let us apply it to the realm of Hebbian research, where both approaches have in fact been used. At first blush, it is difficult to discern any fundamental asymmetry between the two types of studies in this instance. "Rats deprived of vision from birth are inferior in their performance on the Hebb-Williams test of rat intelligence in maturity, relative to normal controls"—thus might read one conclusion from a typical deprivation study (e.g., Hebb, 1949, though it should be noted that the comparison group here was one blinded in maturity). "Rats reared in an environment affording them added visual stimulation, or more varied sensory input, will be superior in their performance on the Hebb-Williams test in maturity, relative to a normal control group" (e.g., Hebb, 1949, p. 299, or Hymovitch, 1952).

Yet, upon closer examination, the evidence of the first type does seem very considerably more potent and incisive in its bearing on Hebbian theory than the second. Hebb considers the presence of patterned sensory stimulation in the environment during the period of development to be a *sine qua non* for the establishment of effective adaptive and intellectual processes in adulthood. Thus, the stress which he lays on the work of Riesen, and on the cases reviewed by Von Senden of humans given sight in later life. If it had turned out that organisms deprived of vision in their early experience had not been substantially impaired in their subsequent performance on perceptual and cognitive tasks, Hebb would clearly have had to abandon his theory; it would have indicated that a factor regarded by the theory as essential for normal development did not in fact play such a role as a necessary cause.

In contrast, from the theoretical standpoint the enrichment work is little more than icing on the cake, and if it had failed to yield positive results, it would not have had nearly as decisive an effect on the theory—it might simply have pointed to a ceiling effect (beyond a certain point, more stimulation ceases to have an effect—just as beyond a certain point, an increase in proteins in the diet would not enhance growth, though proteins are essential to growth).[2]

The Acquisition of Conservation: The Acceleration Approach to the Interpretation of a Developmental Phenomenon

Over the past decade, the topic of conservation has attracted the attention of developmental psychologists perhaps like no other; indeed it is no exaggeration to state that it has become a veritable obsession with them. Whereas the peak of popularity of the problem may have finally been passed, it was not very long ago that the editor of a leading journal in the field complained that the whole forthcoming issue might easily have been filled exclusively with reports of conservation studies.

A large majority of this work has consisted of "training" studies, whose primary concern is in establishing the effectiveness of a particular type or

[2]This distinction between enrichment and deprivation research can be a problematical one, since it rests on the presupposition that a normal baseline has been established against which the effect of either condition can be evaluated. The matter is well illustrated by Hebb's reference to his pet-raised rats as an "enrichment" condition. Undoubtedly it was, relative to the circumstances of daily life in the laboratory. But in a larger biological context, it remains a moot question whether the rats' experience in the household of Professor Hebb—or, for that matter, that of the chimpanzee Vicky in the home of the Hayes (Hayes & Hayes, 1951)—can be considered to be "enriching," relative to that which is normal, that is, typical, for the species. But since the present argument is that research on the effects of enrichment is in any event of subsidiary interest for the study of the role of experience in development, this problem is not as critical as it might seem.

condition of training in turning non- (or rather pre-) conserving children into conservers. Piaget has, with some validity, criticized the virtually exclusive concentration on the part of American psychology with this problem of training, but even he has failed to explicate precisely why this type of study is of such limited value as an approach to unraveling the seeming mystery of the basis for the normal process of acquisition of conservation concepts on the part of the typical child.

Basically, we are in the presence here of a true developmental phenomenon, that is, a change in behavior which occurs in a vast majority of children in the most diverse environments and under the most varied conditions of experience, in most—though apparently not all—cultural groups, and typically within a fairly narrowly delimited age period. Under these circumstances the question arises what, precisely, has been accomplished when we demonstrate that such-and-such a training procedure will cause a child to manifest the concept of conservation? The matter relates directly to the previous discussion of the isolation of necessary as opposed to sufficient conditions. The training-for-conservation study obviously falls under the latter category; it has by now produced a plethora of demonstrations of diverse sufficient conditions for experimentally inducing concepts of conservation. By their very quantity and diversity these studies make it apparent that none of them contains the "magic key" to the secret of conservation, though in the aggregate it is possible that they provide insights into what does in fact take place when a child acquires this concept "naturally," in other words, without benefit of experimental intervention.

The alternative approach to arrive at an explanation of the formation of conservation, that of the deprivation study, is not, strictly speaking, available to the researcher, for the obvious ethical reasons already cited. One example does exist in which a fortuitous "experiment" on the part of our society allowed researchers to examine the contribution of one particular influence which may be regarded as a universal, at least in our culture, to the acquisition of conservation. This concerned the role of formal schooling, which was studied in a sample of black children in a rural county in Virginia who had been systematically deprived of public schooling in the fight over integration. The result, as reported by Mermelstein and Shulman (1967) did not point to any marked inferiority of the nonschooled children in the extent of their development with respect to conservation, suggesting that schooling does not play an essential role in this situation (cf. also Goodnow, 1962). It should be noted that, even if the lack of schooling had been found to result in substantial retardation with respect to this concept, we would still have lacked more specific knowledge concerning the ingredients of this experience that were in fact responsible—for example, vocabulary development, arithmetic, and the like.

TABLE 11–3

Aspects of the Design of Conservation-Training Research, with Comparative Illustrations from Studies by Feigenbaum & Sulkin, 1964, and Bearison, 1969.

Criterion	Feigenbaum and Sulkin	Bearison
TYPE of experience	Focused on criterial concept (with reduction of irrelevant stimuli) and on related concept (addition and subtraction)	Focused on related operation (measurement)
BREADTH of experience	Very limited (series of trials of a single type)	Less limited (graded set of trials of measurement and conservation)
DURATION of experience	Very limited (one set of trials; exact number unspecified)	Limited (one 25- to 45-minute session)
PRETEST	Limited to criterial concept	Included variety of conservation tasks
DIAGNOSIS of level prior to training and selection of Ss for training	Ss giving conservation response on single pretest trial eliminated	Ss dichotomized into total nonconservers and partial or full conservers (at least 1 correct R to all pretest trials). Latter eliminated from study.
CONTROL group	None included	Included (given no training)
POSTTESTS	Limited to criterial concept	Same as in pretest
FOLLOW-UP tests	Ss passing posttest retested for retention one week later	Given six months later

Returning now to the training type of study, let us examine it more closely as a paradigm of experimental-developmental research, to determine just what kind of information we may expect from it, and the problems of design that need to be recognized. A convenient way of doing so is to contrast two prototype studies on the problem, one (Feigenbaum & Sulkin, 1964) dating from the early period of this type of research, while the other one (Bearison, 1969) is more recent. The comparison is best made in the form of a table (Table 11–3), so as to bring out the characteristics of each with respect to a set of criteria for this type of research.[3]

Before looking at the various criteria in turn, along with their exemplifica-

[3]In selecting this particular pair of studies, there is no intent to single them out for special attention, either in a positive or a negative sense, nor to suggest that they are representative in all respects of early versus recent conservation-training research more generally. They have been picked only to provide convenient illustrations of the criteria specified for our discussion of the design of conservation-training research.

tions in the two studies mentioned, let us be clear as to the purpose which research of this type should be designed to serve. As already noted, we cannot hope through such training research to isolate *the* factors thought to be critical for the development of conservation. What we can do, however, is to find out what kinds of factors are relevant to this development, in the sense that where training focused on them is given, development is accelerated. If the factors are chosen so as to bear a plausible relationship to those which may be assumed to be operative in the child's everyday life during the time the concept in question is in process of formation (i.e., for those children acquiring it "naturally"), the value of the finding is to that extent enhanced.

The point just made is relevant to the mode of manipulation of the training conditions, that is, the type, breadth, and duration of the experience given the child. At the same time, if the effects of such training are to be placed in the context of the normal process of cognitive development, appropriate decisions are required with respect to pre- and posttests, the inclusion of a control group, the provision for follow-up tests, and the selection of subjects for inclusion in the main part of the study on the basis of the pretests.

Type of Experience. A large variety of conditions of training, representing diverse theoretical views as to the basis for conservation, have been used in this body of research, with varying success. The choice of the particular type of experience employed has typically been based on the investigator's theoretical predilections, which determined his personal belief as to how a conservation concept might develop in a child (or, in some cases, a comparison among alternative bases, designed to settle a theoretical argument between competing theories). Thus, we have had a parade of training conditions which to varying extents and degrees of consistency have shown themselves to be sufficient to induce conservation, at least given a child within a particular age range. But the relationship between these conditions and the process of conservation as it takes place naturally—that is, the question of the plausibility that these conditions could in fact have been operating in the child's extra laboratory experience—has rarely been examined. If it had been, it would quickly have become apparent that most of them, from rule learning to reversibility training, from cognitive conflict to reinforced practice, are of dubious relevance to that experience.

In this respect, the two studies compared in Table 11–3 turn out to differ less than in most others. Feigenbaum and Sulkin picked two types of training whose effectiveness they were interested in comparing, both of them on theoretical grounds. One was based on the exercise of a cognitive schema (addition and subtraction), which was suggested by previous investigators as possibly implicated as a direct mediator of conservation. The other involved a deliberate attempt to screen out the irrelevant information to which nonconservers respond, by blindfolding the subject. Yet, at least the first of these, which turned out to provide some minimal evidence of success, might conceivably simulate one of the ways in which a child comes to recognize conservation in his everyday experience. For example, the numbers representing a set of elements are entities affected by operations of adding and taking away (and, by implication, have nothing to do with the spatial configuration of the elements). As for the procedure used by Bearison, it was designed more specifically to simulate activities from the child's experience, both in and out of school, that would be expected to establish an attitude or set to respond to a dimension in conceptual rather than perceptual terms.

In one respect there is an important difference, however, between the type of training administered by Bearison and that employed by Feigenbaum and Sulkin. The latter, in both of their conditions, stuck closely to the conservation paradigm for their training items, which always involved transformations of a collection of stimulus elements with or without the addition or subtraction of an element to or from the set, culminating in a judgment of the equivalence between the two collections presented to the subject. Bearison's procedure, on the other hand, involved several initial phases in which the quantity of liquid in one jar was simply poured into a set of unit-sized beakers, and although the question eventually returned to the equivalence between the two quantities of liquid presented at the outset, the procedure remained much less rigidly tied to the conservation paradigm per se.

This point relates to a possible feature of the conservation problem, namely that conservation appears to be acquired indirectly, that is, as a by-product of some other ongoing developmental process rather than through direct confrontation with the problem, which warrants further explicit consideration. In the interests of continuity of the present survey of criteria of conservation research, however, this matter will be deferred to the concluding section of this chapter.

Breadth and Duration of Experience.   One of the severe limitations of much of the research on the acquisition of conservation, although less true of the more recent than of the earlier work, is the restricted extent of the experience provided, both in terms of the type and variety included, and of its duration. As soon as we approach the acquisition-of-conservation problem as an aspect of the child's broadly-scaled cognitive development rather than as the acquisition of a specific, isolated concept, the inadequacy of such an approach as a simulator of ongoing developmental change becomes apparent (cf. Wohlwill, 1966b, 1970c). In this respect neither of the studies being compared comes close to measuring up to the ideal, but there is no question that the 25- to 45-minute intensive sessions administered by Bearison represent a more substantial potential force for cognitive change than the apparently very brief and superficial demonstration sessions arranged by Feigenbaum and Sulkin.

It might be objected that this is an empirical question: To the extent that positive results are obtained in a given study (as they were to a limited degree in the addition and subtraction condition of Feigenbaum and Sulkin's study), to that extent the effectiveness of the condition, however short or "superficial," will have been vindicated. But this argument ignores the larger purpose which presumably stands behind this type of research, that is, to isolate some of the determinants considered to be operative in the normal process by which the child changes from one who denies conservation to one who grants it as a self-evident fact.

This issue is, of course, intimately bound up with the question of transfer, which has been treated at length in the conservation literature (e.g., Brainerd & Allen, 1971; Pascual-Leone & Bovet, 1966; Wohlwill, 1970c) and which will concern us presently, in the consideration of the design of pre- and posttests in conservation studies. Suffice it at this point to note the likelihood of a direct relation between breadth of experience and transfer: At one extreme, highly specific learning is expected to result in little or no transfer (at least in the horizontal sense), while broadly based experience should show a maximum of transfer. Of course, the broader the experience, and the more extensive its duration, the more it would presumably come to approximate the conditions of unstructured, extraexperimental experience (cf. Wohlwill, 1970c).

There is clearly a dilemma here, since, by incorporating more diversity into the program of experience (as might be done in the context of a Head Start type of program, motivated largely by practical aims), one pays the price of reduced ability to specify the particular factors that were operative to produce a given result. The answer would seem to lie in something of a happy medium solution, according to which a particular *type* of experience is used (e.g., counting and measuring, or classifying, or comparing stimuli along alternative criteria, cf. Sigel, Roeper, & Hooper, 1966) but broadly, in the sense of embedding it in diverse contexts, using a variety of stimulus materials, etc., as well as extended in time.

Pretesting. Investigators undertaking a conservation-training study are, of course, forced to administer a pretest, if only to ensure that the subjects to be included in the training and control groups do not already conserve prior to the start of the experiment. This procedure, it should be noted, in and of itself sets this type of study apart from a traditional learning or concept formation study, in which it is simply taken for granted that every subject starts at a zero base line with respect to the response to be acquired, which cannot be expected to become established outside of the laboratory.

As long as the study is conceived of simply in the limited terms of showing that condition X will produce a conservation response in a subject previously not giving it, it is not surprising that the most typical approach (as illustrated in the Feigenbaum and Sulkin example) is simply to dichotomize subjects into conservers and nonconservers, and to exclude the former from the study. This all too common procedure has three unfortunate consequences: It implicitly assumes that conservation once attained cannot be lost, whereas longitudinal studies (Almy, Chittenden & Miller, 1966, pp. 91 ff; Benson, 1966, Appendix B; Wohlwill, Devoe, & Fusaro, 1971) inevitably show a certain number of cases of reversals from one test to the next, even when these are separated over considerable periods of time, that is, several months, so as to go directly counter to the direction of maturational change. Second, it creates a dichotomy between nonconservers and conservers which, even with respect to as discontinuous a variable as this may not be justified.

Finally by limiting oneself to subjects at a single level with respect to conservation on the pretest (namely, total absence of it), all possibility evaporates of relating the process of acquisition to the normal developmental function for this aspect of behavior. Thus, it might be that some conditions (e.g., cognitive conflict) would prove maximally effective for those subjects who had started to move toward conservation already, whereas others might be effective in breaking up the initial nonconservation structure, while only leading to a partial or intermediate level of conservation. Furthermore, the insistence on total nonconservers exclusively for the training and control groups does not even guarantee that all subjects start at the same level, since their closeness to the transition zone might differ. Finally, this selection procedure, by eliminating all variance from the pretests, denies one information that could help to account for interindividual differences in the effectiveness of a given training condition (e.g., Inhelder, Bovet, & Sinclair, 1967).

There is, however, an even more important function to be served by pretesting, which has become increasingly recognized (cf. Inhelder & Sinclair, 1969). It can and should provide a diagnosis of each child's state of development before the onset of the experimental conditions, with respect not just to his understanding of the conservation concept which is the object of the training experience, but to a range of related conservation concepts. It should, preferably, extend to other concepts from the domain of "concrete operations" which can provide a picture of his status with respect to the formation of this stage in its overall structural aspects.

The discussion of the problem of stages in Chapter IX should obviate the need for extended consideration of this point here; let us content ourselves with a brief illustration of its application to the study of the effects of experience. Here again the two studies under review are of limited interest, for while Bearison—in contrast to Feigenbaum and Sulkin— did include a broad range of conservation items in his pretest, he limited himself to children who failed across the board on all of the items, so that the pretest information was not used for diagnostic purposes but only for selection; at most it provided a uniform base line (of zero) for the assessment of transfer effects.

An investigation carried out collaboratively by Carbonneau (1965) and Fournier (1965) as Masters' theses at the University of Montreal represents one of the few instances in which a picture of the standing of the children on a variety of tasks related to the criterion is available on both pre- and posttests. Their work dealt with conservation of area, and included pre- and posttests for four variants of the area-conservation task, as well as length- and substance-conservation items. They exercised a minimal degree of selection, confining themselves to eliminating subjects who on the pretest were at stage 3 of the two conservation items closest to the training situation. Thus, subjects at an intermediary level, stage 2, on these items were retained, as were subjects at either stages 2 or 3 on several transfer items, but experimen-

TABLE 11–4

Frequency-Distribution of Responses in Stages I, II, III, of
Conservation, before, Immediately after, and 3 Months after Training[a]

Conservation item	Group	Pretest			First posttest			Second posttest		
		Stage			Stage			Stage		
		I	II	III	I	II	III	I	II	III
Area conservation	E	17	4	0	3	1	17	7	3	11
(horizontal surfaces)[b]	C	15	6	0	19	2	0	17	3	1
Area conservation	E	10	11	0	1	3	17	4	4	13
(vertical surfaces)	C	10	11	0	12	4	5	11	7	3
Area conservation	E	15	2	4	5	2	14	6	3	12
under shape	C	15	4	2	17	1	3	14	3	3
deformation										
Area conservation (via	E	3	1	17	1	1	20	1	0	21
sectioning of pie)	C	0	3	18	2	1	19	0	2	18
Substance conservation	E	20	0	1	15	1	5	15	1	5
	C	20	1	0	19	2	0	20	0	2
Length conservation	E	18	3	0	15	5	1	11	8	2
	C	19	2	0	18	3	0	18	3	0

[a]Data of Fournier (1965).
[b]Concept used in training.

tal and control groups were effectively matched for performance on the latter. We find, then, the following picture of the distribution of these subjects on the pretest (cf. Table 11–4, which also gives data for an immediate and a delayed posttest).

Looking only at the pretest data, we note that the length and substance conservation items appear to be harder than the area-conservation ones, and that the pie-subdivision item (in effect a special case of area or substance conservation) was by far the easiest. The very fact, however, that such a large proportion of the children conserved on that task suggests that as a group they were moving into the conservation stage at the start of the experiment (unless it represents an artifact of the item or its mode of presentation). More to the point, the transfer exhibited on the first posttest to the various area conservation items, including one, deformation of area, which was quite unlike the training situation, indicates something of the generalizability of the training achieved. At the same time, the lack of transfer to length and substance loses somewhat in importance, in view of the demonstrated higher level of difficulty of those items on the pretest. What we have here, in other words, is a typical gradient of generalization, but it is only the extensive pretesting and the retention of partial conservers in the study that enables us to obtain a valid picture of the effects of the training on the total pattern of the children's responses.

Control Group. No-training control groups are almost invariably provided for in the design of conservation training experiments, the study by Feigenbaum and Sulkin being a rare exception. This point hardly would seem to warrant comment, except that the rationale for including them is rarely made explicit. Presumably it is based on the tacit recognition that changes from nonconservation to conservation responses can occur without benefit of deliberate training—an assumption for which there is ample empirical support in the performance of control-group children from the annals of the conservation-training literature.

Such a change could, of course, occur for reasons quite unrelated to true cognitive change, that is, instability or unreliability of response, response alternation sets, warm-up effects, etc. The use of *sets* of items to test for conservation on pre- and posttests should help in spotting such artifactual changes, as would resort to verbal justification for responses to provide a more stringent, and possibly more reliable criterion for assessing conservation. But generally the inclusion of control groups reflects the investigator's awareness that, in a certain percentage of children, a true change from nonconservation to conservation is to be expected over any interval, even one as short as the typical pre- to posttest interval in a conservation study, which may range between half an hour and one or two days.

There is yet a third interpretation that might be given to such changes. Without denying their possible reality as true changes in cognitive functioning, one might attribute them less to purely spontaneous changes occurring in the interval between the two tests than to the effect of the pretesting experience as such. Thus, Aebli (1963) for one, has emphasized the effect on the child of simply being subjected to questions concerning conservation as a possible instigator of a change in his response. This conjecture is not so far fetched, particularly for those following a cognitive-conflict hypothesis of the acquisition of conservation, in conformance with Piaget's equilibration model (e.g., Smedslund, 1961a,b). Thus, for children who are at an age where perhaps only a minor "stirring-up" of their nonconservation structure is required to disturb the previously stable equilibrium of that structure, confrontation with the conservation question might itself engender the conflict from which the new conservation response could arise.[4]

Lastly, note that the whole conception of the control group becomes altered, once the experiment is viewed, not as one on the acquisition of conservation, but rather as an intervention in the normal process of development. Now the function of the control group, instead of being aimed at assessing test–retest effects or the like, becomes that of determining the developmental function to be expected for the class of responses under investigation in the absence of intervention, over a period of time, so that the effects of the treatment in modifying that function may be revealed. This point will be taken up presently in more detail, in the section on follow-up tests.

Posttests. There are few if any issues relating to the choice of posttests which have not already been considered in the section on pretests. Posttests are of course used to determine the effectiveness of the training, both for the criterial concepts and for transfer. In general, they should correspond directly to the pretest item, though occasionally an investigator might prefer to limit himself to a smaller coverage of tasks on the pre- than on the posttest, in order to cut down on administration time, and avoid extending the pretesting into a potential learning experience in and of itself. In any event, no new issues arise in regard to the posttests.

Follow-up Tests. Just as in our previous discussion of the study of the effects of early experience, it is the provision for follow-up tests to compare the posttreatment changes for the experimental and control groups, and the

[4]Note that this is precisely the sort of effect of pretesting that Solomon and Lessac (1968) alerted us to. Yet, their prescription for nonpretested experimental and control groups is difficult to reconcile with the need for pretest information for screening and matching purposes, and is therefore unlikely to be widely adopted even in this type of short-term experience research, where pretesting may well play a more potent role than in the long-term early experience work.

use made of the information thus obtained, that sets off a true developmental approach to the conservation problem from the traditional learning conception. This point is admirably illustrated by a comparison of Bearison's with Feigenbaum and Sulkin's designs. The latter provide for tests of *retention* of the criterial conservation concept for those children who had acquired it during training; these were given one week following the end of training, and showed that most of the children did maintain their conservation responses over that period of time. Such tests of retention are clearly of value in assessing the stability of the concept learned. But note that particularly as used by Feigenbaum and Sulkin, these tests answer a question which is in effect opposite to the developmental one, i.e., is the response acquired maintained, or does it drop out? The possibility that further development might have taken place over that period, or that a delayed effect of the training might have occurred, is ignored by these authors, first by the failure to test for transfer, and second by limiting these tests to the subjects who had shown learning on the immediate posttest.

Contrast this procedure to that of Bearison. The latter did not in fact administer his *initial* posttests for a period of 3 to 4 weeks following the end of training. Although this procedure was based in part on practical considerations, at the same time it ensured that any positive effects of traning would not represent ephemeral response sets induced by the training procedure. These initial posttests were, furthermore, supplemented by retests following a 6-month interval, thus disclosing the further development over this interval of the training group, in comparison to the control group, with respect to both the criterial and the transfer concepts. Thus, his results indicated that the former maintained its superiority over the latter on the criterial concept of conservation of continuous quantity, as well as on each of the various transfer tests (though in the case of one the difference was no longer significant). Of perhaps greater interest is the fact that, while on the initial posttest there was a clear gradient in the percentage of subjects showing conservation, ranging from 71% for continuous quantity (the object of training) down to 47% for two tests of area conservation, by the second posttest this gradient had flattened considerably. Such evidence, suggesting that over the ensuing 6-month interval the original learning was consolidated in the experimental group, could be interpreted as pointing to the formation of conservation as a structural whole, in accordance with the characteristics of a genuine stage-formation process (see Chapter IX).

Thus Bearison's study, along with the previously cited research of Carbonneau and Fournier, gives testimony to the way in which the investigator, by monitoring the development of his subjects for a period of time following the termination of training, can gain insights into the dynamics of the formation of the criterial concepts, as well as the broader cognitive structures in which they are presumably embedded.

Conclusion: The Dilemma of the Conservation-training Study

Let us review briefly the rationale for the genre of research which has been under discussion. According to the view which underlies the treatment of developmental research in this volume, the attainment of conservation constitutes a general phenomenon of cognitive development, which, given only certain minimal supportive environmental conditions, will run its course predictably (though at varying rates), much as is true of the development of size constancy, the improvement of form discrimination, and the reduction with age in the Müller–Lyer illusion (e.g., Segall, Campbell, & Herskovits, 1966). According to this view, since conservation develops of necessity, the demonstration that it will develop given condition X does not in and of itself add appreciably to our understanding of "what goes into" this phenomenon of cognitive change; only a specification of the necessary conditions for this change in behavior, i.e., via a deprivation study, could hope to do so. The conservation training approach can nevertheless serve a useful function if undertaken along a developmental dimension, that is, by tracing the course of development for the concept under study and others structurally related to it, in the presence and absence of the training condition. Such an approach at least permits us to point to conditions which influence this development, and can thus help to bring into clearer relief the interplay of forces operating in the formation and consolidation of a stage-type concept.

Having said this much, it is unfortunately necessary to do some strenuous backpedaling, in order to arrive at a more sensible view of the conservation phenomenon. When it was stated just previously that this is a "fundamental phenomenon of cognitive development," this statement was intended to refer to the fact that, wherever psychologists have looked for it through suitable tests, they have typically found the shift from nonconservation to conservation responses, within some generally fairly narrow age span, though this span might vary from one culture to another, or even one subgroup to another. Yet a strong case can be made for the view that we are dealing here, not with a basic dimension of cognitive development at all, but rather with an epiphenomenon, or better, a by-product of some other process in which the explanation for this change must be sought. The argument for this view has been presented elsewhere at greater length (Wohlwill, 1966b; Wohlwill, 1970c). Briefly, it is grounded in such considerations as the lack of any obvious common ingredient in children's experience that would lead directly to the realization of conservation, and evidence that suggests that the mere asking of the conservation question (a novelty for most children) itself can sometimes bring about a change in response (cf. the frequent improvement shown by the control group children in conservation-learning studies). Most significant of all, however, is the fact that frequently experiential conditions which do not include any practice with conservation items at all (e.g., Gelman, 1969; Kingsley & Hall, 1967; Sigel, Roeper, & Hooper, 1966) or which present them in conjunction with some other operation (e.g, Bearison, 1969; Winer, 1968), are found to be as effective, or even more effective, than methods which attempt to teach conservation directly.

The evidence from the studies just cited points to the likelihood that conservation develops as a consequence of activities on the part of the child that lead him to respond conceptually to particular stimulus dimensions, independently of other correlated dimensions. The findings from Wohlwill, Devoe, and Fusaro's (1971) longitudinal study in which changes in conservation responses were related to changes in activities of measuring, seriating, and classifying point in the same direction. But the point at issue here is not so much the substantive one regarding the basis for the development of conservation, but the more general one that observed changes in response may occur over the course of development in a purely indirect fashion, that is, as a resultant of changes in other areas to which they are functionally linked. This may be true not only of changes in the domain of conservation responses, but over a much broader array of phenomena, for example, in the field of perceptual development. Thus, it seems highly probable that when we find consistent decreases with age in the strength of the Müller–Lyer illusion (cf. Wohlwill, 1960a) these reflect much more general processes reflected in other perceptual situations, for example, having to do with mode and extensiveness of scanning of stimulus configurations, which happen to reveal themselves, among other ways, in judgments made to the Müller–Lyer figures. All of which brings us back to the problem considered much earlier, in Chapter V, of the definition of developmental dimensions: A meaningful experimental attack on the role of experience in development presupposes that behavioral measures appropriate to the developmentalists' purposes have been selected.

CHAPTER XII
Individual Differences in Development

As we noted in Chapter I, Cronbach (1957) was inclined to place developmental psychology with the differential branch of the field, and given the predilection of developmentalists for the comparative approach there was ample justification for this judgment. Yet, although *child* psychologists have traditionally evinced a strong interest in individual differences, as shown in the amount of child-psychological research represented in such standard differential texts as Anastasi and Foley's (1958), those who have been most active in the study of behavioral development have generally slighted the problem of individual differences. This has been true particularly of the work of Piaget and Werner and their followers, and more generally of the field of cognitive development; though exceptions to this statement could be found, notably from the area of cognitive styles, overall the gap separating the differentialist from the developmentalist appears almost as wide as that which keeps him apart from the experimentalist. This situation has found succinct expression in the sharp distinction which Emmerich (1968) has drawn between the classical and the differential approach to the study of developmental problems.

The real problem appears to be the failure of psychologists at either end to come to grips with the question, how developmental and differential foci may effectively be integrated into a coherent whole. This point is well illustrated in the chapter by Kagan and Kogan (1970) on "Individuality in cognitive performance," in the revision of the *Manual of Child Psychology*. Excellent though it is in its coverage of a broad range of problems in the area of child cognition, notably those relating to cognitive styles, it juxtaposes discussions of developmental changes on cognitive-style type variables and of individual differences in children for the same variables in such a way as to leave these two aspects essentially divorced from one another. The impression conveyed by this chapter is that age changes (read "age *differ-ences*") are regarded as just another source of differences among individuals. In contrast to this seming equation of the two, Kagan and Kogan's introductory overview of theoretical treatments of the concept of differentiation, as used by Lewin, Werner, Witkin, and others, provides a promise of a unifying theme around which the developmental and differential aspects of cognitive functioning might be welded together, but this remains largely unrealized.

There are, fortunately, signs on the horizon for a real change in this picture, in good measure as a result of the growing interest on the part of factor analytically oriented psychologists in the study of developmental change (e.g., Baltes & Nesselroade, 1973; Cattell, 1966b, 1968; Horn, 1970; Nesselroade, 1970). Some of the concepts and techniques emanating from this direction have already been considered in the discussion of the correlational approach to the study of developmental change, which is of course closely related to at least one aspect of the topic to which the present chapter is devoted. But what, precisely, does the study of "individual differences in development" mean? In order to sharpen the issues that arise in this regard, let us look at one area in the study of individual differences in behavior which has become increasingly popular as a subject of investigation by child and developmental psychologists, that of cognitive styles.

The Development of Cognitive Styles: Developmental or Differential?

The concept of cognitive styles, or controls, was originally proposed to refer to aspects or dimensions of performance on perceptual and cognitive tasks on which large and presumably stable and consistent individual differences were encountered. These individual differences are interpreted in diverse ways by the major proponents of cognitive-style dimensions, Gardner and his associates at Menninger, Witkin and his co-workers, and Kagan and his collaborators. The Menninger group (Gardner, Holzman, Klein, Linton, & Spence, 1959; Gardner, Jackson, & Messick, 1960) grounded their approach in the egopsychology and the neopsychoanalytic schools and accordingly saw cognitive controls as adaptive mechanisms in the service of the ego, though Kagan and Kogan note quite aptly that there is nothing in that theoretical framework that would explain why stable and pervasive individual differences should result from the operation of such mechanisms, let alone how they came into being. Kagan's own dimensions of cognitive style, analytic-perceptual (Kagan, Moss & Sigel, 1963), and impulsive-reflective (Kagan, 1966), appear to have been arrived at initially in a more ad hoc fashion, but he has evolved an interpretation stressing the role of the social environment in fostering differential amounts of anxiety and fear of failure in performance on cognitive tasks (cf. Kagan & Kogan, 1970). This view would lead to the prediction of increasing variance with age on this dimension, but not necessarily explain the systematic changes with age found for these measures (Kagan, 1966; Kagan, Rosman, Day, Albert, & Phillips, 1964).

The very use of the term "explain" in regard to the age changes on Kagan's dimensions raises the question whether we are dealing here with basically developmental dimensions, on which individual differences are superimposed, or with dimensions of individual differences which happen to be subject to a certain amount of change with age. In the case of each of Kagan's dimensions, one of the measures he uses gives rise to very marked age changes: number of analytic concepts and Haptic-visual matching. These appear to be basically aspects of children's cognitive development, and it is interesting to note that for boys, number of analytic concepts failed to correlate significantly with any of the other cognitive-style measures used by Kagan (notably those involving response latency), with the single exception of response time on his tests of conceptual style, for one of two conditions under which the tests were administered (Kagan *et al.*, 1964, Tables 4 and 5). The same holds true for the boys of the younger age group of a longitudinal study on which the Haptic-visual matching data are based (Kagan, 1966), the exception in this case being the WISC verbal skills measure. For the older boys there were three additional instances (out of 14) of significant correlations, but none exceeding the .05 level. This pattern admittedly differed in the case of the girls, for both dimensions; yet, interestingly, the *age changes* were less marked for the girls on both of these measures (number of analytic concepts, and errors on haptic-visual matching).

The point of this lengthy foray into the thicket of Kagan's cognitive-style data is to suggest the possibility that there may be an inverse relationship between the suitability of a dimension as an expression of individual differences and its status as a dimension of major developmental change. If true, this would reduce the burden on Kagan to deal with the problem of age in the context of his particular cognitive style concepts; in fact, he might be in a stronger position by systematically eliminating those measures that gave rise to systematic and consistent age changes. As long as they are retained, however, it would seem incumbent on him to tackle the problem of relating them to the individual differences, which are his main concern, and more particularly to investigate these age changes in the context of the total correlation matrices. As it stands, age differences are reported only sporadically for particular subsets of variables, and no information is available on differential patterns of correlations at different ages.

Much the same point could be made in regard to the "cognitive controls" studied by Gardner *et al.* Though they emphasize the importance of age changes, these are reported in similarly incidental fashion, and no attempt is made to integrate this aspect of their data with the individual-difference question [cf. Gardner & Moriarty (1968), for a review of the developmental data]. An attempt in this direction on a small scale has, however, been contributed by Santostefano and Paley (1964); in the light of the discussion of Witkin's work to follow, it is undoubtedly significant that they invoke the latter's differentiation concept to deal with their data on age changes in the controls of "focusing-scanning" and "constricted flexible." At the same time the information on age changes in interindividual *variability* which they present for these two dimensions goes counter to a simple differentiation notion, since the standard deviations consistently *decrease* with age. This is a problem which, as we shall find presently, similarly arises in the work of Witkin *et al.*

Witkin et al.'s Research on Field-Dependence–Independence. In comparison to either Kagan's work or that of Gardner and his associates, Witkin's group has made a much more concerted effort to encompass at once the individual difference and the developmental aspects of their work on the dimension of field dependence versus independence in their theory of cognitive styles (Witkin, *et al.*, 1954; Witkin *et al.*, 1962). They have succeeded in doing so in part by resorting to a basic developmental construct, that of differentiation, to deal with both the developmental data—which are much more extensive than those of Kagan and of the Menninger group—and with the individual differences encountered at the adult level. It is nevertheless ironic that it is the earlier work (Witkin *et al.*, 1954), antedating the use of this concept, which contains most of the data on which an effective integration of developmental and differential aspects is grounded.

There remains, furthermore, a basic question as to the form this integration might take. Logically, it would seem that where individual differences are assimilated to the terms used to describe developmental change, they will turn out to be expressible in terms of differential *rates* of development, leading to differential terminal levels, according to a fanning-out process (cf. Fig. 12–3, Model II). One might put it this way: the individual becomes increasingly differentiated, perceptually, cognitively, etc., as he develops, but some individuals become more differentiated than others. This appears to be the sense in which Witkin intends his developmental conception of individual differences to be taken, as suggested by the following sentence: "It follows from the preceding account of development that children of the same age differ in the extent to which they are differentiated, reflecting individual differences in pace of development in this important dimension [Witkin *et al.*, 1962, p. 16]."

This view is likewise implied in his discussion of psychological individuality in the concluding chapter of the same volume, in which he asserts that "In children, . . . limited differentiation is most often, although not always, the result of some kind of developmental 'arrest.' Among adults, it may also be a consequence of regression, coming after earlier achievement of a more differentiated level of functioning [p. 386]." The evidence for such an interpretation is, however, circumstantial and indirect at best, since it is not backed up by the type of longitudinal information that terms such as "arrest," and especially "regression" demand. Witkin, Goodenough, and Karp (1967) have undertaken a longitudinal study of performance on the rod-and-frame test, but their results actually provide little evidence in favor of a differential-rate-of-development view. Thus, separating out the seven most field independent and the seven most field dependent male subjects (from their longitudinal sample of 27 males and 24 females) they found the following pattern, shown in Fig. 12–1. The altogether parallel course exhibited in these two subgroups points rather to the presence of individual differences at the younger ages operating quite independently of, i.e., uncorrelated with the age changes. The same is suggested by the finding of considerable stability for these data over the period from 8 to 13, and even from 10 to 17 years, yielding stability coefficients of .76 and .72, respectively, for two different groups of males; for females the values are slightly lower: .48 and .62. As Witkin *et al.* (1967) themselves emphasize, the finding of such stability in performance suggests that consistent individual differences along

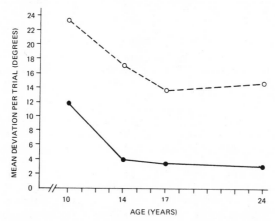

Fig. 12–1. Developmental curves for rod-and-frame test for two extreme groups of field dependent and field independent males studied longitudinally (●——●): 7 most field independent subjects; (o–––o): 7 most field dependent subjects. [From Witkin, Goodenough, & Karp (1967). Copyright by the American Psychological Association and reproduced by permission.]

the field-dependence dimension become established relatively early. It is less consistent with an interpretation in differential developmental-rate terms, if only because the increase in intersubject variability with age which would be expected under such a fanning-out pattern should, through heterogeneity of variance, attenuate the magnitude of the stability coefficients.

This brings up a much more direct source of evidence on this problem, that is, the pattern of the variability data for performance in Witkin *et al.*'s (1954) tasks. Table 12–1 shows the means and standard deviations for their three main tasks, the RFT (rod-and-frame, Series 3, with body erect), the TRTC (Series 2 b of the Body-Adjustment Test of the Tilting Room-Tilting Chair measures), and the EFT (embedded-figures test), taken from the earlier research of Witkin *et al.* (1954). The general pattern here is for the standard deviations to vary roughly in correlation with the means; this is most pronounced in the case of the EFT measures, as would be expected from such a skewed distribution. But nowhere is there a suggestion of an *increase* in variability with age, except for the results for the adult group in comparison to the adolescents on the RFT and EFT. It is well to remember, however, that the data do not extend below the 8-year-old level (in the case of the EFT, 10-year-olds constitute the youngest group). It is conceivable, therefore, that the hypothesized increase in variability as the dimension first becomes established has already occurred before this time. Any attempt to

TABLE 12–1

Means and Standard Deviations for Three Measures of Field Dependence at Different Ages[c]

	Tasks											
	Rod-and-Frame[a] (degrees of deviation from upright)				Tilting Room-Tilting Chair[b] (degrees of deviation from upright)				Embedded Figures Test (time in sec required for location of simple figure)			
	M		F		M		F		M		F	
Age Group	Mean	S.D.	Mean	S.D.	Mean	S.D.	Mean	S.D.	Mean	S.D.	Mean	S.D.
8	17.1	6.2	21.5	6.2	13.3	6.8	12.1	7.1	—	—	—	—
10	15.5	6.8	18.8	8.4	11.2	7.8	10.8	8.5	146.8	53.8	160.0	58.8
13	7.4	4.9	10.0	5.7	7.0	4.4	5.1	3.7	57.8	31.8	73.2	40.8
15	5.2	3.8	7.3	4.7	6.9	4.4	7.2	3.8	41.0	38.2	47.5	26.5
17	4.5	2.3	8.6	3.6	4.5	2.3	7.8	5.4	31.2	31.0	49.2	22.5
Adult	7.4	5.5	11.0	7.0	7.8	6.1	9.5	7.0	39.8	32.0	58.2	38.0

[a] Data shown are those for Series 3 (body erect).

[b] Data shown are those for Series 2b (Body Adjustment Task, with room tilted in direction opposite to body).

[c] Data from Witkin *et al.* (1954).

demonstrate this point would, however, run into the problem of intra-subject variability, or more particularly lack of perceptual differentiation, typically encountered in psychophysical judgments in children (cf. Gibson & Olum, 1960).

In this connection, we might refer to a rare feature of Witkin *et al.*'s (1954) data presentation, which includes tables of the (grouped) frequency distributions for all of their measures. This kind of descriptive data, so generally ignored in our rush to the computer for data analysis, can provide valuable hints as to the nature of our variables, and of group differences found with respect to them. In the present instance, these frequency distributions all show a pattern for the adult groups to include a proportion of cases near the field-independence end of the scale that is roughly comparable to those for the 15- and 17-year-olds, but the adults' distributions are strung out much further down into the field-dependence end of the scale, particularly in the case of the female subjects. (Thus the distributions are markedly skewed.) It is possible that it was this pattern that suggested to the investigators the possibility of a regression phenomenon to account for the reversal in the curves for the means for the adult groups toward greater field dependence—that is, a certain proportion of subjects, and of females in particular, might have been subject to this trend, running counter to the majority of the group, and thus accounting for both the change in mean and in standard deviation. This interpretation was not, however, upheld subsequently in the aforementioned longitudinal study which failed to show any such change toward increased field dependence in the age range from 14 to 24 (cf. Fig. 12–1). Thus selective factors in the composition of the adult group in the original cross-sectional work are presumably implicated in the apparent reversal of the developmental functions.

While in the present instance, then, the regression hypothesis failed to receive support as a possible basis for the increased variability with age, it is well to bear it in mind as a possibility, to the extent that the central tendency data point in that direction. It may point to a source of such increased variability, based on individual differences in the *shape* of the developmental function, that represents a clear alternative to the more obvious basis for such a pattern in individual differences in *rate* of development. Figure 12–2 illustrates these two alternative cases. Attention to the pattern of the means should, in general, allow one to differentiate between these, provided the sampling of age groups covers the age continuum sufficiently well. But ultimately, as already noted, where regression is a real possibility, one will want to verify it via longitudinal data.

There is a final bit of evidence pertinent to this discussion from Witkin *et al.*'s (1954) original data, which concerns the intercorrelations among the several tasks studied by them (RFT, TRTC, and EFT) which are taken

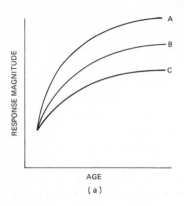 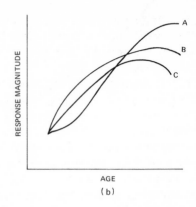

Fig. 12–2. Two models of change in variability with age, based on (a) differential rates of development, and (b) differences in shape of developmental function.

jointly as alternative measures of their central variable of field dependence, and in fact combined into a single perceptual index in the 1962 book. While the pattern of these correlations is not a simple one, they are generally larger for the adolescent and adult groups than for the 8- and 10-year-olds (the data for the former are limited, however, to the RFT versus TRTC correlation, since the 8-year-olds did not receive the EFT test). Here we find, for the first time, some indication of the establishment during the course of development of an internally homogeneous dimension of individual differences; the suggestion is that we have here a case of an emergent factor, much as uncovered in some of the developmental factor-analytic studies (cf. Chapter X; also the following discussion). This is then a kind of developmental trend that is at least conceptually independent of either changes in level or changes in variability, but quite possibly of even greater interest than these latter in arriving at a picture of the way in which developmental processes may operate to produce individual differences. To the extent that this is the case, it provides a strong argument, incidentally, for the value of multivariate designs in this field.

We have dwelled to this extent on Witkin *et al.*'s (1954) research, because it serves to bring out a number of issues in this field, and some of the alternative sources of information regarding them, which will occupy us for the remainder of this chapter—the relationship between developmental changes in level and individual differences at a given level; the differential consistency of response on related tasks at different ages; the stability of individual differences across age. Most of these questions cannot even be profitably asked with respect to the work of either the Menninger group or that of Kagan and his associates, for the reasons already noted.

Note, finally, that in contrast to Witkin, Kagan and Gardner are faced with something of a dilemma resulting from the substantial age changes which some of their variables are subject to. This is because the concept of cognitive styles or "controls" appears to be intended to refer to bipolar variables akin to personality traits and the like, with neither end of the continuum being necessarily to be "preferred" over the other, that is, more adaptive, or indicative of a higher level of functioning or ability. Indeed, Kagan et al. (1964) go to some lengths to attempt to counteract the impression that they regarded the analytic and reflective ends of their cognitive-style dimensions as somehow superior to the nonanalytic or impulsive ends. Yet, given the nature of these measures, to the extent that they are subject to consistent, systematic changes with age this would seem to constitute presumptive evidence for an ability component to these variables, though they may well be separable from those tapped by our standard intelligence tests. The overall picture in regard to the correlation between cognitive-style measures and IQ is confused, varying with the particular measures used on either side, but typically a moderate degree of correlation is found (cf. Kagan et al., 1964). In any event, the age changes point to the character of certain of these measures as directionally biased, rather than bipolar; the picture is one of individual differences superimposed on developmental changes, instead of emerging traitlike independently of the age changes. There may, however, be some measures that do tap a truly bipolar continuum.

With this all too brief consideration of the problem of cognitive styles, we are now ready to follow up more systematically on the question posed at the outset, that is, what does the study of individual differences in development refer to? We will start out by proposing two different, and in some sense opposite foci for such study.

First, there is a differential aspect to the study of developmental change. We may be interested to the study of individual differences as they relate to developmental functions of the type which have been under discussion throughout this volume. The main problem in this approach is to find suitable ways of expressing differences among individuals in terms of the quantitative parameters or qualitative characteristics of a developmental function for some variable; these parameters can then be used either for descriptive purposes, that is, to identify salient aspects of a given child's development, or to relate to other known information about individuals or groups.

The second focus is in a sense the converse of the first. It represents the developmental aspect of the study of individual differences, and concerns itself with such questions as the origin and developmental course of individual differences, the differentiation of psychological abilities and traits as the individual develops, the transformations which dimensions of individual difference undergo over age, and the like. Both methodologically and conceptually this topic poses rather more difficult problems than the first. It has been approached thus far almost entirely through the comparative analysis of factorial structure at different ages, to which reference has been made in Chapter X. This type of study tells us something about the "fate" of a factor or dimension of individual differences over the course of development; on the other hand, very little has been done to answer questions at the level of the individual, to trace the emergence and evolution of differences in measures of temperament, personality, etc.

This last statement similarly applies to the one specific question relating to the development of individual differences that has been asked most frequently, namely: How *constant* or *stable* are they? Note that this question refers essentially to the negative side of the picture, that is, it involves abstracting invariance—typically considered in terms of the preservation of an individual's *relative* standing on some behavioral variable—from developmental change. More to the point, however, is that here again the emphasis has been on the stability of *variables* and *factors*, rather than of the *individual's development*. Here is where we are perhaps most in need of an enlargement of current thinking and traditional methodology. But this question follows naturally from the other two; in fact, as we shall see, the first focus, too, has its negative, or stability side. The treatment of this topic will thus be reserved for the last portion of this chapter.

Individual Differences as an Aspect of Developmental Functions

Various illustrations of the application of developmental-function methodology, to represent differences among individuals or groups in terms of parameters of mathematical growth curves were already given in Chapter VIII. Recall the reference to Vandenberg and Falkner's (1965) application of orthogonal polynomials to describe differences in the degree of homogeneity of fraternal and identical twins with respect to growth in height. Consider also the use of growth rates at particular points in time to differentiate early and late maturers (i.e., in terms of age at maximum growth), and, at a more behavioral level, the work on the correlates of differential patterns of mental growth by Sontag, Baker, and Nelson (1958) and others. In this case we are admittedly not dealing with mathematically determined growth functions, but rather with descriptively presented patterns of IQ change, which would, however, be readily translatable at least into *rates* of growth in MA.

Age-of-attainment data provide a different means of representing individual differences in terms which are directly relatable to developmental function terms [e.g., age of attainment of 80% of mature height, as used by

Nicolson and Hanley (1953)]. They provide a convenient form for expressing the distribution of individual differences, their interrelationship, their stability, and differences among groups, that is of particular value for non-quantitative aspects of development. Nicolson and Hanley's use of age-of-attainment measures to provide information on interrelationship among a variety of stage- or level-type physiological indices was noted in Chapter X. At a more behavioral level, we may refer to Miranda's (1970) determination of age at which preference for the novel stimulus appears in infancy, in differentiating normal from premature infants, as well as a much more ambitious and comprehensive examination of individual patterns of development, based on McGraw's phases of motor development in infancy by Campbell and Weech (1941), which deserves to be examined in more detail.

Campbell and Weech's procedure was to determine for each of 40 infants from McGraw's original sample the mean age of their attainment of each phase, for five different activities: creeping, sitting, walking, reaction to

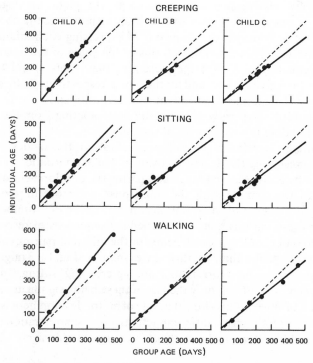

Fig. 12–3. Functions relating individual ages of attainment of phases of creeping, sitting, and walking to corresponding group ages, for three infants. [Reprinted from *Child Development* 1941, **12**, by Campbell & Weech by permission of The Society for Research in Child Development, Inc.]

pinprick, and reaching for a lure. These means were obtained by taking for any given infant the ages at which he displayed a particular phase, and determining a weighted average of these, taking account of unequal time intervals between successive observations. This permitted the authors to represent graphically the development of each child in comparison to the group, by plotting each infant's set of phase ages against the corresponding mean ages at which the same phases were attained by the group as a whole; these plots are shown in Fig. 12–3 for three cases, for the activities of creeping, sitting, and walking.

Two points are apparent from this set of graphs: They tend to follow a linear pattern in most instances, and the slopes of the best-fitting straight lines are similar for all five of the activity areas. The linear character of these plots is probably at least in part an artifact of the weighting method by which the mean phase ages were obtained, which worked much as in a running-averages procedure to smooth out irregularities in the data, and reduced the effect of extreme values. But since these functions are in any case of no more than a purely relative significance, much as MA plots, for instance, this limitation is not a very serious one. It has, furthermore, the considerable advantage of providing a simple means of expressing each infant's rate of progress for any given activity, in terms of the value of the parameter a in the linear equation $t_c = a\theta + c$ representing these plots (t_c and θ being the phase ages for a given infant, and for the group, respectively, and c a constant representing the extent of that infant's acceleration and retardation at the time of his birth—typically obtained by extrapolating from the observed points and finding the y-intercept of the line).

Chief interest centers in the parameter of rate, a. It provides a basis, not only for representing the degree of advancement or retardation of each child relative to the group (as well as for comparing the development of the twins included in this sample with the singletons), but more importantly, for indicating the degree of interrelationship among the developmental time-tables for these various qualitatively defined sequences of responses. The actual values of r for these coefficients for the different pairings of activities turn out to be smaller than the three cases shown in Fig. 12–3 might have led one to believe; the intercorrelations among creeping, sitting, and walking vary between .32 and .44, only the last of these being significant at $p < .01$. Campbell and Weech thus show that rate of motor development is far from a homogeneous affair across different activities—a demonstration that would have been difficult to make without recourse to this age-of-attainment approach.

To return to the more general consideration of the developmental-function approach to the study of individual differences, we have seen how information obtained from such an approach facilitates a purely descriptive formulation of individual differences in development, for example, in terms of rate. But what contribution can this approach make toward a more systematic study of such individual differences? Fundamentally, this particular mode of handling individual differences in development solves the problem of integrating the differential with the developmental aspects of behavior by assimilating the former to the latter. Individual differences are simply conceived as variations around some norm or modal pattern of development, and thus reducible to the terms of the modal function. As will be seen in the third section of this chapter, this conception leads likewise to a formulation of the stability problem in terms relating directly to the individual, which represents a potentially valuable alternative to the traditional approach to this problem.

Developmental Models of Individuation. We should recognize further that the developmental-function approach implicitly assumes that (*a*) different individuals do conform to a single prototype function, and (*b*) that variations around that prototype are uniform or stable over the total period of development. This represents only one among several alternative models of the relationship between individual differences and overall change in

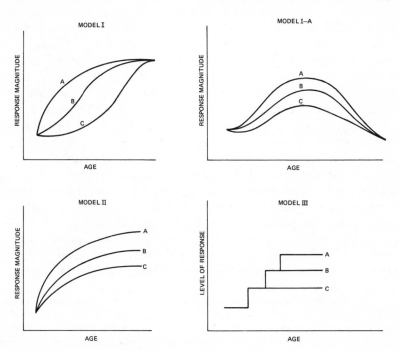

Fig. 12–4. Schematic representation of different models of individuation in behavioral development, modified from Loevinger (1966b).

behavior with age that might be envisaged. Loevinger (1966b) has given us a set of five such models, presented unfortunately in only very sketchy fashion, leaving many issues arising with respect to them unresolved. Only the first three of her five models turn out to be of interest for us. These are shown as Models I, II, and III in Fig. 12–4; for reasons to be noted presently, an important variant of Model I has been added to this set, represented as Model I–A.[1]

Of these several models, II is perhaps the one most typically encountered, at least when dealing with true developmental variables (e.g., vocabulary development). It corresponds to the case just discussed, in which individual differences are treated as variations around some prototype developmental function. Contrast this to Model I, which represents the case of responses whose development takes place over a certain time period, but eventually all children reach the same level with respect to it. Loevinger gives as examples of variables fitting this model the case of skeletal development, and, at the behavioral level, walking, achievement of control over bowel and bladder, and the like. A variety of other simple motor and cognitive skills would presumably follow the same pattern.

This model, along with its variant I-A, is of considerable importance in so for as it indicates that individual differences, rather than either remaining constant or becoming progressively greater with age, may wax and wane. To the extent that this is the case, important implications follow for any research strategies which rely on the presence of pronounced individual differences, as is true of correlational methodologies generally, and the study of stability in particular, as will be shown in the last section of this chapter. What about the distinction between I and I-A? The latter has been inserted here to refer to responses which themselves reach a peak at some intermediate age, only to decline in importance subsequently. A number of instances of this type are to be found in research on responses to stimulation in infancy, for example, crying to a stranger, smiling in response to a visual stimulus, etc. Physical aggression probably represents a similar case, peaking perhaps in early or middle childhood. And if we extend the developmental continuum to later periods of maturity, we could fit a variety of behaviors, for example, engagement in "horseplay," enjoyment of physical activity, involvement in heterosexual pursuits, etc., under this general model. The main point, however, is that in both versions we are faced with a maximiza-

---

[1] Loevinger's Model IV is omitted here since it is defined purely by a nonmonotonic developmental function, i.e., one which reaches a peak before maturity, without reference to individual variation. The same point applies to Model V, intended to represent a sequence of stages (or phases), such as might apply in the area of embryonic development; it is directed more specifically, however, at Erikson's stage system, and in that context deviations from the normal developmental pattern are considered, though not as part of the definition of the model itself.

tion of individual differences at some intermediate value on the continuum of age, with consequences for approaches to data analysis which have already been noted with respect to Model I.

Finally we come to Model III, which represents perhaps an analog of Model II for the case of qualitatively defined variables. Here as in Model I individual differences are represented in terms of the terminal level attained, but the stepwise character of development assumed under this Model does not leave room for taking account of individual differences along the path to the terminal level. This shortcoming could be remedied, however, by shifting to an age-of-attainment focus (i.e., allowing the developmental "staircases" to vary along the horizontal, rather than forcing them onto one common path).

The Developmental Aspect of Individual Differences

We turn now to the focus of the differentialist interested in individual differences, and their developmental history, that is, the course they follow over age. Note that this focus does not require that there be any systematic changes with age on the dimension of interest; rather, to the extent that these exist, the differentialist most typically abstracts from them to look at differences among individuals independent of level. Table 12–2 presents the major problems and issues in this field, in terms of a three-way classificatory

TABLE 12–2

Topics in the Developmental Study of Individual Differences

Focus on:	Single-variable case	Multivariate case
I. Emphasis on change		
The individual	Individual patterns of change in z-scores and similar measures.	Changes in patterns of ipsative relationships among variables.
The dimension	Patterns of change in variability.	Changes in factorial structure; emergence of factors; developmental transformations.
II. Emphasis on stability		
The individual	Invariance of z-scores or other relativized measures at different ages.	Constancy of ipsative patterns; invariance of factor scores.
The dimension	Stability of individual differences for a variable across a time interval.	Invariance of factorial structure across age.

scheme: a focus on the individual, as opposed to the dimension; a univariate as opposed to a multivariate approach; an interest in developmental changes in individual differences, as opposed to stability or invariance of such differences. As already mentioned, the discussion of the stability question is reserved for the final section of this chapter; we will confine ourselves here, therefore, to a discussion of the upper half of the table. At the same time comparison of corresponding entries in the upper and lower halves of the table will bring out the relations between the two facets of change and constancy in this area.

At the outset the distinction between the focus on the individual as opposed to the dimension requires explanation. Within the field of differential psychology there appear to be two quite separate emphases: On the one hand, we have the study of differences among individuals proper, including the comparison of individuals differing in sex, intelligence, socioeconomic status, etc., and the determinants and antecedents of these differences; on the other, we have the study of the interrelationship among variables, through correlational and other multivariate techniques, notably factor analysis. The latter emphasis capitalizes on individual differences for the purposes of a more nomothetic aim, that of determining the structural relations among behavioral variables and, if possible, of identifying "basic" dimensions underlying these variables. To be sure, these two approaches are not incompatible, and may in fact be used in combination. The use of factor scores determined from a factor analysis for the further exploration of individual differences represents a good illustration of such an approach. Yet the difference between these two modes of differential research remains a very real one, as readily illustrated by contrasting the work of a psychologist such as Guilford or Thurstone with that of Witkin or Eysenck, for instance.

This distinction is directly relevant to the topic of the present chapter, since two very different types of research, each with their own set of problems and techniques, are implied by these two emphases. The developmental side of the first emphasis is concerned with the emergence and developmental history of a particular type of individual, whether defined in terms of position on a continuum (e.g., a very "feminine" girl, that is, one occupying a position toward the feminine end of the M–F scale) or in terms of qualitative typology (e.g., a paranoid schizophrenic). The developmental side of the second, on the other hand, relates to an entirely different set of questions, such as the changing factorial structure and composition of abilities at different ages. It has attracted considerably more attention and effort than the first, primarily, one suspects, because it can be approached via cross-sectional data, whereas a developmental focus on the individual necessarily entails longitudinal study.

1. THE FOCUS ON THE INDIVIDUAL

a. *The Developmental History of Individual Differences along a Single Variable.* Most of the concern over the route by which an individual arrives at some terminal point on an individual-differences dimension has been directed at the stability or predictability question: How well does a child's standing on variable X at age T_1 predict his standing on the same or an equivalent variable at age T_2 (e.g., Kagan & Moss, 1962)? In order to obtain information concerning the *pattern of change* which an individual's status on some such dimension undergoes, an extensive series of longitudinal measures is required. The study by Sontag, Baker, and Nelson (1958) referred to in the previous section actually belongs here, since it concerned age changes in the differential variable of IQ, rather than in the developmental variable of MA. The fact that one is directly translatable into the other in this particular case need not obscure the essential difference between them, that is, between the tracing of a particular individual's developmental function compared with that of some reference group, and the tracing of the changes with age displayed by some measure of individual differences, that is, a relativized measure of standing on a differential variable. The latter does not presuppose even the existence of a prototype developmental function for the variable in question; it may concern measures of aggressiveness, or masculinity–feminity, which either are not subject to systematic changes with development at all, or which show changes of a primarily qualitative type, that is, in the *form* that the behavior takes.

As in the case of the study of individual variations in developmental function parameters, however, the present type of research is basically of a descriptive sort, useful in case-study work or in differentiating developmental patterns in the emergence of individual differences that might characterize different types of individuals, or groups marked by contrasting experiential histories. An interesting case in point is to be found in a study of patterns of change in IQ by McCall (1970), using the same data from the Fels study which are the subject of the Sontag *et al.* monograph referred to previously. McCall was concerned with the extent of the resemblance in IQ between siblings, in comparison to unrelated pairs of children, and between parent and child, in comparison with unrelated pairs taken from the same combination of cohorts as the parent-child pairs. He was specifically interested in the resemblance in pattern of IQ change between these pairs, and accordingly used Cronbach and Gleser's (1953) measure of pattern similarity, based on the sum of the squared deviations between corresponding IQ values at each of 10 ages (3 to 12). This measure of pattern similarity differentiated sibling from nonsibling pairs at a high level of significance, but failed to do so for parent-child versus unrelated pairs. As McCall points out, however, even the sibling–nonsibling comparison is greatly affected by overall differences in IQ level between members of a pair, and thus does not reflect the *pattern* of change in IQ as such. Thus two children whose IQ's differed by some constant amount over the age period investigated could obtain the same pattern-similarity score as a pair of children whose mean IQ over this period was equivalent, but who showed contrasting patterns of increases and decreases, the two functions intersecting in the middle. Accordingly McCall repeated his analysis, but taking deviations around each child's overall mean as the basis for the between-pair differences from which the similarity index was calculated. This procedure eliminated the influence of level, leaving him with a measure of pattern similarity in the strict sense. For this measure the profile similarity for siblings no longer differed from that of nonsiblings.

McCall sees these discrepant findings based on level as opposed to pattern as evidence for a differential determination for the two; specifically, he believes level to be inheritable, whereas pattern is more likely determined by specific events and circumstances. It does not detract from the value and interest of McCall's analysis to note that the greater intersibling resemblance in level can be accounted for on grounds other than heredity (in fact, the lack of superior similarity for the parent-child pairs compared to unrelated ones would argue against a simple genetic interpretation). For us, it is McCall's approach that is of interest, pointing as it does to a type of analysis of individual differences similar to that employed by Vandenberg and Falkner (1965) in differentiating identical from fraternal twins with respect to the similarity of their growth-curve parameters. The main difference is that McCall applies his method to an index—IQ scores—whose relativized character precludes a meaningful developmental-function analysis, since it represents an individual-difference variable, rather than a developmental one.

For this very reason one might look for further developments in this approach to be applied to the field of personality. For instance, one might be interested in tracing the developmental history behind a particular girl's status as a late adolescent or young adult on the M–F scale. Figure 12–5 shows graphically three forms that this history might take. All show a girl winding up on the high masculine side of the scale at age 20, but via three different routes: The first is seen moving consistently in that direction since early childhood, reflecting perhaps the combined action of constitutional factors and family constellation; the second arrives at the terminal point over a more erratic course, perhaps indicating long-term conflict or ambivalence in regard to her sex role; the third, finally, shows a sudden shift away from an initially normal feminine pattern, occasioned possibly by some severe identity crisis—such as might be set off by parental divorce—resulting in an altered mode of sex-role identification.

The value of this developmental-profile approach in actual application

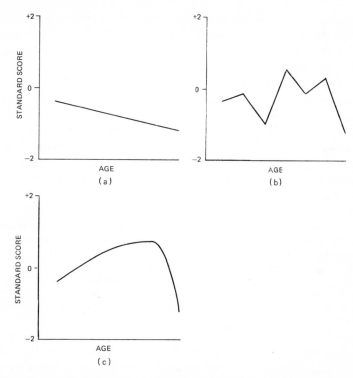

Fig. 12–5. Hypothetical alternative paths that might be taken by different individuals with identical standing on an individual-difference dimension (e.g., the M–F scale) as adults.

to problems of personality development remains to be established, since it has not really been given a try. [A tantalizing abstract by Stutsman (1935) indicates that research of this type was in fact undertaken at the Merrill–Palmer School, but the writer was unable to find any further reports of this work.] Yet it seems reasonable to suppose that we will be able to shed light on relationships between antecedent variables such as child rearing, father absence, and the like by taking account of developmental-pattern information, rather than limiting ourselves to a measure of behavior taken at but a single, frequently arbitrarily chosen point in time. At the same time, it will considerably enlarge our view of the development of personality patterns, which even in the analysis of longitudinal material has been so exclusively tied to the stability coefficient, that is, to the determination of the size of the correlation between equivalent measures obtained at two different age levels. A good illustration of this limitation is to be found in the analysis by Kagan and Moss (1962) of personality data from the files of the Fels Research Institute. This volume contains upward of 350 pages devoted to the reporting and discussion of stability coefficients, interspersed with individual descriptive case-study material; not a single mean is to be found in the whole book, let alone an examination of patterns of change with respect to the variables studied, though the data available would have readily lent themselves to such an analysis. The same point applies to the analysis of the data from the Berkeley Growth Study (Schaefer & Bayley, 1963). As a discussant on a symposium on Personality Consistency and Change, in which results from both of these investigations were reported, Honzik (1964) took rather wistful note of this flood of correlation coefficients, and advocated their supplementation by an analysis of "concomitance and change in growth curves in relation to environmental stress and support [p. 141]." Her conclusion is worth pondering:

> The methodology of analysis of growth data is inherently difficult and requires more thought than it has received. Correlations and case histories help, but what is needed is a highly complicated prediction equation which will take into account many time series, interaction effects, and the combining and partialling of variables simultaneously. It is clear that the answers to the problems are going to come slowly, as did the accumulation of data, and that the only impediments to progress will be analyses which avoid the existing complexity and draw premature conclusions [p. 141].[2]

b. The Developmental History of Patterns of Ipsative Relations within a Variable Set. The multivariate equivalent of the preceding case would relate to changes in the patterns of relations among a given set of variables, considered in an ipsative sense, that is, with the individual himself as a reference point. For instance, given an adult—e.g., a mathematician—with a marked differential between mathematical reasoning and spatial ability, the question arises as to the developmental course out of which this differential arose. Information concerning this course—at what point in childhood did this differential first appear; how consistent was it over the span from childhood through adolescence, etc.—could provide a clue as to the origin of such differentials, in terms of the role of particular school experiences, or alternatively of possible genetic factors.

The ipsative approach has as yet seen little application in differential psychology, except for the efforts of a very few adherents, notably Brover-

---

[2]In a recently published volume Block (1971) has dealt quite specifically with this problem of individual patterns of development with respect to individual-difference variables, but defined in terms of qualitative traits, determined from Q-sorts, rather than quantitative dimensions. This work, however, covers changes only from the junior-high school period to adulthood. [Quotation from M. P. Honzik "Personality consistency and change: Some comments on papers by Bayley, MacFarlane, Moss and Kagan, and Murphy." *Vita Humana* 7: 139–142 (S. Karger, Basel 1964).]

man (1962). Emmerich (1968) has made a persuasive case for including this approach as a major alternative to both the classical and the differential study of developmental patterns, particularly in the study of personality structure. He cites a number of examples where it has been used at least implicitly, in the sense that structural relations among personality variables have been studied on a within-individual basis. One of these, in fact (Martin, 1964), includes a longitudinal dimension, and thus provides a rare example of the particular paradigm being referred to.

Martin obtained time-sample data for children in the nursery school for seven separate behavioral dimensions (dependency, nurturance, aggression, control dominance, autonomous achievement, avoidance withdrawal, and friendship affiliation). These were obtained in four successive semesters, during the children's third and fourth year. The resulting behavior frequency data for each child were converted into proportions of the total number of behavior events in which he was observed; the set of scores for each child, then, represented a profile of the relative incidence of responses falling in the various categories. This procedure provided Martin with scores that were not only comparable from one child to another, independent of the absolute number of behavior events scored for him, but, more important, from one semester to another, independent of the very substantial total increases in behaviors in virtually all categories over time.

The ipsative part of his analysis consists of an analysis of variance carried out on the set of scores for each child individually, with behavior categories and semesters as orthogonal factors, and two replications within each cell, obtained by selecting at random the records for two independent sets of observations taken from the total time sample. Thus for each child a pair of F-values result, one for the differences among behavior categories, the other for the interaction between categories and semesters. (The F for semesters $= 0$, since the total of the proportions for each semester is fixed at 1.0.)

The results show, first, highly significant F-values for categories for all children, ranging from a low of 10.0 to a high of 104.6, indicating simply that for all children the distribution of behaviors in the various categories departed markedly from chance. Second, the F-values for the interaction between semester and category was *non*significant for the large majority of cases, which Martin interpreted as indicative of considerable stability in these response patterns over time.

Martin's approach represents an interesting application of the ipsative approach in this area, but suffers from some obvious statistical difficulties (notably the lack of independence of the observations in the various cells, especially those associated with the semesters variable; thus the data for the individual children fit a chi-square model much more aptly than an analysis of variance), as well as from low reliabilities of the observations for a number of the behavior categories. But the study raises a more substantive question. It appears that, though nominally ipsative, Martin's approach yields information mainly concerning the group as a whole, and more particularly concerning the overall differences in the relative incidence of behaviors among the various categories. Surely this is what is reflected in the inflated F-values for categories obtained for all of the children: Dependency is simply a more frequently observed type of behavior than avoidance withdrawal, for instance. As a matter of fact, Table 10 of Martin's paper, in which the proportional frequency data for each child summed over the different semesters are given, indicates that there was exactly one subject (out of 75) who had a higher proportion in *any* of the other six categories than he did for dependency.

A more interesting way in which these data might have been analyzed to provide a truly ipsative picture of the individual children's response profiles and their changes over time would have been to standardize these values, thus fixing not only the total across categories, but the mean for each category. This is, incidentally, the approach to ipsative research favored by Broverman (1962). It would provide a picture of the patterning of behavior within individual children which would maximize the information concerning individuality of patterning, much as McCall did in his analysis of similarity of profiles of IQ change, with overall level partialled out.

Let us note, finally, that a focus on the structure of behavior at the level of the individual child of a different type is represented in Cattell's *P*-technique discussed in Chapter X. Here the interest is in the interrelations among variables, rather than in profiles showing the relative amounts of each; nonetheless this too appears to qualify as a genuinely ipsative approach. On the other hand, since in this model the time axis is used to generate a sample of occasions across which to intercorrelate the variables, the possibility for demonstrating changes in their interrelationship over age at an individual level is lost. Furthermore, any such ipsative approach must eventually face the problem of how to deal with the results for each individual, that is, what generalizations to draw from them. At the very least this entails finding ways of classifying the individual profiles or patterns (or the changes in these over age) into a manageable set of categories, for use in further correlational or comparative study.

2. The Focus on Dimensions

a. The Study of Age Changes in Individual Differences with Respect to a Single Variable.   Turning from the study of the individual to that of dimensions in our coverage of the various cells of Table 12–2, we come next to the univariate study of changes in dimensions of individual differences across

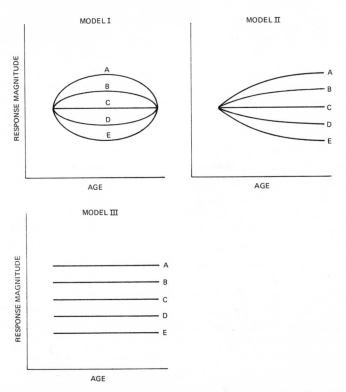

Fig. 12–6. Schematic representation of models of progressive individuation with age along a dimension of individual differences.

development. The only topic that seems to fit under this rubric is that of changes in variability over age for a single variable—a problem which, incidentally, has been too generally neglected in this field, since, as noted in our discussion of Witkin's work as well as of Loevinger's models, different patterns of change in variability correspond to different models of individuation. It would not be difficult, in fact, to develop a set of models to deal with this topic that would be the analog for nondevelopmental variables (or for measures from which information as to level has been removed) of the models of individuation of ontogenetic change which Loevinger has proposed for developmental variables. Thus we might differentiate among the following patterns of change in variability shown in Fig. 12–6.

The first two of these are equivalent to Loevinger's Models I and II. The former represents a case of increasing differentiation reaching a maximum at some intermediate point in development, only to disappear subsequently, while the latter shows rather a pattern of progressively increasing individuation with respect to a particular variable. Model II is presumably widely applicable to a broad range of personality traits for which an absence of individual variation at birth must be assumed, if only in the sense that they are not meaningfully measurable at that time. Model I, on the other hand, suggests the formation of a dimension of individual difference sometime during childhood which ceases to be applicable subsequently. Although it may appear unrealistic to expect such a pattern to occur, it does apply in a limited sense to variables defined in terms of a particular mode of expression of some trait—for instance, physical aggressiveness.

As for the third model depicted in Fig. 12–6, it appears implausible on the face of it, suggesting as it does an invariance in variability across age that is borne of an absence of change as such, that is, stability of behavior in the absolute sense. If, however, we look at patterns of change abstracted from changes in level (e.g., by dealing with deviation scores), the model might conceivably apply to a limited set of functions characterized by stability, along with lack of systematic change in variability. Figure 12–1, showing patterns of change in field dependence based on the rod-and-frame test for two contrasting groups, from the longitudinal study by Witkin, Goodenough, and Karp (1967) represents perhaps one instance in point, though one would want to look at the corresponding functions for subjects in the intermediate range before so deciding.

In a more general sense, there are obviously many instances in which intersubject variability does not undergo systematic change (though our information on this point is much less complete than it might be, as information on changes in variability is frequently not reported). But the models illustrated in Fig. 12–6 are intended to do more than simply portray patterns of change (or lack of change) in variability with age; rather they are intended to represent different routes that individuation with respect to an individual-difference variable may follow. In this sense the pattern of parallel paths shown in Fig. 12–6 is implausible, unless we either assume an innately determined type of behavior or confine ourselves to but a limited portion of the developmental continuum. (Note in this connection that the data of Witkin, Goodenough, and Karp just referred to only start at age 10; presumably individuation has taken place before that time to establish the child's level of field dependence on the 10-year-old test.)

Little has been done thus far to provide evidence on the appropriateness of these models, the areas of their applicability, etc. The topic of developmental changes in intersubject variability has not even generally been recognized as a methodological issue, in its consequences for factor-analytic research, for the interpretation of stability coefficients, etc. Progress in this direction has been further hampered by the use of scales such as the Stanford-Binet which are constructed so as to yield variances that are approximately constant across age, as well as the more general problem of the noncomparability of scales (especially of individual-difference scales) used to assess the same variable at different ages. Finally, statistical constraints operate here, which work on this problem will have to take into account, as seen in Witkin's perceptual data (cf. Table 12–1). Here we find large changes in variability, largely as a result of the skewed nature of the score distributions and the attendant correlation of means and variances, so that the pattern of changes with age in variability is devoid of significance for bringing out intrinsic characteristics of evolving individual differences.

   b. The Multivariate Study of Age Changes in Individual Differences.   This topic, dealing with a developmental analysis of changing patterns of interrelationships among variables studied contemporaneously, as well as of patterns of relationships between variables studied at different ages, has already been treated at length in Chapter X. It concerns such problems as the differentiation of abilities or traits with age, age changes in the number of factors extracted from batteries of tests or personality scales, and the comparability of factorial matrices in terms of the identity of component factors. Although the presentation in Chapter X was intended primarily for the treatment of interrelations and factorial structure for developmental variables, the procedures outlined there apply equally to true individual-difference dimensions, such as measures of personality (cf. Coan, 1966). In fact, some of the problems relating to the dilemma of "what to do about age" vanish when we deal with variables for which overall age changes are negligible, and Cattell's conception of time, as well as the value of P-technique favored by him, assume greater cogency under these circumstances.

   Most important, perhaps, is the enhanced feasibility and meaningfulness, where age changes in level on the component variables are minimal, of undertaking a single factor analysis including all of the age groups, as Black (1965) has done with respect to a set of 54 personality variables assessed via teacher ratings. Black describes a method suggested by Tucker (unpublished) for dealing with such data, and the possible inferences to be drawn from such an analysis, as follows:

> In this method, a single set of factors is obtained for all age levels. The variance accommodated by the factors at each age level, and the intercorrelations among the factors at each age level, are estimated. The variance of a factor is generally taken as an indication of the size, or importance, of that factor relative to other factors (Harman, 1960; Peterson, 1960). In the same manner, the variance, in Tucker's method, is used as an indication of the size, or importance, of a factor in one age group, relative to that in other age groups. To the extent that a factor is degenerating with age, its variance would be expected to decrease systematically with age; to the extent that a factor is emerging with age, its variance would be expected to increase systematically with age; to the extent that two factors are differentiating with age,

their intercorrelation would be expected to decrease systematically with age; to the extent that two factors are merging with age, their intercorrelation would be expected to increase systematically with age. Discovery that variance is concentrated in a single factor for young children and diffused among many factors at later ages might assume some interest in the light of related principles of growth. A shift in variance concentration from one set of factors to another over the course of time could lead to the formation of new principles of personality development, with empirical specifications established from the beginning [p. 770].

In the case of Black's own results, a considerable degree of apparent constancy of factorial structure across age was found, from nursery school through the end of high school, at least in the sense that neither the amount of variance accounted for by either of the two factors extracted from the analysis nor the correlation between them showed very consistent changes with age. (The pattern for the variance for Black's Factor 1 actually does show a fairly regular rise between Grades 1–2 and 5–6, with a subsequent drop to a lower level for the older age groups, which Black tentatively attributes to the onset of adolescence.) At the same time the limitations of teacher-rating data are emphasized; Black mentions the possibility that the apparent constancy of these indices of factorial structure with age is a function more of the characteristics of the ratings themselves (and of the raters) than of the children's behavior. In this connection the fact that no more than two factors emerged from this analysis should be noted, suggesting a general diffuseness and lack of differentiation across these ratings, as Black points out.

The Study of Stability and Continuity in Behavior

The problem of the stability of behavior over age has attracted an enormous amount of attention on the part of developmental researchers, both in the domain of intelligence and abilities and in the personality area. It has virtually preempted, in fact, the field of long-term longitudinal research, such as that carried out at Berkeley and Fels. It almost seems as though those studying the development of behavior were in need of reassurance that, amid all the obvious and not so obvious changes in behavior that take place over the course of development, something identifiable remains *un*changed, so that the individual can indeed be shown to retain his identity.

The intensity of this concern appears, unfortunately, to have exceeded the imaginativeness of the approaches taken to investigate this question. With only very few exceptions, work on stability, as already pointed out, has consisted in the endless proliferation of correlation coefficients, to indicate the degree of relationship between measures of behavior obtained over some given time interval. We have already pointed to the limiting effect of this narrow approach in the realm of personality development, but a perusal of Bloom's (1964) comprehensive review of the literature on stability, including physical characteristics, intelligence and abilities, achievement data and interests and attitudes, as well as personality measures, shows that this limitation extends across the whole field. The result has been that we have learned a little about the "behavior" of *variables* over age, but nothing concerning the behavior of individuals. Furthermore, even at the level of the focus on dimensions, the information contained in bare correlation coefficients is meager at best, and conveys little sense of a system undergoing change—or, for that matter, remaining invariant in the midst of change.

1. VARIETIES OF BEHAVIORAL STABILITY

The most general, and certainly the most neutral definition of stability, whether applied to behavior or any other process, is probably one which equates it with *predictability*. This is most readily seen in the case of the negative: "Unstable" necessarily means unpredictable. But predictability

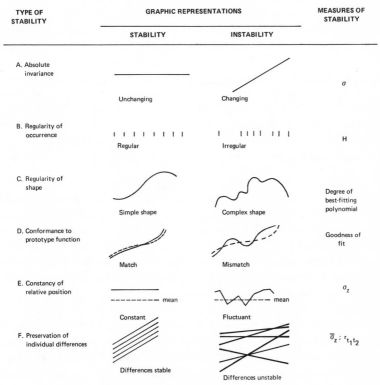

Fig. 12–7. Different types of stability.

can arise in several different ways. Let us look at some of the main ones; they are represented graphically in Fig. 12–7. Note that, in terms of the schema of Table 12–2, we are dealing here with the single variable side exclusively. At the same time the types of stability to be considered cut across not only the distinction between the focus on the individual versus that on the dimension, but even across the more general one running through this chapter, between the study of individual differences in developmental functions and that of the development of individual differences. In particular, of the six types of stability to be considered, the first two actually deal with invariance in an absolute sense, and are thus difficult to fit into the scheme of this chapter at all, but are included mainly for the sake of completeness. The next two types concern the individual's developmental function, from the vantage point of its conformance to a prototype, rather than individual variations around it. It is only the last two of the six types that bring us back to the development of individual differences, and to the schema of Table 12–2; of these two, the fifth remains on the side of the focus on the individual, while the last alone concerns the focus on the dimension.

a. Absolute Invariance. Behavior may be stable over time in an absolute sense, that is, remain unchanged. This is true, for example, of much of learned behavior, once it is acquired, notably in the field of motor skills, habits, or other highly overlearned chains of behavior; it may be equally true of a variety of sensory and perceptual processes. These would appear to be of little interest to the developmental psychologist, except for the possible bearing they may have on the hypothesis of innately determined behavioral attributes (cf. the Gestalt interpretation of perceptual constancy) or, alternatively, on the role of early experience in laying down patterns of behavior that remain unchanged subsequently (cf. psychoanalytic conceptions of fixations).

b. Regularity of Occurrence. One sense in which the term "stability" is applicable in the study of behavior generally refers to the distribution in time of the occurrence of some event, and particularly the periodic or aperiodic nature of this distribution. In this sense the phases of the moon are a stable phenomenon, the occurrence of sun spots less so, and the falling of a meteor least. Similar examples could readily be given from the field of psychophysiology. This type of stability is necessarily less pertinent to the developmental psychologist. It is difficult to envisage many discrete behavioral events that would occur at repeated intervals over an extended span of development, except for such trivial cyclic responses as eating and sleeping. The issue of stability in this sense could be studied more meaningfully with respect to such events as the occurrence of dreaming, or engagement in sexual intercourse.

c. Regularity of Form of Change. It is stability in the context of change that is of primary interest for the developmental psychologist. One form that such stability may take is that of regularity—that is, smoothness of the developmental function. An analogy from the movement of objects in space may be helpful: The movement of a jet crossing the continent can be considered highly stable; the opposite is true of that of a fighter engaging another in a dogfight. Applied to the developmental area, it seems safe to assert that growth in height during middle childhood follows a highly stable pattern, that for weight somewhat less so, and that for scores on the embedded-figures test still less.

d. Consistency Relative to a Prototype Function. This aspect of stability is closely related to the preceding, but would be assessed in a different way, since it refers to the degree of correspondence between an individual's developmental function and some prototype curve, derived either on empirical or theoretical grounds. Thus, while an individual's total pattern of growth in height is in fact unstable in the sense of the previous definition—since no single mathematical function can be fitted to it—it is generally stable in the present sense, that is, in the correspondence between the pattern shown by any given child and the modal or prototype growth curve determined for this aspect of growth for the human individual in general.

e. Constancy of Relative Position. Yet another way of representing stability for an individual's course of development is to consider the constancy of his standing relative to some referent group across age, abstracted from any developmental change that may take place. This is the most generally applicable definition to deal with the stability problem at an individual level, since it does not require the postulation of a developmental function, and may in fact be employed with reference to variables measured on different scales at different ages, or even directly via the use of rankings.

f. Preservation of Individual Differences. With this definition we turn the corner from a focus on the individual to that on the dimension. It is the definition which has been assumed for 99.9% of the work on the problem. It is obviously closely related to the preceding, but provides information concerning a *group* of developing individuals. It, thus, tells us about the stability of a given aspect of behavior in general, rather than referring to stability as a characteristic of the development of the individual.

Take, for instance, the typical finding that measures of intelligence in infancy or very early childhood show either no or only very low correlation with measures taken in adolescence. This tells us something about lack of continuity between these respective measures of intelligence. The significance of this finding, on the other hand, for our understanding of the development of intelligence in the individual child is much more doubtful.

We will return to this question, and to the interpretation of this type of stability data at the end of this chapter. At this point, suffice it to mention one further important difference between the stability obtained for a group of individuals on the basis of the intercorrelation between measurements taken at two different ages, and the other types of stability. Stability in this sense is dependent on the choice of the particular initial and final ages over which it is measured. Thus, given some initial age of testing, one can generate a "developmental function" describing the change in the magnitude of the correlations between the initial test and subsequent tests administered at successive ages (cf. Bloom, 1964, for a variety of illustrations of such functions). For the measures of stability based on the individual, on the other hand, one may readily determine a single value describing stability for the total course of development of a given child. We will consider possible alternatives to the traditional stability coefficient that likewise apply to the entire period of development in the section on the measurement of stability to follow.

2. The Measurement of Stability

Measures of Absolute Stability (Types A, B, and C).   For these cases one would presumably choose a dimensionless measure of variability around expected values. In the case of Absolute Invariance (Type A), the coefficient of variability is satisfactory; if several observations at each age are available to provide an error term, F-ratios may be used to yield significance values. In the case of Type B, chi-square tests would be indicated, to test for deviation from equal distribution of events over time. Type C presents a more difficult problem; one solution might be simply to use the highest order coefficient of the best-fitting polynomial as an index of regularity, or, if multiple observations at each age are available, the highest significant component in a trend analysis. More sophisticated approaches are available, for example, by applying procedures from the field of time-series analysis.

Unlike the coefficient of stability (i.e., Pearson r) all of these indices unfortunately lack an upper bound, but this feature does not detract from their value in comparing the stability of developmental functions among individuals or groups.

One particular caution is in order with reference to the assessment of absolute stability of Type A. Behavior may remain stable over time in level or type either for lack of within-group variance in the behavior, or for reasons of individual stability in the face of interindividual variation. It is presumably the latter that the developmental psychologist is interested in, yet there are cases where the stability encountered is of the former kind, that is, largely due to an artifact of the selection of measures. One such instance, the observational study by Martin (1964) of nursery school children was referred to previously, in the section on ipsative models of developmental research on individual differences. The other is the investigation by Thomas, Birch, Chess, Hertzig, and Korn (1963) of infants observed over their first two years of life, in which three-point rating scales for nine different activity dimensions were obtained on five occasions over this interval. As an index of stability, the percentage of cases in which the infant's dominant responses on these three-point scales remained invariant was used; yet for seven of the nine categories, better than 70% of the ratings (and better than 80%, in the case of several) fell into one of these three categories—that is, there was little interindividual variation on these ratings.

Stability as Fit to a Prototype Function (Type D). A standard measure of goodness of fit, for example, one based on a least-squares procedure, is obviously indicated here. In view of a family of such curves for a group of individuals, furthermore, we could readily determine whether there are significant individual differences around the prototype function which would suggest the need for a number of different such functions.

Constancy of Relative Position (Type E). A straightforward index of individual variability suitable with virtually any kind of data is the variance of a set of relativized measures obtained at successive ages. These could take the form of quotients (e.g., IQ), percentile ranks, or most generally, standard scores. The latter have in fact been employed by Bayley (1949), who reports individual "lability coefficients" (i.e., sigmas of a set of standard scores obtained from an individual) from her longitudinal data on IQ.[3]

One shortcoming of the proposed index, that is, the standard deviation of a set of z-scores, should be noted. It fails to differentiate between shifts in relative position that are random and those that are systematic, since the order of the scores is not taken into account. For instance, one subject might have IQ's at successive ages of 85, 90, 95, 100, 105, 110, and 115, while another's IQ's at the same ages might be 90, 115, 100, 105, 85, 95, and 110. Both of these subjects' lability coefficients would of course be identical, even though the development of the second child is clearly much more erratic.

[3]The author has applied this statistic to 12 cases (six boys and six girls) taken from the Berkeley Growth Study, for the variable of height, weight, and strength, as published by Tuddenham and Snyder (1954). Despite the small number of cases, the data are consistent in at least two respects: The median values of the lability coefficients are higher for girls than for boys for all three variables, and (for both sexes combined) they are also higher for weight and strength than for height—as one would expect.

Measures of Group Stability (Type F). Since the stability coefficient (correlation between measures taken at two different ages) is the most frequently employed measure of stability, it warrants the closest attention. Apart from the one limitation noted already, that is, that any stability coefficient applies only to the particular pair of points on the age continuum over which the correlation is obtained, we should also note the fact that such coefficients are necessarily affected by changes with age in the variance of a distribution. Curiously, Bloom (1964, p. 21f) has taken note of the effect of selection due to attrition in longitudinal samples on variability, and of the resultant influence on the magnitude of the stability coefficient, and attempted to correct for this factor in comparing different samples by calculating an adjusted common terminal variability. Yet he has failed to recognize the more general problem posed by changes in variability in the measure of interest over the interval studied. Here again the use of standard instead of raw scores commends itself, since it will result in equivalent variances at all ages. Bayley's (1949) report, just cited in connection with the measurement of individual stability, likewise represents one of the rare instances in which group stability coefficients were calculated following such a standardization procedure.

One modification of the traditional stability coefficient that could be suggested to provide a single measure of stability for the age continuum as a whole would be via the use of Kendall's coefficient of concordance—that is, a measure of the overall agreement among the set of n rankings of the group of subjects obtained at the n occasions of testing. There is, however, a more satisfactory approach available, which has the advantage of being directly relatable to the measure of individual stability in the relative-position sense (Type E). We noted that the standard deviation of an individual's standardized scores obtained from his raw scores for successive ages served as a convenient index of individual stability, or lability to use Bayley's term. For a group as a whole it would be necessary only to average these standard deviations, or preferably to use the square root of the mean squared deviation, to obtain a group index of within individual variation across time.

It should be noted that this index is still influenced by the interval of time separating successive tests, just as is true of stability coefficients: The mean variability of z-scores obtained from a coarse sampling of the age variable will generally be larger than that obtained from a dense sampling. Without considerable further mathematical analysis of this index it is not possible to relate it to the corresponding matrix of stability coefficients which it is designed to supplant. It is not even clear just what the index's upper bound is, though it is obvious that for the special case of a set of perfectly correlated measures its value is zero, since each individual's set of z-scores would be constant. It is interesting to note that the measure suggested is directly related to the subjects x treatments variance estimate in a repeated-measurements analysis of variance (i.e., the error term used in testing for the significance of the treatment variable—in this instance, the age variable).

The Interpretation of Stability Coefficients.   It is well to remind ourselves, with respect to both individual and group measures of stability of the type cited in the preceding two sections, that they entail abstracting invariance of relative position from change in behavior over age in either level or form. This point is too readily forgotten in interpreting such stability data. This is not to say that the magnitude of stability coefficients is completely independent of the magnitude of the developmental changes taking place in the interval over which stability is measured, but rather that the relationship between them is by no means a simple one. Under very special circumstances, however, this relationship can be stated in rather precise form, namely, where development can be assimilated to a simple accretionary growth model.

When given a variable X_1, made up of, or determined by N_1 elements, and a variable X_2 by $N_1 + \Delta N$ elements, it can be shown that $r_{X_1 X_2} = \sqrt{N_1 / (N_1 + \Delta N)}$ (cf. Kelley, 1924, p. 190). This relationship represents a generalized statement of the "overlap hypothesis," that is, the correlation between two quantities related to each other as part to whole. Anderson (1939) has applied it to the particular case of stability coefficients obtained from longitudinal data, stating it in the form $r_{12} = \sqrt{\overline{X}_1 / \overline{X}_2}$. By this formula, stability is shown to be directly proportional to the square root of the proportion of the growth at the later age that has been attained at the earlier one, or the proportion of terminal growth, if t_2 is taken at maturity. In order for this relationship to apply, however, one must be dealing with a variable conforming to the accretion of independent elements. Translated into a form applicable to behavioral variables for which such elements are not specifiable, the equivalent condition that has to be met is that the magnitude of the gain from t_1 to t_2 be uncorrelated with the individual's level at t_1. This is, however, a fairly stringent assumption, since frequently for developmental measures without a fixed ceiling there will be a positive correlation between these two quantities, just as it is typically negative in educational measurements where a ceiling effect (and a consequent regression phenomenon) is operative.

Even for physical measurements for which a ready meaning can be assigned to the quantity $\overline{X}_1 / \overline{X}_2$, the fit of stability data to those predicted from the overlap hypothesis has been found to vary from very close to very poor. Bloom (1964) presents evidence from data collected by Tuddenham and Snyder (1954) which shows the prediction to be excellent for the case of height, as one might expect given the nature of that particular variable. For weight, the fit is considerably poorer, whereas for strength it has reached the vanishing point. (For the latter, between ages 10 and 14 the stability coefficients actually decline, from .75 to .68, at a time for which the overlap hypothesis predicts an increase from .62 to .78.) Bloom is inclined to invoke the role of extraneous factors—diet and health, in the case of weight; motivational factors and unreliability, in the case of strength—to explain these departures from discrepancies between the observed stabilities and those predicted from the overlap hypothesis. Although these factors are undoubtedly important, the more basic question to begin with is whether the nature of these variables is such as to justify the application of Anderson's formula.

The limited validity of the overlap hypothesis even to the area of physical growth should caution one against a blithe acceptance of it with respect to a psychological dimension such as intelligence. Yet this is precisely what Bloom (1964) has done, to the point of translating stability coefficients into statements of proportion of mature intellectual growth attained at different ages, as in the following passage:

> Using either Bayley's correlation data (r_2) or the Thorndike absolute scale (both of which yield essentially the same results), it is possible to say, that in terms of intelligence measured at age 17, at least 20% is developed by age 1, 50% by about age 4, 80% by about age 8, and 92% by age 13. Put in terms of intelligence measured at age 17, from conception to age 4, the individual develops 50% of his mature intelligence, from ages 4 to 8 he develops another 30% and from ages 8 to 17 the remaining 20%. This differentially accelerated growth is very similar to the phenomenon we have noted in Chapter 2 with regard to height growth.
>
> With this in mind, we would question the notion of an absolutely constant I.Q. Intelligence is a developmental concept, just as is height, weight, or strength. There is increased stability in intelligence measurements with time. However, we should be quick to point out that by about age 4, 50% of the variation in intelligence at age 17 is accounted for. This would suggest the very rapid growth of intelligence in the early years and the possible great influence of the early environment on this development.
>
> We would expect the variations in the environments to have relatively little effect on the I.Q. after age 8, but we would expect such variation to have marked effect on the I.Q. before that age, with the greatest effect likely to take place between the ages of about 1 to 5 [p. 68].[4]

As this quote indicates, Bloom places a heavy burden on the tenability of the overlap hypothesis, from which he draws far-reaching inferences as to the modifiability of intelligence at different ages. The reference to "Thorndike's absolute scale" represents Bloom's attempt to validate the translation of the stability coefficients into values of proportion of mature intelligence attained at different ages, by recourse to a scale with a presumed absolute unit. But he neglects to mention that the major part of Thorndike's curve is obtained

[4] From *Stability and change in human characteristics* by B. S. Bloom. Copyright 1964, Wiley. By permission of John Wiley and Sons, Inc.

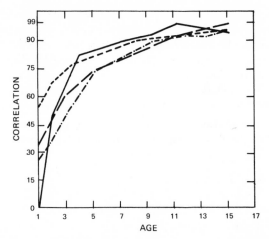

Fig. 12–8. Magnitude of stability coefficients between different ages and age 18 for measures of IQ, based on data of Bayley (1949), compared to stability coefficients predicted from overlap hypothesis for absolute-unit growth functions proposed by Thorndike *et al.* (1927), Thurstone (1928), and Heinis (1924). (————): Bayley (Point Attenuated); (—·—·—): Heinis; (————): Thorndike; (— — —): Thurstone. [From *Stability and change in human characteristics* by B. S. Bloom, 1964, Wiley. By permission of John Wiley and Sons, Inc.]

purely by extrapolation, since no data on the CAVD intelligence scales appear to have been available below the age of 10 years (Thorndike *et al.*, 1927)! Furthermore, the fit between the correlations predicted from either Thorndike's function, or from similar absolute unit scales constructed by Thurstone (1928) and Heinis (1924) to the stability coefficients reported by Bayley (1949) for the Stanford-Binet is far from close below the age of about 7, as shown in Fig. 12–8. It will be noted that the stability values start well below the predicted ones, but rise much more steeply. This is an important point, since it is what happens in this period, during which the stability values rise from zero to over .80, that is presumably most critical for the question of the plasticity of intelligence, both from a theoretical and a practical standpoint.

This critique of Bloom's analysis is not intended to detract from the strong case that can be made for the proposition that the influence of the environment as a determinant of intellectual ability is maximal at an early age, and declines subsequently—a proposition implicit in the rationale for the major programs for compensatory education at the preschool level of which we have been hearing so much in the past decade. Bloom does in fact review some of the evidence in regard to this point, and succeeds in presenting a convincing argument in support of this thesis. The point of the present discussion is only to demonstrate the equivocal bearing of the stability data on this argument.

Stability in the Multivariate Sense

From the preceding discussion, it becomes apparent that stability in the traditional sense tells us more about the nature of our developmental dimensions than about the development of individuals. Yet, in order to obtain a full picture of the "behavior" of developmental dimensions over age, and specifically of the degree to which they measure some stable, invariant entity at different ages, a multivariate approach is in fact necessary. This point is brought out in the analysis of the problem which Emmerich (1964) has given us.

Stability versus Continuity. Emmerich differentiates between *continuity* and *stability* of dimensions; the former refers to the identity of the structural relationships among a set of variables, whereas the second refers to the preservation of individual differences from one measure of a variable to one taken subsequently. Continuity, in this sense, has most typically been investigated in a factor-analytic context, by applying one of the various means of factor matching (cf. Nesselroade, 1970; Nunnally, 1973, for discussions of this problem in the context of behavior changes over age). In view of the still problematical character of factor matching, the signal advantages of a longitudinal design bear emphasizing, since they permit one to obtain a direct measure of factor continuity across age, simply by intercorrelating the factor scores for the same subjects measured at different ages. This is precisely the approach followed by Emmerich (1964) in his study of personality traits of nursery-school children assessed through observation of free-play behavior over four consecutive semesters. Thus Emmerich found evidence for two partially overlapping "longitudinal networks" of factors, that is, constellations of factors extracted from the data for the four semesters, such that intercorrelations among factors (including both intra- and inter-semester relations) are all significant.[5] Two dimensions identified at each semester (positive versus negative attitudes, and interpersonal versus impersonal orientation) accounted for the nucleus of both of these networks. Emmerich's study included a further analysis, supplementing the preceding, to assess the extent of the *applicability* of each of the three bipolar scales derived from the factor analyses for each semester. The measure of applicability was obtained from the factor variance at each semester, weighted by "meaningfulness" scale values, these indicating the consistency with which a set of judges rated each of the variables loading on a factor as

---

[5] Emmerich's criterion of significance, that is, $p < .05$, though understandable in view of the nature of the data he was dealing with, is a rather lenient one to use as a basis on which to establish the stability of a factor across age. One would look for something more than simply beating chance by an eyelash in this type of situation.

connoting one or the other pole of the psychological dimension identified with that factor. This measure disclosed that one of the dimensions, "interpersonal versus impersonal orientation," declined in applicability from the second to the fourth semester, while another, active-passive, increased from the first to the third; a third dimension, "positive–negative attitude" was subject to lesser change.

Developmental "Transformations." Of particular interest in Emmerich's analysis is the isolation of what he terms developmental "transformations," that is, instances of stability of individual differences along some dimension combined with lack of continuity in the structural network defining that dimension, that is, a change in its meaning. There are, however, several alternative ways of defining such a situation operationally, each of which would carry its own set of implications concerning the underlying dynamics. Let us start out with the one which is probably easiest to grasp and interpret, and which was in fact employed by Emmerich (1966) in a subsequently reported study of personality development of nursery-school children carried out concurrently with that just described, but based on teacher ratings rather than direct observation. According to this definition, evidence for a transformation consists of a combination of *stability of the factors*, established in terms of the intercorrelation among the factor scores for the individuals in a sample for successive occasions, with *discontinuity in the loadings* of the component variables on these factors. Thus, in the teacher-rating study, Emmerich found factor stability of a fairly high order for the three main factors uncovered in this analysis, though decreasing as the time interval separating the ratings increased. Specifically, for an aggression-dominance factor, the stability coefficients for semesters 1–2, 1–3, and 1–4 were .84, .47, and .47, respectively; for a dependency factor, the corresponding values were .83, .61, and .48, and for the third factor, autonomy, they were .78, .44, and .54. Yet, over the interval from the first to the third semester, for which dependency factor scores showed a .61 correlation, the scale which showed the highest loading on that factor in the first-semester ratings ("asks teacher to do what teacher asks child to do") dropped from a loading of .84 to one of only .33 by the third semester, while the same scale's loading on the autonomy factor changed from − .14 to − .69 (cf. Emmerich, 1966, Table 3). Another item, "seeks help from teacher," showed a similar though less marked shift from the dependency to the autonomy factor, while two further items relating to destructiveness and physical aggression correspondingly decreased in their (negative) loadings on autonomy.

According to this sense of a developmental transformation, then, we have here an instance where children show a fair degree of consistency with regard to their status on a personality dimension over time, but where

certain of the particular behavioral manifestations of that dimension undergo change. We will return to this meaning of the concept shortly, when we
consider an extension of Emmerich's analysis by Baltes and Nesselroade
(1973), as well as Kagan's (1969, 1971) distinction between "homeotypic"
and "heterotypic" continuity. Meanwhile let us return to Emmerich's
(1964) original study of free-play observations which reveals a developmental transformation of a different kind, or at least one based on a different
criterion. It is defined by the appearance of a factor which, though significantly intercorrelated across time with other factors (thus forming part of the
same longitudinal network) is nevertheless not identifiable in meaning with
any of the prior-occasion factors in the network, in terms of the items loading
on it; thus it appears to represent a developmental emergent.

In Emmerich's case, he found two factors in his fourth-semester matrix,
labeled 44 and 45, which could not be identified with any of the three bipolar
scales defined by the rest of the network (positive versus negative attitude,
interpersonal versus impersonal orientation, and active–passive mode), in
terms of the "meaningfulness" scale values for the items defining these new
factors (cf. the description of Emmerich's procedure). On the basis of the
nature of these items, Emmerich was inclined to see in this pattern of data
the emergence of a dimension of interpersonal poise and mastery versus
hesitance and insecurity. This pattern represented a transform of a combination of the interpersonal–impersonal and positive–negative attitude factors
from the previous semesters, the latter of which declined sharply in importance (i.e., in terms of its "applicability" index) from the second to the
fourth semester. Thus Emmerich conjectured that children who earlier had
been marked by an impersonal positive mode of relating to others turned
into rather insecure children as the socialization process in the nursery school
ran its course, whereas others marked by an interpersonal orientation with a
more negative attitude gained in poise and mastery of their emerging social
relationships.

Emmerich's strategy in this study places a heavy load on factor interpretation, even though his meaningfulness scaling strengthened his hand in this
regard (his criterion of agreement for 10 of 13 judges in assigning the same
directionally labeled meaning to each item is rather lenient, however). The
nature of the "items" which provided the data for the factor analyses,
furthermore, represents a somewhat shaky foundation on which to base
inferences of this sort. (They were the same data used by Martin in the study
previously referred to, i.e., observations of children's free-play behavior,
in terms of a set of 33 subcategories, whose reliabilities ranged between 1.00
and .21, with a median of .62.) It also seems that Emmerich could have used a
rather more direct method, by examining the pattern of loadings of the items
on corresponding factors for different semesters. Thus the three items which

most strongly define Factor 44 ("Destruction to inanimate objects," "offering, touching or holding," and "securing positive attention") do not as a group load significantly on any single factor for any of the three preceding semesters. In fact, there is only one factor, at the third semester, which loads on even any two of these three items. Exactly the same finding applies to the other of the "transformation" factors, 45. It thus appears—assuming that we can rely on the rotation method used—that we are witnessing the formation of new dimensions here, even though the intercorrelation of this factor with other factors for the previous semesters suggests a modicum of stability.

Turning finally to a third possible criterion for a developmental transformation, we may suggest that individual *variables* may retain stability over time, yet change in the factors on which they load. This particular criterion does not seem to have been applied in the literature, and may in fact turn out to be of lesser interest for the developmentalist; it corresponds in fact to the type of continuity which Kagan (1971) has designated as "homeotypic" (cf. below), and which he constrasts to "heterotypic" continuity which is embodied in the first criterion.

Emmerich's distinction between continuity and stability has been developed further by Baltes and Nesselroade (1973), who propose a four-fold classification of patterns of temporal change in factor-analytic data. This classification is based on the distinction between stable versus fluctuant factor *scores* for individuals, and invariant versus unstable patterns of factor *loadings* for tests. This classification is intended, however, to describe temporal change over relatively short intervals; the authors argue in fact that the particular combination of the above categories that applies will itself change over the course of development. Thus early in life they maintain that the combination of score fluctuation and pattern instability will generally prevail, reflecting the pervasiveness of behavioral oscillation and variability typically found in infancy. This changes to a condition of *state* stability, represented by the combination of fluctuant factor scores and invariant patterns; finally *trait* stability, corresponding to stable factor scores and invariant patterns, obtains.

The multivariate longitudinal data that would be required to verify this conception are still lacking. It appears to be most promising in application to the realm of personality variables and other noncognitive measures, since the factor scores from a single factor analysis carried out on all ages combined would be expected to show stability (in the sense of lack of change, in this instance) only for variables not subject to systematic changes with age. For ability measures and the like, on the other hand, the model would be applicable to describe temporal change over only very brief intervals.

In conclusion, we should refer to Kagan's (1971) distinction between homeotypic and heterotypic continuity, and his attempt to relate these to a more general version of Emmerich's concept of developmental transformations. Kagan actually differentiates among three types of continuity, i.e., "complete," "homeotypic," and "heterotypic" (cf. also Kagan, 1969), referring, respectively to continuity with respect to both overt behavior and underlying process or motivational dynamics, to continuity of behavior with change in underlying process, and to continuity of process with change in form of behavior. Curiously, Kagan believes that complete continuity is confined largely to behavior following the termination of ontogenetic development, i.e., after puberty, while he considers the homeotypic variety a kind of "fool's gold," visible particularly in infancy, as in the case of crying behavior, which may be observed at different ages but for very different reasons.

It is the third type of continuity, however, that is of most concern to us, since Kagan attempts to identify it with Emmerich's developmental transformations; at the same time he enlarges it to encompass any case in which measures of the same variable X_1 and X_2 at times t_1 and t_2 fail to correlate, while X_1 does correlate with a different measure, Y_2 at time t_2. As examples, Kagan refers to an unpublished honors thesis by Byram, based on observations of children over the age range from $3\frac{1}{2}$ to 5 years, which indicated that aggression at age 3 in boys failed to correlate with aggression at age 5, but did show a significant correlation with two other variables at the later age: masculine role play ($r = .49$) and assertiveness with others ($r = .50$). Data of a similar kind were found in his analysis of the Fels data (Kagan & Moss, 1962), where passivity under stress in boys in the elementary school years failed to correlate with passivity in adulthood, but did predict several other kinds of adult personality traits, for example, avoidance of competitive activities and vocations and lack of heterosexual attachments.

The question arises whether instances of this kind are in fact comparable to Emmerich's case. There is a major difference between the type of data cited by Kagan, and Emmerich's, namely that the latter was working within a multivariate framework, and could thus differentiate between factorial stability and factorial continuity, according to the criteria he devised. Kagan, on the other hand, is limited to a univariate model, and to cases in which measures of a single variable at different ages fail to correlate with one another. At the very least this represents a much weaker criterion for a developmental transformation; although his evidence, like Emmerich's, points to changes in meaning of a response across age (cf. also Lewis, 1967 for further cases in point), he does not deal with the problem of the changing structural relationships among variables, as Emmerich does. In fact, much of the heterotypic-continuity evidence is traceable to the patent fact that behavior changes in form with age, that is, what is labeled aggression at age

3 is more apt to be identified as assertiveness in a more nearly socialized kindergarten age child. It is also interesting to note that according to this rather loose criterion, homeotypic and heterotypic continuity are simply opposite sides of the same coin. This may be shown with reference to the example of crying, cited previously. We saw that Kagan identifies homeotypic continuity with cases where the behavior remains the same, but serves a different function. But this very fact means that, generally speaking, there will be little stability between measures of this variable over time, in other words, crying at age 6 months and age 36 months, and this is in fact what has been shown (cf. Lewis, 1967). In other words, whereas crying at 36 months may be observed in some children under particular circumstances (e.g., frustration), it is *dis*continuous with crying at age 6 months, in the stability sense. At the same time this discontinuity creates the possibility at least for heterotypic continuity, i.e., for a correlation with some other variable at the later age. This again was what Lewis (1967) found for crying in infancy (6 months) which correlated significantly with aggression to a barrier at age 13 months—a correlation which suggests that the earlier measure of crying reflects general emotionality.

Conclusion. In sum, the field of stability and continuity is one strewn with roadblocks of the investigators' own making, arising from the purely correlational sense in which the terms are typically taken, combined with the all too human tendency to lose sight of this limitation in discussions of the subject. (It is interesting to note that the same difficulty is encountered in the field of educational measurement, in the interpretation of test–retest correlations between successive measures of a single test; cf. Hilton, 1971.) Kagan (1971) himself has pointed to one contributory factor in this regard, that is, the fact that continuity of behavior represents an assumption that would be difficult to eliminate from the thinking, not only of the developmental psychologist, but more particularly of the layman. As he points out, under these circumstances even equivocal evidence in favor of continuity (based on stability coefficients) will be taken at a discount. It is unfortunate, however, that this attachment to the stability view appears to have blocked a clearer understanding of the basic issue in this area, that of conceptualizing the meaning of continuity when it is abstracted from the much more obvious and visible evidence of developmental *change* in behavior.

Concluding Comments

a. Alternatives to Factor Analytic Approaches. The treatment of the multivariate side of the development of individual differences, and of the stability question, has relied heavily on factor-analytic models of research. These appear to have virtually preempted the approach to the treatment of data in this area, but it is by no means clear that they are ideally suited to the developmentalist's problem of tracing changes in the structural relationships among his variables. Not only are the problems of analytic criteria for factor rotation, and factor matching in particular, as yet insufficiently resolved to warrant undue confidence in the meaningfulness of factor analytically determined structures of variables, but the problems involved in adapting the model for the study of structural change have not received attention until lately (cf. Chapter X). Thus possible alternative models, such as that of facet analysis (Foa, 1965), which involves a search for a determinate ordering of variables in terms of a proximity relationship, e.g., conforming to Guttman's simplex or circumplex, deserves serious consideration. Foa (1968) has more recently indicated its relevance to the study of behavior change, though not specifically with respect to developmental problems. Emmerich (1971) has, however, begun research applying a similar approach to the study of personality patterning in childhood.

b. The Study of the Correlates of Individual Differences. Much of the treatment of the developmental aspects of individual differences in this chapter may strike some as irrelevant to a more functionally based approach to the study of such differences. The case of cognitive-style research represents a good case in point. There we find much effort going into the specification of the antecedents and correlates of individual differences, ranging from experimental studies in which an attempt is made to modify some aspect of cognitive style through special training, to correlational research of diverse kinds. This includes work relating cognitive-style differences to child-training variables, diverse aspects of mother-child interaction and interpersonal behavior variables, and comparative studies of different socioeconomic, ethnic, and cultural groups (cf. Kagan & Kogan, 1970 for a comprehensive review of much of this research).

This type of work is not included in the treatment of this chapter, since it raises few new issues of a methodological nature—it is of course heir to all of the difficulties of correlational research—and above all since most of it is not pertinent to the problem of the developmental aspect of individual differences which is the focus of this chapter. Nevertheless the potential bearing of the present treatment to this type of research deserves brief comment, in the form of two points.

First, much as the correlational study of development was considered to be a valuable precursor of, or at least complement to research on the effects of special experience on development, so too the approaches to the study of the developmental patterning of individual differences should aid in forging a more effective mode of attack on the functional basis for cognitive-style differences in children. The reason is, basically, the same in both cases: We need to know more concerning the structural relationships among our behavioral variables and the changes which they undergo during development, in order to arrive at the most appropriate indicator of the variables we are interested in for the functional analysis. Specifically, instead of correlating antecedent conditions and the like with individual measures, it would be advantageous to employ a multivariate design, making use of the individual's scores on the factors to maximize our chances for obtaining a more robust relationship to the independent variables. One illustration of the need for an approach of this sort comes from the study by Sears (1961) concerning child-rearing antecedents of aggression in 12-year-old children. In this study, the choice of the particular set of pencil-and-paper scales selected to measure aggressiveness at this age legel was not based on any expirical or even theoretical analysis of the structural changes occurring with respect to this dimension in the interval between 5 and 12 years. It was inspired rather by a theoretical framework based in large measure on the frustration-aggression hypothesis, from which five subscales directed at aggression anxiety, projected aggression, self-aggression, prosocial aggression and antisocial aggression, were derived. Since these scales were only minimally correlated with the earlier measure of aggression (with the single exception of aggression anxiety for girls, which was, however, *negatively* correlated with age-5 aggression!), it is hardly surprising to find the relationship to the child-rearing variables emerging from the use of these aggression scales to be tenuous at best, and quite unilluminative in their meaning.

This leads to the second point, which is once again a plea for a broader developmental focus in this area, looking at determinants of individual differences not in terms of some arbitrarily chosen single age level, but in terms rather of the child's movement with age along individual-difference dimensions. This is, in effect, what Sontag, Baker, and Nelson (1958) did in their attempt to determine some of the correlates in the child's family history and experience to his pattern of change in IQ. As suggested in our example cited of differential routes to the attainment of a given adult status on the masculinity–femininity scale (cf. Fig. 12–5), a similar approach can be profitably applied in the realm of personality development. Such a developmental focus will at the same time lead to a more effective choice of sets of behavior measures at any given age level to bring out relationships to independent variables, at their maximal strength.

CONCLUSION

The steady diet of methodologically oriented discussion and analysis of the preceding chapters has perhaps some of the flavor of a meal of vitamins and other synthetic nutrients. It can hardly aspire to capture the flavor of live research on substantive questions that developmental psychologists, whatever their theoretical inclinations and favored methodological approaches, are engaged in. The field is indeed tremendously alive, and the rate of progress being made on a diversity of fronts impressive, both quantitatively and qualitatively. Yet it may be that the very liveliness and accelerating rate of output characterizing the field have inhibited the focusing of attention on questions of methodology and approach to data analysis which is required to provide more definite answers to the questions which are being posed. The area of conservation research presents a good illustration of this point.

No attempt will be made at this point to review the arguments presented throughout this volume for the relevance of the treatment of methodological issues presented in this volume for the study of particular substantive questions; such a review would be redundant in the extreme, and hardly profitable. A rather more interesting focus for these closing pages is to look at the relationships of developmental psychology both to the psychological discipline at large, and to other developmental disciplines, and to examine some of the institutional constraints in the academic and research establishment which are operating on the field, and their consequences.

In their chapter on Developmental Psychology for the 1963 *Annual Review of Psychology*, Rheingold and Stanley (1963) voiced the view that there was no fundamental difference between the method and theory of developmental psychology and that of psychologists in general. In Chapter II, we examined some of the trends current in the field that are a reflection of this point of view, notably the influence of the Skinnerians, and of the experimentalists generally. Although those with a different orientation, upholding a developmental view that insists on a separation of the field from that of psychology proper could certainly be found—e.g., the Wernerians; Riegel (1972), and of course those approaching the field from a psychoanalytic, or a psychobiological standpoint (e.g., Nash, 1970)—the "center of gravity" of the discipline has undoubtedly shifted toward the former position, with important and far-reaching side effects resulting.

Let us look at some of these, as they relate in particular to the institutional structure of the discipline and the training of graduate students. In regard to the first, the Society for Research in Child Development represents an interesting example of this shift. Founded originally as an interdisciplinary Society of scientists studying human growth and development in all of its aspects, and thus serving equally the fields of biology of growth, pediatrics and developmental medicine, the Society has today become so strongly dominated by psychologists that it is difficult to distinguish it from the Division on Developmental Psychology of the American Psychological Association, and indeed the officers of the two groups are to a considerable extent drawn from the same small pool of psychologists.

The preempting of the field of Child Development by psychologists is particularly apparent in the journal, *Child Development*, chief organ of publication of the Society for Research in Child Development, along with its companion, the *Monographs* of the SRCD. Thus, whereas for the years 1936 through 1961, 44 of 184 or 24% of the papers appearing in *Child Development* dealt with physiological development or physical growth, the 1969 and 1970 volumes of this journal show only 3 of 202 or 1.5%. Similar though less striking statistics apply to the *Monograph* series: Of #1–30, (1936–1941), 10 out of 30 dealt with physiological development or physical growth; of #110–139, (covering 1967 to 1970), 5 of 20 fall in the same category.

These statistics reflect, at the very least, the growing estrangement of the developmental psychologist from his colleagues in the physical and biological area. Certain trends might seem to counteract this shift—notably the interest in infancy, where behavioral and biological processes are frequently so closely interdependent that they could not meaningfully be studied in isolation one from the other (e.g., work on attentional states, on conditioning, on reflexes). But it is nevertheless safe to say that the field of biological and physical growth has become to a very large extent separated from and autonomous of that of behavioral development, and little is being done at present to foster interaction and interchange of ideas and information among behaviorally and biologically minded developmentalists, outside of medical settings perhaps.[1] This situation is reinforced by the institutional

[1] It is significant that, according to the Spring, 1972 issue of the Newsletter of Division 7 of the American Psychological Association, SRCD has organized a Long Range Planning Committee, with the view, among other aims, of strengthening the interdisciplinary character

structures for research and graduate training in the developmental area in the Universities. Whereas in the 1930s child development was generally placed in Institutes of Child Development or Welfare, Colleges of Home Economics and the like, today most of the significant work in the field (with a few exceptions, such as the Institute of Child Development at the University of Minnesota) is being carried on under the auspices of Departments of Psychology. While few would deny that this change has on the whole resulted in a marked rise in the quality of the work in the field, and particularly in the theoretical sophistication inspiring it, it has at the same time contributed to the assimilation of child development, child psychology, or developmental psychology (the three terms represent roughly three epochs in the history of the field) to the mold of general psychology.

This is perhaps most evident in the training of graduate students in this field. The heavy preponderance of experimental work and the reluctance to define the field in any terms that would allow it a substantive status in its own right has resulted in most departments treating students interested in the field of developmental psychology in terms basically equivalent to the trainee in general-experimental psychology. True, many departments have evolved more or less formal training programs in the developmental area, but in most instances these have not involved any specifically developmental curriculum, for example, in terms of methodology, or even theory. Coverage might be given to theorists such as Piaget and Werner, of course, but the emphasis has, with few exceptions, been on sound training in general behavioral methodology and theory, with a subsequent specialization on particular problems of research with infants, children, or perhaps adolescents. Such research may require its own techniques and instrumentation (notably for work in infancy) but only in the same sense that that of the psychophysicist or psychophysiologist does.

Above all, the net result has been a virtually complete atrophy of the ties between developmental psychology and other developmental and child-related disciplines. Work on physical growth, or, at the opposite end, on sociological aspects of child life is rarely considered as part of the developmental trainee's training. This has resulted not only in a narrowing of the range of variables and processes relating to the development of the child to

---

of the Society. Among recommendations in this direction, the Newsletter cites the following: "... an increase in the page allocation of *Child Development* to incorporate research reports from other fields, reviews of research areas outside of child psychology, and reprints of the contents of related journals; institutes and study groups for interdisciplinary training and research, interdisciplinary symposia at SRCD meetings; SRCD symposia for other societies." It is apparent, then, that the concerns voiced in this chapter are shared by at least some of the leaders in the field.

which the trainee is exposed, but more fundamentally in the constriction of his thinking in regard to the operation of developmental processes, the selection of methodologies for studying developmental problems and the extra-behavioral matrix within which these problems are situated.

What alternative institutional models for developmental training and research may be envisaged? One that may be proposed is that of an inter-departmental program, such as some institutions are starting to inaugurate for work on environmental problems, and other subject matters that tran-scend the confines of a single academic discipline. In this type of program the student would remain identified with his parent department (e.g., of Psychology) and acquire a general background of that discipline during the early stages of his training. At the same time he would be brought together with students and faculty from other disciplines converging on the develop-mental area (biology, anthropology, and possibly sociology, as well as certain more applied fields such as education and pediatrics), and would thus obtain an opportunity to approach the study of behavioral development within a broader framework, bringing to bear concepts and techniques that may be borrowed, or rather adapted from other disciplines as these may prove relevant.

The obstacles to such a program are well known to those familiar with the academic scene. Though they may freely admit the arbitrariness of disciplinal boundaries and definitions of departmental activities and curricula defined along disciplinal lines, academicians are notoriously suspicious of relin-quishing any part of their authority and control over the training experience of a graduate student to share it with colleagues from another department or academic unit. Thus interdepartmental programs are difficult to institute and administer, and are apt to create in the student a feeling of being squeezed between competing sets of expectations, demands, and definitions of his program.

The conception of interdisciplinary work on developmental problems which we are arguing for here is founded on an assumption that some may find debatable: that a thorough understanding of developmental processes in the behavioral realm requires an intensive exposure to developmental phe-nomena and mechanisms in the physical and biological realm, as well as at the very least an appreciation of the sociological and cultural forces that are modulating the development of the human individual. A tall order, this, if it is taken seriously, admittedly. Furthermore, it flies in the face of the trend toward increasing specialization, and of the subsumption of developmental phenomena under general-psychological processes, which the experi-mentalists and the behaviorists' influence have brought to our field.

Yet it is encouraging to note that efforts at such broad-scaled attacks on developmental problems have in fact been launched at the level of programmatic research. One good example is to be found in the Harvard-Florence research project, a longitudinal cross-cultural study of human development being undertaken jointly by the Harvard School of Public Health and several Italian universities under the directorship of H. Boutourline Young, as indicated by the statement of Purpose published in recent issues of *Research Relating to Children*: "To observe the long-term effects of environment on growth and health; i.e., the influence of environmental factors upon physical and mental development, and their mode of action and interaction with genetic endowment." This rather conventional-sounding aim is being implemented via a most interesting approach to sample selection, by studying a sample of males whose ancestral origin is Southern Italy, and who are currently living in different geographic and cultural enviornments, namely, Boston, Rome, and Palermo (Sicily). Unfortunately the study starts with the main sample in pre-adolescence; furthermore, the major publications of this project thus far (Barron & Young, 1970; Young & Knapp, 1966; Young, Tagiuri, Tesi, & Montemagni, 1962; Young, Zoli, Gallagher, & Rothwell, 1963) do not give much evidence of either the interdisciplinary or the longitudinal focus seemingly built into the study.

At the research level, this type of project is apt to remain rare as a prototype of developmental research, if only because of the difficulties of funding such range-scope long-term projects (e.g., Klivington, 1970; Woodside, 1970). Yet there is no reason why work of this type could not be carried out on a smaller scale, fitted into a shorter time span, without sacrificing entirely the multi-faceted approach and developmental perspective which is at issue here. Above all, through exposure to and involvement in such research, and one would hope eventually through institutional support in the form of training programs, curricula and staffing arrangements, a valuable complement would become available to the model of developmental research assimilated to the paradigm of experimental psychology which dominates our field today. It is to this vision, modest though it be, that this volume is dedicated.

REFERENCES

Abravanel, E. The development of intersensory patterning with regard to selected spatial dimensions. *Monographs of the Society of Research in Child Development*, 1968, 33, (2, Whole No. 118).

Aebli, H. *Über die geistige Entwicklung des Kindes*. Stuttgart: Klett, 1963.

Ahammer, I., & Baltes, P. B. Objective versus perceived age differences in personality: How do adolescents, adults, and older people view themselves? *Journal of Gerontology*, 1972, 27, 46–51.

Akishige, Y. Experimentelle Untersuchungen über die Struktur des Wahrnehmungsraumes. II. *Mitteilungen der Juristisch-Literarischen Fakultät, Kyushu University*, 1937, 4, 23–118.

Alexander, H. W. A general test for trend. *Psychological Bulletin*, 1946, 43, 533–557.

Almy, M., Chittenden, E., & Miller, P. *Young children's thinking: Studies of some aspects of Piaget's theory*. New York: Teacher's College, Columbia Univ. 1966.

Ames, B., & Ilg, L. The developmental point of view with special reference to the principle of reciprocal neuromotor interweaving. *Journal of Genetic Psychology*, 1964, 105, 195–210.

Anastasi, A., & Foley, J. P. Jr. *Differential psychology: Individual and group differences in behavior*. (Rev. ed.) New York: Macmillan, 1949.

Anastasi, A., & Foley, J. P. Jr. *Differential psychology: Individual and group differences in behavior*. (3rd ed.) New York: Macmillan, 1958.

Anderson, J. E. The limitations of infant and preschool tests in the measurement of intelligence. *Journal of Psychology*, 1939, 8, 351–379.

Anderson, J. E. Methods of child psychology. In L. Carmichael (Ed.), *Manual of child psychology*. (2nd ed.) New York: Wiley, 1954. Pp. 1–59.

Anderson, J. E. Child development: An historical perspective. *Child Development*, 1956, 27, 2, 181–196.

Ausubel, D. P. *Theory and problems of child development*. New York: Grune & Stratton, 1958.

Ausubel, D. P., Schiff, H. M., & Gasser, E. B. A preliminary study of developmental trends in socioempathy: Accuracy of perception of own and others' sociometric status. *Child Development*, 1952, 23, 111–128.

Baer, D. M. An age-irrelevant concept of development. *Merrill Palmer Quarterly*, 1970, 16, 238–245.

Baldwin, A. L. *Theories of child development*. New York: Wiley, 1967.

Baltes, P. B. Longitudinal and cross-sectional sequences in the study of age and generation effects. *Human Development*, 1968, 11, 145–171.

Baltes, P. B., Baltes, M. M., & Reinert, G. The relationship between time of measurement and age in cognitive development of children: An application of cross-sectional sequences. *Human Development*, 1970, 13, 258–268.

381

Baltes, P. B., & Goulet, L. R. Exploration of developmental variables by manipulation and simulation of age differences in behavior. *Human Development*, 1971, **14**, 149–170.

Baltes, P. B., & Nesselroade, J. R. Multivariate longitudinal and cross-sectional sequences for analyzing ontogenetic and generational change. A methodological note. *Developmental Psychology*, 1970, **2**, 163–168.

Baltes, P. B., & Nesselroade, J. R. Cultural change and adolescent personality: An application of longitudinal sequences. *Developmental Psychology*, 1972, **7**, 244–256.

Baltes, P. B., & Nesselroade, J. R. The developmental analysis of individual differences on multiple measures. In J. R. Nesselroade & H. W. Reese (Eds.), *Life-Span developmental psychology: Methodological issues*. New York: Academic Press, 1973. Pp. 219–251.

Baltes, P. B., & Reinert, G. Cohort effects in cognitive development of children as revealed by cross-sectional sequences. *Developmental Psychology*, 1969, **1**, 169–177.

Bandura, A. Social-learning theory of identification processes. In D. A. Goslin (Ed.), *Handbook of socialization theory and research*. Chicago Illinois: Rand McNally, 1969. Pp. 213–262.

Barker, R., & Wright, H. F. *One boy's day: A specimen record of behavior*. New York: Harper, 1951.

Barron, F., & Young, H. B. Rome and Boston: A tale of two cities and their differing impact on the creativity and personal philosophy of Southern Italian immigrants. *Journal of Cross-Cultural Psychology*, 1970, **1**, 91–114.

Bayley, N. The development of motor abilities during the first three years. *Monographs of the Society of Research in Child Development*, 1935, **1**, (1, Whole No. 1).

Bayley, N. Consistency and variability in the growth of intelligence from birth to intelligence. *Journal of Genetic Psychology*, 1949, **75**, 165–196.

Bayley, N. Individual patterns of development. *Child Development*, 1956, **27**, 45–74.

Bearison, D. J. Role of measurement operations in the acquisition of conservation. *Developmental Psychology*, 1969, **1**, 653–660.

Bell, R. Q. Convergence: An accelerated longitudinal approach. *Child Development*, 1953, **24**, 145–152.

Bell, R. Q. An experimental test of the accelerated longitudinal approach. *Child Development*, 1954, **25**, 281–286.

Bell, R. Q. A reinterpretation of the direction of the effects in studies of socialization. *Psychological Review*, 1968, **75**, 81–95.

Benson, F. A. M. An examination over an eight-month period of Piaget's concept of number development and the presence or absence of certain interrelated tasks in a group of first grade children. Unpublished Ed.D. dissertation, University of Oregon, 1966.

Bentler, P. M. Evidence regarding stages in the development of conservation. *Perceptual & Motor Skills*, 1970, **31**, 855–859.

Bentler, P. M. Monotonicity analysis: An alternative to linear factor and test analysis. In D. R. Green, M. P. Ford, & G. B. Flamer (Eds.), *Measurement and Piaget*. New York: McGraw-Hill, 1971. Pp. 220–244.

Bereiter, C. Some persisting dilemmas in the measurement of change. In C. W. Harris (Ed.), *Problems in measuring change*. Madison: Univ. of Wisconsin Press, 1963. Pp. 3–20.

Berlyne, D. *Structure and direction in thinking*. New York: Wiley, 1965.

Bertalanffy, L. v. *Theoretische biologie*. Vol. II: *Stoffwechsel, wachstum*. (2nd ed.) Bern: Francke, 1951.

Bertalanffy, L. v. Remarks in discussion on general systems theory and the behavioral sciences. In J. M. Tanner & B. Inhelder (Eds.), *Discussions on child development*, Vol. 4. New York: International Univ. Press, 1960. Pp. 155–176. (a)

Bertalanffy, L. v. Principles and theory of growth. In V. W. Nowinski (Ed.), *Fundamental aspects of normal and malignant growth*. Amsterdam: Elsevier, 1960. (b)

Bertalanffy, L. v. *General systems, theory: Foundations, development, applications.* New York: Braziller, 1968.

Bijou, S. W. Child behavior and development: A behavioral analysis. *International Journal of Psychology,* 1968, **3**, 221–238.

Bijou, S. W., & Baer, D. M. *Child development.* Vol. 1: *A systematic and empirical theory.* New York: Appleton, 1961.

Bijou, S. W., & Baer, D. M. Some methodological contributions from a functional analysis of child development. *Advances in Child Development & Behavior,* 1963, **1**, 197–231.

Bijou, S. W., & Baer, D. M. *Child development.* Vol. II: *Universal stage of infancy.* New York: Appleton, 1965.

Birch, H. G., & Lefford, A. Intersensory development in children. *Monographs of the Society of Research in Child Development,* 1963, **28** (5, Whole No. 89).

Birch, H. G., & Lefford, A. Visual differentiation, intersensory integration, and voluntary motor control. *Monographs of the Society of Research in Child Development,* 1967, **32** (2, Serial No. 110).

Black, M. S. The development of personality factors in children and adolescents. *Educational & Psychological Measurement,* 1965, **25**, 767–785.

Block, J. *Lives through time.* Berkeley, California: Bancroft, 1971.

Bloom, B. S. *Stability and change in human characteristics.* New York: Wiley, 1964.

Bohrnstedt, G. W. Observations on the measurement of change. In E. F. Borgatta (Ed.), *Sociological methodology.* San Francisco: Jossey-Bass, 1969. Pp. 113–136.

Bonner, J. T. *Morphogenesis: An essay on development.* Princeton, New Jersey: Princeton Univ. Press, 1952.

Bower, T. G. R. Slant perception and shape constancy in infants. *Science,* 1966, **151**, 832–834.

Braine, M. D. S. The ontogeny of certain logical operations: Piaget's formulation examined by nonverbal methods. *Psychological Monographs,* 1959, **73** (5, Whole No. 475).

Brainerd, C. J., & Allen, T. W. Experimental inductions of the conservation of "first-order" quantitative invariants. *Psychological Bulletin,* 1971, **75**, 128–144.

Broadbent, D. E. *Perception and communication.* Oxford: Pergamon, 1958.

Brody, S. *Bioenergetics and growth.* Princeton, New Jersey: Van Nostrand-Reinhold, 1945.

Broverman, D. M. Normative and ipsative measurement in psychology. *Psychological Review,* 1962, **69**, 295–305.

Brown, R. W., & Berko, J. Word association and the acquisition of grammar. *Child Development,* 1960, **31**, 1–14.

Brunswik, E. *Perception and the representative design of psychological experiments.* Berkeley: Univ. of California Press, 1956.

Burt, C. L. *The factors of the mind: An introduction to factor analysis in psychology.* New York: Macmillan, 1941.

Burzlaff, W. Methodologische Beiträge zum Problem der Farbenkonstanz. *Zeitschrift für Psychologie,* 1931, **119**, 177–235.

Bush, R., & Mosteller, F. *Stochastic models for learning.* New York: Wiley, 1955.

Campbell, D. T. From description to experimentation: Interpreting trends as quasi-experiments. In C. W. Harris (Ed.), *Problems in measuring change.* Madison: Univ. of Wisconsin Press, 1963. Pp. 212–244.

Campbell, D. T., & Fiske, D. W. Convergent and discriminant validation by the multitrait-multimethod matrix. *Psychological Bulletin,* 1959, **56**, 81–105.

Campbell, D. T., & Stanley, J. C. Experimental and quasi-experimental designs for research in teaching. In N. L. Gage (Ed.), *Handbook of research on teaching.* Chicago: Rand McNally, 1963. Pp. 171–246.

Campbell, R. V. D., & Weech, A. A. Measures which characterize the individual during the development of behavior in early life. *Child Development*, 1941, **12**, 217–236.

Carbonneau, M. Apprentissage de la notion de conservation de surfaces. Unpublished thesis (lic. philos.), University of Montreal, 1965.

Carroll, J. B. The nature of the data, or how to choose a correlation coefficient. *Psychometrika*, 1961, **26**, 347–372.

Cattell, R. B. *The description and measurement of personality.* Yonkers, New York: World Book, 1946.

Cattell, R. B. *Personality and motivation structure and measurement.* Yonkers, New York: World Book, 1957.

Cattell, R. B. The structure of change by P-technique and incremental R-technique. In C. W. Harris (Ed.), *Problems in measuring change*. Madison: Univ. of Wisconsin Press, 1963. Pp. 167–198.

Cattell, R. B. The data box: Its ordering of total resources in terms of possible relational systems. In R. B. Cattell (Ed.), *Handbook of multivariate experimental psychology*. Chicago, Illinois: Rand McNally, 1966. Pp. 67–128. (a)

Cattell, R. B. Patterns of change: Measurement in relation to state-dimension, trait change, lability, and process concepts. In R. B. Cattell (Ed.), *Handbook of multivariate experimental psychology*. Chicago, Illinois: Rand McNally, 1966. Pp. 355–402. (b)

Cattell, R. B. Continuity of personality and ability concepts in researches over the life-span. Paper presented at the American Psychological Association Convention, San Francisco, August 1968.

Charlesworth, W. R., & Zahn, C. Reaction time as a measure of comprehension of the effects produced by rotation of objects. *Child Development*, 1966, **37**, 253–268.

Child, I. L. Socialization. In G. Lindzey (Ed.), *Handbook of social psychology*. Vol. II. Reading, Massachusetts: Addison-Wesley, 1954. Pp. 655–592.

Coan, R. W. Child personality. In R. B. Cattell (Ed.), *Handbook of multivariate experimental psychology*. Chicago: Rand McNally, 1966. Pp. 732–752.

Cohen, W., Hershkowitz, A., & Chodack, M. Size judgment at different distances as a function of age level. *Child Development*, 1958, **29**, 473–479.

Comalli, F. E. Jr., Wapner, S., & Werner, H. Interference effects of Stroop color-word test in childhood, adulthood and aging. *Journal of Genetic Psychology*, 1962, **100**, 47–53.

Coombs, C. H. Psychological scaling without a unit of measurement. *Psychological Review*, 1950, **57**, 145–158.

Coombs, C. H. A theory of data. *Psychological Review*, 1960, **67**, 143–159.

Coombs, C. H., & Smith, On the detection of structure in attitudes and developmental processes. Unpublished ms., University of Michigan, 1972.

Cooper, L. M., & London, P. The development of hypnotic susceptibility: A longitudinal (convergence) study. *Child Development*, 1971, **42**, 487–503.

Count, E. W. Growth patterns of human physique: Part 1. *Human Biology*, 1943, **15**, 1–32.

Count, E. W. Brain and body weight in man: Their antecedents in growth and evaluation. *Annals of the New York Academy of Sciences*, 1947, **46**, 993–1122.

Courtis, S. A. *The measurement of growth.* Ann Arbor, Michigan: Brumfield & Brumfield, 1932.

Cronbach, L. J. The two disciplines of scientific psychology. *American Psychologist*, 1957, **12**, 671–684.

Cronbach, L. J. Year-to-year correlations of mental tests: A review of the Hofstaetter analysis. *Child Development*, 1967, **38**, 283–289.

Cronbach, L. J., & Gleser, G. C. Assessing similarity between profiles. *Psychological Bulletin*, 1953, **50**, 456–473.

Curtis, H. A. A study of the relative effects of age and of test difficulty upon factor patterns. *Genetic Psychology Monographs*, 1949, **40**, 99–148.

Damon, A. Discrepancies between findings of longitudinal and cross-sectional studies in adult life: Physique and physiology. *Human Development*, 1965, **8**, 16–22.

Darwin, C. A biographical sketch of an infant. *Mind*, 1877, **2**, 286–294.

Davis, E. A. The development of linguistic skill in twins, singletons with siblings and only children from age five to ten years. University of Minnesota, Institute of Child Welfare, *Monograph Series*, No. 14, 1937.

Day, E. J. The development of language in twins: I. A comparison of twins and single children. *Child Development*, 1932, **3**, 179–199.

Dearborn, W. F., & Rothney, J. W. M. *Predicting the child's development*. Cambridge, Massachusetts: Sci-Art, 1941.

Dearborn, W. F., Rothney, J. W. M., & Shuttleworth, F. K. Data on the growth of public school children. *Monographs of the Society of Research in Child Development*, 1938, **3** (1, Whole No. 14).

Deming, J. Application of the Gompertz curve to the observed pattern of growth in length of 48 individual boys and girls during the adolescent cycle of growth. *Human Biology*, 1957, **29**, 83–122.

Dennis, W. Historical beginnings of child psychology. *Psychological Bulletin*, 1949, **46**, 224–235.

Deutsche, J. M. *The development of children's concepts of causal relations*. Minneapolis: Univ. of Minnesota Press, 1937.

Dodwell, P. C. Children's understanding of spatial concepts. *Canadian Journal of Psychology*, 1963, **17**, 141–161.

Educational Testing Service. *Disadvantaged children and their first school experiences: Theoretical considerations and measurement strategies*. Princeton, New Jersey: Educational Testing Service, 1968, PR-68-4.

Educational Testing Service. *Disadvantaged children and their first school experiences: From theory to operations*. Princeton, New Jersey: Educational Testing Service, 1969, PR-69-12.

Elkind, D. Children's discovery of the conservation of mass, weight, and volume. *Journal of Genetic Psychology*, 1961, **98**, 219–227.

Ellis, H. *The transfer of learning*. New York: Macmillan, 1965.

Emmerich, W. Continuity and stability in early social development. *Child Development*, 1964, **35**, 311–332.

Emmerich, W. Continuity and stability in early social development: II. Teacher ratings. *Child Development*, 1966, **37**, 17–27.

Emmerich, W. Personality development and concepts of structure. *Child Development*, 1968, **39**, 671–690.

Emmerich, W. *Structure and development of personal-social behaviors in preschool settings*. Princeton, New Jersey: Education Testing Service, 1971, PR 71–20.

Endsley, R. C. Effects of forced reward–nonreward ratios on children's performance in a discrimination task. *Journal of Experimental Child Psychology*, 1968, **6**, 563–570.

Engelmann, S. Cognitive structures related to the principle of conservation. *Ontario Institute for Studies in Education, Research Series*, 1967, No. 2, 25–51.

Erikson, E. H. Identity and the life cycle: Selected papers. *Psychological Issues*, 1959, **1** (1, Whole No. 1).

Escalona, S. K., & Corman, H. H. The validation of Piaget's hypothesis concerning the development of sensorimotor intelligence: Methodological issues. Paper presented at meeting of Society for Research in Child Development, New York City, March, 1967.

Estes, W. K. A statistical theory of learning. *Psychological Review*, 1950, **57**, 94–107.

Estes, W. K. The problem of inference from curves based on group data. *Psychological Bulletin*, 1956, **53**, 134–140.

Evans, G. T. Factor analytic treatment of growth data. *Multivariate Behavioral Research*, 1967, **2**, 109–134.

Fantz, R. L., & Nevis, S. The predictive value of changes in visual preferences in early infancy. In J. Hellmuth (Ed.), *The special child.* Vol. 1. Seattle: Special Child Publications, 1967. Pp. 394–414.

Feffer, M. H., & Gourevitch, V. Cognitive aspects of role-taking in children. *Journal of Personality*, 1960, **28**, 383–396.

Feigenbaum, K. D., & Sulkin, H. Piaget's problem of conservation of discontinuous quantities: A teaching experience. *Journal of Genetic Psychology*, 1964, **105**, 91–97.

Ferguson, G. A. The factorial interpretation of test difficulty. *Psychometrika*, 1941, **6**, 323–329.

Flavell, J. H. Concept development. In P. H. Mussen (Ed.), *Carmichael's manual of child psychology.* (3rd ed.) Vol. I. New York: Wiley, 1970. Pp. 983–1060.

Flavell, J. H. Stage-related properties of cognitive development. *Cognitive Psychology*, 1971, **2**, 421–453.

Flavell, J. H. An analysis of cognitive-developmental sequences. *Genetic Psychology Monographs*, 1972, **86**, 279–350.

Flavell, J. H., Beach, D. H., & Chinsky, J. M. Spontaneous verbal rehearsal in a memory task as a function of age. *Child Development*, 1966, **37**, 283–299.

Flavell, J. H., & Draguns, J. A microgenetic approach to perception and thought. *Psychological Bulletin*, 1957, **54**, 197–217.

Flavell, J. H., & Wohlwill, J. F. Formal and functional aspects of cognitive development. In D. Elkind & J. H. Flavell (Eds.), *Studies in cognitive development: Essays in honor of Jean Piaget.* London and New York: Oxford Univ. Press, 1969, Pp. 67–120.

Foa, U. G. New developments in facet design and analysis. *Psychological Review*, 1965, **72**, 262–274.

Foa, U. G. Three kinds of behavioral changes. *Psychological Bulletin*, 1968, **70**, 460–473.

Forgays, D. G. The development of differential word recognition. *Journal of Experimental Psychology*, 1953, **45**, 165–168.

Forgays, D. G., & Forgays, J. W. The nature of the effect of free environmental experience in the rat. *Journal of Comparative & Physiological Psychology*, 1952, **47**, 332–328.

Forgus, R. H. The effect of early perceptual learning on the behavioral organization of adult rats. *Journal of Comparative & Physiological Psychology*, 1954, **47**, 331–336.

Forgus, R. H. Early visual and motor experience as determiners of complex maze-learning ability under rich and reduced stimulation. *Journal of Comparative & Physiological Psychology*, 1955, **48**, 215–220.

Fournier, E. Generalisation intranotionnelle et internotionelle d'un apprentissage empirique de la notion de conservation de surface. Unpublished thesis (lic. philos.), University of Montreal, 1965.

Frank, H. Untersuchung über Sehgrössenkonstanz bei Kindern. *Psychologische Forschung*, 1925, **7**, 137–145.

Freeman, F. N., & Flory, C. D. Growth in intellectual ability as measured by repeated tests. *Monographs of the Society of Research in Child Development*, 1937, **2** (2, Whole No. 9).

Fusaro, L. A. An experimental analysis of the roles of measurement and compensatory operations in the acquisition of conservation. Unpublished M.A. thesis, Clark University, 1969.

Gagné, R. M. The acquisition of knowledge. *Psychological Review*, 1962, **69**, 355–365.

Gagné, R. M. Contributions of learning to human development. *Psychological Review*, 1968, **75**, 177–191.

Gagné, R. M. Structured experience and pre-planned learning. *Interchange*, 1970, **1**, 114–116.

Gardner, R. W., & Moriarty, A. E. *Personality development at preadolescence*. Seattle: Univ. of Washington Press, 1968.

Gardner, R. W., Holzman, P. S., Klein, G. S., Linton, H. B., & Spence, D. P. Cognitive control: A study of individual consistencies in cognitive behavior. *Psychological Issues*, 1959, **1** (4, Whole No. 4).

Gardner, R. W., Jackson, D. N., & Messick, S. J. Personality organization in cognitive controls and intellectual abilities. *Psychological Issues*, 1960, **2** (4, Whole No. 8).

Garrett, H. E. A developmental theory of intelligence. *American Psychologist*, 1946, **1**, 372–378.

Gellerman, L. The double alternation problem. II. The behavior of children and human adults in a double alternation temporal maze. *Journal of Genetic Psychology*, 1931, **39**, 197–226.

Gelman, R. Conservation acquisition: A problem of learning to attend to relevant attributes. *Journal of Experimental Child Psychology*, 1969, **7**, 167–187.

Gesell, A. L. Maturation and infant behavior pattern. *Psychological Review*, 1929, **36**, 307–319.

Gesell, A. L. Reciprocal interweaving in neuromotor development: A principle of spiral organization shown in the patterning of infant behavior. *Journal of Comparative Neurology*, 1939, **70**, 161–180.

Gesell, A. L. The ontogenesis of infant behavior. In L. Carmichael (Ed.), *Manual of child psychology* (2nd ed.). New York: Wiley, 1954. Pp. 335–373.

Gesell, A. L., & Ames, L. B. The ontogenetic organization of prone behavior in human infancy. *Journal of Genetic Psychology*, 1940, **56**, 247–263.

Gewirtz, J. L. Mechanisms of social learning: Some roles of stimulation and behavior in early human development. In D. A. Goslin (Ed.), *Handbook of socialization theory and research*. Chicago, Illinois: Rand McNally, 1969. Pp. 57–212.

Gibson, E. J. *Principles of perceptual learning and development*. New York: Appleton, 1969.

Gibson, E. J., & Olum, V. Experimental methods of studying perception in children. In P. H. Mussen (Ed.), *Handbook of research methods in child development*. New York: Wiley, 1960. Pp. 311–373.

Gibson, J. J. Adaptation, after effect, and contrast in the perception of tilted lines: II. Simultaneous contrast and the areal restriction of the after effect. *Journal of Experimental Psychology*, 1937, **20**, 553–569.

Goldfarb, N. *An introduction to longitudinal statistical analysis*. Glencoe, Illinois: Free Press, 1960.

Gollin, E. S. Organizational characteristics of social judgment: A developmental investigation. *Journal of Personality*, 1958, **26**, 139–154.

Gollin, E. S. A developmental approach to learning and cognition. *Advances in Child Development and Behavior*, 1965, **2**, 159–186.

Gollin, E. S. An organism oriented concept of development. *Merrill Palmer Quarterly*, 1970, **16**, 246–252.

Goodman, L. A., & Kruskal, W. H. Measures of association for cross classifications. *Journal of the American Statistical Association*, 1954, **49**, 732–764.

Goodman, L. A., & Kruskal, W. H. Measures of association for cross classifications. II. Further discussion and references. *Journal of the American Statistical Association*, 1959, **54**, 123–163.

Goodnow, J. J. A test of milieu effects with some of Piaget's tasks. *Psychological Monographs*, 1962, **76** (36, Whole No. 555).

Goulet, L. R., & Goodwin, K. S. Development and choice behavior in probabilistic and problem-solving tasks. *Advances in Child Behavior and Development*, 1970, **5**, 214–254.

Grant, D. A. Analysis-of-variance tests in the analysis and comparison of curves. *Psychological Bulletin*, 1956, **53**, 141–154.

Gray, J. The kinetics of growth. *British Journal of Experimental Biology*, 1929, **6**, 245–274.

Green, B. F. Attitude measurement. In G. Lindzey (Ed.), *Handbook of social psychology*, Vol. I. Reading, Massachusetts: Addison-Wesley, 1954. Pp. 335–369.

Green, B. F. A method of scalogram analysis using summary statistics. *Psychometrika*, 1956, **21**, 79–88.

Griffiths, R. *The abilities of babies: A study in mental measurement.* New York: McGraw-Hill, 1954.

Grinder, R. A. *A history of genetic psychology.* New York: Wiley, 1967.

Guilford, J. P. *Psychometric methods.* New York: McGraw-Hill, 1954.

Gulliksen, H. *Theory of mental tests.* New York: Wiley, 1950.

Guttman, L. A basis for scaling qualitative data. *American Sociological Review*, 1944, **9**, 139–150.

Guttman, R., & Guttman, L. A new approach to the analysis of growth patterns: The simplex structure of intercorrelations of measurements. *Growth*, 1965, **29**, 219–232.

Harlow, H. F., Harlow, M. K., Dodsworth, R. O., & Arling, G. L. Maternal behavior of rhesus monkeys deprived of mothering and peer association in infancy. *Proceedings of the American Philosophical Society*, 1966, **110**, 58–66.

Harman, H. H. *Modern factor analysis.* Chicago, Illinois: Univ. of Chicago Press, 1960.

Harris, C. W. Some problems in the description of change. *Educational & Psychological Measurement*, 1962, **22**, 303–320.

Harris, C. W. Canonical factor models for the description of change. In C. W. Harris (Ed.), *Problems in measuring change.* Madison: University of Wisconsin Press, 1963. Pp. 138–155. (a)

Harris, C. W. (Ed.) *Problems in measuring change.* Madison: Univ. of Wisconsin Press, 1963. (b)

Harter, S. Discrimination learning set in children as a function of IQ and MA. *Journal of Experimental Child Psychology*, 1965, **2**, 31–43.

Hayes, K. J., & Hayes, C. The intellectual development of a home-raised chimpanzee. *Proceedings of the American Philosophical Society*, 1951, **95**, 105–109.

Hays, W. L. *Statistics for psychologists.* New York: Holt, 1965.

Hebb, D. O. *Organization of behavior.* New York: Wiley, 1949.

Hebb, D. O., & Williams, K. A method of rating animal intelligence. *Journal of General Psychology*, 1946, **34**, 59–65.

Heinis, H. La loi du développement mental. *Archives de Psychologie (Genève)*, 1924, **74**, 97–128.

Held, R., & Hein, A. Movement-produced stimulation in the development of visually guided behavior. *Journal of Comparative & Physiological Psychology*, 1963, **56**, 872–876.

Hersh, A. H. Allometry and anthropometry. *Annals of the New York Academy of Sciences*, 1955, **63**, 484–490.

Hertzman, M. The effects of the relative difficulty of mental tests on patterns of mental organization. *Archives of Psychology*, NY, 1936, **28** (9, Whole No. 197).

Hilton, T. L. Predictability and determinants of change—some comments on the interpretation of correlations. Paper presented at Symposium on Problems in the analysis and interpretation of change, Meetings of American Psychological Association, Washington, D. C., September, 1971.

Hilton, T. L., & Myers, A. E. Personal background, experience, and school achievement: An investigation of the contribution of questionnaire data to academic prediction. *Journal of Educational Measurement*, 1967, **4**, 69–80.

Hoffman, H. N. A study in an aspect of concept formation with subnormal, average, and superior adolescents. *Genetic Psychology Monographs*, 1955, **52**, 191–240.

Hofstätter, P. R. The changing composition of intelligence: A study in T-technique. *Journal of Genetic Psychology*, 1954, **85**, 159–164.

Holtzman, W. H. Statistical models for the study of change in the single case. In C. W. Harris (Ed.), *Problems in measuring change.* Madison: Univ. of Wisconsin Press, 1963. Pp. 199–211.

Holtzman, W. H. Cross-cultural longitudinal research in child development: Studies of American and Mexican school children. In J. P. Hill (Ed.), *Minnesota symposia on child psychology,* Vol. 2. Minneapolis: Univ. of Minnesota Press, 1969. Pp. 125–159.

Holway, A. H., & Boring, E. G. Determinants of apparent visual size with distance invariant. *American Journal of Psychology,* 1941, **54,** 21–37.

Honzik, M. P. Personality consistency and change: Some comments on papers by Bayley, Macfarlane, Moss and Kagan, and Murphy. *Vita Humana,* 1964, **7,** 139–142.

Horn, J. L. Organization of data on life-span development of human abilities. In L. R. Goulet & P. B. Baltes (Eds.), *Life-span developmental psychology.* New York: Academic Press, 1970. Pp. 423–466.

Horst, P. *Factor analysis of data matrices.* New York: Holt, Rinehart, & Winston, 1965.

House, B., & Zeaman, D. Reversal and nonreversal shifts in discrimination learning in retardates. *Journal of Experimental Psychology,* 1962, **63,** 444–451.

Howard, K. I., & Krause, M. S. Some comments on "techniques for estimating the source and direction of influence in panel data." *Psychological Bulletin,* 1970, **74,** 219–224.

Hunt, J. McV. The effects of infant feeding frustration upon adult hoarding in the albino rat. *Journal of Abnormal & Social Psychology,* 1941, **36,** 338–360.

Hymovitch, B. The effects of experimental variations in early experience on problem solving in the rat. *Journal of Comparative & Physiological Psychology,* 1952, **45,** 313–321.

Inhelder, B., & Piaget, J. *The growth of logical thinking from childhood to adolescence.* New York: Basic Books, 1958.

Inhelder, B., & Sinclair, H. Learning cognitive structures. In P. H. Mussen, J. Langer, & M. Covington, *Trends and issues in developmental psychology.* New York: Holt, 1969. Pp. 2–21.

Inhelder, B., Bovet, M., and Sinclair, H. Développement et apprentissage. *Revue Suisse de Psychologie,* 1967, **26,** 1–23.

Israelsohn, J. Description and modes of analysis of human growth. In J. M. Tanner (Ed.), *Human growth.* (Symposia of the Society for the Study of Human Biology, Vol. III). New York: Pergamon Press, 1960. Pp. 21–42.

Jeffrey, W. E. Variables in early discrimination learning: I. Motor responses in the training of left-right discrimination. *Child Development,* 1958, **29,** 269–275.

Jenkin, N., & Feallock, S. Developmental and intellectual processes in size-distance judgments. *American Journal of Psychology,* 1960, **73,** 268–273.

Jenkins, J. G., & Dallenbach, K. M. Obliviscence during sleep and waking. *American Journal of Psychology,* 1924, **35,** 605–612.

Jenkins, J. J., & Palermo, D. S. Mediation processes and the acquisition of linguistic structure. *Monographs of the Society of Research in Child Development,* 1964, **29** (1, Whole No. 92).

Jenss, R. M., & Bayley, N. A mathematical method for studying growth in children. *Human Biology,* 1937, **9,** 556–563.

Jersild, A. T. Emotional development. In L. Carmichael (Ed.), *Manual of child psychology.* New York: Wiley, 1954. Pp. 833–917.

Jones, H. E. Problems of method in longitudinal research. *Vita Humana,* 1958, **1,** 93–99.

Jones, M. H., & Liverant, S. Effects of age differences on choice behavior. *Child Development,* 1960, **31,** 673–680.

Jöreskog, K. G. Factoring the multitest-multi-occasion correlation matrix. Educational Testing Service (Princeton, N.J.) *Research Bulletin,* 1969, No. 69–62.

Kagan, J. American longitudinal research on psychological development. *Child Development,* 1964, **35,** 1–32.

Kagan, J. Developmental studies in reflection and analysis. In A. H. Kidd & J. L. Rivoire (Eds.), *Perceptual development in children*. New York: International Univ. Press, 1966. Pp. 487–522.

Kagan, J. The three faces of continuity in human development. In D. A. Goslin (Ed.), *Handbook of socialization theory and research*. Chicago, Illinois: Rand McNally, 1969. Pp. 983–1002.

Kagan, J. *Change and continuity in infancy*. New York: Wiley, 1971.

Kagan, J., & Kogan, N. Individual variation in cognitive process. In P. H. Mussen (Ed.), Carmichael's *Manual of child psychology* (3rd ed.). Vol. I. New York: Wiley, 1970. Pp. 1273–1365.

Kagan, J., & Moss, H. A. *Birth to maturity: A study in psychological development*. New York: Wiley, 1962.

Kagan, J., Moss, H. A., & Sigel, I. E. Psychological significance of styles of conceptualization. In J. C. Wright & J. Kagan (Eds.), *Basic cognitive processes in children. Monographs of the Society of Research in Child Development*, 1963, **28** (2, Whole No. 86).

Kagan, J., Rosman, B. L., Day, D., Albert, J., & Phillips, W. Information processing in the child: Significance of reflective attitudes. *Psychological Monographs*, 1964, **78** (1, Whole No. 578).

Keeney, T. J., Cannizzo, S. R., & Flavell, J. H. Spontaneous and induced verbal rehearsal in a recall task. *Child Development*, 1967, **38**, 953–966.

Kelley, T. L. *Statistical method*. New York: Macmillan, 1924.

Kempler, B. Developmental level and serial learning. Unpublished Ph.D. dissertation. Clark University, 1964.

Kendler, T. S. Development of mediating responses in children. In J. C. Wright & J. Kagan (Eds.), *Basic cognitive processes in children. Monographs of the Society for Research in Child Development*, 1963, **28** (2, Whole No. 86).

Kendler, T. S. Verbalization and optional reversal shifts among kindergarten children. *Journal of Verbal Learning & Verbal Behavior*, 1964, **3**, 428–436.

Kendler, T. S. Developmental laws and theory construction. Paper presented at Symposium on Approaches to Experimental-Developmental Research in Child Psychology, Meetings of Society for Research in Child Development, Minneapolis, Minnesota, March, 1965.

Kerlinger, F. N. The statistics of the individual child: The use of analysis of variance with child development data. *Child Development*, 1954, **25**, 265–275.

Kerpelman, L. C. Preexposure to visually presented forms and nondifferential reinforcement in perceptual learning. *Journal of Experimental Psychology*, 1965, **69**, 257–262.

Kessen, W. Research design in the study of developmental problems. In P. H. Mussen (Ed.), *Handbook of research methods in child development*. New York: Wiley, 1960. Pp. 36–70.

Kessen, W. "Stage" and "structure" in the study of children. In W. Kessen & Kuhlman, C. (Eds.) Thought in the young child. *Monographs of the Society of Research in Child Development*, 1962, **27** (2, Whole No. 83). Pp. 65–82.

Kessen, W. *The child*. New York: Wiley, 1965.

King, J. A. Parameters relevant to determining the effect of early experience upon the adult behavior of animals. *Psychological Bulletin*, 1958, **55**, 46–58.

Kingsley, R. C., & Hall, V. C. Training conservation through the use of learning sets. *Child Development*, 1967, **38**, 1111–1126.

Klein, S. D. A developmental study of perceptual integration within and across sensory modalities. Unpublished M.A. thesis, Clark University, 1960.

Klein, S. D. A developmental study of tactual perception. Unpublished Ph.D. dissertation, Clark University, 1963.

Klivington, K. Funding for multidisciplinary research by a private foundation. Paper presented at Symposium on "The developmental sciences: State and fate of research funding," at meetings of AAAS, Chicago, December, 1970.

Kodlin, D., & Thompson, D. J. An appraisal of the longitudinal approach to studies of growth and development. *Monographs of the Society of Research in Child Development*, 1958, **23** (1, Whole No. 67).

Koffka, K. *The growth of the mind: An introduction to child psychology.* New York: Harcourt, 1924.

Kofsky, E. Developmental scalogram analysis of classificatory behavior. Unpublished doctoral dissertation, University of Rochester, 1963.

Kohen-Raz, R. Scalogram analysis of some developmental sequences of infant behavior as measured by the Bayley Infant Scale of Mental Development. *Genetic Psychology Monographs*, 1967, **76**, 3–21.

Kohlberg, L. State and sequence: The cognitive-developmental approach to socialization. In D. A. Goslin (Ed.), *Handbook of socialization theory and research.* Chicago, Illinois: Rand McNally, 1969. Pp. 347–480.

Kounin, J. S. Experimental studies of rigidity: II. The explanatory power of the concept of rigidity as applied to feeble-mindedness. *Character & Personality*, 1941, **9**, 273–282.

Kragh, U. The actual genetic model of perception-personality. University of Lund, *Studia Psychologica et Paedagogica*, 1955, Series 2, VII.

Kramer, R. B. Changes in moral judgment response pattern during late adolescence and young adulthood: Retrogression in a developmental sequence. Unpublished Ph.D. dissertation, University of Chicago, 1968.

Kuenne, M. R. Experimental investigation of the relation of language to transposition behavior in young children. *Journal of Experimental Psychology*, 1946, **36**, 471–490.

Lambercier, M. Recherches sur le développement des perceptions: VI. La constance des grandeurs en comparaisons sériales. *Archives de Psychologie (Genève)*, 1946, **31**, 1–204.

Langer, J. Werner's comparative organismic theory. In P. H. Mussen (Ed.), *Carmichael's manual of child psychology* (3rd ed.) Vol. I. New York: Wiley, 1970. Pp. 733–771.

Laurendeau, M., & Pinard, A. Une méthode rationelle de localisation des tests dans les échelles d'age. *Canadian Journal of Psychology*, 1957, **11**, 33–45.

Lee, L. C. The concomitant development of cognitive and moral modes of thought: A test of selected deductions from Piaget's theory. *Genetic Psychology Monographs*, 1971, **83**, 93–146.

Leibowitz, H. W., Pollard, S. W., & Dickson, D. Monocular and binocular size matching as a function of distance at various age-levels. *American Journal of Psychology*, 1967, **80**, 263–268.

Leik, R. K., & Mathews, M. A scale for developmental processes. *American Sociological Review*, 1968, **33**, 62–75.

Lessac, M. S., & Solomon, R. L. Effects of early isolation on the later adaptive behavior of Beagles: A methodological demonstration. *Developmental Psychology*, 1969, **1**, 14–25.

Levin, J. Three-mode factor analysis. *Psychological Bulletin*, 1965, **64**, 442–452.

Lewin, K. Behavior and development as a function of the total situation. In L. Carmichael (Ed.), *Manual of child psychology* (2nd ed.). New York: Wiley, 1954. Pp. 918–970.

Lewis, H. P. The relationship of picture preference to developmental status in drawing. *Journal of Educational Research*, 1963, **57**, 43–46. (a)

Lewis, H. P. Spatial representation in drawing as a correlate of development and a basis for picture preference. *Journal of Genetic Psychology*, 1963, **102**, 95–107. (b)

Lewis, M. The meaning of a response or why researchers in infant behavior should be oriental metaphysicians. *Merrill Palmer Quarterly*, 1967, **13**, 7–18.

Lingoes, J. C. Multiple scalogram analysis: A set-theoretic model for analyzing dichotomous items. *Educational & Psychological Measurement*, 1963, **23**, 501–524.

Loevinger, J. A systematic approach to the construction and evaluation of tests of ability. *Psychological Monographs*, 1947, **61** (4, Whole No. 285).

Loevinger, J. The technique of homogeneous tests compared with some aspects of scale analysis and factor analysis. *Psychological Bulletin*, 1948, **45**, 507–529.

Loevinger, J. The meaning and measurement of ego development. *American Psychologist*, 1966, **21**, 195–206. (a)

Loevinger, J. Models and measures of developmental variation. *Annals of the New York Academy of Sciences*, 1966, **134**, 585–590. (b)

Lord, F. M. Further problems in the measurement of growth. *Educational & Psychological Measurement*, 1958, **18**, 437–451.

Lord, F. M., & Novick, M. R. *Statistical theories of mental test scores*. Reading, Massachusetts: Addison-Wesley, 1968.

Lovell, K. A follow-up study of Inhelder and Piaget's "The growth of logical thinking." *British Journal of Psychology*, 1961, **52**, 143–153.

Lovell, K., & Ogilvie, E. A study of the conservation of weight in the junior school child. *British Journal of Educational Psychology*, 1961, **31**, 138–144.

Luchins, A. S., & Luchins, E. H. *Rigidity of behavior: A variational approach to the effect of Einstellung*. Eugene: Univ. of Oregon Press, 1959.

Lunzer, E. A. Some points of Piagetian theory in the light of experimental criticism. *Journal of Child Psychology & Psychiatry*, 1960, **1**, 191–202.

Maccoby, E. E., & Konrad, K. W. Age trends in selective listening. *Journal of Experimental Child Psychology*, 1966, **3**, 113–122.

Maccoby, E. E., & Konrad, K. W. The effect of preparatory set on selective listening: Developmental trends. *Monographs of the Society of Research in Child Development*, 1967, **32** (4, Whole No. 112).

Magoun, H. W. *The waking brain*. Springfield, Illinois: Thomas, 1958.

Martin, W. Singularity and stability of social behavior. In C. B. Stendler (Ed.), *Readings in child behavior and development*. New York: Harcourt, 1964. Pp. 448–466.

Maxwell, A. E. *Analysing qualitative data*. London: Methuen, 1961.

McCall, R. B. Intelligence quotient pattern over age: Comparison among siblings and parent-child pairs. *Science*, 1970, **170**, 644–648.

McCandless, B. R., & Spiker, C. C. Experimental research in child psychology. *Child Development*, 1956, **27**, 75–80.

McCarthy, D. Language development in children. In L. Carmichael (Ed.), *Manual of child psychology* (2nd ed.). New York: Wiley, 1954. Pp. 492–630.

McDonald, R. P. A general approach to nonlinear factor analysis. *Psychometrika*, 1962, **27**, 397–415.

McGraw, M. B. *Growth: A study of Johnny and Jimmy*. New York: Appleton, 1935.

McGraw, M. B. *The neuromuscular maturation of the human infant*. New York: Columbia Univ. Press, 1943.

McLaughlin, G. H. Psychologic: A possible alternative to Piaget's formulation. *British Journal of Educational Psychology*, 1963, **33**, 61–67.

McNeill, D. The development of language. In P. H. Mussen (Ed.), *Carmichael's manual of child psychology* (3rd ed.), Vol. I. New York: Wiley, 1970. Pp. 1061–1161.

McNemar, Q. *The revision of the Stanford–Binet scale: An analysis of the standardization data*. Boston, Massachusetts: Houghton Mifflin, 1942.

McTavish, D. G. Perceptions of old people: A review of research methodologies and findings. *Gerontologist*, 1971, **11** (4, Pt. II), 90–102.

Melzack, R. The genesis of emotional behavior: An experimental study of the dog. *Journal of Comparative & Physiological Psychology*, 1954, **47**, 166–168.

Meredith, H. V. Longitudinal anthropometric data in the study of individual growth. *Annals of the New York Academy of Sciences*, 1955, **63**, 510–527.

Mermelstein, E., & Shulman, L. S. Lack of formal schooling and the acquisition of conservation. *Child Development*, 1967, **38**, 39–52.

Merrill, M. The relationship of individual growth to average growth. *Human Biology*, 1931, 3, 37–70.

Meyer, W. J., & Bendig, A. W. A longitudinal study of the Primary Mental Abilities test. *Journal of Educational Psychology*, 1961, **52**, 50–60.

Meyers, C. E., Dingman, H. F., Orpet, R. E., Sitkei, E. G., & Watts, C. A. Four ability-factor hypotheses at three preliterate levels in normal and retarded children. *Monographs of the Society of Research in Child Development*, 1964, **29** (5, Whole No. 96).

Milgram, N., & Goodglass, H. Role style versus cognitive maturation in word associations of adults and children. *Journal of Personality*, 1961, **29**, 81–93.

Milholland, J. E. Four kinds of reproducibility in scale analysis. *Educational & Psychological Measurement*, 1955, **15**, 478–482.

Millard, C. V. The nature and character of pre-adolescent growth in reading achievement. *Child Development*, 1940, **11**, 71–115.

Miller, D. J., Cohen, L. B., & Hill, K. T. A methodological investigation of Piaget's theory of object concept development in the sensory-motor period. *Journal of Experimental Child Psychology*, 1970, **9**, 59–85.

Miranda, S. B. Visual abilities and pattern preferences of premature infants and full-term neonates. *Journal of Experimental Child Psychology*, 1970, **10**, 189–205.

Misumi, J. Experimental studies on the development of visual size constancy in early infancy. *Bulletin of the Faculty of Literature, Kyushu University*, 1951, **1**, 91–116.

Moran, L. J. *Repetitive psychological measures*. Austin: Univ. of Texas Press, 1959.

Mosteller, F. Association and estimation in contingency tables. *Journal of the American Statistical Association*, 1968, **63**, 1–28.

Munn, N. L. Learning in children. In L. Carmichael (Ed.), *Manual of child psychology* (2nd ed.). New York: Wiley, 1954.

Munn, N. L. *The evolution and growth of human behavior* (2nd ed.). Boston, Massachusetts: Houghton Millfin, 1965.

Mussen, P. H. (Ed.) *Handbook of research methods in child psychology*. New York: Wiley, 1960.

Mussen, P. H. (Ed.) *Carmichael's manual of child psychology* (3rd. ed., 2 Vols.). New York: Wiley, 1970.

Nash, J. *Developmental psychology: A psychobiological approach*. Englewood Cliffs, New Jersey: Prentice-Hall, 1970.

Nassefat, M. *Etude quantitative sur l'évolution des opérations intellectuelles*. Neuchatel: Délachaux & Niestlé, 1963.

Neimark, E. D., & Lewis, N. Development of logical problem solving: A one-year retest. *Child Development*, 1968, **39**, 527–536.

Nesselroade, J. R. Application of multivariate strategies to problems of measuring and structuring long-term change. In L. R. Goulet & P. B. Baltes (Eds.), *Life-span developmental psychology*. New York: Academic Press, 1970. Pp. 193–207.

Nicolson, B., & Hanley, C. Indices of physiological maturity: Derivation and interrelationships. *Child Development*, 1953, **24**, 3–38.

Nunnally, J. C. *Psychometric theory*. New York: McGraw-Hill, 1967.

Nunnally, J. C. Research strategies and measurement methods for investigating human development. In J. R. Nesselroade & H. W. Reese (Eds.), *Life-span developmental psychology: Methodological issues*. New York: Academic Press, 1973. Pp. 87–109.

O'Bryan, K. G., & Boersma, F. J. Eye movements, perceptual activity, and conservation development. *Journal of Experimental Child Psychology*, 1971, **12**, 157–169.

Offenbach, S. I. Studies of children's probability learning behavior. I. Effect of reward and punishment at two age levels. *Child Development*, 1964, **35**, 709–716.

Offenbach, S. I. Studies of children's probability learning behavior. II. Effect of method and frequency at two age levels. *Child Development*, 1965, **36**, 951–962.

Olson, W. C., & Hughes, B. O. The concept of organismic age. *Journal of Educational Research*, 1942, **36**, 525–527.

Oostlander, A. M. The development of the weight-volume illusion. *Journal of Experimental Child Psychology*, 1967, **5**, 237–248.

Osler, S., & Kofsky, E. Structure and strategy in concept learning. *Journal of Experimental Child Psychology*, 1966, **4**, 198–209.

Osterrieth, P. (Ed.) *Le problème des stades en psychologie de l'enfant*. Paris: Presses Univ. de France, 1956.

Palermo, D. S., & Jenkins, J. J. *Word association norms: Grade school through college*. Minneapolis: Univ. of Minnesota Press, 1964.

Paraskevopoulos, J., & Hunt, J. McV. Object construction and imitation under differing conditions of rearing. *Journal of Genetic Psychology*, 1971, **119**, 301–321.

Parker, J. F. Jr., & Fleischman, E. A. Ability factors and component performance measures as predictors of complex tracking behavior. *Psychological Monographs*, 1960, **74**, (16, Whole No. 503).

Parrish, M., Lundy, R. M., & Leibowitz, H. W. Effect of hypnotic age regression on the magnitude of the Ponzo and Poggendorff illusions. *Journal of Abnormal Psychology*, 1969, **74**, 693–698.

Parten, M., & Newhall, S. M. Social behavior of preschool children. In R. C. Barker, J. S. Kounin, & H. F. Wright (Eds.), *Child behavior and development*. New York: McGraw-Hill, 1943. Pp. 509–525.

Pascual-Leone, J., & Bovet, M. C. L'apprentissage de la quantification de l'inclusion et la théorie opératoire. *Acta Psychologica*, 1966, **25**, 334–356.

Pascual-Leone, J., & Smith, J. The encoding and decoding of symbols by children. A new experimental paradigm and a neo-Piagetian model. *Journal of Experimental Child Psychology*, 1969, **8**, 328–355.

Patterson, G. R., Littman, R. A., & Bricker, W. Assertive behavior in children: A step toward a theory of aggression. *Monographs of the Society of Research in Child Development*, 1967, **32**, (5, Whole No. 113).

Pelz, D. C., & Andrews, F. M. Detecting causal priorities in panel study data. *American Sociological Review*, 1964, **29**, 836–848.

Peterson, D. R. Age generality of personality factors derived from ratings. *Educational & Psychological Measurement*, 1960, **20**, 461–474.

Piaget, J. *The moral judgment of the child*. London: Paul, 1932.

Piaget, J. *The child's conception of number*. New York: Humanities Press, 1952. (a)

Piaget, J. *The origins of intelligence in children*. New York: International Univ. Press, 1952. (b)

Piaget, J. Ce qui subsiste de la théorie de la Gestalt dans la psychologie contemporaine de l'intelligence et de la perception. *Revue Suisse de Psychologie*, 1954, **13**, 72–83. (a)

Piaget, J. *The construction of reality in the child*. New York: Basic Books, 1954. (b)

Piaget, J. Les stades du développement intellectuel de l'enfant et de l'adolescent. In P. Osterrieth (Ed.), *Le problème des stades en psychologie de l'enfant*. Paris: Presses Univ. de France, 1956, Pp. 33–42.

Piaget, J. *Psychology of intelligence*. Patterson, New Jersey: Littlefield & Adams, 1960.

Piaget, J. *The mechanisms of perception*. New York: Basic Books, 1969.

Piaget, J., & Lambercier, M. Recherches sur le développement des perceptions: III. Le problème de la comparaison visuelle en profondeur (constance de la grandeur) et l'erreur systématique de l'étalon. *Archives de Psychologie (Genève)*, 1943, **29**, 253–308.

Piaget, J., & Lambercier, M. Recherches sur le développement des perceptions: XXIX. Grandeurs projectives et grandeurs réelles avec étalon eloigné. *Archives de Psychologie (Genève)*, 1956, **35**, 257–280.

Pick, H. L. Jr., & Pick, A. D. Sensory and perceptual development. In P. H. Mussen (Ed.), *Manual of child psychology*, (3rd ed.), Vol. 1. New York: Wiley, 1970. Pp. 773–847.

Pinard, A., & Laurendeau, M. "Stage" in Piaget's cognitive-developmental theory: Exegesis of a concept. In D. Elkind & J. H. Flavell (Eds.), *Studies in cognitive development. Essays in honor of Jean Piaget*. London and New York: Oxford Univ. Press, 1969. Pp. 121–163.

Pineau, H. *La croissance et ses lois*. Paris: Laboratoire d'anatomie de la Faculté de Médécine de Paris, 1965.

Pinneau, S. R., & Newhouse, A. Measures of invariance and comparability in factor analysis for fixed variables. *Psychometrika*, 1964, **29**, 271–281.

Prader, A., Tanner, J. M., & von Harnack, G. A. Catch-up growth following illness or starvation. *Journal of Pediatrics*, 1963, **62**, 646–659.

Preyer, W. *Die Seele des Kindes*. Leipzig: Grieben, 1882.

Rand, G., Wapner, S., Werner, H., & McFarland, J. H. Age differences in performance on the Stroop Color-Word test. *Journal of Personality*, 1963, **31**, 534–558.

Rapoport, J. L. Attitude and size judgment in school-age children. *Child Development*, 1967, **38**, 1187–1192.

Rapoport, J. L. Size-constancy in children measured by a functional size-discrimination task. *Journal of Experimental Child Psychology*, 1969, **7**, 366–373.

Reese, H. W. Verbal mediation as a function of age level. *Psychological Bulletin*, 1962, **59**, 502–509.

Reeve, E. C. R., & Huxley, J. S. Some problems in the study of allometric growth. In W. E. LeG. Clark & P. B. Medawar (Eds.), *Essays on growth and form*. London and New York: Oxford Univ. Press, (Clarendon), 1945. Pp. 121–156.

Reinert, G. Comparative factor analytic studies of intelligence throughout the human life span. In L. R. Goulet & P. B. Baltes (Eds.), *Life-span developmental psychology*. New York: Academic Press, 1970. Pp. 467–484.

Rheingold, H. R., & Stanley, W. C. Developmental psychology. *Annual Review of Psychology*, 1963, **14**, 1–28.

Riegel, K. F. Time and change in the development of the individual and society. In *Advances in Child Development and Behavior*, 1972, **7**, in press.

Riley, D. A. Memory for form. In L. Postman (Ed.), *Psychology in the making*. New York: Knopf, 1962. Pp. 402–465.

Rozelle, R. M., & Campbell, D. T. More plausible rival hypotheses in the cross-lagged panel correlation technique. *Psychological Bulletin*, 1969, **71**, 74–80.

Russell, D. H. *Children's thinking*. Boston, Massachusetts: Ginn, 1956.

Russell, W. A. An experimental psychology of development: Pipe dream or possibility? In D. B. Harris (Ed.), *The concept of development*. Minneapolis: Univ. of Minnesota Press, 1957. Pp. 162–174.

Sandell, R. G. Note on choosing between competing interpretations of cross-lagged panel correlations. *Psychological Bulletin*, 1971, **75**, 367–368.

Sanders, B. S. *Environment and growth*. Baltimore: Warwick and York, 1934.

Santostefano, S. G., & Paley, E. Development of cognitive controls in children. *Child Development*, 1964, **35**, 939–949.

Scammon, R. E. The first seriatim study of human growth. *American Journal of Physical Anthropology*, 1927, **10**, 329–336.

Scammon, R. E. The measurement of the body in childhood. In J. A. Harris, C. M. Jackson,

D. G. Paterson, & R. E. Scammon, *The measurement of man*. Minneapolis: Univ. of Minnesota Press, 1930.

Schaefer, E. S., & Bayley, N. Maternal behavior, child behavior and their intercorrelations from infancy through adolescence. *Monographs of the Society of Research in Child Development*, 1963, **28**, (3, Whole No. 87).

Schaie, K. W. A general model for the study of developmental problems. *Psychological Bulletin*, 1965, **64**, 92–107.

Schaie, K. W. A reinterpretation of age related changes in cognitive structure and functioning. In L. R. Goulet & P. B. Baltes (Eds.), *Life-span developmental psychology*. New York: Academic Press, 1970. Pp. 485–507.

Schaie, K. W., & Strother, C. R. The effect of time and cohort differences on the interpretation of age changes in cognitive behavior. *Multivariate Behavioral Research*, 1968, **3**, 259–294. (a)

Schaie, K. W., & Strother, C. R. A cross-sectional study of age changes in cognitive behavior. *Psychological Bulletin*, 1968, **70**, 671–680. (b)

Schuessler, K., & Strauss, A. A study of concept learning by scale analysis. *American Sociological Review*, 1950, **15**, 752–762.

Sears, R. R. Relation of early socialization experiences to aggression in middle childhood. *Journal of Abnormal & Social Psychology*, 1961, **63**, 466–492.

Sears, R. R., Whiting, J. W. M., Nowlis, V., & Sears, P. S. Some childrearing antecedents of aggression and dependency in young children. *Genetic Psychology Monographs*, 1953, **47**, 135–236.

Segall, M. H., Campbell, D. T., & Herskovits, M. J. *The influence of culture on visual perception*. New York: Bobbs-Merrill, 1966.

Sekuler, R. W., & Rosenblith, J. F. Discrimination of direction of line and the effect of stimulus alignment. *Psychonomic Science*, 1964, **1**, 143–144.

Shantz, C. U., & Smock, C. D. Development of distance conservation and the spatial coordinate system. *Child Development*, 1966, **37**, 943–948.

Shirley, M. M. *The first two years: A study of twenty-five babies. Vol. I: Postural and Locomotor development*. Minneapolis: Univ. of Minnesota Press, 1931. (a)

Shirley, M. M. The sequential method for the study of maturing behavior patterns. *Psychological Review*, 1931, **38**, 507–528. (b)

Shirley, M. M. Locomotor and visual-manual functions in the first two years. In C. Murchison (Ed.), *A handbook of child psychology* (2nd ed.). Worcester, Massachusetts: Clark Univ. Press, 1933. Pp. 236–270.

Shock, N. W. Growth curves. In S. S. Stevens (Ed.), *Handbook of experimental psychology*. New York: Wiley, 1951. Pp. 330–346.

Sholl, D. A. Regularities in growth curves, including rhythms and allometry. In E. J. Boell (Ed), *Dynamics of growth processes*. Princeton, New Jersey: Princeton Univ. Press, 1954. Pp. 224–241.

Shuttleworth, F. K. Sexual maturation and the physical growth of girls age six to nineteen. *Monographs of the Society of Research in Child Development*, 1937, **2**, (5, Whole No. 12).

Sidman, M. A note on functional relations obtained from group data. *Psychological Bulletin*, 1952, **49**, 263–269.

Siegel, S. *Nonparametric statistics for the behavioral sciences*. New York: McGraw-Hill, 1956.

Sigel, I. E., Roeper, A., & Hooper, F. H. A training procedure for acquisition of Piaget's conservation of quantity: A pilot study and its replication. *British Journal of Educational Psychology*, 1966, **36**, 301–311.

Simpson, G. G. The study of evolution: Methods and present status of theory. In A. Roe & G. G. Simpson (Eds.), *Behavior and evolution*. New Haven, Connecticut: Yale Univ. Press, 1958. Pp. 7–26.

Smedslund, J. The acquisition of conservation of substance and weight in children. I. Introduction. *Scandinavian Journal of Psychology*, 1961, **2**, 11–20. (a)

Smedslund, J. The acquisition of conservation of substance and weight in children. V. Practice in conflict situations without external reinforcement. *Scandinavian Journal of Psychology*, 1961, **2** , 156–160. (b)

Smedslund, J. Concrete reasoning: A study of intellectual development. *Monographs of the Society of Research in Child Development*, 1964, **29**, (2, Whole No. 93).

Solomon, R. L., & Lessac, M. S. A control group design for experimental studies of developmental processes. *Psychological Bulletin*, 1968, **70**, 145–150.

Sontag, L. W., Baker, C. T., & Nelson, V. L. Mental growth and personality development, a longitudinal study. *Monographs of the Society of Research in Child Development*, 1958, **23**, (2, Whole No. 68).

Spiker, C. C. The hypothesis of stimulus interaction and an explanation of stimulus conditioning. *Advances in Child Development & Behavior*, 1963, **1**, 233–264.

Staats, A., & Staats, C. K. *Complex human behavior: A systematic extension of learning principles*. New York: Holt, 1963.

Staats, A. W., Minke, K. A., Finley, J. R., Wolfe, M., & Brooks, L. O. A reinforcer system and experimental procedure for the laboratory study of reading acquisition. *Child Development*, 1964, **35**, 209–231.

Stahl, W. R. Similarity and dimensional methods in biology. *Science*, 1962, **137**, 205–212.

Stevenson, H. W., & Weir, M. W. Variables affecting children's performance in a probability learning task. *Journal of Experimental Psychology*, 1959, **57**, 403–412.

Stevenson, H. W., & Weir, M. W. Developmental changes in the effects of reinforcement and nonreinforcement of a single response. *Child Development*, 1961, **32**, 1–5.

Stevenson, H. W., & Zigler, E. F. Probability learning in children. *Journal of Experimental Psychology*, 1958, **56**, 185–192.

Strauss, A. L., & Schuessler, K. F. Socialization, logical reasoning, and concept development in the child. *American Sociological Review*, 1951, **16**, 514–523.

Stutsman, R. Constancy in personality trends. *Psychological Bulletin*, 1935, **32**, 701–702.

Suppes, P., & Ginsberg, R. A fundamental property of all-or-none models, binomial distribution of responses prior to conditioning, with application to concept formation in children. *Psychological Review*, 1963, **70**, 139–161.

Sutton-Smith, B. Developmental laws and the experimentalist's ontology. *Merril Palmer Quarterly*, 1970, **16**, 253–259.

Tanner, J. M. *Educational and physical growth*. London: Univ. of London Press, 1961.

Tanner, J. M. *Growth at adolescence* (2nd ed.). London: Blackwell, 1962.

Tanner, J. M. The regulation of human growth. *Child Development*, 1963, **34**, 817–848.

Tanner, J. M., Healy, M. J. R., Lockhart, R. D., Mackenzie, J. D., & Whitehouse, R. H. Aberdeen growth study. I: The prediction of adult measurements from measurements taken each year from birth to 5 years. *Archives of Disease in Childhood*, 1956, **31**, 372–381.

Terrell, G. , Jr. The role of incentive in discrimination. *Child Development*, 1958, **29**, 231–236.

Thomae, H. Theory of aging and cognitive theory of personality. *Human Development*, 1970, **13**, 1–16.

Thomas, A., Birch, H. G., Chess, S., Hertzig, M. E., & Korn, S. *Behavioral individuality in early childhood*. New York: NY Univ. Press, 1963.

Thompson, W. R. Early experiential and genetic influences on flexibility. In O. J. Harvey (Ed.), *Experience, structure and adaptability*. New York: Springer Publ., 1966. Pp. 67–94.

Thorndike, E. L., Bregman, E. O., Cobb, M. V., & Woodyard, E. *The measurement of intelligence*. New York: Teachers College, Columbia Univ. 1927.

Thurstone, L. L. A method of scaling psychological and educational tests. *Journal of Educational Psychology*, 1925, **16**, 433–451.

Thurstone, L. L. The absolute zero in intelligence measurement. *Psychology Review*, 1928, **35**, 175–197.

Thurstone, L. L. Theory of attitude measurement. *Psychology Review*, 1929, **36**, 222–241.

Thurstone, L. L., & Ackerson, L. The mental growth curve for the Binet tests. *Journal of Educational Psychology*, 1929, **20**, 569–583.

Thurstone, L. L., & Thurstone, T. G. *SRA primary abilities for ages 11–17*. Chicago Illinois: Science Research Associates, 1947.

Thurstone, L. L., & Thurstone, T. G. *SRA primary abilities for ages 7–11*. Chicago Illinois: Science Research Associates, 1948.

Thurstone, L. L., & Thurstone, T. G. *SRA primary abilities for ages 5–7*. Chicago, Illinois: Science Research Associates, 1953.

Torgerson, W. J. *Theory and methods of scaling*. New York: Wiley, 1958.

Tucker, L. R. Implications of factor analysis of three-way matrices for measurement of change. In C. W. Harris (Ed.), *Problems in measuring change*. Madison: Univ. of Wisconsin Press, 1963, Pp. 122–137.

Tucker, L. R. Learning theory and multivariate experiment: Illustrations by determination of generalized learning curves. In R. B. Cattell (Ed.), *Handbook of multivariate experimental psychology*. Chicago, Illinois: Rand McNally, 1966. Pp. 476–501.

Tucker, L. R. Three-mode factor analysis of Parker-Fleishman complex tracking behavior data. *Multivariate Behavioral Research*, 1967, **2**, 139–151.

Tucker, L. R., Damarin, F., & Messick, S. A base-free measure of change. *Psychometrika*, 1966, **31**, 457–473.

Tuddenham, R. D., & Snyder, M. M. Physical growth of California boys and girls from birth to eithteen years. *University of California Publications in Child Development*, 1954, **1**, 183–364.

Turiel, E. Developmental processes in the child's moral thinking. In P. Mussen, J. Langer, & M. Covington (Eds.), *Trends and issues in developmental psychology*. New York: Holt, 1969. Pp. 92–133.

Tyler, F. T. Organismic growth: *P*-Technique in the analysis of longitudinal growth data. *Child Development*, 1954, **25**, 83–90.

Uzgiris, I. C. Situational generality of conservation. *Child Development*, 1964, **35**, 831–841.

Uzgiris, I. C., & Hunt, J. McV. An instrument for assessing infant psychological development. Progress report, U. S. Public Health Service Grant, 1966.

Vandenberg, S. G., & Falkner, F. Heredity factors in human growth. *Human Biology*, 1965, **37**, 357–365.

Van den Daele, L. D. Qualitative models in developmental analysis. *Developmental Psychology*, **1**, 1969, 303–310.

Van der Vaart, H. R. Adult age, an investigation based on certain aspects of growth curves. *Acta Biotheoretica*, 1953, **10**, 139–211.

Vinh-Bang. Evolution des conduites et apprentissage. In A. Morf, J. Smedslund, Vinh-Bang, & J. F. Wohlwill, *L'apprentissage des structures logiques*. Paris: Presses Univ. de France 1959. Pp. 3–13. (Etudes d' épistémologie génétique, IX).

Vurpillot, E. Development of scanning strategies and their relation to visual differentiation. *Journal of Experimental Child Psychology*, 1968, **6**, 632–650.

Waddington, C. H. The biological foundations of measurements of growth and form. *Proceedings of the Royal Society of London, Ser. B*, 1950, **137**, 509–515.

Walters, A. A genetic study of geometrical-optical illusions. *Genetic Psychology Monographs*, 1942, **25**, 101–155.

Wapner, S. An organismic-developmental approach to the study of perceptual and other cognitive operations. In C. Scheerer (Ed.), *Cognition: Theory, research, promise.* New York: Harper, 1964. Pp. 6–44.

Wapner, S., & Werner, H. *Perceptual development.* Worcester, Massachusetts: Clark Univ. Press, 1957.

Watson, R. I. *Psychology of the child* (2nd ed.). New York: Wiley, 1965.

Webb, E. J., Campbell, D. T., Schwartz, R. D., & Sechrest, D. *Unobtrusive measures.* Chicago, Illinois: Rand McNally, 1966.

Weinbach, A. P. Some physiological phenomena fitted to growth equations: III. Rate of growth of brain potentials (alpha frequency) compared with rate of growth of the brain. *Growth*, 1938, **2**, 247–251.

Weinbach, A. P. Some physiological phenomena fitted to growth equations: IV. Time and power relations for a human infant climbing inclines of various slopes. *Growth*, 1940, **4**, 123–134.

Weinstein, E. A. Development of the concept of flag and the sense of national identity. *Child Development*, 1957, **28**, 167–174.

Weir, M. W. Developmental changes in problem-solving strategies. *Psychological Review*, 1964, **71**, 473–490.

Weiss, P., & Kavanau, J. L. A model of growth and growth control in mathematical terms. *Journal of General Physiology*, 1957, **41**, 1–47.

Wenar, C., & Coulter, J. B. A reliability study of developmental histories. *Child Development*, 1962, **33**, 453–462.

Werner, E., & Bayley, N. The reliability of Bayley's revised scale of mental and motor development during the first year of life. *Child Development*, 1966, **37**, 39–50.

Werner, H. Process and achievement: A basic problem of education and developmental psychology. *Harvard Educational Review*, 1937, **7**, 353–368.

Werner, H. Experimental genetic psychology. In P. H. Harriman (Ed.), *Encyclopedia of psychology.* New York: Philosophical Library, 1946. Pp. 219–236.

Werner, H. The concept of development from a comparative and organismic point of view. In D. B. Harris (Ed.), *The concept of development.* Minneapolis: Univ. of Minnesota Press, 1957. Pp. 125–148.

Werner, H., & Kaplan, B. The developmental approach to cognition: Its relevance to the psychological interpretation of anthropological and ethnolinguistic data. *American Anthropologist*, 1956, **58**, 866–880.

White, B. L. The initial coordination of sensorimotor schemas in human infants—Piaget's ideas and the role of experience. In D. Elkind, & J. Flavell (Eds.), *Studies in cognitive development: Essays in honor of Jean Piaget.* London and New York: Oxford Univ. Press, 1969. Pp. 237–256.

White, B. L. *Human infants: Experience and psychological development.* Englewood Cliffs, New Jersey: Prentice-Hall, 1971.

White, B. W. & Saltz, E. Measurement of reproducibility, *Psychological Bulletin*, 1957, **54**, 81–99.

White, S. H. The learning–maturation controversy: Hall to Hull. *Merrill Palmer Quarterly*, 1968, **14**, 187–196.

Whiting, J. W., & Child, I. L. *Child training and personality.* New Haven, Connecticut: Yale Univ. Press, 1953.

Winer, G. A. Induced set and acquisition of number conservation. *Child Development*, 1968, **39**, 195–205.

Witkin, H. A., Dyk, R. B., Faterson, H. F., Goodenough, D. R., & Karp, S. A. *Psychological differentiation.* New York: Wiley, 1962.

Witkin, H. A., Goodenough, D. R., & Karp, S. A. Stability of cognitive style from childhood to young adulthood. *Journal of Personality & Social Psychology*, 1967, **7**, 291–300.

Witkin, H. A., Lewis, H. B., Hertzman, M., Machover, K., Meissner, P. B., & Wapner, S. *Personality through perception.* New York: Harper, 1954.

Wohlwill, J. F. A study of the development of the number concept by scalogram analysis. *Journal of Genetic Psychology*, 1960, **97**, 345–377. (a)

Wohlwill, J. F. Developmental studies of perception. *Psychological Bulletin*, 1960, **57**, 249–288. (b)

Wohlwill, J. F. The development of "overconstancy" in space perception. *Advances in Child Development and Behavior*, 1963, **1**, 265–312. (a)

Wohlwill, J. F. The measurement of scalability for non-cumulative items. *Educational & Psychological Measurement*, 1963, **23**, 543–555. (b)

Wohlwill, J. F. Piaget's system as a source of empirical research. *Merrill Palmer Quarterly*, 1963, **9**, 253–262. (c)

Wohlwill, J. F. Texture of the stimulus field and age as variables in the perception of relative distance in photographic slides. *Journal of Experimental Child Psychology*, 1965, **2**, 163–177.

Wohlwill, J. F. Piaget's theory of the development of intelligence in the concrete-operations period. In M. Garrison, Jr. (Ed.), *Cognitive models and development in mental retardation. American Journal of Mental Deficiency, Monograph Supplement*, 1966, 70 **(4)**, 57–78. (a)

Wohlwill, J. F. Vers une reformulation du role de l'expérience dans le développement cognitif. In *Psychologie et epistémologie génétiques: Thèmes Piagétiens.* Paris: Dunod, 1966, Pp. 211–222. (b)

Wohlwill, J. F. The place of structured experience in early cognitive development. *Interchange*, 1970, **1** (2), 13–27. (a)

Wohlwill, J. F. Methodology and research strategy in the study of developmental change. In L. R. Goulet & P. B. Baltes (Eds.), *Life-span developmental psychology.* New York: Academic Press, 1970. Pp. 150–191. (b)

Wohlwill, J. F. The age variable in psychological research. *Psychological Review*, 1970, **77**, 49–64. (c)

Wohlwill, J. F. The concept of experience: S or R? *Human Development*, 1973, **16**, in press.

Wohlwill, J. F., & Wiener, M. Discrimination of form orientation in young children. *Child Development*, 1964, **35**, 1113–1125.

Wohlwill, J. F., Fusaro, L., & Devoe, S. Measurement, seriation, and conservation: A longitudinal examination of their interrelationship. Paper presented at the meeting of the Society for Research in Child Development, Santa Monica, California, March, 1969.

Wohlwill, J. F., Devoe, S. & Fusaro, L., Research on the development of concepts in early childhood. Final Report for NSF Grant G-5855, 1971.

Wolfe, R. The role of conceptual systems in cognitive functioning at varying levels of age and intelligence. *Journal of Personality*, 1963, **31**, 108–123.

Wolff, G. A. study on the trend of weight in white school children from 1933 to 1936. *Child Development*, 1940, **11**, 159–180.

Woodrow, H., & Lowell, F. Children's association frequency tables. *Psychological Monographs*, 1916, **22** (5, Whole No. 97).

Woodside, G. L. Funding of developmental research by NICHHD. Paper presented at Symposium on "The developmental sciences: State and fate of research funding," at meetings of AAAS, Chicago, December, 1970.

Woodward, M. The behavior of idiots interpreted by Piaget's theory of sensori-motor development. *British Journal of Educational Psychology*, 1959, **29**, 60–71.

Woodward, M., & Stern, D. J. Developmental patterns of severely subnormal children. *British Journal of Educational Psychology*, 1963, **33**, 10–21.

Yarrow, L. J., Campbell, J. D. & Burton, R. V. Recollections of childhood: A study of the retrospective method. *Monographs of the Society of Research in Child Development*, 1970, **35** (5, Whole No. 38).

Yates, A. J. Hypnotic age regression. *Psychological Bulletin*, 1961, **58**, 429–440.

Yee, A. H., & Gage, N. L. Techniques for estimating the source and direction of causal influence in panel data. *Psychological Bulletin*, 1968, **70**, 115–126.

Young, H. B., & Knapp, R. Personality characteristics of converted left handers. *Perceptual & Motor Skills*, 1966, **22**, 35–40.

Young, H. B., Tagiuri, R., Tesi, G., & Montemagni, G. Influence of town and country upon children's intelligence. *British Journal of Educational Psychology*, 1962, **32**, 151–158.

Young, H. B., Zoli, A., Gallagher, J., & Rothwell, M. D. Events of puberty in 111 Florentine girls. *American Journal of Diseases of Children*, 1963, **106**, 568–577.

Zeaman, D., & House, B. J. Mongoloid MA is proportional to log CA. *Child Development*, 1962, **33**, 481–488.

Zeigler, H. P., & Leibowitz, H. Apparent visual size as a function of distance for children and adults. *American Journal of Psychology*, 1957, **70**, 106–109.

Author Index

Numbers in italics refer to the pages on which the complete references are listed.

403

Subject Index